LIBRARY OF SECOND TEMPLE STUDIES

100

Formerly Journal for the Study of the Pseudepigrapha Supplement Series

Editor
Lester L. Grabbe

Founding Editor
James H. Charlesworth

Editorial Board
Randall D. Chesnutt, Philip R. Davies, Jan Willem van Henten,
Judith M. Lieu, Steven Mason, James R. Mueller, Loren T. Stuckenbruck,
James C. VanderKam

HORIZONS OF ANCESTRAL INHERITANCE

Commentary on the Levi, Qahat, and Amram Qumran Aramaic Traditions

Andrew B. Perrin

LONDON • NEW YORK • OXFORD • NEW DELHI • SYDNEY

T&T CLARK
Bloomsbury Publishing Plc
50 Bedford Square, London, WC1B 3DP, UK
1385 Broadway, New York, NY 10018, USA
29 Earlsfort Terrace, Dublin 2, Ireland

BLOOMSBURY, T&T CLARK and the T&T Clark logo
are trademarks of Bloomsbury Publishing Plc

First published in Great Britain 2022
Paperback edition published 2024

Copyright © Andrew B. Perrin, 2022

Andrew B. Perrin has asserted his right under the Copyright, Designs and Patents Act, 1988, to be identified as Author of this work.

For legal purposes the Acknowledgments on pp. vii constitute an extension of this copyright page.

All rights reserved. No part of this publication may be reproduced or transmitted in any form or by any means, electronic or mechanical, including photocopying, recording, or any information storage or retrieval system, without prior permission in writing from the publishers.

Bloomsbury Publishing Plc does not have any control over, or responsibility for, any third-party websites referred to or in this book. All internet addresses given in this book were correct at the time of going to press. The author and publisher regret any inconvenience caused if addresses have changed or sites have ceased to exist, but can accept no responsibility for any such changes.

A catalogue record for this book is available from the British Library.

Library of Congress Cataloging-in-Publication Data

Names: Perrin, Andrew B., author.
Title: Horizons of ancestral inheritance : commentary on the Levi, Qahat, and Amram Qumran Aramaic traditions / Andrew B. Perrin.
Description: New York : T&T Clark, 2022. | Series: The library of Second Temple studies; 100 | Includes bibliographical references and index. | Summary: "A transcription of and commentary upon three priestly pseudepigraph from the Dead Sea Scrolls; Aramaic Levi Document, Words of Qahat, and Visions of Amram"-- Provided by publisher.
Identifiers: LCCN 2022000355 (print) | LCCN 2022000356 (ebook) | ISBN 9780567705433 (hardback) | ISBN 9780567705471 (paperback) | ISBN 9780567705440 (pdf) | ISBN 9780567705464 (epub)
Subjects: LCSH: Levi document. | Dead Sea scrolls--Criticism, interpretation, etc. | Apocryphal books (Old Testament)--Criticism and interpretation. | Manuscripts, Aramaic.
Classification: LCC BM488.L48 P47 2022 (print) | LCC BM488.L48 (ebook) | DDC 296.1/55--dc23/eng/20220129
LC record available at https://lccn.loc.gov/2022000355
LC ebook record available at https://lccn.loc.gov/2022000356

ISBN:	HB:	978-0-5677-0543-3
	PB:	978-0-5677-0547-1
	ePDF:	978-0-5677-0544-0
	ePUB:	978-0-5677-0546-4

Series: Library of Second Temple Studies, volume 100

Typeset by Duncan Burns

To find out more about our authors and books visit www.bloomsbury.com and sign up for our newsletters.

Contents

Acknowledgments   vii

Chapter 1
INTRODUCTION   1
  1.1. On Mixed Metaphors   1
  1.2. The Ongoing History of a Perceived Priestly "Trilogy"   2
  1.3. Commentary Structure and Approach   5

Chapter 2
ARAMAIC LEVI DOCUMENT   8
  2.1. The Figure of Levi in Texts and Traditions   8
  2.2. Publication History   9
  2.3. Material Quality and Scribal Features   11
  2.4. Prominent Themes and Noteworthy Structures   12
  2.5. Genre   17
  2.6. Compositional Date and Social Setting   19
  2.7. Text and Commentary: 1QLevi (1Q21)   23
  2.8. Text and Commentary: 4QLevi^a (4Q213)   26
  2.9. Text and Commentary: 4QLevi^b (4Q213a)   43
  2.10. Text and Commentary: 4QLevi^c (4Q213b)   57
  2.11. Text and Commentary: 4QLevi^d (4Q214)   60
  2.12. Text and Commentary: 4QLevi^e (4Q214a)   67
  2.13. Text and Commentary: 4QLevi^f (4Q214b)   75

Chapter 3
WORDS OF QAHAT   81
  3.1. The Figure of Qahat in Texts and Traditions   81
  3.2. Publication History   81
  3.3. Material Quality and Scribal Features   82
  3.4. Prominent Themes and Noteworthy Structures   83
  3.5. Genre   85
  3.6. Compositional Date and Social Setting   87
  3.7. Text and Commentary: 4Q542   88

Chapter 4
VISIONS OF AMRAM 122
4.1. The Figure of Amram in Texts and Traditions 122
4.2. Publication History 123
4.3. Material Quality and Scribal Features 123
4.4. Prominent Themes and Noteworthy Structures 125
4.5. Genre 129
4.6. Compositional Date and Social Setting 130
4.7. Text and Commentary: 4QVisions of Amram^a (4Q543) 132
4.8. Text and Commentary: 4QVisions of Amram^b (4Q544) 148
4.9. Text and Commentary: 4QVisions of Amram^c (4Q545) 168
4.10. Text and Commentary: 4QVisions of Amram^d (4Q546) 184
4.11. Text and Commentary: 4QVisions of Amram^e (4Q547) 194

Chapter 5
CONCLUSION 204
5.1. Pseudepigraphal Texts and Pseudepigraphic Traditions:
     Rethinking the "Trilogy" Question for *ALD*, *WQ*, and *VA* 204
5.2. Conceptual and Compositional Correlations 205
5.3. Codicological Considerations 209
5.4. Cultural Contexts 213
5.5. Switching Metaphors: From Trilogy to Constellation 216

Bibliography 219
Index of References 237
Index of Authors 255

Acknowledgments

This volume was made possible by the resources, opportunities, and time provided through a Social Sciences and Humanities Research Council Insight Grant, the Canada Research Chair in Religious Identities of Ancient Judaism at Trinity Western University, and an Alexander von Humboldt Fellowship. For the latter, I am particularly grateful to Professor Loren Stuckenbruck who was an exceptional host during my time at Ludwig Maximilians Universität München in 2018.

Aspects of Chapters 1 and 5 overlap significantly with my essay in the forthcoming volume of the 2019 Proceedings of the International Organization for Qumran Studies. Thanks to both Brill and Bloomsbury for permitting this shared use of content.

During this project, I benefited greatly from the collaborative work and editorial assistance of several graduate assistants at Trinity Western University. Thanks to Monika Andrassyova, Shelby Bennett, Brandon Diggens, Brian Felushko, Matthew Hama, and Kyle Young for their involvement. Thanks also to the many colleagues in many venues who heard and critiqued my work en route to this outcome.

Much of this project was researched and written at Trinity Western University. Special thanks to Dr. Eve Stringham for creating and caring for the research environment of the university. And to Dr. Dirk Büchner, for co-suffering in commentaries written on cryptic ancient texts. I'm also grateful to my new colleagues at Athabasca University for their interest and encouragement in the completion of this book.

As always, family is more important than work. Kudos to the Perrin home team (Tanya, Emma, and Jude), frankly, for putting up with me but graciously going well beyond that on a daily basis. To my parents, Daryl and Rosanne, it's an honor to dedicate the book to you for your ongoing encouragement and support in life. Apologies, Mom and Dad, that this book is so expensive and technical. I hope the next book is a heretical best-seller.

Andrew B. Perrin
July 2021
Lanark Highlands, Ontario, Canada

Chapter 1

INTRODUCTION

1.1. *On Mixed Metaphors*

I admit it: the title of this book is a mixed metaphor. But for good reason. An inheritance is always handed down from the past. It is both a gift with inherent value and an opportunity for molding and maintaining the identity of the next generation. A horizon is ever-ahead, meaning it points to prosperity or peril depending on the reality brought by the dawn or perception of the one gazing toward it. Horizons are never met yet they are constantly read. Reflecting on the past while projecting the future is the space in which the writers of the priestly Aramaic texts among the Dead Sea Scrolls (DSS) found themselves.

While there are priestly topics and writings that cut across the Qumran collection, this volume focuses on three writings: *Aramaic Levi Document* (*ALD*), *Words of Qahat* (*WQ*), and *Visions of Amram* (*VA*). By capturing or creating authoritative voices from figures of the remote past, the priestly scribes who crafted these traditions drew upon ideas from the past, extended them into the present, and constructed both identities to maintain the integrity of future generations and ideas to guide their thought and practice.

Images of leveraging an inheritance while looking to the horizon are, in some ways, domestic to these materials. In one instance, Qahat underscored that the ancestral inheritance was precious and to be protected from outsiders (4Q542 1 i 4–6). Elsewhere in the tradition, we find Levi lifting hands and eyes heavenward in prayer for protection against further waywardness, promiscuity, and satanic forces (4Q213a 1 8–12). In these samples, the pseudepigraphic perspectives from the past spoke into a priestly present of the mid-Second Temple period and beyond. So perhaps this mixed metaphor is not such a stretch for the priestly scribes who cultivated this tradition.

This looking back while looking ahead, however, raises several questions about the position of the writers of *ALD*, *WQ*, and *VA* in time and space: Who were these priests? Where did they live? When did they write? Did they craft the texts independently or in interrelation? Good questions. As I describe in individual commentary chapters below, unfortunately, there are few firm answers on many of these fronts. Yet reading the texts together reveals that—regardless of these unknowns—the three texts both constitute and participate in an emerging priestly tradition in the centuries leading up to the turn of the Common Era. The aims of this commentary are to cast a greater light on that formative tradition, to work toward answers to the above-listed unknowns, to provide a departure point for more sustained work on these often-overlooked writings, and to enable their uptake into larger areas of study beyond the niche within a niche of research on the Qumran Aramaic texts.

But before exploring what these texts say in the commentary chapters below, it is important to establish why they are routinely studied together. This commentary is selective. It encompasses only the fragmentary Qumran manuscripts for *ALD*, *WQ*, and *VA*. The project could have cast a still wider net to include several other ancient Aramaic texts interwoven with priestly topics and themes. For instance, the visionary blueprint of the eschatological city and cult of *New Jerusalem* and bifurcated list of priests and kings in 4QPseudo-Daniel[c] are undeniably priestly. So why single out the three priestly pseudepigrapha here and not others? While there is a need for the development of resources to enable advanced and ongoing study of several Aramaic texts among the Qumran finds, the three selected here have both a heritage in past scholarship for joint study and potential for ongoing research as a group. Therefore, to make the most of the commentaries on the individual Levi, Qahat, and Amram *texts* below it is important to outline the shape and scope of this emerging *tradition* of priestly pseudepigrapha. In the spirit of looking back and looking ahead, I set this context first through a history of research on these writings as a group, then point to the book's conclusion that proposes a new way forward for conceiving of *ALD*, *WQ*, and *VA* as a constellation of texts in a pre-canonical world. At the close of this introductory chapter, I describe the structure and approach of the commentaries that follow.

1.2. *The Ongoing History of a Perceived Priestly "Trilogy"*

From an early time in research, *ALD*, *WQ*, and *VA* were described or approached as a tripartite group. After initial work on some of these materials by J. Starcky, publication of the bulk of the Aramaic texts fell to J. T. Milik. Following the publication of DJD 1 and a number of partial and preliminary editions of Cave Four Aramaic materials, Milik undertook several studies that included individual textual analyses and syntheses of groups of Aramaic texts. In an essential *Revue Biblique* article, Milik (1972a) advanced the case that the Aramaic Levi, Qahat, and Amram texts were alluded to in *Apostolic Constitutions* VI 16.3 as τῶν τριῶν πατριαρχῶν. The texts, he averred, are connected in their shared styles of patriarchal discourse and transmission of priestly teaching, which presents a cascading of the tradition. Milik (1976: 95 n. 9) indicated his plans to publish a monograph on the Aramaic Levi traditions attested at Qumran, a task he did not complete before his passing. Aspects of his unpublished work on the Levi traditions are increasingly coming to light in posthumous publications (Kapera 2007; Schattner-Rieser 2007; Drawnel forthcoming).[1]

In these years Milik also developed a complex theory of another group of Aramaic writings, namely the now infamous Enochic Pentateuch championed in his 1976 volume *The Books of Enoch*. He also perceived yet another ancestral anthology at Qumran, involving ancient Jewish testaments of Jacob, Levi, Judah, Joseph, and Amram (Milik 1978: 106). While the former theory won few adherents and the latter has been almost entirely forgotten, it seems Milik was interested in clumping rather than splitting.

In most cases, the history of scholarship has proceeded with variations of acceptance of this clustered approach. De Jonge's (Hollander and De Jonge 1997: 22) critique of Milik's work focused on genre, yet affirmed that the three texts "form a series" of priestly texts read by the Qumran group but likely authored elsewhere in other "priestly sectarian circles." To my knowledge, Milik never used the term "trilogy" to refer to *ALD*, *WQ*, and *VA* in his published works. However, Kugel (1993) first drew the association between Milik's proposal of a priestly group with the concept. While Kugel focused on the shape and forms of early Levi traditions, he referenced the Qahat and Amram materials as "the other two parts of a priestly trilogy" (Kugel 1993: 45). Cook (1993: 207) proposed that the three works may share a *Sitz im Leben* and "have formed some of the earliest literature of the 'Asideans' (I Macc. 2:42)." Puech (2001: 258–62) accepted core elements of Milik's theory and developed it in his Aramaic edition of the Qahat and Amram texts in DJD 31. Based on *ALD*'s existence also in Greek translation, Puech inferred *WQ* and *VA* likely also circulated in translation, enabling their Christian reception. Compositionally, he also stated that *WQ* and *VA* depended on *ALD* for elements of their content and outlook, specifically regarding dualism, calendar, and priestly outlooks. Drawnel (2004: 87) noted the "general acceptance" of Milik's prescribed approach of reading and interpreting the texts together and noted that *ALD* has without a doubt "influenced the vocabulary and content and, most probably, the literary form of the latter two priestly works." Following a summary of some literary and formal qualities of the works, Greenfield, Stone, and Eshel (2004: 31; see also Stone and Eshel 2013: 1490) made the following remark:

> We should stress the relationship between *ALD*, *4QTestament of Qahat* and *4QVisions of Amram*, works associated with the generations of Levi down to Aaron, the direct father of the priestly line of Israel. *ALD* is the oldest of these three and the other two works might be related to it and perhaps even depend on it to some extent. *4QTestament of Qahat* and *4QVisions of Amram* might have been written on the pattern of *ALD* to legitimate the continuity of the priestly line and its teaching.

---

1. Thanks to Henryk Drawnel for sharing a prepublication draft of his study.

Though Goldman's (2013: 246) study compared aspects of *VA* with Tobit—including presentations of endogamous marriage—her conclusion referenced the broader patterns of similarity with our priestly pseudepigrapha, "which appear to have been composed in the same circle."

The only study to engage the trilogy issue directly is that of Tervanotko (2014). Tervanotko evaluated several items of similarity and difference between the texts. The similarities collected from scholarship on the texts include items related to: discourse style, literary themes, linguistic proposals, and compositional dates. Following brief considerations of these, Tervanotko (2014: 44) reached the tentative conclusion that the "linguistic and thematic connections between *ALD*, *TQahat* and *VA* provide the strongest arguments for the association of these texts. Moreover, the three texts are roughly dated to the same era. They were written in the third or second century BCE." Proposed differences include: potential variation in use or popularity by virtue of manuscript counts for each composition, unsettled or unknown provenance of the three works, variation on themes shared by all texts (e.g., views of outsiders and the preferred means of knowledge transmission), and either debated or indeterminate genre. In view of analysis of these items, Tervanotko (2014: 49–50) wrote:

> All in all, the research history results in a more detailed understanding of what the similarities and differences are between *ALD*, *VA*, and *TQahat*. There is growing scholarly consensus that *ALD*, *VA*, and *TQahat* do reflect common themes, and are connected through their shared literary family lineage. This is virtually accepted by everyone. In contrast to the affinities, other thematic details and especially the material evidence (number of copies and their date and circulation) argues against a common origin between the texts. Furthermore, most scholars working in this area assume that *ALD* reflects an earlier situation than the other two texts. Therefore, it seems that these texts were not composed together. Meanwhile inquiries concerning their genre or provenance remain open for the time being. Importantly, these observations do not contradict or exclude the idea that *TQahat* was read together with the other two texts or that the other two texts inspired it.

Reflecting on this history of research, it is evident that there is a general appreciation of the cogency, coherence, or continuity between *ALD*, *WQ*, and *VA*. However, in many cases, this impression was developed on the basis of a limited set of perceived features. Revising our understanding of the potential correlations or connectedness of these Aramaic pseudepigrapha traditions discovered among the scrolls requires a refined and sustained analysis of each of the texts. Only after delving into the details of each can we stand back and reassess our understanding of the ways in which *ALD*, *WQ*, and *VA* are at once distinct yet exhibit their shades of similarity.

A commentary is one of the tools needed to advance toward an answer to the "connection question" of *ALD*, *WQ*, and *VA*. Such a resource enables a focused reading of each writing while also providing the opportunity to gather insights along the way that can help assess possible indicators of unity or disunity. Following the individual analyses in the body chapters of this book, it will become apparent that there are at least three criteria that help gauge the types of interactions or interrelations we discover when reading the texts together. These include: conceptual and compositional correlations, codicological considerations, and cultural contexts. To look ahead, these three criteria will be explored further at the close of the study. The conclusion will provide a new way of understanding the formation and emergence of this tradition using the metaphor of "constellations" of texts that comprise a wider tradition of Aramaic, priestly, pseudepigrapha.

1.3. *Commentary Structure and Approach*

The bulk of this volume magnifies its focus on individual fragments of *ALD*, *WQ*, and *VA* in commentary form. While this genre is no doubt familiar, a commentary on incomplete and understudied texts from Qumran presents both problems and prospects. Therefore, to provide a map to this challenging landscape, I here outline key aspects of my method and presentation of the commentary chapters below. This will not only assist a reader of large sections of the work but also ensure those looking for detail of a specific text, fragment, or even line are able to access as much information as possible in a focused engagement.

Scope

While my focus is on a larger tradition that encompasses *ALD*, *WQ*, *VA*, I treat each of the texts separately with commentaries presented sequentially by Qumran manuscript and fragment numbers using the common referencing system established in DJD. In part, this is to ensure ease of use. Presumably, users of this volume will not read cover to cover—save for the few (un)lucky reviewers for academic journals—but will read selectively and strategically based on interest in a specific composition or even fragment represented at Qumran. I do not undertake significant reconstructions (e.g., of *ALD* in light of the Aramaic Cairo Genizah texts) or eclectic editions (e.g., of *VA* known in at least five fragmentary manuscripts at Qumran). This is not to say that such a task is impossible or cannot be revisited anew in view of new approaches or technologies (e.g., Holst 2020). But it is to acknowledge that my immediate task in this volume is to shed light on fragmentary remains of manuscripts unfortunately ravaged by time. That is, to push yet another metaphor, I am interested here in the puzzle pieces without assuming or arguing for what image was originally on the front of the box.

Introduction

The volume introduction here contextualizes the three writings as a group. The sections on *ALD*, *WQ*, and *VA* below are framed with a specialized introduction on open-questions and current issues related to each work's compositional origins (social location, date, and place), key literary or thematic features, and scribal characteristics or material quality of the manuscripts. These are meant to provide a current state of research for each writing and a secure point of departure for the detailed analyses of the commentary itself.

Transcription and Translation

The commentary on each fragment begins with a fresh transcription based on multiple sets of images made publicly available on the Leon Levy Digital Dead Sea Scrolls Library (https://www.deadseascrolls.org.il). This remarkable and open-access resource enabled the parallel consideration of several stages of photographs captured using different technologies. In general, my method was to use at least three images for each transcription: a scan of early infrared images taken at the Palestinian Archaeological Museum in the 1950s and 1960s (PAM plates) and both a more recent infrared and full-color digital image captured for the preservation and study of the manuscripts, many of which for *ALD*, *WQ*, and *VA* were taken in the early 2010s. I include a list of key images used at the outset of my critical notes for each fragment (see next). These new transcriptions served as the basis for a fresh English translation. When dealing with such fragmentary materials, the balance between a cogent or intelligent English rendering and authentically representing idioms and syntax of the underlying Aramaic is not always an easy, or even possible, task. Yet the aims of this aspect of the work is to walk that line to provide a sufficient and stable basis for the commentary proper.[2]

Critical Notes

For each fragment I present a selective list and focused discussion of items that relate to textual, scribal, and material aspects of the text in question. Many of

---

2. A note on sources for additional writings: Unless otherwise indicated, all English translations of the Hebrew Bible, Apocrypha, and New Testament are from the NRSV. Septuagint translations are drawn from NETS, with accompanying Greek texts from the Göttingen editions. Apart from transcriptions and translations of the *ALD*, *WQ*, and *VA*—which are my own—other primary language and renderings of the DSS are predominantly from those of the DJD series. A key exception to this throughout is the *Genesis Apocryphon*, for which I draw from the recent edition by Machiela and VanderKam (2018). Additional DSS sources are indicated in the critical notes when pertinent. Sources of other commonly used ancient texts include: *1 Enoch* (Nickelsburg and VanderKam 2012), Aramaic inscriptions (Schwiderski 2004; 2008), *ALD* Cairo Genizah and Mt. Athos materials (Drawnel 2004), *Jubilees* (VanderKam 2018), and *Testaments of the Twelve Patriarchs* (de Jonge 1978).

these items pertain to revised or problematic readings of the Aramaic. As such, this component of the commentary provides a space for evaluation of transcription options from several other main editions of the texts. The notes section, however, is not exhaustive so cannot be considered a full catalogue of alternate proposals or comprehensive critical apparatus. In most cases, my threshold for highlighting an item was if my proposed reading departed from that of the majority of editions or aligned with a minority position for a given reading currently on offer. I also use this section to comment on more technical matters of codicology when relevant.

Commentary

The heart of the project is a line-by-line commentary. The depth and scope of the commentary was often determined by the nature of the fragment under consideration. In cases where fragments are too small or in such an advanced state of decay where a full commentary is not possible, I highlight potential significance of extant terms in an introductory summary of the manuscript in question. For those fragments included in the commentary proper, my aim was to account for the content and context of *ALD*, *WQ*, and *VA* from several angles. These included: description of narrative units in their literary context, insofar as it can be known; discussion of stylistically difficult or intriguing Aramaic linguistic constructions (e.g., new lexical items, idioms, and syntactical configurations); consideration of the potential referential background for concepts, practices, and traditions in the Hebrew Bible; situation of the work within broader ancient cultural and literary traditions; exploration of terminological or ideological analogies with other contemporary Aramaic literature attested at Qumran or other known Jewish writings from the Second Temple period; explanation of noteworthy scribal features (e.g., methods for correcting errors, use of non-traditional scripts to pen divine epithets, and marginal symbols); and evaluation of similarities and differences between overlapping or related materials in the Qumran Aramaic texts.

While the writings of *ALD*, *WQ*, and *VA* are at times frustratingly fragmentary, they provide a unique opportunity to unlock new insights into the Aramaic intellectual culture of Judaism in the Second Temple period. While some once called this period "the years of silence," betraying a two-testament biblical anachronism, materials such as the Aramaic texts found among the Dead Sea Scrolls reveal that this period was in fact very loud. My hope in this project is to amplify some of the voices speaking in this period, thus enabling a better understanding of the patterns of life, thought, and identities in that era.

Chapter 2

ARAMAIC LEVI DOCUMENT

2.1. *The Figure of Levi in Texts and Traditions*

The figure of Levi is foundational for the ongoing formations of priestly identity and priesthood functions in the Hebrew Scriptures and beyond. Despite his prime position in the ancestral origins of the priestly line, Levi's profile in Genesis is cluttered with questions over his motivations and actions in response to Shechem raping Dinah in Genesis 34. While Levi and Simeon viewed their plot and violence against the Shechemites as a justified response to sexual assault, their father Jacob viewed it merely as unrestrained, juvenile rage (Gen. 34:30–31). Genesis 49:5–7 includes what is likely an early reception of this tradition, where the patriarch Jacob has the final word. He comments negatively on the character and heritage of Levi and Simeon—it is defined by bloodshed and brutality. Though the motif of priestly violence crops up intermittently in other episodes in the Pentateuch (Exod. 32:26–29; Num. 25:7–13), for the memory of Levi enshrined in Genesis, this conduct was hardly becoming of a priestly patriarch.

The rest of the Hebrew Scriptures are silent on the impact or outcomes of the injustice against Dinah. In the longer arc of reception history, Dinah's fate and future is limited with but a few sources indicating her marriage to Job (*T. Job* 1:5–6; *Job Tg.* 2:9; *Gen. Rab.* 57:4; *y. B. Bat.* 1:7, 15b). The reception and reinterpretation of the lingering loose-ends of Genesis 34 and 49, however, sparked questions and creative solutions related to the figure of Levi. This is particularly evident in the later Greek *Testament of Levi* (see Kugel 1992). One such early interpretation is found in *ALD*, dated to between the late-third and mid-second centuries BCE (see the section on compositional dating below). The earliest of the Qumran *ALD* fragments come from the tail end of this range, indicating that the Levi materials in Caves One and Four are from an early point in the transmission history of the tradition.

The narrative structure of *ALD* at Qumran is not fully known because of the fragmentary evidence. However, the scribes who developed this material were clearly not only concerned with justifying Levi's violence in Genesis 34 or overturning the negative ruling of Genesis 49. At best, this was one of many sources of inspiration and aims. *Aramaic Levi Document* presents Levi as a dynamic character who is: an authorized and authoritative founder of the subsequent priestly lineage; a source for privileged ancestral lore and wisdom; a receiver of otherworldly revelation; a comprehensive knowledgebase of sacrificial requirements and processes; an embodied model for essential practices for forming and maintaining priestly identity; and a reliable guide for preserving the priestly inheritance and societal position. In these ways, Levi's portfolio in *ALD* extends well beyond the brash youth presented in Genesis. In this early Aramaic memory, Levi is a sage, seer, scribe, and sacrificial expert.

2.2. Publication History

Before the discovery of Aramaic fragments of *ALD* at Qumran, the work was known in a variety of witnesses and languages from several collections. While the commentary offered below focuses on the Qumran fragments, contextualizing these in the larger set of *ALD* witnesses helps situate the present study. For more detailed descriptions and textual comparisons across the *ALD* witnesses, see Greenfield and Stone (1979), Drawnel (2004: 29–32), and Greenfield, Stone, and Eshel (2004: 1–6).

The most extensive *ALD* materials were recovered from the Cairo Genizah and include Aramaic folia of a medieval codex. These materials are now held in the Bodleian Library of the University of Oxford (Ms Heb c 27 f 56) and Cambridge University Library (T-S 16.94). Pass and Arendzen (1900) first published the Cambridge fragment and Charles and Cowley (1907) published the *editio princeps* of the Oxford materials. Charles (1908; cf. Charles 1913) reprinted both universities' manuscripts shortly thereafter. Citing the report of Beit-Arie, Stone and Greenfield (1979: 216) indicate the script of these materials locates their production before the year 1000 CE, suggesting they are among the earliest strata of texts recovered from the Cairo Genizah. More recently, Bohak (2011; 2013) identified an overlooked *ALD* fragment of the Cairo Genizah in the Rylands Library of the University of Manchester.

A section of a Greek translation of *ALD* was also recovered as an interpolation into a codex of the *Testaments of the Twelve Patriarchs* at the Koutloumousiou monastery on the north-eastern side of Mount Athos. The manuscript (E 2,3; MS Koutloumousiou 39) dates to the tenth century CE (Greenfield and Stone 1979: 215) yet it is unknown when the Aramaic text was rendered into Greek (de Jonge 1985: 19). The Greek material is valuable both for reconstructing the text of *ALD*, since it contains text otherwise lost in the Aramaic witnesses, and for exploring the transmission and reception of *ALD*, since it evidences both translation and geographical distribution.

The reception and translation histories of *ALD* extend in one final direction on account of the Syriac fragment of a small amount of text held in the British Library (B Add. 17,193). As with the Greek sample above, this material provides an important, though partial, view of the reach of *ALD* into unknown translation initiatives.

The discovery and identification of *ALD* fragments among the Dead Sea Scrolls provided original language witnesses from before the Common Era and in a location presumably much closer to the point of origin of the tradition. In total, fragments of seven Aramaic copies of *ALD* were identified among the collection. These include: 1QLevi (1Q21), 4QLevi^a (4Q213), 4QLevi^b (4Q213a), 4QLevi^c (4Q213b), 4QLevi^d (4Q214), 4QLevi^e (4Q214a), and 4QLevi^f (4Q214b).

Shortly after the discovery of Qumran Cave One, Milik published 1Q21 in DJD(J) 1 (1955a: 87–91). Though his notes were brief, the title "Testament de Lévi" suggested his early understanding of the relationship to, or relevance of, the newly discovered Aramaic materials to the later Greek composition. In an early *Revue Biblique* article, Milik (1955b) specified the Cave One materials were in fact from the same composition as *ALD* known from the Aramaic, Greek, and Syriac witnesses noted above. In this study, he also hinted at the identification of three Aramaic manuscripts of the same work among the then-recently acquired Cave Four materials (1955b: 399). Milik described the material and scribal quality of the texts in brief and presented a preliminary edition of Levi's prayer as found in 4Q213a 1–2 in comparison with the partially overlapping text in the Mt. Athos manuscript.

The significance of these new finds for studies on *ALD* and other ancient Jewish and Christian literature was evident early on but took decades to materialize in view of the largely unpublished collection. Grelot (1956) refined and problematized the transmission and reception histories of the witnesses of *ALD* in light of the *Testament of Levi*—at that time, he did not have access to the Cave Four materials—as well as opened the question of the relationship to parallel traditions in *Jubilees*.

As Milik continued to work on the *ALD* fragments, he published samples of 4Q213 3–4 in his *The Books of Enoch* (1976: 23; cf. 1971: 344–45), where he proposed that the fragments contain the "earliest allusion to the Book of Watchers." (On closer evaluation, however, the reading at 4Q213 4 2 is problematic and Milik's proposal unlikely; see the commentary below.) Milik (1976: 24; 1978: 95 n. 9) recognized the complexities presented by the newly discovered *ALD* materials and indicated his goal of addressing such matters in a planned monograph. As noted in the introduction to this volume, some of Milik's work on that project has now come to light.

The task of publishing the Cave Four *ALD* materials eventually fell to Greenfield and Stone (1996), who divided the fragments into six separate manuscripts and established the sigla now accepted in scholarship. In between these early studies and the eventual complete critical edition are several other important selective presentations of the Qumran *ALD* fragments.

Coordinating all of the *ALD* manuscript witnesses and fragments into a cohesive structure and presentation is challenging. At present, Drawnel's (2004) reconstruction is the most compelling because of its adoption of a standard referencing system for *ALD*. For this reason, when referring to sections of *ALD* as a composition, I utilize Drawnel's system and rely on his edition for all primary texts beyond the Qumran materials. For alternate reconstructions and versification systems, see Kugler (1996a) and Greenfield, Stone, and Eshel (2004), as well as hints of Milik's developing understanding (Kapera 2007; Schattner-Rieser 2007; 2011).

Preliminary, partial, and complete editions of the Qumran *ALD* fragments may be found in the following: Milik (1955a: 88–91; 1955b: 398, 400), Beyer (1984: 193–97, 208–209; 1994: 104–10; 2004: 71–78), Eisenman and Wise (1992: 136–41), Kugler (1996a), Stone and Greenfield (1996: 1–72), García Martínez and Tigchelaar (1998 2:56–59), Fitzmyer and Harrington (2002: 80–91), Drawnel (2004), Greenfield, Stone, and Eshel (2004), Parry and Tov (2005: 378–401), and Schattner-Rieser (2008: 446–67).

2.3. *Material Quality and Scribal Features*

Given the scope of materials included and individual qualities of the *ALD* fragments, it is beyond the bounds of a commentary to undertake a full analysis of their material and scribal quality. Nonetheless, to give an impression of the whole, I overview salient and noteworthy features of the fragmentary scrolls. For detailed descriptions, see the edition of Stone and Greenfield (1996).

2.3.1. *Codicological Characteristics*

Our knowledge of the material character of the original complete scrolls is limited and dictated by the fragments that have come down to us. I do not undertake a full reconstruction of any of the scrolls here; rather, I venture only impressions of the material philological features of the extant fragments.

The preservation of stitching is evident on some fragments. 4Q213 1, 2 retains stitching that adjoins partial columns. 4Q213a 1–2 bears the marks of a similar lost connection. Other fragments include the remnants of stitching or edges marked by holes indicating now-missing strands and adjoining sheets (4Q213 2, 3, 4, 5, 6; 4Q213b). Some fragments of 4Q213 include inscribed texts running well into the leftmost margin, in some instances with text encroaching upon the stitching to optimize the space available on the presumably prepared scroll (4Q213 1 i 7–11; 2 13, 15; 3 2; 4 8–9; 5 1–2). While the original structure and scope of the scrolls is difficult to discern, in the case of 4Q214b the presence of vertical creases in the texts suggest the placement and orientation of the manuscript as having been "rolled up and squashed" for some duration (Stone and Greenfield 1996: 61).

2.3.2. *Paleographical Profile*

Script analysis of the *ALD* fragments suggests their production from the mid-second century BCE to the turn of the Common Era. More detailed discussions of palaeography are available in the DJD editions (Milik 1955a: 87–88; Stone and Greenfield 1996: 34, 27, 37, 44, 54, 62). Greenfield, Stone, and Eshel (2004: 4) summarized the paleographical dates as follows: 1Q21 (100–1 BCE),

4Q213 (50–25 BCE), 4Q213a (75–50 BCE), 4Q213b (75–50 BCE), 4Q214 (75–50 BCE), 4Q214a (50–25 BCE), and 4Q214b (150–30 BCE). However, van der Schoor (forthcoming) has now problematized the paleographical profiles of these Cave Four fragments, which may indicate those materials relate to as few as four copies of *ALD*.[1]

While the traditional analyses are generally helpful, the limit of a twenty-five-year margin for the Cave Four materials certainly extends beyond the reasonable precision provided by paleographic study. Furthermore, a larger production date range for the fragments is suggested by the results of radiocarbon analysis for 4Q213, which span the mid-fourth to mid-first century BCE (see compositional dates below). For the possibility that the same scribe penned 4Q213a and 4Q213b, see the conclusion to this volume for codicological considerations. Finally, Stone and Greenfield (1996: 37) indicated that Cross opined 4Q213a and 4Q213b might have been written by the same scribe. Ultimately, their independent analysis concluded otherwise.

2.3.3. Scribal Interventions

Instances of scribal interventions across the Qumran *ALD* fragments are minimal yet instructive. These include interactions both within the text as well as around it. The presence of a marginal hook between 4Q213 1 ii–2 10–11 and 4Q213b 2 10–11 may indicate a section notation by the scribe or a later user, which invites comparison with a similar marking in *WQ* (4Q542 1 ii 8–9). The evidence for corrections is moderate. There is a scribal dot above the final *pe* in אלף at 4Q213 1 i 14 marking a correction, which Stone and Greenfield proposed was made "by the original scribe" (1996: 1). This is not to be confused with several other dots across the manuscripts caused by an ink spatter in antiquity, a phenomenon also apparent on some fragments of 4Q214a and perhaps 4Q214b (Stone and Greenfield 1996: 1, 53, 61). Finally, there are few instances of supralinear insertions or corrections (4Q213 1 ii 9; 4 5; 4Q213a 1 13; 4Q214 3 2).

2.4. Prominent Themes and Noteworthy Structures

Although the Qumran *ALD* witnesses are fragmentary, their brittle and broken remains retain content from several key themes and topics of the larger composition. To maintain the focus on the Qumran materials, I highlight four items that are evident among the fragments. Threads of each of these emphases are woven throughout the commentary that follows.

---

1. I am grateful to Hanneke van der Schoor for sharing a prepublication version of her study, aspects of which were also shared at 2019 International Organization of Qumran Studies meeting in Aberdeen.

2.4.1. Levi's Revelatory Election to the Priesthood

The number and setting of Levi's dream-visions in the original composition is a matter of debate. Though his full account remains unpublished, Milik reportedly understood *ALD* as including three dream-visions (Schattner-Rieser 2007: 141; 2011: 806). Kugler (1996a: 52–59) argued that the Qumran *ALD* fragments attest to a stage in the compositional development where Levi had but a single revelatory account. In this, Kugler was pushing back against readings and reconstructions of *ALD* that were overly influenced by the tandem dream-visions of the later Greek *T. Levi* 2:5–5:7; 8. Kugel (1993) offered a source-critical analysis of *ALD* that parsed the tradition into at least two pre-existing works. However, his source-critical evaluation is highly theoretical and unlikely. As research on these materials progressed, most have accepted the likelihood that *ALD* in its earliest form indeed featured dual dream-visions, even if the content of much of the accounts themselves is largely lost at the fringes (de Jonge 1985: 19; 1999; Drawnel 2004: 54–55; 2005; Davila 2013: 125; Perrin 2015a: 63). Others would say the Qumran *ALD* fragments are indeterminate on this issue (Greenfield, Stone, and Eshel 2004: 13).

Though the content of the dream-visions is limited, several fragments demonstrate that Levi's priestly status was at the core of these revelatory encounters. 4Q213b 1 1 includes the first-person words of an angelic figure stating to Levi that רביתך מן כל בשר[א ("I made you greater than all fles[h"). This content comes immediately before an awakening formula. The tradition of Levi's otherworldly installment to the priesthood is shared with Jub. 32:1, received in *T. Levi* 2:6–10; 4:2; 5:2; 8:1–18, and reworked and applied to Aaron in *VA* (4Q545 4; cf. 4Q213b 1 6). 4Q213a 2 14–18 may also include fragmentary material related to Levi's heavenly elevation and encounter with an angel. This encounter perhaps extended to 4Q213a 6 1, which may include a soundbite of some lost conversation with the *angelus interpres*. The angelic ordination of Levi's priesthood also makes sense in light of the reference to כהנות עלמא ("eternal priesthood") in 4Q213a 5 i 3.

The added dynamic of the religious-political profile of the priesthood is evident in 1Q21 1 2, which references the מלכות כהנותא רבא ("the kingdom of the high priesthood"). The priestly kingdom is also juxtaposed in duration and quality with the kingdom of the sword (1Q21 3 1; cf. *ALD* 4–6). Levi's wisdom discourse also interweaves themes of the royal and priestly character of the family line (4Q213 1 ii–2 15).

The content of Levi's second dream-vision is more fleeting still. It is likely that the revelation in some way related to forecasting and endorsing Levi's rage at the rape of Dinah (4Q213a 3–4; cf. *T. Levi* 5:3–4). On this limited content, see the commentary below.

The full content and context of Levi's dream-visions is unknown in these early Aramaic fragments of *ALD*. Yet the surviving materials retain enough internal clues and allow for sufficient external comparisons to conclude that *ALD* deployed dream-visions to endorse and authorize Levi's priestly position. So how did the scribes of the Levi tradition enable this growth? Through a form of creative, philologically oriented exegesis that uncovered new dynamics in Levi's profile based on hints within the Hebrew Scriptures.

As with select other texts among the Aramaic DSS—not least *GenAp* and *1 Enoch*—the redrawing of ancestors as Aramaic dreamers is rooted in recovering *potential* meanings of Hebrew phrases (Perrin 2015a: 123–57). For Levi, it seems at least two exegetical hooks enabled this development. First, the phrase "he revered me" (*niphal* נחת) in Mal. 2:5 was taken with some linguistic liberty to suggest Levi "descended" (Aramaic root נחת; Kugel 1993: 33). Added to this, the phrase "he walked with me" (הלך אתי) in Mal. 2:6 perhaps implied a career of otherworldly ventures *à la* Enoch (Perrin 2015a: 152–56). Second, if taken to allude to Levi, the phrase "I revealed myself" (הנגלה נגליתי) in 1 Sam. 2:27 could have provided a complementary clue that Levi was the recipient of a divine revelation alluded to, yet untold, in the Hebrew Scriptures.

In these ways, recovering the threads of Levi's dream-vision career in *ALD* must account for the internal themes among the fragments, external context of broader traditions associating Levi with revelatory episodes, as well as the style of exegesis in Aramaic scribal culture that seems to have reinvested in the profiles of ancestral figures by investigating the curious and convenient philological gaps of the Hebrew Scriptures.

2.4.2. *The Pursuit and Inheritance of Scribal Craft, Instruction, and Wisdom*

Among the many currents that run through Levi's prayer, wisdom poem, and dream-visions, one that recurs throughout is the emphasis on the triad of ספר ("scribal craft"), מוסר ("instruction"), and הכמה ("wisdom"). These dominant elements were subsequently received as part of Levi's heritage in *T. Levi* 13:2.

In Levi's wisdom poem—a separate unit from Levi's revelations—he admonishes his children to pursue these invaluable and irreplaceable ideals as a means of attaining יקר עלם ("everlasting glory"; 4Q213 1 i 10). In that context, Levi also encourages his progeny to consider the great and successful model of Joseph who, by embodying these attributes, brought glory and greatness even to royalty (4Q213 1 i 11–12). Though his reading is not secure, Drawnel (2004: 201) proposes that Levi's poetic discourse later references a partial triad—מֹוסֹר[חֹכֹ]מה ("ins]truction, wis[dom")—when describing the impenetrable sapiential city (4Q214b 8 3).

The content of 4Q213 1 ii–2 8–9 // 4Q214a 2–3 ii 5 takes this rhetoric to the next level, literally. Drawnel's (2004: 199) re-evaluation of these fragments suggests these three items were also the subjects of a dream-vision, as Levi remarked, חזית בחזרין די [תֹרתון אנון ("I saw in visions that]you will inherit them"; 4Q213 1 ii–2 9; cf. 4Q214a 2 ii 6). Though fragmentary, the most natural antecedent for the pronoun is the partially extant reference to the triad of qualities in 4Q213 1 ii–2 8. These fragmentary texts, then, retain inklings of the notion that the priestly inheritance is not only ancestral in origin but also in some way relates to an otherworldly disclosure.

In one instance, the prayer of Levi at 4Q213a 1 14 features an alternate threefold reference to ח[כּמה ומנדע וגבורה ("[w]isdom and knowledge and might"). This suggests that wisdom was coordinated with other ideals and that *ALD* exhibits a trend for tripling virtues or desirable characteristics. That this trend extends beyond the Levi tradition is evident from similar triads in other Aramaic writings among the Qumran finds. *Genesis Apocryphon* (1Q20) 19 25 includes a similar set of qualities and proficiencies: סָפְרָא וְחָכְמְתָא וְקוּשְׁטָא ("scribal craft, wisdom, and truth"). The focus on textuality and scribalism extends also to both *WQ* (4Q542 1 ii 9–13) and *VA* (4Q543 1a–c 1; 4Q547 9 8), suggesting that their priestly inheritance in some way also included such items.

The Aramaic DSS emphasize scribalism and booklore in many and diverse ways (see the comment below on 4Q213 1 ii–2 12). In the context of the priestly pseudepigrapha, however, it is clear that the memory of the founding figures of the priesthood are overlaid with a dominant set of scribal qualities (e.g., reading, writing, and teaching) to underscore the importance of the transmission of tradition and to inspire future generations of priests to maintain their status and role by cultivating such practices.

2.4.3. *Ancestral Instruction in the "Law of the Priesthood"*

Though the inheritance of *ALD* is connected with the three aptitudes discussed above, the bulk of the instruction included in the narrative pertains to priestly purity and sacrificial processes. In the more complete witnesses, this content clusters under the larger category of the דין כהנותא ("the law of the priesthood"; *ALD* 13, 15; MS A, Bodl. b 8 7–8, 13–14). The antiquarian, even antediluvian, origins of this ancestral knowledge is claimed through a multi-tiered, authority claiming strategy. Isaac instructs Levi in the teachings and model of Abraham (*ALD* 22; 25a; 4Q214b 2–3, 4, 5–6 i 2–6), who in turn claims a heritage and access to booklore associated with Noah (*ALD* 57).

Though fragmentary, Isaac's instruction on priestly processes not only secured ancestral authority, it also ensured the orderliness and consistency of priestly procedures at the altar (*ALD* 31; 4Q214 2 10). In this light, Drawnel's (2004: 275) emphasis on the priestly-instructional quality of *ALD* and its metro-arithmetical knowledge is well-warranted. However, as discussed below, this topic is but one aspect of the complex makeup of *ALD* and should not be elevated as a theme governing the interpretation of the entire tradition. Regarding the priestly teaching retained in the Qumran fragments, the largest blocks of extant text pertain to three procedures of the sacrificial process. These have been compared with both a presupposed pentateuchal referential background (e.g., Kugler 1996a) or in light of later rabbinic materials (e.g., Schiffman 2005). What I wish to highlight here, however, is that *ALD*'s sacrificial prescriptions should be contextualized in the complex of traditions emerging in ancient Judaism reflecting on and reimagining sacrificial processes, regardless of perceived antecedents or later iterations.

First, 4Q214 2 and 4Q214b 2–3 relate primarily to the preparations and delivery of the bovine offering. While we might first compare these items to Leviticus 1, as Kugler (1996a: 105) observed, "there are considerable differences" (e.g., specificity of salt in the process, order of elements prepared, and stages of washing). At points, *ALD's* treatment of this topic parallels the Aramaic *New Jerusalem* text (e.g., 11Q18 13) and invites comparison with a larger suite of writings rethinking the traditions related to bull offerings (e.g., *GenAp* [1Q20] 10 17; *Temple Scroll* [11Q19] 34 9–12; *Ant.* 3.227; *m. Tamid* 4:3). In this way, *ALD may* represent an early reception and interpretation of the foundational sacrificial prescriptions of Leviticus 1. But, more importantly, this material relates to a broader scope of traditions exploring, imagining, and describing patterns of sacrificial processes in a variety of literary and interpretive contexts.

Second, the Qumran texts include wine in the sacrificial process. Here too, there is potential for gauging varieties among early representations. Most significantly, *ALD* does not seem to refer to a receptacle for holding the wine, as is the case in *New Jerusalem* (11Q18 13 4–5), but shares the understanding with the *Temple Scroll* (11Q19 34 13) and *Jub.* 7:3–5 that the wine is poured over the sacrifice in its entirety. Though not extant in the Qumran fragments, *ALD* also detailed and updated the measurements for wine (and oil) offerings using post-exilic measurements. On this approach, *ALD* and *New Jerusalem* again align in their strategy for expressing sacrificial measurements in a contemporary system.

Third, *ALD* includes a list of acceptable wood species for use on the altar (4Q214b 2–6 i 4–6). Though wood is necessary for burnt offerings—unless you are Elijah calling down divine fire!—the Hebrew Scriptures are generally ambivalent about the types of wood for fueling sacrifice (Lev. 1:12, 17; 3:5; 4:12; 6:12; 14:6; cf. Lev. 14:49–52; Num. 19:6). While several Hebrew texts of the Second Temple period develop traditions around schedules or celebrations related to supplying wood for altar use (e.g., Neh. 10:34; 13:31; 4QPentateuch^c [4Q365] 23 4–12; *Temple Scroll* [11Q19] 23 1–3), only *ALD* and a parallel tradition in *Jub.* 21:12–14 enumerate the types of wood permitted for use on the altar.

On these points, it is evident that aspects of *ALD*'s "law of the priesthood" at once reflect other innovations of sacrificial law that developed throughout the Second Temple period and, in a closer way, relate to developing priestly traditions among the DSS collection. Feldman (2020: 346) recently argued that "sacrifice in Aramaic Levi cannot be explained simply as revision, rewriting, or gap-filling vis-à-vis Leviticus and should not be read as proto-rabbinic." In view of the larger complex of traditions highlighted briefly here, it is now clear that *ALD*'s sacrificial imagination is an early one, though not necessarily a Levitical interpretation.

2.4.4. *Discourses against Promiscuity and Demonic Temptation*

In various sections, *ALD* develops constructs that maintain priestly identity as a safeguard against waywardness. One strategy involves deploying a two-ways motif. In a discourse delivered to his children, Levi references a group who strays from the א[וֹרחת קשׁטא ("ways of truth"; 4Q213 4 5), a direction seemingly associated with darkness (4Q213 4 1, 6–7). Thus, Greenfield, Stone, and Eshel

(2004: 218) perceive the structure of "light-dark dualism," yet this is not clear in the available text. In Levi's prayer, however, it is evident that the imagined world of the text is one where malevolent beings persuasively draw humans from the [אָרחת קשט ("ways of truth"; 4Q213a 1 12).

By the end of the fragment, Levi prays, וְ[אַל תשלט בי כל שטן ("let not any satan rule over me"; 4Q213a 1 17). This phrase represents another contribution of the Levi tradition for documenting developments in demonology. The reference appears to entail a category of beings (i.e., satans) rather than a specific red bastard with a pointy tail and pitchfork subsequently known by that name. Though many contemporary conceptions of angels and demons are a by-product of medieval imaginations inherited in current Western culture—such as the one of the foregoing sentence—the Aramaic DSS make an important contribution to recovering the development of the realms, roles, and realities of otherworldly figures in Second Temple period thought. These demonic forces in *ALD*, therefore, are assigned roles that could compromise the integrity of the priestly line if wayward behavior is not avoided.

The impulse for waywardness in Levi's prayer, however, is not only from without. One of the themes cautioned against in the prayer and beyond is the avoidance of זנו, typically rendered "fornication." Conceivably, זנו implies promiscuity that could compromise the sexual or marital purity of the priesthood (e.g., 4Q213a 1 13; cf. *ALD* 16). In this term and focus, *ALD* shares a common concern with *WQ* (4Q542 3 ii 12). Damascus Document associates Levi with cautions against the שלושת מצודות בליעל ("three traps of Belial"), one of which is זנו (*CD* 4 14–19). At a minimum this reference attests to an early memory of Levi speaking against promiscuity, perhaps in relation to the larger caution against the enticement of demonic forces. For discussion of the intertextual dynamics of this reference, see the commentary on 4Q213a 1 13.

2.5. *Genre*

The question of genre for the Aramaic materials related to Levi extends back to the very beginnings of research on the Cairo Genizah and Qumran texts and perhaps earlier still with hints in the translation and reception history of the work itself. As is also the case with *WQ*, the biggest question in this regard is whether or not the composition is a testament.

As noted above, in his publication of the Cave One materials and initial discussions of the Cave Four texts, Milik (1955a: 87; cf. 1955b; 1976: 24) presented the texts under the title "Testament de Lévi." This understanding also extended to his consideration of the Qahat and Amram materials as constituting the group of three testaments and perhaps even related to a patriarchal pentateuch (Milik 1972a). That Milik's determinations on the genre of *ALD* were still developing is evident from his passing reference to the texts as "Testament (ou des Visions) de Levi" in other publications (Milik 1978: 95). This openness is likely due to the dream-vision elements of *ALD* and his parallel study of the *VA* fragments, which carries an internal title marking their visionary character (4Q543 1a–c 1–4

// 4Q545 1a i 1–4 // 4Q546 1 1–2). Beyer (1984: 188) also retained the testament classification. He noted, however, that the work's testamentary quality is not due to its ancestral discourse (a feature common to the Greek *Testaments of the Twelve Patriarchs*) but to Levi's potential delivery of the material from a near-death perspective. As Frey observed (2010: 363), the testamentary association of *ALD* in relation to the later Greek *T. Levi* was part of the early discussions of the Cairo Genizah materials. Apparently, this connection even precedes modern scholarship on the tradition as the excerpter of the Syriac fragment "tells us that the quotation comes from the 'testament' of Levi" (Davila 2013: 123).

Milik's preliminary genre assessments, however, were challenged from an early time. Burchard (1965: 283 n. 2) asserted that the Aramaic Levi materials are primarily ancestral discourses akin to writings such as *Jubilees* and *GenAp*, not the later testaments. Though Greenfield and Stone at first continued the use of testamentary language to describe the Aramaic Levi materials at Qumran and in the Cairo Genizah, their progress toward publishing the Cave Four materials included a re-evaluation of genre and adoption of the more neutral, and now standard, title *Aramaic Levi Document* (cf. Greenfield and Stone1979; and 1985: 457–69; 1990).

To be sure, the text is important for understanding the development of testamentary literature that comes into its own much later. Yet as many have rightly underscored, *ALD* is not a testament (Drawnel 2004: 87; Frey 2013: 366; Davila 2013: 124; Hillel 2019: 262). As Kugler (1996a: 24) remarked, the revision to the modern title is necessary for at least two methodological reasons and enables a reorientation around what is most central to the text:

> First, as it turns out, *Aramaic Levi* is probably not a testament, lacking as it does the formal characteristics of that genre, most conspicuously a deathbed context for Levi's words. Second, it is misleading to call it by the name of the document for which it served as a source. The designation betrays the bias built into most study of *Aramaic Levi*, and obscures its independent existence prior to *Testament of Levi*. Therefore, it is necessary to adopt a new term. The difficulty in doing so lies in *Aramaic Levi*'s fragmentary nature, and the concomitant uncertainty whether we possess its beginning and conclusion. Because those parts of a document are essential for defining positively its genre, and thus classifying it accurately, a name that includes genre designation must be avoided. We settle on the name *Aramaic Levi*, since it captures the document's character—an Aramaic text about Levi, son of Jacob—and avoids the use of genre terminology.

In this respect, any characterization of *ALD* must recognize both the diverse themes and genres embedded within—dream-visions, a wisdom poem, a prayer, an address to Levi's children, biographical information, legal instruction on priestly matters, and eschatologically oriented content—as well as the single entity that binds them together: the figure of Levi. Elevating a single element among this diversity over the others to assign genre risks both flattening the complex expressions of the work and obscuring the centrality of Levi's persona as the common denominator across the composition. In this regard, while Drawnel (2004: 93–96) is correct to underscore the sapiential and didactic qualities of the work, these thematic elements do not override the entire work as we know it (cf. Hillel 2019: 262).

While identifying *ALD*'s orbit around Levi may not resolve the genre question, it does advance our understanding of the scribal use of a pseudepigraphic perspective as a compositional strategy. The work is dominated by Levi's first-person voice and utilizes his figure as an anchor for both drawing upon and extending his authority as a significant ancestral figure for the founding of the priesthood. Part of the *ALD*'s agenda was to reconceive Levi's memory from the dismal record given in Gen. 49:5 (Drawnel 2004: 87; Davila 2013: 124; Hillel 2019).

In addressing these concerns in the formation of a parascriptural narrative, the scribe(s) behind the text developed memories of Levi that extended well beyond the initial exegetical interest of reimagining the impulse and outcomes of the Shechem episode. One should approach the text as a scribal venture in extending Levi traditions. Recognizing the expansion of the lore, revelation, wisdom, instruction, and priestly profile of this ancestor forces us to see the diverse directions Levi's position as a founding figure of the priesthood enabled. In this way, Lange and Mittmann-Richert's (2002: 117–18, 123) primary categorization of *ALD* as "parabiblical"—a category they understand as inherently comprised of different genres based upon different interests and items in antecedent writings—is perhaps the most helpful way forward. Of course, the modest nuance of opting for the term "parascriptural" is necessary to skirt the challenges of canonical anachronism.

2.6. *Compositional Date and Social Setting*

The emerging consensus in research on *ALD* is that the composition likely dates to the third to early second century BCE (Greenfield, Eshel, Stone 2004: 19; Kugler 1996a: 134; 2010: 884–85). Drawnel (2004: 63–75) inches into the late fourth century BCE. Based on Schattner-Rieser's (2007: 143) study of Milik's monograph notes, he apparently suggested a potentially earlier date in the Persian exile, specifically for the underlying text of 4Q213a, which he reportedly dated to the fifth or sixth centuries BCE! The compositional dates preceding the third to early second centuries BCE are speculative. It is far more likely that *ALD* took shape in the mid-Second Temple period. Determining a likely compositional date range involves coordinating several pieces of information related to *ALD*'s paleographical, ideological, intertextual, and linguistic characteristics.

Paleographically, 4QLevi^f is the oldest manuscript of the Cave One and Four *ALD* materials (ca. 150–30 BCE), providing a *terminus ante quem* of the early to mid-second century BCE. The radio carbon dates of 4QLevi^a, dated by its scribal hand to ca. 50–25 BCE, are also instructive for establishing some broad parameters for the production of the manuscript: 197–105 BCE (1σ range, with 68%

confidence) and 344–324/203–48 BCE (2σ range, with 95% confidence) (Doudna 1998–9: 468). Unquestionably, the compositional date precedes the exemplars at Qumran.

Aramaic Levi Document's internal ideologies and external intertextual dynamics also suggest the third- to second-century BCE range. As Kugler commented (1996a: 135), the priestly rhetoric of *ALD* is relatively neutral, lacking both sharp critiques of priestly controversies and accentuated insider language of sectarian thought, both of which crescendo in mid- to late second-century BCE writings. Kugel (2012: 346, 357) argued that the blended royal-priestly language of *ALD* signals its collection and composition by the hand of a pro-Hasmonean writer. However, as VanderKam (2018: 92) responded, it is not until the tenure of Aristobulus I in 104–103 BCE that a Hasmonean ruler takes on the title of king (cf. *J.W.* 1.70; *Ant.* 13.301). Prior to this, Hasmoneans were essentially "civil rulers." Therefore, the royal-priestly claims of the late second century BCE cannot explain the ideology of *ALD* since this would conflict with the paleographical date of 4QLevi^f.

Part of the debate over the date of *ALD* pertains to its potential avenues of interaction with other texts and traditions in ancient Judaism. Determining these directions is neither easy nor always possible. Yet it does seem that Aramaic Levi traditions were formative to other known writings of the period, not least *Damascus Document*, certainly *WQ* and *VA*, and perhaps *Jubilees*.

While Kugel (2012) argued for *ALD*'s dependence on *Jubilees*, I find VanderKam's (2018: 90–93) proposed reliance of both texts on a common set of traditions more compelling. This explanation accounts for the most variables (i.e., the limits of our knowledge based on fragmentary texts, precision in the use of political ideologies to date texts, a broad network of literary similarities in structure and detail, and the setting for the rewriting of ancestral traditions in the mid-Second Temple period [cf. Machiela 2012]) while creating the fewest problems (i.e., it does not demand a theoretical source-critical proposal, which is inadvisable given our incomplete knowledge of the forms of *ALD* among the Aramaic DSS). In this way, the compositional date of *Jubilees* in 161–152 BCE (VanderKam 1997) provides at least one important parameter for *ALD*'s compositional date as no later than the mid-second century BCE.

As Stone (2002: 318–19) argued, the composition in Aramaic supports a date as early as the third century BCE, since the now-known larger suite of Jewish writings in this language at Qumran emerged in this era. Linguistically, there is general agreement that the idiom of *ALD* reflects the linguistic setting of Aramaic in the late-second millennium BCE (Greenfield and Stone 1979: 227–29; Fitzmyer 2000: 244–45). However, Norin's (2013) philological comparison of the Qumran and Cairo Genizah witnesses is a healthy reminder that early and late linguistic forms crop up at intervals in transmission history, which presents challenges for methods based only on linguistic dating.

In terms of social location and provenance, there have been a range of proposals from specific to unknown. In several instances, Milik (1971: 345; 1976: 24; 1978: 96, 106; cf. Schattner-Rieser 2011: 806) alluded to or outlined his case for the Samaritan origin of *ALD*, which he implied extended also to *WQ* and *VA*. For *ALD*, this identification was based largely on a perceived concentration of northern toponyms, especially אבל מין ("Abel Mayin") in 4Q213a 2 13. Kugler (1996a: 137) viewed this proposal as "remarkably attractive," and augmented it by arguing that *ALD* was partially developed out of a form of Leviticus that had affinities to the sacrificial regulations of the Samaritan Pentateuch, exhibited a shared concern for intermarriage that would fit with a Samaritan context, and elevated the figure of Joseph, which may relate to the Samaritan theology of a laity descending from Joseph (Kugler 1996b). While he proposed that these preliminary findings may hint at support for a Samaritan priesthood against the Jerusalem establishment (1996a: 127–28, 137), Kugler is aware that the textual, social, and theological potential of this hypothesis is limited by the fragmentary evidence (Kugler 1996a: 104 n. 155, 137; 1996b: 358). Duke (2005: 121) accepted such arguments as "good cases for the Samaritan province for the Levi material" with little critical evaluation.

Regarding the geography depicted within *ALD*, a literary setting or theological orientation cannot be mistaken with authorial social location. The extension of this social location to the Qahat and Amram materials is more problematic still and should not be retained. Additionally, it is likely that Milik's identification of the location "Abel Mayin" is confused (see the comment below on 4Q213a 2 11–13). The possibility of interaction with a proto-Samaritan text of Leviticus does not demand such a provenance. The presence of a diversity of pentateuchal materials within the Qumran library exhibiting degrees of scribal harmonization mitigate against this point (see Knoppers 2017: 167–72). In short, while intriguing, the likelihood of *ALD*'s northern provenance is slim.

It may be that so-called proto-Samaritan scriptures provided the scribes of parascriptural Aramaic literature with convenient points of departure for their exegetical strategies for expanding traditions (cf. VanderKam 1978 for a proto-Samaritan textual substructure of *GenAp*). This, however, would say more about the *ways* in which scribes worked than about the locations *where* they undertook such activities. Joseph may have ascended to a special status for priestly memory in later Samaritan tradition. But in view of the fully published Qumran Aramaic corpus, the scribes of these writings clearly participated in extending memories of a host of ancestors for their priestly potential. In these ways, then, none of the hints at a Samaritan origin of *ALD* hold water.

Other proposals on the origins of *ALD* have been less oriented on geography and more conscious of social location. In this regard, the pervasive priestly tone of the work has lent itself to both specific and generic proposals. The following scholarly proposals plot *ALD*'s potential production at numerous sites across the ancient Near East or spaces within Judaean society.

In a study of the potential origins of the Greek *Testaments of the Twelve Patriarchs*, Becker (1970: 149–51) outlined eleven ideological-literary points in the texts, including the Levi materials, that led him to see the texts as originating in Hellenistic Judaism but not Qumran specifically. Focusing on the figure of Levi in early Aramaic materials and *Jubilees*, Hultgård (1977: 15–81) deduced that

ALD is likely a pre-Essene Zadokite work which may have influenced the thought of the Qumran group. (For synopses of Becker's and Hultgård's proposals in the context of research on *T. Levi*, see de Jonge [1985: 24–25].) Beyer (1984: 189) read the priestly discourses of *ALD* against the impacts of Hellenism on the priesthood in the mid-second century BCE. As noted above, Kugler's (1996a: 137) suggestion read *ALD*'s rhetoric as indicating a competing priesthood in Samaria. In these ways, many scholars posit Hellenistic Judaea as the plausible point of origins for *ALD*.

Others, however, gauged *ALD*'s perceived literary and theological emphases as related to some priestly group. Greenfield, Stone, and Eshel (2004: 20–22) outline seven features of the work that may "hint at the character of the group that produced it." Their items include: solar calendar, priesthood, purity, generational transmission of knowledge, dualisms and demonology, the paradigmatic role of Joseph, and the lack of sectarian language. In view of this outline, they suggest the writers of *ALD* were "priestly in character, though one might query whether *ALD* comes from a group connected with the Jerusalem temple, or an opposition group of some kind, though no polemical characteristics can be detected" (2004: 22). Drawing on their work, Hillel (2019: 262) concluded, "[t]he provenance of *ALD* remains unknown; the document contains no direct indications of its origins." Kugel (2012: 357) argued that *ALD* was a composite work developed in support of the Hasmonean royal-priestly status, with the aim of both emphasizing the Levites's right to the priesthood and grandfathering the clan's royal claim "back to the time of Levi himself." Emphasizing ancient Near Eastern influence on both the knowledge and didactic models upon *ALD*, Drawnel (2004: 94) determined that "the [*Aramaic Levi*] *Document* probably grew in the Levitical milieu in which priestly education, metro-arithmetical training, and scribal ideas were transmitted." Such proposals attempt to capture something of the social milieu of *ALD* from its conceptual contours. Of course, these are susceptible to much interpretation, although *ALD*'s priestly quality is undeniable.

Finally, at least two scholars have found a tighter association between *ALD* and Qumran. With little in the way of independent argumentation, Schattner-Rieser (2007: 144) wrote that "[t]he various literary elements in the Aramaic Levi Document had probably been shaped into a 'testamentary' narrative by the Essenes or Qumran copyists." Kugler (2008) also proposed sectarian intervention into 4Q213b 1 1, which he suggested bore the marks of a Qumran scribal approach of "revoicing" traditions from a divine perspective. Both of these scholarly proposals, however, fail to convince.

As this overview demonstrates, there is a surprising diversity of perspectives for the compositional beginnings of *ALD*. As with the Qahat and Amram materials, the authorial origins of *ALD* are unknown and allusive. It is undeniable that *ALD* took shape in a priestly scribal group that was well-versed in ancestral traditions related to sacrificial processes and practices of purity. The group was also adept at extending these traditions in light of a changing cultural context and their broader scientific knowledge of the ancient world. Anything beyond this is speculation.

The emphasis on "origins," however, easily overlooks the earliest historical instance of the reception of the tradition in the known socio-historical context of Qumran. Judging from *Damascus Document*'s allusion to a Levi tradition (see the comment on 4Q213a 1 13), it is evident that Levi traditions formed some aspects of sectarian thought and identity. It is unknown if the *ALD* copies were produced elsewhere and received at Qumran or were transmitted within that scribal community. The paleographical dates of the manuscripts suggest a continued transmission of the texts in some locale in the centuries after its composition. Thus, a myopic pursuit of authorial origins risks missing the far more certain indicators of the tradition's appeal and use at Qumran and perhaps beyond in the mid-Second Temple period.

2.7. *Text and Commentary: 1QLevi (1Q21)*

The material remains and photographs of 1Q21 are particularly unforgiving. At present, digital images exist only of the earlier PAM plates, which are themselves rather disorganized and frustratingly unclear. Given this situation, my commentary below is based primarily on the transcriptions of DJD 1 (Milik 1955a: 87–91). Even the best-preserved fragments reveal but a few words or phrases that can be identified with known content from other *ALD* witnesses. As Drawnel (2004: 22) summarized, while Milik (1955a: 87) gathered these fragments mostly for their paleographical similarities, only four (1Q21 1, 3, 4, 45) "unequivocally overlap" with known materials of *ALD*. While it is certainly true that, in some cases, the Qumran witnesses attest to previously unknown content of *ALD*, interpreting all these fragments along those lines is inadvisable. To further complicate matters with this manuscript, Schattner-Rieser (2007: 146) reported that Milik "seems to have identified other fragments of 1Q[21] not published in DJD," which are presently unidentified.

Given the fragmentary nature of the materials of 1Q21, the commentary below focuses only on 1Q21 1, 3, and 4. 1Q21 5, while possibly associated with *ALD* 26, retains but a single word (יצחק, "Isaac") and is thus insufficient for commentary. For the sake of general impressions, however, it is worth overviewing the nature and content of other fragments. In even the best cases, these involve mere characters, stray words, or, in a very few instances, partial phrases.

The largest fragment, 1Q21 8, is clearly set in a first-person address. 1Q21 7 2, of similar size, includes the phrase תִּמְלֹךְ עִם ("you will rule people/with"). Several names and nouns are among the smaller unplaced fragments, such as יַעֲקֹ[ב אֲבִי ("my father [Jaco]b"; 1Q21 29; cf. 19) and זְרַע ("seed"; 1Q21 28), which may be remnants of Levi's discourse on the ancestral line. This may relate to the reference of [יִ]שראל ("[I]srael"; 1Q21 58). Mentions of ראשא ("the head"; 1Q21 45) and כדניא ("the jugs"; 1Q21 59 2) may suggest additional content on priestly offerings and processes. The reference to טעותא ("the idol"; 1Q21 31) may also reflect a warning against waywardness or idolatry. The mention of שמיא ("the heavens"; 1Q21 32 1) could relate to either Levi's posture in prayer or his dream-vision experience. The phrase מן קרבא ("from the war"; 1Q21 51 1) may refer to a memory or expectation of battle. Finally, the fragments include an intriguing cluster of verbs such as לוט ("to curse"; 1Q21 12 1), בָרֵךְ ("to bless"; 1Q21 50), חזה ("to see"; 1Q21 54 1), and רחם ("to love"; 1Q21 57 2).

The scattering of fragments that comprise 1Q21 remind us that we cannot always recover the full scope of Aramaic literature recovered in the caves in the Judaean wilderness. These fragments either indicate that the *ALD* tradition extended further than we can discern based on the limited evidence available or attest to the large number of small Aramaic fragments relating to unknown works.

2.7.1. *The Political-Religious Profile of the Priesthood (1Q21 1)*

This is the largest of the puzzle pieces of 1Q21, here including the apparent juxtaposition of the political-religious profile of the high priesthood with other kingdoms. The fragment does not overlap with any specific passage of the Cairo Genizah texts, but may relate to Levi's dream-vision.

1 [...] מֹ[ן די לֹהוין תלתין [...]
2 [...]בִّיךְ מלכות כהנותא רבא מן מלכות[...]
3 [...]לֹ[...]לֹ[...]לֹ[...]

1. [...]because they will be three[...]
2. [...]...kingdom of the high priesthood than [the] kingdoms of[...]
3. [...]...[...]...[...]...[...]

Commentary

Line 1: *because they will be three*. Greenfield, Stone, and Eshel (2004: 141) noted the possible relevance of *T. Levi* 8:14. However, *T. Levi* 8:11 may provide the closer comparison, since it references the division of Levi's posterity into three offices.

Line 2: *kingdom of the high priesthood than [the] kingdoms of*. Drawnel (2004: 111–12) and Greenfield, Eshel, and Stone (2004: 66–67) located this fragment in the context of Levi's dream-vision, confirming the priestly context and otherworldly confirmation of Levi's priesthood. *Visions of Amram* participates in a similar idea by underscoring the angelic ordination and continuity of the priestly line (Perrin 2015a: 166–70).

This seems to be the only Qumran fragment referencing the high priestly office. Greenfield, Stone, and Eshel (2004: 141) noted the additional reference at *ALD* 67, spelled in the Cairo Genizah text as בְּהֹנֻּתא רבתא (MS A, Cambr. c 7 1). *Aramaic Levi Document* 9 refers to Levi as the ראש [כהנו]תֹה ("the head of the [high priest]hood"; MS A, Bodl. a 8 16–17; cf. 4Q213b 1 5) in the narrative of his priestly installation in the Jacob encounter.

The pairing of priestly and political language here implies that the office has some dynastic quality (cf. 4Q213 1 ii–2 15). Though the context and content of the present line are limited, the particle מן seems to be juxtaposing, comparing, or positioning this high priestly domain with that of other kingdoms. As Drawnel (2004: 112) commented, this points to "a contrast between two kingdoms, with the prevalence on the side of the priestly rule." *Testament of Judah* 21:2–4 includes a similar idea, though developed to parallel the dynamics between priestly vs. royal power with heavenly vs. earthly rules.

This recalls the concept of a ממלכת כהנים ("kingdom of priests") from Exod. 19:6 that later writings picked up and developed. Perhaps the closest tradition-historical connection is with *Jub.* 16:18, which uses similar language when looking ahead to the priestly quality of Isaac's lineage. At Qumran, this phrase also likely occurred within a fragmentary line of the *War Scroll* (4Q491 16 3). In a highly fragmentary Aramaic text, the phrase ונתא[כֹּהֹ]מל[כֹּוֹת ("king]dom of pr[iests"; 4Q582 1 5) also occurs. Already in DJD 1, Milik (1955a: 88) noted thematic similarities with later Christian texts (e.g., Rev. 1:6; 5:10; 1 Pet. 2:5–9).

2.7.2. *Glimpses of Levi's Dream-Vision of Ascent (1Q21 3)*

The fragment includes phrases from Levi's dream-vision of heavenly ascent relating to the destitution of the kingdom of the sword. The content here relates to that of *ALD* 4–6.

1 [...]וּקֹ[רבא [...]
2 תֹּעמל וזמנין תנֹ]וח...[
3 [...] עָֹלמֹֹא [...]

1. [...] the [ba]ttle [...]
2. It will labor and at times [it] will re[st...]
3. [...]etern[al...]

Textual, Scribal, and Material Notes
Line 1: וקֹ[רבא ("and] the [ba]ttle") – The form is read here in view of the corresponding form in *ALD* 4 (MS A, Bodl. a 8 3; cf. Drawnel 2004: 112). Milik (1955a: 88–89) read ח[רבא ("the [s]word") but noted the reading לקרבא ("for battle") as a possibility.

Line 3: עָֹלמֹֹא ("etern[al") – Both the fragment and photos are difficult at this point. Milik (1955a: 88) read the remains of two words: ש]לם עָלמֹ[א ("eter[nal pe]ace". This reading is possible and would reflect the content of *ALD* 6. However, the more conservative reading included here better accounts for the available ink traces (cf. Drawnel 2004: 112).

Commentary
Lines 1–3: *and] the [ba]ttle [...]It will labor and at times [it] will re[st...] etern[al...].* This material comes from the penultimate section of Levi's dream-vision, immediately before his elevation by an angelic revealer and picks up on

the notion of juxtaposed kingdoms from 1Q21 1. The addition here is a partial description of the stark struggle and dire conditions of what *ALD* 4 describes as מלכות חרבא ("the kingdom of the sword"; MS A, Bodl. a 8 2). It is possible that this language builds on the framework of a two-ways motif, which is prominent in Levi's wisdom discourse.

2.7.3. *The Tithe of Jacob (1Q21 4)*

Limited content of *ALD* 9, which references Jacob's tithe and recognition of Levi as the head of the priesthood. The overlap with 4Q213b 1 4 involves a variant reading.

1 [...]אבי יע[קב מעשר...]
2 [...]ל[...]

    1. [my father Ja]cob tithed[...]
    2. [...]...[...]

Commentary

Line 1: *my father Ja]cob tithed.* The content here comes from one of the few places of internal overlaps in the Aramaic DSS and is one of still fewer variant readings among the Qumran *ALD* witnesses (Perrin and Diggens 2020c). Where 1Q21 4 reads אבי יע[קב מעשר, the overlapping materials in 4Q213b 1 4 include a modest syntactical variation, יעקוב אבי מעשר ("Jacob, my father, tithed"). In the corresponding Cairo Genizah text, a gap in the manuscript suggests that the later witness agreed with the phrasing of the Cave Four fragment (Grelot 1956: 404; Drawnel 2004: 113; *contra* Stone and Greenfield 1996: 39).

2.8. *Text and Commentary: 4QLeviᵃ (4Q213)*

This manuscript survives in but five fragments, all of which preserve enough content for commentary. Fragments 4Q213 3–5 include content not previously known from the later witnesses, thus providing new insight into the earliest form(s) of *ALD*. For a material description of the fragments of 4Q213, see Stone and Greenfield (1996: 1).

2.8.1. *Wisdom Discourse on Success and Scribal Status (4Q213 1 i)*

A portion of Levi's wisdom discourse underscoring how right living, wisdom, and scribal knowledge lead to honor and success. All of these are described as the treasures of wisdom. The material in this fragment corresponds to *ALD* 82–95.

2. Aramaic Levi Document

Top Margin
1 [...] *vacat*
2 [...]מֹית בה
3 [...]אֹ∘נון
4 [...]לֹבֹנֹיֹ
5 [...]אֹנה לבֹן
6 [...רא]שֹׁ כל עבדכֹן
7 [...]∘ֹ [...] צדקתא וקשטא
8 [...ברי]בֹה דזרע טב טב מעל
9 [...זר]עֹה *vacat* וכען ספר ומוסר וחכמה
10 [...]∘ ליקר עלם די אלף חכמה יקר
11 [...לב]סֹרון ולשיטו מתיהב חזו לכן בניׁ
12 [...ומוס]רֹ חכמה ליקר ולרבו ולמלכין
13 [...]אל תמחלו חכמתא למאלף
14 [...]רֹ״סֹ גברֹ די אלף חכמה כל
15 [...ל]הֹ לכל מת ומדינה די יהך לה
16 [...]רֹ בה ולא דמא בה לנכרי ולא
17 [...י]הֹבין לה בה יקר בדי כלא צבי
18 [...רחמו]הי שגיאין ישאלי שלמה רבֹרבֹיֹןֹ
19 [...]לֹלֹ[...] ∘[...]זֹ למשמע מליֹ חכֹמֹתֹהֹ[...]
20 [...]ידעיה ושימה טֹבֹה
21 [...קֹשֹׁיֹטֹאֹ]...[תֹ ועם]∘ [הֹ]∘ [ ]∘

1. [...] *vacat*
2. [...]he died in it
3. [...]...them
4. [...]to my sons
5. [...]I to you
6. [...Foremost,] all of your deeds
7. [...]...[...] upright character and truth
8. [...bless]ed. He who sews goodness brings goodness
9. [...]his [se]ed. *vacat* And now, scribal craft, instruction, and wisdom
10. [...]...for everlasting glory. The one who teaches wisdom attains glory
11. [...]is given [to dis]dain and to scorn. Observe for yourselves, my sons
12. [...and instruct]ion, wisdom for glory and greatness and to kings
13. [...]do not neglect to learn wisdom
14. [...]...a man who learns wisdom, all
15. [...to] him to any land or nation that he goes about
16. [...]... in it and he will not be like a stranger in it and will not
17. [... wi]ll give him in it honor, for all will desire
18. [... h]is [friends] *are* many and well-wishers abundant
19. [...]...[...]...[...]...to hear his words of wisdom
20. [...]those who know her and fine treasure
21. [...]truth[...]...and people...[...]...[...]

Textual, Scribal, and Material Notes

Primary images for transcription: PAM M41.405; PAM M43.241; B-295984; B-295402.

Line 7: וּקְשׁטָא ("and truth") – The *tet* and *aleph* are inscribed over the stitching of the sheets, suggesting the scribe penned the text on an already prepared scroll.

Line 8: בְרִי[כָּה ("bless]ed") – The form here is read and reconstructed in light of בריכה in *ALD* 86 (MS A, Cambr. e 6 14; cf. Stone and Greenfield 1996: 5, 9; Drawnel 2004: 156; Greenfield, Stone, and Eshel 2004: 102).

Line 9: וכען ("And now") – The Cairo Genizah materials reveal a textual variant here in the form of a plus not evident in the Qumran fragment. *Aramaic Levi Document* 88 (MS A, Cambr. e 8 17) reads וּכְעַן בני ("And now, my sons"). The plus sets a more intentional scene of Levi gathering his children for instruction. Note that in both witnesses the variant phrase is preceded by a *vacat* indicating a sense division.

Line 10: יקר ("glory") – There is a minor syntactic variant here with the Cairo Genizah text. *Aramaic Levi Document* 89 (MS A, Cambr. e 6 20) adds a conjunctive *vav* in the form ויקר ("and glory").

Line 11: לְב[סְרון ("[to dis]dain") – This partial word is read and reconstructed in view of לבשרון in *ALD* 89 (MS A, Cambr. e 6 14; cf. Stone and Greenfield 1996: 5, 9; Drawnel 2004: 156; Greenfield, Stone, and Eshel 2004: 102). The reconstruction assumes a common sibilant variation between the Qumran and Cairo Genizah materials.

Line 12: וּמוֹסֵ[ר ("and instruct]ion") – A partial *resh* of a lost form is likely at the fringe of the fragment, suggesting the form ומוסר found in the corresponding text of *ALD* 90 (Stone and Greenfield 1996: 9; Drawnel 2004: 156; Greenfield, Stone, and Eshel 2004: 102).

Line 14: רֵיֹסׁ גְבַֿר ("…a man") – The form is damaged here and bears the marks of a scribal intervention above the line. At present, the meaning of the first form is unintelligible. The *yod* and final *nun* penned above the line are in a stronger hand and/or by a stylus with a blunted end resulting in thicker ink strokes. Both the original and corrected text of the Qumran fragment are unknown. The Cairo Genizah materials here read די מאלף ("whoever teaches"), which does not cohere with the ending of the form in the 4Q213. Drawnel (2004: 159, 337) proposed the correction here was to the form [די] מְהֹלֵּךְ ("[whoever] guides"), which "seems to be a scribal correction from מאלף." The limited ink traces available for the supralinear text, however, are insufficient to support this reading and the proposed sequence of correction. More conservatively, Stone and Greenfield (1996: 9) included כ[לׄ∘∘יׄגְבַֿר in their reconstructed and combined text, yet do not comment on the apparent difference with the Cairo Genizah materials. At most, we can say there are the remnants of a scribal correction implying a variant reading with later known witnesses.

Line 14: הכמה ("wisdom") – Stone and Greenfield (1996: 5–6) transcribe a dot over the *mem* here and suggest it "might be part of an ink splatter." They transcribe a similar dot over the final *peh* of the preceding form אלף, yet do not comment on this aspect of the text. New digital images (B-295402, January 2012 [full-colour]; B-295984, April 2012 [infrared]) confirm that the perceived dot over the *peh* is a tiny circular hole in the fragment and the proposed spatter over the *mem* is small.

Line 16: ‎ר̇[בה ("]... in it") – Stone and Greenfield (1996: 5, 9) read an uncertain character at the edge of the fragment. The partial ink stroke is a possible *resh* (see B-295984, April 2012 [infrared]). At this point, the Cairo Genizah text of *ALD* 91 (MS A, Cambr. f 6 8) reads: מ]תנכר הוא בה (see Drawnel 2004: 161 for context and translation). If the *resh* in the Qumran text is to be understood as the final character of the form מ]תנכר, then there would be a textual variant here with the later witness.

Line 19: חכֹמתֹה ("of his wisdom") – The form is highly fragmentary on the manuscript. Yet the reading is likely in view of the ink traces and insight from the Cairo Genizah materials for *ALD* 93 (MS A, Cambr. f VI 15; cf. Stone and Greenfield 1996: 5, 9; Drawnel 2004: 159; Greenfield, Stone, and Eshel 2004: 104).

Line 20: ידעיה ושׂימֹה טֹבֹה ("those who know her and fine treasure") – There is a variant reading here with the Cairo Genizah text at *ALD* 94, which reads the shorter phrase וסימא טאבא ("a fine treasure"; MS A, Cambr. f 6 15). Note also the sibilant variation of *sin* and *samek* from the Qumran to Cairo Genizah witnesses.

Line 21: קֹשׁיטא ("truth") – My reading here differs from other editions but is based on improved digital images of the fragment (B-295984, April 2012).

Commentary

Line 2: *he died in it.* This phrase relates to a temporal marker of Levi's age of 137 in the year of Joseph's death (*ALD* 81–82). As Greenfield, Stone, and Eshel (2004: 206) noted, "Joseph's death was regarded as a significant turning point in Patriarchal history from Exodus 1:6 and 1:8 and on" (cf. *Jub.* 34:15; *T. Sim.* 1:1, Heb. 11:22; *City of God* 7).

Lines 3–5: *]them[...]to my sons[...]I to you.* While there is little remaining text in the upper section of the fragment, this content clearly sets the discourse in a context of first-person discourse from the patriarch to his gathered progeny. This motif is shared also with *VA* and *WQ* and extends to a larger network of Aramaic writings at Qumran. For discussion, see the comment on 4Q542 1 i 4.

Lines 6–8: *all of your deeds[...]...[...]upright character and truth[... bless]ed. He who sews goodness brings goodness.* These forms and phrases relate to the fundamental principles of Levi's teaching: if קשט ("truth") and צדקה ("upright character") are the guiding ethic of one's actions, one reaps good things. Formally, these items are presented in poetic parallel (Drawnel 2004: 327; Greenfield, Stone, and Eshel 2004: 203; Lee 2015: 213–27). The limited materials that have survived in the Qumran fragment, therefore, represent the positive half of a two-ways wisdom metaphor that is spelled out more fully in the Cairo Genizah witnesses. For discussion of these two nouns in the context of the Aramaic DSS, see the comment on 4Q542 1 i 12.

Qahat's instruction to his children invests a great deal in virtue and ethics as captured in the list of qualities he presents to his children. The first two items of that list are the same two qualities underscored here in *ALD*, which may suggest Qahat's discourse is constructed on the fundamental wisdom principles of Levi's teaching. Drawnel (2004: 327) noted another instructional dynamic at play within *ALD*, as the theme of "truth" is equally central to Isaac's instruction, suggesting "Levi's teaching of the truth should be interpreted in light of Isaac's instructions."

Line 9: *And now, scribal craft, instruction, and wisdom.* The content here begins a new section, as indicated by the *vacat* in the manuscript. The later Cairo Genizah text also uses a blank space as a section marker at *ALD* 88 (MS A, Cambr. e; pl. 6 17).

The triad of terms is partially retained in 4Q213 1 i 12, there in the context remembering Joseph's character and capabilities in the Egyptian court (cf. 4Q214a 2–3 ii 5). In this way, scribal craft, instruction, and wisdom represent the core of ancestral inheritance handed down through the priestly generations and, therefore, champion the priestly lineage as embodiments of these proficiencies and ideals. For *ALD*, priestly identity is rooted in these areas of knowledge both in its memory and projection. *Testament of Levi* 13:2 also receives and advances this notion.

The specialized sense of ספר here refers to neither a "document" as an object holding text nor the mere facility with a script of language—it is a calculated use of the form to represent the prominent scribal profile and proficiencies of key figures. *Testament of Levi* 13:2 here reads νόμος ("law"), which "may be indicative of the editorial tendencies" of the later Greek tradition (Greenfield, Stone, and Eshel 2004: 209; cf. Greenfield and Stone 1996: 3).

The term מוסר ("instruction") is a Hebraism (Stadel 2008: 42). Other occurrences of the form in the Aramaic DSS include the calque in 11Q10 27 4 (Job 36:10) and a possible fragmentary occurrence in 4Q534 7 1.

References to חכמה ("wisdom") are far more numerous in the Aramaic DSS than the first two items in this triad. See: 1Q20 6 4; 19 25; 20 7; 4Q212 1 iv 13; 4Q213 1 i 9, 10, 12, 13, 14, 19; 1 ii + 2 5; 4Q213a 1 14; 4Q531 2 + 3 10; 4Q534 1 i 8; 4Q536 2 i + 3 5; 4Q541 7 4; 4Q543 2a–b 2; 11Q10 30 2; 33 7; 37 4; cf. 4Q541 7 4; 4Q574 1 8.

In the larger context of the Aramaic DSS, some of these categories were essential to memories of other founding figures or expectations of the eschatological age. *Genesis Apocryphon* locates Abraham in the Egyptian court instructing nobles in ספרא וחכמתא וקושטא ("scribal craft, wisdom, and truth"; 1Q20 19 25). He derives this learning from an Enochic writing, which implies Enoch too was invested with these qualities in the memory of Aramaic scribal culture.

The pair חכמה ומדע ("wisdom and knowledge") are qualities attached to the eschatological elect in the revelatory Enochic tradition (4Q212 1 iv 13 [*1 En.* 93:10]). As Greenfield, Stone, and Eshel (2004: 208) noted, the threefold reference in *ALD* is similar to *Jub.* 4:17, which states Enoch's branches of learning as "writing and knowledge and wisdom." Finally, as Greenfield (1993: 43) noted, these three items bring to mind the Aramaic Ahiqar tradition, wherein Ahiqar, the "wise and skillful scribe" (col. 1, line 1 recto; cf. col. 3, lines 35–36, 42), trains his adopted son in חכמתי ועטתי ("my wisdom and [my] couns[el]"; col. 2, line 19).

Line 10: *for everlasting glory. The one who teaches wisdom attains glory.* The initial phrase indicates the rewards of pursuing scribal craft, instruction, and wisdom as described in the previous line. The second unit expresses that the ongoing acquisition and transmission of wisdom results in glory. The model of Joseph is again in the purview, as line 12 underscores his ascent ליקר ולרבו ("for glory and greatness") on account of his wise character and instructional talent.

Greenfield, Stone, and Eshel (2004: 202) highlighted the didactic tone of the wisdom poem, achieved in part by the threefold use of the verb אלף ("to teach"; 4Q213 1 i 10, 13–14). The present use is likely a *pael* verb, indicating a pedagogical call to action rather than the acquisition of wisdom (compare the *peal* forms in 4Q214 1 i 13–14 indicating "learning"). In the present line, Levi exhorts the priestly progeny not only to receive knowledge but to transmit and mobilize it for future generations. *Words of Qahat* continues this model (4Q542 1 ii 1). The concept may derive generally from an earlier model in the Israelite wisdom tradition (Prov. 15:33) or, as Greenfield, Stone, and Eshel (2004: 208) noted, derive from the linkage between priestly instruction and judgment (Deut. 33:10, Mal. 2:7; Sir. 45:17).

Lines 11–12: *is given [to dis]dain and to scorn. Observe for yourselves, my sons[…and instruct]ion, wisdom for glory and greatness and to kings.* The end of the clause at line 11 comes from a phrase outlining the eventual outcomes of a life despising wisdom, which is undergirded by a two-ways wisdom motif.

The imperative חזו ("observe") draws attention to the exemplary model of Joseph as a wise ancestor and teacher, whose personality is apparent in the more complete Cairo Genizah materials. For discussion on the terms that are the content of Joseph's teaching here, see the comment on line 9. That Joseph was not only capable but also influential in the foreign court is indicated by the partially extant phrase indicating his enjoinment to the thrones of rulers. As Drawnel (2004: 336) noted, "the link between the teaching and sitting on the throne is well attested in *A.L.D.* 93" and received later in the Greek *T. Levi* 13:9. In this section of 4Q213, then, we have one of our earliest receptions of the Joseph tradition in Aramaic. Drawnel (2004: 335) proposed that the emphasis on Joseph instructing royalty is based on an interpretation of Gen. 45:8, which states Joseph was designated as אב לפרעה ("father to Pharaoh"; cf. 2 Kgs 6:21; 13:14). He continues, "for the author of the [*Aramaic Levi*] *Document*, this expression could only mean that Joseph was the pharaoh's tutor and the pharaoh was his disciple."

In the context of the Aramaic DSS, it should also be emphasized that the figure of Joseph is also received, reworked, and ultimately reimagined in the Aramaic Daniel tradition (von Rad 1976; Gnuse 1990; Segal 2016: 48–51) and possibly in 4Q539. The reception of the figure of Joseph in the Aramaic DSS, then, involves both memory of a founding figure and formation of new characters.

Lines 13–14: *do not neglect to learn wisdom[…]…a man who learns wisdom, all.* The two-ways wisdom concept continues here with the contrast between one who pursues wisdom and another who disregards it for another course. The verb מחל carries the idea of "neglect" or "abandon," coming from the basic meaning "to let drop" (Cook 2015: 137). The more complete Cairo Genizah text of *ALD* 91

(MS A, Cambr. f; pl. 6 4–6) spells out the positive outcomes of living in pursuit of wisdom as longevity of life and fame.

Line 15–17: *to] him to any land or nation that he goes about[...] in it and he will not be like a stranger in it and will not[... wi]ll give him in it honor, for all will desire.* The benefits of a wise life continue. As with the model of Joseph, *ALD* emphasizes that wisdom is the key to a kind reception and success in foreign contexts. While the narrative of *ALD* does not feature a court tale episode, this statement provides a rubric for success in such settings. Even though Jews would be foreigners is such a context, they will be treated as natives. The term נכרי here is also used to describe an outsider in *WQ* (see the comment on 4Q542 1 i 5 for lexical analysis).

Lines 18–19: *h]is [friends] are many and well-wishers abundant[...]... to hear his words of wisdom.* These partial lines come from a unit affirming the ripple effects of attaining wisdom in one social sphere. Not only does it win favor and prominence among royalty, wisdom wins friends and good will. Royalty and common folk alike will flock to Levi's wise progeny to glean from their teaching and knowledge. This language continues the comparison of the one who disdains the pursuit of wisdom, who will be a stranger to others (4Q213 1 i 16).

Drawnel (2004: 338) sees this idea as extending from the sapiential concept that activities of teaching contribute to constructing friendly and healthy relationships. In the shadow of the recent memory of the Joseph tradition, Greenfield, Stone, and Eshel (2004: 211) drew attention to Wis. 10:13–14, which draws a tight connection between Joseph's living wisely and winning favor with those around him in his upward mobility from prison to the top of the Egyptian political system.

Line 20: *those who know her and fine treasure.* Attaining wisdom is equated with discovering a priceless treasure trove. The form שימה ("treasure") is exclusively bound to wisdom in *ALD*. Here the metaphor of discovery captures the worth of wisdom (cf. Prov. 3:15; 8:21; 16:16; Col. 2:2–3). Shortly after, 4Q213 1 ii–2 3 elevates wisdom as a sought-after city full of riches and fortified for protection. The Hebrew manuscript of the book of Tobit at Qumran underscores שימה טוֹבָה ("good treasure") as the outcome of generosity and alms giving (4Q200 2 9 [Tob. 4:9]). Limited occurrences in other Hebrew writings of the period (4Q504 7 9; Sir. 40:18; 41:12) likely point to Aramaic influence.

2.8.2. *The Sapiential City (4Q213 1 ii–2)*

Levi's wisdom discourse continues, now underscoring the scribal and pedagogical pursuits of wisdom, her enshrinement in a metaphorical city, and the outcomes of everlasting glory for a royal-priestly kingdom. The initial phrase of line 1 overlaps slightly with *ALD* 96. Otherwise, the text continues beyond all other witnesses. Overlap: 4Q214a 2–3 ii; **4Q214b 8.**

2. Aramaic Levi Document

TOP MARGIN

1 מטמוריה ולא יעלון תרעיהֿ ולא [...]
2 ישכחון למכבש שוריה [...] ולאֿ [...]
3 יחזון שיֿמֿתה שימתֿה ○[...]○דֿ[...]
4 ולא **איתי כֿ**]ול [מֿחור נגדה ○[...]
5 בעא חכמהֿ[...]○מֿת[...]○○[...]
6 **מטמרה מנהֿ**[...]○אלֿ○[...]
7 ולא חס[...]○[...]הֿ כל בעלֿ[...]
8 אֿקֿשטֿ [...]**ובען בני** [**סֿפר ומוסר**
9 הֿ]כֿ[מֿה ד אלֿ○[**חזית בחזוין דיֿ**]תֿרתון אנון
10 י○[...]רבה תתנון
11 [...]קֿרֿ *vacat*
12 א○[...]אֿף בספריא
13 קרֿהֿ[...]זֿן ראשין ושפטיֿן
14 דֿהֿ[...]ב ועבדין
15 [...]אֿף כהנין ומלכין
16 ת○[...]○[...]זֿ מלכותכן
17 תהֿוֿאֿ[...]דֿ ולא איתי סוף
18 לֿוֿ○[...]תֿעבר מנכן עד כל
19 ○[...]○ בֿיקר רבֿ
20 [...]
21 ○[...]

1. her hidden places and they will neither enter her gates nor [...]
2. they will *not* be able to flatten her walls ...[...]and not[...]
3. they will see her treasure, the treasure ...[...]...[...]
4. and there is no price equal to it ...[...]
5. seeking wisdom[...]...[...]
6. to hide it from him[...]not...[...]
7. and not...[...]...[...]...all who seek
8. and truth [...And now my sons,] scribal craft and instruction
9. wi[sd]om that...[I saw in visions that]you will inherit them
10. ...[...]great you will give
11. [...g]lory *vacat*
12. ...[...]also in the books
13. ...[...]... heads and judges
14. knows[...]...and servants
15. [...]also priests and kings
16. ...[...]...[...]...your kingdom
17. it will be[...]...and without end
18. ...[...]will pass from you until every
19. ...[...]...with great glory
20. [...]
21. ...[...]

Textual, Scribal, and Material Notes

Primary images for transcription: PAM M41.405; PAM M43.241; B-295984; B-295402; B-295987; B-295405. To aid in interpretation below, I present the fragments jointly. For configurations of the underlying Aramaic texts, see Stone and Greenfield (1996: 17–20) and Drawnel (2004: 163–4). Even within these arrangements, however, it is clear that content is missing between the extant sides of the column. Where there is no overlap with the later witnesses, I do not venture any reconstructions beyond what can be recovered from the Qumran fragments themselves.

Line 1: תרעיה ("her gates") – The ink dot above the final character of this form is an "editorial dot" (Stone and Greenfield 1996: 14; cf. 4Q213 1 ii 16).

Lines 11: While the Aramaic text is nearly entirely lost here, save for a sole *aleph* and an indecipherable ink trace, the margin of 4Q213 1 ii–2 11 includes a small fishhook-like scribal marking, a *paragraphos*. A *vacat* that runs to the end of line 11 suggests the scribe signaled the end of a discourse unit. See similar interventions in 4Q213a 2 10–11 (*paragraphos*) and 4Q542 1 ii–2 8–9 (horizontal line). For additional comment on this feature in the priestly literature and Aramaic DSS, see the textual notes to the *WQ* occurrence.

Line 16: ת ("...") – Though much of this form is lost at the very outset of the line, it is clear an ink dot was placed above the initial character of the word, perhaps indicating the character was part of a correction (cf. 4Q213 1 ii 1).

Commentary

Lines 1–3: *her hidden places and they will neither enter her gates nor [...]they will not be able to flatten her walls ...[...]and not[...]they will see her treasure, the treasure.* The beginning of this fragment marks the end of overlap with other known witnesses to Levi's wisdom poem. The phrase מטמוריה ולא ("her hidden places and they will neither") overlaps with the final words of *ALD* 96 (MS A, Cambr. f; pl. 6 23). The hiding places are for safekeeping the treasure introduced in 4Q213 1 i 20.

As hinted above, the content of these lines likens wisdom to a city that will not be conquered or plundered by any foe. Greenfield, Stone, and Eshel (2004: 203) remarked that "[t]his image is rather unusual." At the very least, it is unprecedented. The Hebrew Scriptures contain select references to the protection offered by wisdom (Prov. 4:6–7; Eccl. 7:12) and a single instance of wisdom building her own dwelling (Prov. 14:1). In the DSS, elaborate architectural descriptions of cities are typically eschatologically oriented and related to a renewed Jerusalem (e.g., *Temple Scroll*, *New Jerusalem*, Tob. 13), which is, of course, also evident in the Hebrew Scriptures (Ezek. 40–48).

For *ALD*, the city is metaphorical. Enemies will neither be able to break through her clad gates nor vanquish her indestructible walls. As wisdom was previously epitomized as fine treasure, her embodiment in the architecture and defenses of the fortress make the imagined city equally precious and invaluable as well as an awe-inspiring sight even to her assailants. As the inheritors of Levi's wise teachings, perhaps his priestly progeny are the implied protectors of this city constructed of wisdom, inviting another comparison to the idea of protecting the ancestral inheritance in *WQ*. Given the heritage of Levi's protecting the priestly family with violence, this concept of a priestly guard is intriguing.

Line 4: *and there is no price equal to it.* The phrase overlaps with 4Q214b 8 1. As the inheritance of wisdom is passed down and protected by the priestly progeny, outsiders will recognize its invaluable quality when they approach the imagined city. The term מחיר ("price") occurs only in these overlapping *ALD* fragments at Qumran and is likely a Hebraism (Stadel 2008: 42).

Commenting on the nature of this "treasure," Greenfield, Stone, and Eshel (2004: 213) gathered an impressive list of passages that either connect riches with the fruit of wisdom (Wis. 7:14; Sir. 29:11–12; *2 En.* 50:5) or liken wisdom to treasure (Isa. 13:10; 22:6). They note also the relevance of 4Q525 2 iii 2–3, which indicates wisdom "will not be acquired with gold o[r with silver...]with all precious stones" (cf. Job 28:18; Prov. 8:11; 16:16).

Lines 5–7: *seeking wisdom[...]...[...]to hide it from him[...]not...[...]and not...[...]...[...]...all who seek.* The phrase מטמרה מנה ("to hide it from him") in line 6 overlaps with 4Q214b 8 2. Though the content of 4Q213 here is limited, the available phrases and forms suggest either a continuation of the allure of the sapiential city and the inability to overtake her or a shift into a reiteration of the advantages of acquiring and safeguarding wisdom for the insider priestly lineage. The motif of the "hiddenness" (√טמר) of wisdom surfaces again here (cf. 4Q213 1 ii–2 1), as does the emphasis on "seeking" (√בעי) wisdom.

Line 8: *and truth [...And now, my sons,]scribal craft and instruction.* The materials here come from the same line but are on separate fragments, which requires a gap between the extant content. The overlap with 4Q214a 2–3 ii 5 is instructive in that the reference to וֹכְעַן בֹּנִי ("And now my sons") indicates a shift in discourse. This confirms that the reference to קשט ("truth") is not from the same unit as the content later in the line. The references to ספר ומוסר ("scribal craft and instruction"), then, are the initial pair of a threefold reference that is completed by the mention of חֹ[כ]מֹה ("wisdom") in line 9 (cf. 4Q214b 8 3). The terminological triad already occurred in 4Q213 1 i 9, suggesting that the terms here echo the earlier portion of the wisdom poem and form a sort of inclusio to the section. Here "Levi is made to be not only a sacerdotal functionary, but now also a scribal figure" (Kugler 1996a: 130).

Line 9: *wi[sd]om that ...[I saw in visions that]you will inherit them.* We can infer, despite the broken context, that the core of the ancestral inheritance for the priestly line is in fact "scribal craft, instruction, and wisdom" (lines 8–9), since the verb ירת ("to inherit") immediately follows this repeated triad. The supplied phrase in the reconstruction comes from the overlapping materials in 4Q214a 2–3 ii 6, which connects the priestly inheritance with divine revelation.

The second-person plural reference to the audience and the topical shift to inheritance suggest this content marks a move back into paraenesis, which continues for the rest of the fragment with other second-person plural suffixes in subsequent lines (Stone and Greenfield 1996: 20). The concept of the transmission and retention of a priestly inheritance is central also to *WQ* (see nominal forms of ירותה at 4Q542 1 i 5, 12), which suggests a shared understanding of the importance of privileged knowledge to identity formation and maintenance of this insider priestly group. Drawnel (2004: 341) commented that the likely interaction of Levi and Qahat traditions here "assure the transmission of this tradition" to the next generation.

Lines 10–11: *great you will give[...g]lory.* The text in these lines is damaged but suggestive. The initial partial verbal phrase hints at the impact of the priestly progeny on account of their wisdom profile. A *vacat* and corresponding marginal hook signal the end of this section of the wisdom poem. The possible mention of יְקָ[ר ("glory") here suggests a reiteration of the elevation of the priestly progeny if they are successful in acquiring, pursuing, and protecting the ancestral inheritance of wisdom, scribal craft, and instruction (cf. 4Q213 1 i 10–12). Like the metaphorical sapiential city, the progeny too will attain glory for their wise character.

Line 12: *also in the books.* The idea of scribal learning as part of the inheritance seems to be connected in some way to ancestral lore. Greenfield, Eshel, and Stone (2004: 214) and Drawnel (2004: 342) suggested that Levi is referencing something gleaned from "books I re[ad." Although possible, the reading and reconstruction of the verb at the outset of line 13 are conjectural. It is more likely that the reference here is not to lore accessed in the past but lore passed down to the priestly genealogy. While wisdom, scribal craft, and instruction are no doubt the core of this tradition, the full scope of knowledge embedded in this imagined booklore is technically unknown (cf. Drawnel 2004: 324–43). This is the only reference to booklore using the form בספריא in the Qumran *ALD* fragments, but the connection between a priestly inheritance and received writings is much more evident in *WQ* (4Q542 1 ii 9–13) and in *VA* (4Q543 1a–c 1; 4Q547 9 8). If this interpretation is correct for *ALD*, 4Q213 1 ii–2 12 would include the earliest clue of a memory of the priestly forefathers cultivating scribal knowledge as an ideal in tandem with transmitting scribal lore down through their generations. Motifs of priestly scribal expertise extend also into *VA*, which draws a close association between revealed knowledge and inscribing revelation (4Q547 9 8).

Scribal acts and artefacts of writing occur throughout the imagined, narrative worlds of the Qumran Aramaic texts, beyond the priestly pseudepigrapha studied here. Intriguingly, key examples demonstrate that this theme is threaded into narrative settings from both the antediluvian days and exilic diaspora (Perrin 2018b; cf. Tigchelaar 2007; Dimant 2010; García Martínez 2014). The samples that follow are not exhaustive of the Aramaic corpus; rather, they are illustrative of the more diverse scribal imagination that obtains across a network of the Aramaic DSS.

Looking to the antediluvian past, the small fragment of 4Q203 8 1–5 encapsulates many terms and themes that show the retrojection of scribal qualities onto the ancestors. There Enoch is lauded as a סָפַר פרשא ("scribe of interpretation"; cf. 4Q530 2 ii + 6–12 14) in the context of references to many forms of inscribed media including: סִפְ[ר ("boo[k"), תִנְ[יָ]נָא די אִי[גרתא ("a copy of the s[ec]on tablet of the le]tter"), and בִּכְ[תָ]ב ("a document"). Enoch's scribal profile in the emerging Aramaic tradition, of course, is celebrated in *GenAp*, where Abram reads from an Enochic artefact before a captive audience of Egyptian nobles (1Q20 19 25–26) as well as in *Words of Michael*, which nods to an otherworldly writing likely accessed or inscribed in the course of Enoch's tour de universe (4Q529 1 1, 6). And this is to say nothing of the equally large and looming question of purported Noachic booklore, which was also cast in a new light due to notations such as that of 1Q20 5 29.

Examples of scribalism and writtenness from the other side of the narrative divide in the Aramaic corpus include scenes in both court tales and apocalypses. Acts of writing and resulting books are part of the Aramaic Danielic traditions (e.g., Dan. 7:1 [cf. 12:4]; 4Q243 6; 4Q245 1 i 4). *Jews in the Persian Court* is shot through with references to scribal objects and even offices. In one instance, Bagasraw is concerned of imperial repercussions, as "the fear of בית ספרא fell on him" (4Q550 2 4). Alternatively, a Jewish courtier is referenced for his scribal reliability after reading before the king: "And [I] wa[nt]ed [to introduce you to] this good [scri]be (ספ[רא טבא), a good man, a servant of the [lord] of the [kingd]om" (4Q550 5 + 5a 3–4). *Jews in the Persian Court* (4Q550 1–2) also depicts the deposit and access of imperial records in scribal archives using terms and tropes analogous to Ezra 6:1–2.

While references to scribes and scrolls are generally in short supply in the Qumran Hebrew texts, the opposite of this trend is true in the Aramaic materials. The sketch here could be developed into a more complete portrait. For the immediate purposes, however, it provides a preliminary context for understanding both the centrality of scribal actions and artifacts in the Aramaic DSS, to which *ALD*, *WQ*, and *VA* contributed.

Lines 13–14: *heads and judges… knows[…]… and servants*. With little context for the forms in these and subsequent lines it is difficult to discern how these items relate to the attainment of wisdom. It is possible that they refer to those whom the priestly progeny will ascend over, similar to the model of Joseph in the previous section. The second office, שפט ("judge"), is a *hapax legomenon* in the Aramaic DSS and is likely a Hebraism (Stadel 2008: 43). The paired reference in the initial phrase of this line resembles Josh. 14:1; 23:2 (cf. Deut. 29:9; Mic. 3:11; so Greenfield, Eshel, and Stone 2004: 214). Drawnel (2004: 343) noted the similarity to *Jub.* 31:15, where Isaac declares Levi's sons as "princes, and judges, and chiefs." Greenfield, Stone, and Eshel (2004: 214) are also correct that the form עבדין could refer either to "servants" or "making."

Line 15: *priests and kings*. The pairing of royalty and priesthood is unique, though, as Greenfield, Stone, and Eshel (2004: 38) describe, it comes "in a sadly fragmentary context." Elsewhere, Stone (1997: 135) proposed that this language and address to Levi's lineage—including Qahat—suggests that the continuance of the line will "incorporate royal attributes in his [i.e., Qahat's] priestly character. This is a very distinctive conception." Levi's dream-vision in 1Q21 1 2 also hints at the royal connotation of the priestly office by juxtaposing מלכות כהנותא רבא ("the kingdom of the high priesthood") with other kingdoms. In the Cairo Genizah materials, *ALD* 67 explains the origins of Qahat's name as significant for his rising to the high priesthood and that "he and his seed will be a supreme kingship, a priesthood for [all Israel" (MS A, Cambr. c; pl. 7 7). If that reference to the ascendency of Qahat to offices with priestly-royal significance is in view here, the mention of priests and kings in Levi's discourse may relate to a particular word spoken to Qahat about the offices his lineage will occupy.

Lines 16–19: *your kingdom... it will be[...]... and without end... [...]will pass from you until every... [...]... with great glory.* The second-person plural suffix on the form מלכותכן ("your kingdom") suggests that Levi is addressing the collective priestly lineage and describing the nature of their kingdom (cf. 1Q21 1 2; 4Q213 1 ii–2 16). If the following phrases are glimpses of the descriptors of this kingdom, its endurance and unsurpassable nature suggest an eschatological projection of the royal-priestly kingdom. As with the praise of wisdom, this kingdom too will culminate in יקר רב ("great glory"; cf. *ALD* 88).

2.8.3. *Astrological Terminology or Symbolism (4Q213 3)*

A fragment of uncertain placement including astrological terminology or symbolism.

TOP MARGIN
1 [...]ל° כל עממיא
2 [...ש]הׄרא בׄוכביא
3 [...]מן
4 [...]לׄשׄהרה

1. [...]...[...]... all the peoples
2. [...m]oon and stars
3. [...]from
4. [...]to the moon

Textual, Scribal, and Material Notes
Primary images for transcription: PAM M43.241; B-295985; B-295403.

Commentary
Line 1: *all the peoples.* The context of this phrase is unknown. Elsewhere in the Qumran *ALD* fragments, the phrase כול עמה ("all her people") is used to communicate the enduring revilement of an ancestral name due to the rape of Dinah (4Q213a 3–4 6). Variations on this phrase, however, occur in several writings in the Aramaic DSS (1Q20 15 18; 4Q534 1 i 8; 4Q537 15 1; 4Q553 3 + 2 ii + 4 6) and Hebrew Scriptures (Dan. 3:7, 31; 5:19; 6:26; 7:14; Ezra 7:25).

Lines 2–4: *m]oon and stars[...]from[...]to the moon.* The astrological terms in these lines do not occur in any other known sections of *ALD*. In the Qumran Aramaic texts, this pairing occurs also in *GenAp*: כול מזלת שמיא שמשא שהרא וכוכבׄיׄאׄ וׄעׄיׄרׄיא ("every heavenly body: the sun, the moon, and the stars, and the

Watchers"; 1Q20 7 2; cf. Ps. 148:3; Ep. Jer. 60). Based on this listing, Drawnel (2004: 168) follows Milik (1976: 23) by reconstructing שמשא ש[הרא וֹכוכביא here. Additional references to שהרא ("the moon") are extant in Enochic astrological revelation (4Q209 7 iii 6; cf. 4Q210 1 iii 3, 7; 4Q531 2 + 3 1). In this light, it is also possible that the language here relates to dream-vision symbolism. Astrological symbolism is also a core element of the largely lost account of the so-called Son of God text (4Q246 1 ii 1–2). Of course, Joseph's dream-vision in Gen 37:6–10 also includes some analogous terminology, which may be relevant to the present text given *ALD*'s elevation of Joseph's profile earlier in the wisdom sections.[2]

Based on this astrological terminology here and the apparent two-ways or dualistic language of 4Q213 4, Milik (1976: 23; cf. 1971: 344–45) boldly claimed these Qumran *ALD* fragments contain "[t]he earliest allusion to the Book of Watchers." But, as seen in the commentary for the following fragment, critical elements of this proposed allusion are far from secure in the transcription. For the present fragment, Milik's (1976: 23) added observation of the similarity to the Greek *T. Levi* 14:1–3 is possible. However, as Stone and Greenfield (1996: 21) noted, "the two texts are clearly far from identical." The Cave Eleven Job translation includes additional occurrences of the terms (11Q10 9 8; 19 1 [Job 25:4; 31:27]).

2.8.4. *Levi's Discourse on a Two-Ways Motif (4Q213 4)*

A fragment including Levi's continued discourse to his children, here with an apparent theme of binaries and/or a two-ways motif. This may suggest a future orientation to the end of Levi's exhortation.

1 [...]ן תחשכון [...]
2 [...]א הלא קבל ○[...]○ד [...]
3 [...]נֿא ועל מן תהוא חובתאֿ[...]
4 [...]הֿלא עלי ועליכן בני ארו יֿדֿעֿוֿנה
5 [...]אׄ֯רֿחת קשטא תשבקוֿןֿ[...]○כל שֿבֿיֿלֿי
6 [...]תֿמחלון ותהכון בחשוךֿ[...]שֿׁ○○○
7 [...]תֿקֿ חֿ[ש]וֿכה תתא עליכֿוֿןֿ[...]זֿ וֿתהֿכון
8 [...]שֿׁגֿיֿא...[בּֿעֿןֿ זֿמֿ[...]תהוון לשפלין
9 [...] בּֿ ○[...]קֿ[שיט]יֿן...[○בֿ○]○[...]

1. [...]...you will become dark [...]
2. [...]...did he not receive...[...]...[...]
3. [...]us and upon whom will come the guilt[...]
4. [...]is it not upon me and you, my sons, behold, they will know it
5. [...]you will leave the [w]ays of truth [...]all paths of
6. [...]neglect and proceed in darkness[...]...[...]

2. Thanks to Kyle Young for this reference and possibility.

7. [...]...dar[k]ness will come over you[...]...and you will proceed
8. [...]gre[at...]now...[...]you will become low
9. [...]...[...t]rut[h...]...[...]

Textual, Scribal, and Material Notes
Primary images for transcription: PAM M43.241; B-295986; B-295404.
Line 2: ךֹ‎ ֹ‎ ֹ‎[– The end of this line retains the lower sections of at least three characters, which are too scant to venture a plausible reading. These have been transcribed variously. The most intriguing proposal, however, is Milik's (1976: 23) reading, חֹנוֹךֹ ("Enoch"). Kugler (1996a: 121) and Wise, Abegg, and Cook (2005: 312) accepted Milik's reading. Nevertheless, the reconstruction seems to be informed more by the reference to Enoch in the later Greek *T. Levi* 14:1 than by the actual material remains of the Aramaic manuscript. A more certain reference to the figure of Enoch outside of Enochic traditions in the Aramaic DSS is found in the so-called *Pseudo-Daniel* text of 4Q243 9 1. Due to the limited text available, I read the text here with Stone and Greenfield (1996: 21).

Incidentally, the fragmentary remains at the start of the following line have invited another ancestral speculation. Greenfield, Stone, and Eshel (2004: 218) suggested that "נח at the start could be read more plausibly as 'Noah' that the final *kaph* preceding as חנוך 'Enoch.'" This too, however, goes beyond the available evidence. For comparison's sake, note the reference to Noah in a small fragment of *VA* (4Q547 5 3).

Line 5: קשׁ״א ("truth") – There is a superscripted character here, which Stone and Greenfield (1996: 21) confused as קט״א.

Line 6: בחשוּךֹ ("in darkness") – The reading of this form is difficult, but the proposal of this form by Drawnel (2004: 169) fits both the content and limited ink traces available. Stone and Greenfield (1996: 212) read בֹהֹ ∘ ∘. Later in the line Kugler (1996a: 121) rendered "in the darkness of satan," similar to Drawnel's reading שׂטן ("satan"). These proposals, however, extend beyond the reach of the available evidence.

Line 7: חֹ[שׁ]וֹּכֹה ("darkness") – Cook is correct that the reading is "very uncertain." While it reasonably coheres with available ink traces, the fragment is highly damaged at this point. More likely language of darkness occurs in lines 1 and 6 of the fragment.

Line 7: וֹתהֹכון ("and you will proceed") – Drawnel's (2004: 169) transcription, accepted here, offers an improved reading of the text.

Line 8: שֹׁגֹּ[...]יא[...]בֹּעֹן זֹמֹן[...]תהוון לשפּלין ("gre[at...]now and...[...]you will become low") – The reading of this line adopted here is more modest than most. It draws on the best of Drawnel's (2004: 169) work, while retaining insightful aspects of Stone and Greenfield's (1996: 22) transcription.

Line 9: קֹ[שׁיט]ן ("truth") – The line is highly fragmentary. While Drawnel (2004: 169) offers a more ambitious reading, the form included here is the only word that can be reasonably recovered from the ink traces at the lower reaches of the fragment.

Commentary
Line 1: *you will become dark*. The fragment includes language related to darkness in at least three places (4Q213 4 1, 6–7). In the present case, this includes a verbal form of the root √חשׁך, used only here and in an unidentified fragment from Aramaic Job (11Q10 A11 2). Inflected nominal forms of חשׁוך ("darkness") occur shortly after in 4Q213 4 6–7. This language may represent the remains of some form of dichotomy in the foretold future of Levi's progeny.

Lines 3–5: *us and upon whom will come the guilt[...]is it not upon me and you, my sons, behold, they will know it[...]yo[u] will leave the [w]ays of truth from all paths of*. This language seems to project a future time of wrongdoing or waywardness and raises the question of who is responsible for this misdirection. The issue of חובה ("guilt") emerges in line 3. This invites comparison with 4Q542 1 ii 6, which underscored the eternal guilt of the outsider before the judgment of priests.

Line 5 seems to indicate the innocence of the patriarch and his progeny. If this is the case, line 5 implies a bifurcation in the priestly progeny as some will depart from [א]ֹרחת קשׁטא ("the [w]ays of truth"; cf. line 9). Greenfield, Stone, and Eshel (2004: 217) observed that this theme connects the discourse with the same terminology used in Levi's prayer (4Q213a 1 12), the only difference being that in the other section, "the surviving text mentions only one way." Drawnel (2004: 347) noted that this phrase closely parallels those in 4Q212 1 ii 18; 1 v 25 (*1 En.* 91:18; 94:1) as well as fuller expressions in 4Q212 1 iv 22 (*1 En.* 91:14) and 4Q246 1 ii 5. Added to these, note the likely occurrence of the phrase אורחת ק[ושטא ("paths of t[ruth") in a so-called *Pseudo-Daniel* fragment (4Q243 7 3). Though its Semitic language *Vorlage* is lost at this point, it is possible that Tob. 1:3 also deployed similar terminology based on the Greek: ὁδοῖς ἀληθείας ("ways of truth").

The juxtaposition of darkness and guilt with a path of truth suggests this fragment draws upon or develops a dichotomy or two-ways motif. Like 4Q213 4, *GenAp* presents a similar patterning of darkness language with a path of falsehood (1Q20 6 3). Based on this analogy, Greenfield, Eshel, and Stone (2004: 218) proposed a more extensive reconstruction of the end of 4Q213 4 5 so that it likewise refers to [אמת עלמא] וֹכל שבילי ("all paths of [eternal truth]"). If this proposal is accepted, it would amplify and extend the nature of duality in Levi's discourse.

Lines 6–7: *dar[k]ness will come over you[...]and you will proceed*. As described in the textual note above, Drawnel (2004: 347) read a mention of satan here. In view of this, he proposed that the "unique expression חשׁוך שׂטן ['darkness of satan'] proves that the [*Aramaic Levi*] *Document's* eschatology is related to the light–darkness opposition, characteristic of a dualistic view of the spiritual world." This assertion extends beyond the available evidence. A more secure reference to שׂטן occurs in 4Q213a 1 17. Even without this reading, Greenfield, Stone, and Eshel (2004: 218) assert that the darkness language of the fragment "is related, of course, to contrastive light–dark dualism." The motif of walking in darkness is found in both Qumran Hebrew texts (1QS 3 21; 4 1; 11 10; 1QM 13 12) as well as in biblical literature (Isa. 9:2; John 8:12; 12:35; 1 John 2:11;

cf. Luke 1:79). The question of the origins, definition, and extent of this type of thought in *ALD* and the Aramaic DSS, however, remains an open question.

2.8.5. *Malevolent Beings against the Priestly Progeny (4Q213 5)*

A very limited fragment, with a possible reference to a malevolent being in some opposition to Levi's lineage.

1 [...]בֿ[ר]שׁׁעׁא עִׁמְּהֹוֹן בֿ[ר]שׁׁעׁא
2 [...]בֿאיכן אדין יר∘[ ]בכן
3 [...]∘שנון בכן מן כל בֿ[...]∘∘

1. [...]with them/their people by the [e]vil one
2. [...]...you, then ...[...]with you
3. [...]...with you from all ...[...]...

Textual, Scribal, and Material Notes
Primary images for transcription: PAM M43.241; B-295988; B-295406.

Line 1: עִׁמְּהֹוֹן בֿ[ר]שׁׁעׁא ("with them/their people by the [e]vil one") – The top of the fragment includes only the bottom portions of lost words. Greenfield and Stone (1996: 23) read]בֿ[ ]∘עׁא]∘∘∘[. Drawnel (2004: 170), however, rightly deduced some of the lost forms based on better images of the text. As such, I accept his readings here.

Line 2:]בֿאיכ[("...you") – The form, read here with Stone and Greenfield (1996: 23), seems to be a partial word. The initial partial character is most likely *bet*, although Drawnel's (2004: 171) reading שׁ[נֿאיכן ("those who h]ate you") introduces an intriguing possibility. Similarly, later in the line the extant characters יר' are also most likely from a lost word (Stone and Greenfield 1996: 23). Drawnel there proposed reconstructing יר'[ם ("he will aris[e]"), which seems to imply demonic opposition by the evil figure referenced in line 1. That reading is not certain.

Line 3: ∘שנון – I read this partial word with Stone and Greenfield (1996: 23). Drawnel (2004: 171) proposed לשני ("languages"). However, the penultimate extant character is a *vav* and the proposed *lamed* is known only by an ink speck in a location too low for that character.

Commentary
Line 1: *with them/their people by the [e]vil one.* If the reference to בֿ[ר]שׁׁעׁא ("the [e]vil one") is accepted, it may reflect yet another demonic figure in *ALD*. The reading, however, is far from secure. Elsewhere, the text references שׁטן as a class of beings (4Q213a 1 17), which makes the specific, determinative reference in the present line significant. *Visions of Amram* also contributes to the naming of malevolent beings with its reference to Melchi-resha and likely other lost names (4Q544 2 13; cf. 4Q280 2 2).

2.9. Text and Commentary: 4QLevi*ᵇ* (4Q213a)

Six fragments comprise the remains of 4Q213a. Of these, four are assigned to known sections of *ALD* based on the later witnesses. 4Q213a 5 i–ii references the [כֹּהנות עלמא ("eternal priesthood"), which, as noted below, opens up potentially new vistas for the enduring quality of priesthood in the worldview of *ALD*. 4Q213a 6 is too limited to warrant full commentary. The phrase]אמרת מא ("I said, 'What'") in 4Q213a 6 1 may relate to lost discourse between Levi and an *angelus interpres*, but without greater context this remains only a possibility. For a full description of the material character of the fragments, see Stone and Greenfield (1996: 25–27).

2.9.1. Levi's Prayer for Protection from Satanic Temptation (4Q213a 1)

A fragment of Levi's prayer emphasizing protection from waywardness and evil with an added petition for flourishing. This material overlaps with *ALD* 1a, known from a Greek translation inserted after *T. Levi* 2:3 in the Mt. Athos manuscript.

5 [...]דֹּן
6 [...]אָנה
7 [...]אתרחעֹ[תֹ וכל
8 [...] נטלת לשמיא
9 [...]וֹאצבעת כפי ודי
10 [...וֹ]אמרת מרי אנתה
11 [...אֹ]נֹתה בלחודיך ידע
12 [...]אֹרחת קשט ארחק
13 [...בֹ]אישˣ וזנותא דחא
14 [...חֹ]כֹמה ומנדע וגֹבורה
15 [...לֹא]שכחה רחמיך קדמיךֹ
16 [...]דֹּשפיר ודטב קדמיך
17 [...וֹ]אֹל תשלט בי כל שטן
18 [...עֹ]לֹי מֹרֹי וקרבני למהוא לכה
Bottom Margin

5. [...]this
6. [...]I
7. [...]I [washed] and all
8. [...]I lifted to the heavens
9. [...]...and the fingers of my hands and my hands
10. [...and]I said, "My Lord, you
11. [...y]ou and you alone know
12. [...]ways of truth. Remove
13. [...e]vil and repel fornication
14. [...w]isdom and knowledge and might
15. [...to f]ind mercy before you

16. [...]which is beautiful and good before you
17. [...And] let not any satan rule over me
18. [...up]on me, my Lord, and draw me near to become for you

Textual, Scribal, and Material Notes
Primary images for transcription: PAM M41.405; PAM M43.242; PAM M42.363; B-281216; B-295997; B-295425. 4Q213a 1 forms the lower left section of a column which was originally joined to 4Q213a 2 by stitching. Judging from the first photographs (PAM M42.363, May 1957) the separation of the two fragments occurred at an early time. Both fragments include a generous lower margin. 4Q213a 1 includes almost no left margin, while 4Q213a 2 has a moderate intercolumnar margin on the right. I have accepted several of Drawnel's (2004: 174–75) minor reconstructions of some partial forms at the fringes of fragments.

Lines 7, 10, 13–15, 17–18: Minor reconstructions to complete forms for sense are accepted here (see Stone and Greenfield 1996: 28 and Drawnel 2004: 172). Note that for the reading in line 7, אתרח[עת ("I [washed]"), the form is restored on the basis of the Greek ἔπλυνα (Mt. Athos E 2,3 1; Stone and Greenfield 1996: 28; Drawnel 2004: 172).

Commentary
Lines 7–9: *I [washed] and all[...]I lifted to the heavens[...]and the fingers of my hands and my hands.* Though the Qumran Aramaic fragment is damaged, the more complete witness to the passage in the Mt. Athos manuscript clarifies that Levi engaged in ablutions of his body and clothes to ensure priestly purity. Flannery-Dailey (2004: 159) proposed that these activities are to be understood as an incubation ritual for inducing a revelatory experience. This close connection is possible for the latter Greek *T. Levi* 2:4–5, which presents Levi's dream-vision on the heels of a reference to his prayer for deliverance. However, it is unclear in *ALD* that these actions are related to, or are the catalyst for, the subsequent dream-vision of Levi's priestly elevation. As Stone and Greenfield (1996: 28) commented, it is unclear if the "order of events in the two documents was the same." In this way, the content here is not evidence of incubation but a portrayed posture of purity in prayer.

Drawnel (2004: 211) observed that lifting one's eyes towards the heavens (Dan. 4:31; 1 Esd. 4:58; *4 Bar.* 6:2 [4]; John 11:41) or gazing in the direction of the temple (1 Kgs 8:38; Ps. 28:2; 134:2) are common *topoi* in prayer texts. In the context of the Aramaic DSS, Sarah exhibits a similar posture of prayer in 4Q196 6 8 (Tob. 3:11; cf. 4Q200 1 ii 5), ע[ליך אנפי ועינ]י נ[טלת ("my face [to]ward you and I [li]fted [my] eyes"), perhaps while looking toward the city of Jerusalem. Greenfield, Stone, and Eshel (2004: 124) highlighted that the idiom of extending one's palms upward in prayer is also common in prayer texts (Exod. 9:29; Ezra 9:5; Pss. 28:2; 154 [11QPs^a 23 3–4]; Job 1:13; *Jos. Asen.* 11:19; *Sib. Or.* 4:166).

Line 10: *and I said, "My Lord, you*. These lines retain the beginnings of Levi's first-person supplication. The phrase מרי ("my Lord," κύριε MS E, Mt. Athos) here and in 4Q213a 1 ii 18; 2 6 is a reference in the Aramaic DSS to God (1Q20 22 32). *Genesis Apocryphon* also uses this divine address in the context of a prayer (1Q20 20 12–15). Elsewhere it is used to reference angelic interlocutors (4Q546 8 5) as well as spouses in filial dialogues (1Q20 2 9, 13). For additional comments on divine titles in this Aramaic literature, see 4Q542 1 i 2.

Line 11: *y]ou and you alone know*. The subject of God's lauded knowledge is lost in the Aramaic fragment. From the Greek text, we learn that Levi spoke of God's unique awareness and insight into human thoughts. Greenfield, Stone, and Eshel (2004: 124) acknowledged a similar turn of phrase in the Aramaic *Book of Giants* (4Q203 9 3): די כל רזיא יד[ע אנתה ("Because [you] kno[w] all the mysteries"). Similar language also occurs in 4Q534 1 i 8 (Stuckenbruck 1997: 95).

Line 12: *ways of truth. Remove*. The phrase אׄרחת קשט ("ways of truth") invites the question of the degrees of dualistic thought and adaptations of two-ways metaphors in *ALD*. This language figures elsewhere in *ALD*, as seen in Levi's discourse to his children (4Q213 4 5). The immediate object of the *aphel* imperative ארחק ("to remove") is not clear in the available Aramaic text. But from the following partial lines and the more complete Greek text, it is clear that the prayer was for protection against spiritual, cognitive, and sexual waywardness.

Line 13: *e]vil and repel fornication*. The Greek here has a longer text, with the inclusion of καὶ ὕβριν ("and pride") in between these items (MS E 2,3 10–11 7). The initial item included in the Aramaic fragment is בא[ישׁ ("evil"), which undoubtedly refers to an evil inclination. The final item, זנות ("fornication"), is likely the object of the imperative דחא ("repel"). In this item, the prayer underscores the expulsion of sexual promiscuity away from the priestly line as well as the distancing of evil thoughts that lead to waywardness. Drawnel (2004: 214) notes this pairing also occurs in Mt. 15:19.

The warning against זנו is well-established in *ALD*. In *ALD* 16, Isaac's instruction to Levi emphasizes avoiding promiscuity: "First of all, beware, my son, of every *fornication* (זנו{ת} [MS A, Bodl. b 8 14–16]; πορνεία [MS E, Mt. Athos]) and impurity of every harlotry." This reference recalls the terms of Levi's earlier priestly prayer in *ALD* 1a, which includes his request that God remove pride and "fornication" from him. The Mt. Athos Greek text here reads a doublet πονηρὸν καὶ πορνείαν, likely a later development of the simpler idiom and reference to זנותא, as found at Qumran (4Q213a 1 13). Cautions against promiscuity for the priestly line are also essential to the insider vs. outsider rhetoric of *WQ* (4Q542 1 i–ii 12), suggesting a jointly developed motif for the Aramaic priestly literature. The Greek Tobit traditions also reference πορνείας in a caution against sexual promiscuity (Tob. 4:12). That Levi was understood as a figure advocating against this form of sexual waywardness is evident in *CD* 4 14–19. That passage draws upon a Levi tradition as a lens for Isa. 24:17 and states:

> The true meaning (פשרו) of this verse concerns the three traps of Belial about which Levi son of Jacob said that Belial would catch Israel in, so he directed them toward three kinds of righteousness. The first is fornication (זנות); the second is wealth (הון); the third is defiling the sanctuary (טמא המקדש). Who escapes from one is caught in the next; and whoever escapes from that is caught in the other.

There has been much debate over whether or not this passage cites, alludes to, or is aware of the specific tradition of *ALD*. Most often, however, this issue is argued and analyzed from the perspective of intertextuality. Before the Qumran *ALD* were known, Shechter (1910: xxxv n. 17) proposed *CD* likely had the *T. Levi* in mind, a position accepted and adopted also by Charles (1913: 2:790). Rabin (1958: 16; cf. Kosmala 1978: 115; VanderKam 1998: 395) cautioned, however, that the phrasing of *CD* does not bear exact resemblance to anything in the known traditions of *T. Levi*. As publication of the Qumran materials proceeded, Greenfield (1988) made the connection between *CD* and *ALD*. He argued that the Hebrew text indeed quoted the Aramaic work, yet the philological parallels between the three terms were skewed by a scribal error in the late transmission history of *CD*. Hanan Eshel (2007) later adapted this position, maintaining that while *CD* did cite *ALD* here, there are conceptual and exegetical links between the triads in the two texts that do not demand Greenfield's theory of textual corruption.

While I am inclined to see an intertextual relationship here between *CD* and an Aramaic Levi tradition, at least three issues inhibit a final conclusion on this matter at the level of detecting allusions. (1) The Aramaic materials for this portion of *ALD* at Qumran are highly fragmentary. Gauging textual dependence, use, or allusion in view of such fragmentary sources is problematic or even impossible. (2) While the later Greek Mt. Athos text is helpful, assessing intertextuality based on a translated text from a much later time compounds challenges rather than enhances clarity. We lack a full understanding of the original shape of *ALD*, have limited knowledge of the transmission and reception of the tradition from Aramaic into Greek, and already see in the passage at hand that there are variations between the two witnesses. (3) The traditional tools of assessing citations or allusions typically require certain thresholds for probability based on multiple criteria—sequences or series of words, phrases, or unique terminology. Yet these are limited in *CD* as the posterior text and cannot be verified in the Qumran *ALD* fragments as the anterior text. In view of these problems, I concur with Drawnel (2004: 214): "It is difficult to be sure that *CD* referred to our composition [*ALD*]."

There is, however, a way forward from this stalemate. The debate thus far has fixated on *textual* relation. Yet there is a clear common denominator to these materials: Levi as he exists as a figure beyond a single composition. *Aramaic Levi Document* is developing a new profile of the ancestor Levi. Part of that profile involved drawing a close connection between this redrawn patriarch with a deep and dire concern for priestly purity understood in part as avoiding sexual promiscuity. This idea is instantiated in *ALD*, yet it is more important to see how this ideal is enshrined, even embodied, in the remembered figure of Levi. That is, *ALD* is a text within a larger tradition oriented around a figure remembered and remade.

In this respect, the question is not "are the texts related?" but "how do both texts cultivate this aspect of Levi's persona?" While *CD* cites this teaching as some sort of speech act from Levi, this is not necessarily a citation formula of a quoted text. It is equally possible, even probable given the explosion of ancestral pseudepigraphy in this era and the Aramaic DSS, that this was a mechanism for mobilizing this memory of a patriarch committed to purity by harnessing the authority of his voice. Levi "spoke" on this matter—it is that authoritative voice that is leveraged in *CD*.

This perspective also opens up a larger question of how other ideas shared by *ALD* and *CD*, especially the purity of priestly space, connect to larger conceptual frameworks. For instance, the concern for freedom from promiscuity in priestly-oriented texts extends into *WQ*. Though the context is limited, 4Q542 3 i–ii 12 also connects the teaching of Levi's son Qahat with either caution about, or deliverance from, זנו. On the association between Levi's warnings against promiscuity with varied demonological references in *ALD* and *CD*, see also comment on 4Q213a 1 17.

Line 14: *w]isdom and knowledge and might.* This content marks a slight shift in the discourse as Levi is no longer asking for distance from negative actions or attitudes but beseeching God for his provision of positive qualities and capacities. The first of these items, ח[כמה ומנדע וגבורה ("w]isdom and knowledge and might") comes in a triad. There are several potential scriptural backgrounds for this phrasing (Kugler 1996a: 73 n. 48). However, Drawnel (2004: 214) is correct that the closest correspondence is Isa. 11:2. Greenfield, Stone, and Eshel (2004: 128) add that there is "a similar accumulation of positive language" in 1QS 4 2–8 as well as in *1 En.* 93:10 (4Q212 1 iv 13).

In the immediate context of *ALD*, this list calls to mind Levi's admonishment to ascend to the threefold items: "scribal craft, instruction, and wisdom" (4Q213 1 i 9, 12; cf. 4Q214a 2–3 5; 4Q214b 8 3). Though the content shares but one item, the packaging of three elements together in praise or admonishment indicates a formal similarity and pattern. The pattern possibly extends to the threefold reference to negative qualities or behaviors, as in *ALD* 16 (cf. *CD* 4 15–18; Eph. 4:19; 5:3; cf. Mic. 6:8; Mt. 23:23).

Lines 15–16: *...to f]ind mercy before you[...]which is beautiful and good before you.* The Qumran fragment provides insight into the original phrasing of *ALD* in two main ways. First, the root רחם ("mercy") in the Aramaic was perhaps theologized, or at least took on a new dynamic, in the later Mt. Athos Greek text as χάρις ("grace"; MS E 2,3 10–11 9). Of course, the theology of both the process and project of the Greek translations of ancient Jewish texts remains a contentious issue (see Young 2020). Second, the phrase דשפיר ודטב קדמיך ("which is beautiful and good before you") was either different in the lost *Vorlage* of the Mt. Athos text or was altered in the process of translation. This is evident by the reading ποιῆσαι τὰ ἀρέσκοντά σοι ("to do what pleases you"; MS E 2,3 10–11). The Qumran text, however, emphasizes right behavior in order to ascend and pursue what is good and beautiful, not necessarily to please God. In this way, the original Aramaic tradition pertained largely to virtue. While the reference to beauty has no parallel elsewhere in *ALD*, the pursuit of good echoes the wisdom poem's statement דזרע טב מעל טב ("He who sews goodness brings goodness"; 4Q213 1 i 8). With these, compare also the emphasis on virtues associated with Levi in the list of *WQ* (4Q542 1 i 12–13), which points further to a likely association of priestly ideas advanced in Levi and Qahat materials.

Line 17: *And] let not any satan rule over me.* Greenfield, Stone, and Eshel (2004: 129) remarked: "At this point the prayer turns to a plea for divine protection." This content is significant for both textual and theological reasons.

Textually, this language is generally recognized as a development of Ps. 119:133 with one critical difference. Whereas the material there asks for freedom from the dominion of און ("iniquity"), the prayer passage here in *ALD* exchanges this for שטן ("satan"). In this way, the resulting Aramaic content of Levi's prayer, שטן, is remarkably similar to the Hebrew content of the *Plea of Deliverance* in 11QPs[a] (11Q5) 19 15 (cf. 11Q6 4–5 16), which reads אל תשלט בי שטן ("Let satan have no dominion over me"). This indicates that both texts are likely aware of, and interacting with, a larger body of psalm-like materials in the Second Temple period that was itself generated by the ongoing formation and reformation of traditional materials through exegetical development (cf. Flint 1997; Mroczek 2016).

Theologically, the reference to שטן is a development beyond the traditional idea of the noun signifying an adversarial being (cf. Zech. 3:1–2; Job 1–2; 1 Chron. 21:1) toward the idea of a class of malevolent beings. This is signaled by Levi's reference to *any* satan. As Stuckenbruck (2011: 134) commented, "the placement of *kol* before *saṭan* leaves little doubt that a proper name is not in view." Early on in research, Stone and Greenfield (1993: 252) correctly noted that, "[c]onsidering the early date of this document, this is a significant insight into Jewish demonological ideas." The Aramaic DSS seem to be the first place this concept takes shape, of course, in a still broader complex emerging ideas around otherworldly beings.

Similar understandings are found in *1 En.* 40:7; 65:6, although the Enochic tradition seems to have a more focused understanding of a satanic figure (*1 En.* 41:9; 53:3; 54:6). It is possible that the Aramaic notion of a class of satans informed the thought of *Jubilees* (40:9; 46:2 [2Q20 1 2]; 50:5). Greenfield, Stone, and Eshel (2004: 129) added that a similar understanding is found in the *Hodayot* in the phrase תֹּגְﬠַר בכול שטן משחית ("you will rebuke every destructive satan"; 1QH[a] 22 25). Drawnel (2004: 216) suggested that the term שטן is associated with darkness in 4Q213 4 6, which "recalls the angel of darkness," Melchiresha, in *VA*. However, as outlined in the textual note to that fragment above, Drawnel's reading is problematic, making the connection with darkness in this or other texts problematic.

The present tradition makes yet another contribution to the multi-faceted study of demonology in ancient Judaism (see also extensive contextual comment on names beings at 4Q544 2 13). The demonologies of the Aramaic materials, particularly Enochic traditions, were foundational and formative for the theologies of evils spirits, malevolent beings, or angels in the Hebrew DSS (Alexander 1999: 341–42; Stuckenbruck 2011). Regarding the particular theological developments related to satanic figures in the DSS and beyond, Reynolds (2013) proposed an arc involving at least two stages: (1) the transformation of generic beings into a species of demons; (2) the tendency to promote a single named figure to the position of chief demon. Who doesn't love a promotion?! It was already noted above how *ALD* coheres with the first phase. Yet *ALD* may include important information for also understanding the second phase. To make this connection, we must recall the association between the Levi traditions of *ALD* and *CD* described above (see the comment on 4Q213a 1 13).

I argued above that, for all the uncertainties related to the Levi quotation or allusion in *CD* 4 15, the latter text is drawing upon a tradition or memory of Levi that already drew a tight association between the patriarch and warnings against promiscuity and impurity. In the context of *ALD*, these warnings are made in the proximity of a call for protection against "any satan" (i.e., a class of beings). In *CD*, however, the warnings against these issues are understood as traps of Belial (i.e., a specific and chief malevolent figure).

Dimant (2011: 255–56) observed that, while "Belial" is "overwhelmingly attested in sectarian texts," the Aramaic DSS "employ other appellations." In this light, *CD* is not only an early repository for the reception of this Aramaic Levi tradition, or one like it, it also represents a stage in theological development of demonic profiles. Whereas waywardness in the form of promiscuity in *ALD* was due to the broad pull of malevolent forces, for *CD* these issues were brought into the profile of a specific figure, the chief demon of sectarian thought: Belial. This may also be considered in light of the Enochic tradition's increasing naming of specific evil beings and their association with types of revealed and illicit knowledge in the watchers myth.

Line 18: *up]on me, my Lord, and draw me near to become for you.* The fragmentary nature of the Qumran text at this point leaves us with an incomplete thought. However, the Mt. Athos text (MS E 18,2) indicates that this sentence concluded with a petition for God to keep Levi on the right path to become a δοῦλος ("servant"). This idea crops up again in 4Q213a 2 8, 10, which features a corresponding Aramaic term, עבד. The Hebrew Scriptures abound with references to the prophets (e.g., 2 Kgs 9:7; Jer. 26:5; Ezek. 38:17; Dan. 9:10; Zech. 1:6) and founding figures (e.g., Exod. 14:31; 32:13; Deut. 34:5; Josh. 24:29; 1 Chron. 6:49 [34]; Ps. 78:70) as servants to God.

The occurrence here in *ALD* seems to be the earliest application of this language for an elect priest of God. As Drawnel (2004: 217) observed, the expression of "drawing near" refers to Levi's "future priestly elevation." Use of the verb קרב in this sense foreshadows Isaac's priestly blessing in *ALD* 18 (Bodl. b. 8 21) as well as draws on precedents in the Hebrew Scriptures of priests who "draw near" to God in their service (e.g., Exod. 40:12; Lev. 8:6; Num. 16:9–10; cf. Ezek. 44:13; 48:11). In these ways, the scribe of *ALD* has reshaped the memory of Levi not only as a founding priestly figure but as a servant of the Lord. For divine name and reference terminology in the Aramaic DSS, see the comment on 4Q542 1 i 1–2.

2.9.2. *A Revelatory Encounter and Elevation at Abel Mayin (4Q213a 2)*

This fragment includes the end of Levi's prayer, which also relates to *ALD* 1a, known from the insertion following *T. Levi* 2:3 in the Greek Mt. Athos witness. 4Q213a 2 also includes the opening lines of Levi's first dream-vision, wherein he was elevated to the heavenly gates and encountered an angel.

5 לֹעֹ[...]
6 מרי בֹּ[...]רכת
7 זרע דקֹ[...]שט
8 צלות עב[ד]דֹ[...]
9 דין קשט לֹבֹ[...]ל
10 לבר עבדך מן קֹ[...]דם
11 באדין נגדת ב[...]
12 על אבי יעקוב וכדֹ[...]י
13 מן אבל מין אדיֹן[...]
14 שכבת ויתבת אנה על[...]ל
15 *vacat* אדין חזיון אחזיתֹ[...]
16 בחזית חזויא וחזית שמֹ[...]יא
17 תחותי רם עד דבק לשמיֹ[...]א
18 לי תרעי שמיא ומלאך חדֹ[...]

BOTTOM MARGIN

5. ...[...]
6. My Lord, [you] b[lessed...]
7. [a] seed of tr[uth...]
8. prayer of [your] serv[ant...]
9. true judgment for al[l...]
10. the son of your servant from be[fore...]
11. Then I carried on[...]
12. to my father Jacob and whe[n...]
13. from Abel Mayin. Then[...]
14. I laid down and I stayed[...]
15. *vacat* Then I saw a vision [...]
16. in the display of the vision and I saw the heaven[s...]
17. beneath me, high until it reached the heave[ns...]
18. to me the gates of the heavens and a single angel[...]

Textual, Scribal, and Material Notes

Primary images for transcription: PAM M41.405; PAM M43.242; PAM M42.363; B-281216; B-295997; B-295425. See the previous fragment for material description of the fragments as it relates to image plates and minor reconstructions.

Lines 10–11: There is a fishhook-like marking in between these lines that corresponds with a sense division from the conclusion of Levi's prayer to the continuation of his travel itinerary. For other marginal markings in the priestly texts, see 4Q213 1 ii–2 10–11 and 4Q542 1 ii 8–9, with additional commentary provided for the *WQ* reference in the next chapter.

Commentary

Lines 6–7: *My Lord, [you] b[lessed...a] seed of tr[uth.* This content relates to the covenantal promise of an ancestral seed for Abraham and Sarah (*ALD* 15b–16 [Mt. Athos, MS E 18,2]). The language of "a] seed of tr[uth" extends beyond the fundamentals of the blessing of innumerable descendants (e.g., Gen. 12:2; 13:16; 15:5; 16:10; 17:7; 22:17). Though the Aramaic reading זרע דק[שט is fragmentary, it is plausible in view of the Greek σπέρμα δίκαιον (Mt. Athos, MS E 18,2). This pair of terms is unique to ALD and does not occur in other known writings.

The collocation provides a new angle on the reception and reinterpretation of the Abrahamic covenant by reframing the divine promise in light of the Enochic motif, "a plant of truth" (see the comment on 4Q542 1 ii 12). In view of this, it is significant that *1 En.* 93:10 features the terminology of righteousness and eternal planting in the context of the ascendancy and covenant of Abraham. *1 Enoch* 10:16 may also establish a connection between the Abrahamic blessing and the righteous plant motif (Nicklesburg 2001: 226). The present text, then, not only redraws Levi, it remembers a core component of Abraham's profile by including Enochic undertones to provide an eschatological orientation.

Line 8: *prayer of [your] serv[ant.* See the comment on 4Q213a 1 8.

Lines 9–10: *true judgment for al[l...]the son of your servant from be[fore.* These two phrases come from a context in the prayer relating to the request for ongoing blessing for Levi's children. The initial request is for Levi and his sons' ability to offer דין קשט ("true judgment") eternally. The second phrase, however, narrows the focus to one particular son, presumably Qahat. The nature of the prayerful directive over Qahat's life is lost in the Qumran fragment. Yet the Mt. Athos materials indicate that Levi asked God to not turn his face away from Qahat for all eternity (MS E 18,2 19). In this respect, Levi's prayer over Qahat echoes an earlier point in the prayer where he requested the same provision over his own life (MS E 18,2 15a). Although these fragmentary lines do not name Qahat explicitly, they participate in the development of a figure that otherwise is entirely flat and voiceless in the Hebrew Scriptures. Part of this characterization process involved modeling Qahat in a form similar to Levi.

Lines 11–13: *Then I carried on[...]to my father Jacob and whe[n...] from Abel Mayin. Then[.* These lines mark the narrative segue of Levi's journey to Jacob. The toponym אבל מין ("Abel Mayin") has a larger significance in both antecedent and later literature. The Greek *Testament of Levi* includes a pair of dream-visions. The first of these revelatory encounters occurs at Ἀβελμαούλ ("Abelmaoul"; *T. Levi* 2:3). Given that the following lines in 4Q213a relate Levi's dream-vision, the later Greek tradition has certainly received and reworked this earlier Aramaic episode.

As noted in the introduction above, there is some debate on the actual location of the place referenced here in *ALD*. However, it is most likely that Abel Mayin is to be identified with the mid-country location of אבל מחולה ("Abel-Meholah") in the vicinity of Shechem and to the west of the Jordan river (Judg. 7:22; 1 Kgs 4:12; 19:16; 1 Sam. 18:19; 2 Sam. 21:8). For arguments in support of this identification, see: Hollander and de Jonge 1985: 145; Baarda 1992; Eshel and Eshel 2003; Suter 2003; Drawnel 2004: 135–38; and Perrin 2015a: 64.

The Enochic tradition includes a similar, though easily confused reference. After Enoch received his dream-vision of judgment on the fallen watchers, he retires to Ἐβελσατά ("Abel-Main") to relate the judgment of doom upon the wayward angels (*1 En.* 13:9; cf. 1 Kgs 15:20; 2 Kgs 15:29; 2 Chron. 16:4). For advocates of understanding Levi's and Enoch's revelations occurring at the same locale, see: Milik 1956: 403–404; Kugel 2011: 10–11, 60; Nickelsburg 2001: 246; and Flannery-Dailey 2004: 158.

Lines 14–15: *I laid down and I stayed[…]vacat Then I saw a vision.* In his classic work, *The Interpretation of Dreams in the Ancient Near East* (1956), Oppenheim observed some common trends in formal markers of the beginning and ends of revelatory accounts. This "dream frame" often included introductory formulae that set the context of a revelation, typically noting the posture or location of the dreamer (cf. Flannery-Dailey 2004: 114–19). For a sample of such introductory formulae in ancient Near Eastern, Jewish, and classical writings, see Perrin (2015a: 96). In line 14, Levi adopts a position for sleep that is a common posture for narrative dreams in antiquity and the Aramaic DSS. Other dreamers reclining before receiving divine revelation include Enoch (*1 En.* 83:3; cf. *1 En.* 13:9), Noah (*GenAp* [1Q20] 12 19), and Daniel (Dan. 4:5 [2]; 7:1) (Perrin 2015a: 101; cf. Eshel 2009).

Line 15 begins with a *vacat* signaling a sense division as the narrative introduces the content of Levi's dream-vision at Abel Mayin. The language of "seeing" a dream, here from the Aramaic root חזי, is both common to the Aramaic DSS and coheres with broader patterns of dream-vision revelation in the ancient world, predominantly perceived as visual visitations or portrayals of otherworldly realities (Oppenheim 1956: 225–27; Gnuse 1984: 12; Bar 2001: 10–13; Bergman 2003: 421–32; Flannery-Dailey 2004: 24–25; Noegel 2007: 263–65; Perrin 2015a: 94–95). The visual nature of Levi's dream-vision is emphasized again in 4Q213a 2 16. See the introduction above for discussion of the number of dream-visions in *ALD*'s narrative structure and the exegetical underpinnings of Levi's profile as a dreamer.

Lines 16–18: *in the display of the vision and I saw the heaven[s…]beneath me, high until it reached the heave[ns…] to me the gates of the heavens and a single angel.* Unfortunately, very little of the actual content of Levi's dream-vision in

ALD has survived and the later witnesses are of little help. Based on these partial lines, we can make only preliminary observations on the content and scope of the episode.

The piling on of visionary terms—both nouns and verbs—from the root √חזי in lines 15–16 underscore the visual nature of the revelatory account. The Aramaic DSS alternate between the terminologies of "dreams" (חלם) and/or "visions" (חזו; for complete lexical data, see Perrin 2015a, 92). In the present context, it is noteworthy that *VA* also references Amram's experience using forms of the Aramaic חזו (4Q543 1 a–c 1; 4Q545 1 a i 1; 4Q547 9 8).

Levi's dream-vision clearly involved a revelatory ascent to the heavenly gates. The motif of entrance into the divine throne room via τὰς πύλας τοῦ οὐρανοῦ ("gates of heaven") also occurs in Levi's dream-vision at *T. Levi* 5:1. Though the text is even more fragmentary than *ALD* here, an unidentified fragment from Cave Four also featured an encounter at the heavenly gates (4Q574 1 4–5). Both texts include the Aramaic phrasing תרעי שמיא. The motif of heavenly gates is also prominent in Enochic revelations and views of the cosmos in the *Book of Watchers* (*1 En.* 9:1; 14:12; 33:2–3; 34:2–3; 35:1; 36:2). References to otherworldly gates continue in subsequent Enochic writings, which even include references to "gates of hell" (*2 En.* 42:0–1).

The available text does not retain any discourse with the angelic figure, although this figure presumably dialogued with Levi in the now-lost content. For discussion on the remnants of angelic discourse in Levi's dream-visions, see the comment on 4Q213b 1 1.

2.9.3. *Allusion to the Rape of Dinah and Rhetoric against Outsiders (4Q213a 3–4)*

The reception of the rape of Dinah from Genesis 34 underscores *ALD*'s concern for forming and maintaining boundaries against outsiders. Here, the tale is used to illustrate the broader perils and implications of unions with outsiders for the ancestral name and ongoing heritage of the priesthood.

11 [...]י̊ו̊ו̊[...] ו̊ו̊[...]ו̊ו̊ו̊ו̊ו̊[...]
12 [...]מן נק[ב]תא̊[...]א וכען ו̊[ע]ל̊ו מכתשׁי גבריא
13 [...]ת̊אבין חוב[...]א̊נתה ותהלל שמה ושם אבוה
14 [...]ע̊ל̊[י̊]ה̊ ל̊מ̊ע̊[נ]כ̊ה̊ [...]ו̊ו̊ו̊ו̊[...] א̊ב̊ה̊תא וכל
15 [...]בתו̊[לה זי חבלת שמה ושׁם א̊בהתה ואבה̊תת לכל אחיה
16 [...]אבוה̊{א̊} ולא מת̊מחא שם ח̊סדה מן כול עמהא לעלם
17 [...]ל̊י̊ט לכל דרי עלמא ומ̊[ן̊...]ה̊° קדושי̊ן מן עמא
18 [...]ל̊ וד̊[...]מ̊עשר קודש קרבן לאל מ̊ן
BOTTOM MARGIN

11. [...]...[...]...[...]...[...]
12. [...]from the women[...]...And now, let the plagues of men be[fa]ll
13. [...]guilty of a sin[...]a woman and she ruins her name and the name of her father

14. [...]...[...]...[...]...[...]ove[r] her to answer her...the ancestors and all
15. [...virg]in who corrupted her name and the name of her father and the ancestors for all her brothers
16. [...] her father and the name of her reproach will not be wiped out from all her people forever.
17. [...]...for all the generations of eternity and from[...]...holy ones from the people
18. [...]...[...]a holy tithe, and offering to God from

Textual, Scribal, and Material Notes
Primary images for transcription: PAM M42.363; PAM M43.242; PAM M43.610; B-295639; B-295085; B-359985; B-359984.

Line 12: א[וכען ֯י[ע]ל֯ו מכתשׁי֯ גבריא ("And now, let the plagues of men be[fa]ll") – Drawnel's (2004: 108) reading of this line improves on previous attempts in several respects. The reading of the penultimate word is uncertain but possible. Stone and Greenfield (1996: 33) read this line as [א֯שׁ֯בען ו֯]...[○ומס גבריא]...[○ה֯ ("he beswore us and[...]...[...] men").

Line 14: א֯ב֯ה֯תא ("the fathers") – The form here follows Drawnel (2004: 108). Stone and Greenfield (1996: 33) read בהתא ("shame"). Apart from the final two words of this line, all preceding materials are known only by ink traces of partial characters and forms. As such, the reading of the beginning of the line presented above is tentative.

Line 15: בתו[ל]ה ("virg]in") – While only the final *lamed* and *he* are extant, I preliminarily accept the reconstruction by Drawnel (2004: 108; cf. Cook 2015: 40). For a more reserved transcription of only the extant letters, see Stone and Greenfield (1996: 33).

Line 16: חסדה ("reproach") – Read with Drawnel (2004: 108; cf. Kugler 1996a: 36; Cook 2015: 88). Stone and Greenfield (1996: 33) read חסיה ("righteous"), which inverts the apparent meaning of the phrase and passage!

Line 16: עמהא ("the her people") – The definite article is struck out with a vertical line to correct the form.

Line 18: לאל מן ("to God from") – The text is partially effaced, but there is likely a space between the set of words (Drawnel 2004: 108). Stone and Greenfield (1996: 33) read the cluster as לאלפ֯ן ("for teaching [?]").

Commentary
Line 12: *And now, let the plagues of men be[fa]ll.* While this fragment shares the subject matter of the rape of Dinah with *Jub.* 30:5–7, there does not seem to be a "textual parallel" between the two traditions (Stone and Greenfield 1996: 33). This topic is also an important element of both Levi's first dream-vision in *T. Levi* 5:3–4 and the narrative of *T. Levi* 6–7. While the exact narrative location of this fragment is unknown, Drawnel's (2004: 58; 2005: 7–17) reconstruction locates the material within Levi's second dream-vision, which seems most plausible (cf. Perrin 2015a: 53–34).

The opening adverbial phrase, וכען, likely signals an internal shift in discourse. Without greater context for this and the preceding lines, it is difficult to discern the sense and narrative situations of this content. The phrases מכתשׁי גבריא ("the plagues of men") seems to be unique to *ALD* and may refer to the anticipated and endorsed judgment upon the Shechemites. Variations on the notion of divinely mandated destruction for the Shechemites are found in *Jub.* 30:5–6; *T. Levi* 6:8–7:1; *Jos. Asen.* 23:14; and Eusebius, *Praep. ev.* 9.22.9.

Lines 13–15: *guilty of a sin[...]a woman and she ruins her name and the name of her father[...]...[...]...[...]...[...]ove[r] her to answer her...the ancestors and all[...virg]in who corrupted her name and the name of her father and the ancestors for all her brothers.* Though Dinah is not named here, this material likely represents one of our earliest known receptions of the rape of Dinah known from Genesis 34. It seems that the interpretation offered uses the tragic episode in order to galvanize the importance of not intermarrying with foreigners to retain the integrity and purity of the priestly line. On the early reception and cultural framework of that tradition, see Pummer (1982), Collins (1980), and more recently (1998: 403–36) and Tikva (2002: 179–98).

There is a dual emphasis on the profanation (√חלל, line 13) and corruption (√חבל, line 15) of both the (assumed or implied) name of Dinah and "her father" (שם אבוה, line 13; שׁם אבהתה, line 15). The defamation of the name of her father in the immediate context refers to Jacob, who is presented in *ALD* 9 as the forefather who inaugurates Levi's priesthood. In this way, the tradition connects the potential blending with foreigners as a risk for the foundations of the priesthood. *Aramaic Levi Document* also extrapolates this risk for its implications for the name of "the ancestors" (אֲבָהָתא; line 14; אבהתה line 15). *Words of Qahat* demonstrated an understanding of participating in the priestly inheritance by modeling its virtues and protecting it from outsiders (4Q542 1 i 5–13). The interpretation of Genesis 34 was seemingly put to a similar purpose here: mingling with outsiders in this incident not only compromised the immediate family's name (i.e., the father and brothers), it had the potential of disrupting the ongoing ancestral heritage of priestly purity.

In these ways, the reception of Genesis 34 in *ALD* is not exegetically oriented to the many essential and unsettling aspects of this tradition for Dinah; rather, it leverages the assault to develop larger constructions regarding priestly purity issue from Levi. This reference underscores the importance of endogamous marriage and relates to a larger trend in the Aramaic DSS where founding figures are affirmed for their endogamous unions.

Lines 16–17: *her father and the name of her reproach will not be wiped out from all her people forever. [...]...for all the generations of eternity and from... [...]...holy ones from the people.* The implications of contamination of the priestly line now concern חסדה ("her reproach"). Here too, the concern is less about Dinah than for the male priestly members and the ongoing effects of the incident through the generations. For them, the shame brought about by an illicit union would be indelible. In this way, the warning has a broader application to all members of the priestly progeny. As above in 4Q213a 3–4 3–5, the correlations with *WQ* are significant. For both texts, ruptures to the priestly line are understood as having a lasting, even eternal, impact (4Q542 1 ii 3–4).

Line 18: *a holy tithe, and offering to God from.* The reference to [מֹעשׂר קודש ("a holy tithe") recalls Jacob's tithe in 4Q213b 1 4 // 1Q21 4 1. For discussion on this motif in *ALD*, see the commentary on 4Q213b 1 4. The tithe and offering are made to אל ("God"), which parallels the terms and themes of 4Q213b 1 6. This singular divine name occurs only here in the Aramaic DSS. All other occurrences of אל are in some combined form, such as the reference to אל אלין ("God of gods") in 4Q542 1 i 1.

2.9.4. *Hints at the Eternality of the Priesthood (4Q213a 5 i)*

A solitary reference to the eternality of the priesthood, perhaps connected with Levi's angelic installation as a priest in a revelatory setting.

[...] 1
2 [...]אֹ עם א[...]ֹ[...]אֹ[...]ֹֹמֹת[...]
3 [...]כֹהנות עלמא *vacat*
BOTTOM MARGIN

1. [...]
2. [...]...with/people...[...]...[...]...[...]
3. [...]eternal priesthood. *vacat*

Textual, Scribal, and Material Notes

Primary images for transcription: PAM M42.363; PAM M43.242; B-295640; B-295086. This small fragment retains but a few words at the lower left of a column (4Q213a 5 i) and an intercolumnar margin followed by a couple of characters (*mem* and *tav*) from the following column (4Q213a 5 ii). Given this situation, the translation is only of 4Q213a 5 i.

Commentary

Line 3: *eternal priesthood.* The later Greek tradition of *T. Levi* 5:2 pairs the language of priestly election and blessing in the context of Levi's dream-vision of priestly confirmation. The occurrence of the phrase כהנות עלמא ("eternal priesthood") indicates that the understanding in the Greek has an ancient precedent in the earlier Aramaic Levi traditions.

As Stone and Greenfield (1996: 35) noted, the phrasing here in *ALD* also has a background in Exod. 40:15 and Num. 25:13. Drawnel (2004: 111) is cautious about over-interpreting the fragment yet notes that there may be "a connection with Levi's heavenly elevation in his second vision," which included an anointing of שלם עלמא ("eternal peace") at *ALD* 7 (MS A, Bodl. a 8 8–9; 1Q21 3 3). This may indicate that 4Q213a 5 i–ii 3 "could be seen as the angelic statement about Levi's priestly status."

In the context of the Aramaic DSS, the Levi, Qahat, and Amram materials share the impression of the eternal nature of both priests and priesthood. *Words of Qahat* speaks of ברכת עלמא ("everlasting blessings") that will rest upon the priesthood that will endure for דרי עלמין ("eternal generations") if they retain their grasp on the priestly inheritance (4Q542 1 ii 3–4). *Visions of Amram* also operates on this understanding, though in the more specific sense of emphasizing the eternality of Aaron's role and service as כהן עלמין ("an eternal priest"; 4Q545 4 19).

2.10. Text and Commentary: 4QLevi^c (4Q213b)

A single fragment of this manuscript has survived. The paleographical profile and skin coloration of the fragment differentiate it from the fragments assigned to other copies (Stone and Greenfield 1996: 37; see *ad loc.* for further remarks on the material quality of the fragments).

2.10.1. Awakening from an Angelic Endorsement of Levi's Priestly Line (4Q213b 1)

Levi receives an angelic endorsement and elevation of his priestly position before awakening from a second dream-vision and receiving a this-worldly blessing from Jacob. The material here corresponds to *ALD* 7–9. Overlap: 4Q214b 7 1; 1Q21 4.

1 [א...]כֹּהֹ רֹבִּיתך מן כל בשׂרֹ[...]
2 [...וֹ]אֹנה אתעירת מן שנתי אדין
3 [...וטמר]תֹ אף דן בלבבי ולכל אנש לא
4 [...כ]דֹי הֹוה יעקוב אבי מעשר
5 [...]ה ולי מן בנוהי יהב
6 [...לא]ל עֹלֹיוֹןֹ ∘∘[...]

1. [...]how I made you greater than all fles[h...]
2. [...And] I awoke from my sleep. Then
3. [...and I hi]d this too in my heart and did not to anyone
4. [...w]hen Jacob, my father, tithed
5. [...].... And to me from his sons he gave
6. [...to Go]d Most High

Textual, Scribal, and Material Notes

Primary images for transcription: PAM M42.363; PAM M43.242; B-295641; B-295087.

Line 1: רֹבִּיתך ("I made you greater") – This word is extant only by the lower portions of its initial letters. While a variety of proposals have been advanced for the lost form, the general consensus is that the reading רביתך is to be preferred, with varying uses of diacritical markings over the first two characters (Puech

2002: 523; Drawnel 2004: 181; Kugler 2008: 11; Schattner-Rieser 2004: 548). Greenfield and Stone (1996: 39) assert that the reading רְעִיתָךְ "is quite certain in the MS" and suggest that the stem change from √רבי to √רעי may have arisen as a graphic variant (cf. Greenfield, Stone, and Eshel 2004: 68; García Martínez and Tigchelaar: 1998, 1:450). Kugler (2008: 12) rightly critiques their reading, since a crack in the leather "obscures the full extension to the left of the long bottom stroke characteristic of *bet* in this fragment." Note that the corresponding Cairo Genizah text reads רבינך ("we have made you") at this point (MS A, Bodl. a 8 7).

Line 1: כל בשׂר]א ("all fles[h") – This phrase reveals a variant with the later Cairo Genizah text, which includes the shorter reading כולה ("all"; MS A, Bodl. a 8 8).

Line 5: מן ("from") – The later Cairo Genizah witness has a small plus here, reading מכל ("from all"; MS A, Bodl. a 8 18).

Line 6: לא]ל עֶלְיוֹן ("to Go]d Most High") – The form here is known only by the tops of letters, making any reading and reconstruction tenuous. This is compounded by the fact that the Cairo Genizah materials have a series of corrections (MS A, Bodl. a 8 20). For full discussion of the original and resulting readings in the later witness, see Drawnel (2004: 113). Numerous proposals have been made for the Qumran fragment. Stone and Greenfield (1996: 38) suggested a singular reading עֶלְמָֿאָ. Drawnel (2004: 181) proposed stages of correction: עלמין < עלמיא < עליון. While corrections cannot be ruled out, there is insufficient text to verify anything other than a likely final form.

Commentary

Line 1: *how I made you greater than all fles[h.* The discourse is delivered in the first person. Judging from the awakening formula of the next line, the content here is spoken by a figure, likely an angel in Levi's second dream-vision. Note that an angelic figure was present in Levi's first dream-vision (4Q213a 2 18). The limited text of 4Q213a 6 1, אמרת מא ("I said, 'What'"), might include other lost aspects of Levi's dialogue with the *angelus interpres* in either dream-vision (cf. *T. Levi* 2:9). Though the context is equally uncertain, 4Q214 3 may relate to such dialogue.

The topic of the revelation is not fully known, but the language here implies an otherworldly endorsement of Levi and his progeny's priestly profile. The priestly elevation of Levi is a subject shared by both dream-visions in the later Greek *T. Levi* 5:2; 8:18. Such an association is already established in *Jub.* 32:1. The otherworldly endorsement of the priestly line is also a key feature of Amram's dream-vision in *VA* (4Q545 4), which presents Aaron as a high priestly figure drawing on the terminology of the Levi tradition.

Lines 2–3: *And] I awoke from my sleep. Then[... and I hi]d this too in my heart and to anyone not.* The Aramaic of these lines reads as follows: ו[אנה אתעירת מן שנתי אדין]...וטמר[ת אף דן בלבבי ולכל אנש לא. While 4Q213a 2 14–15 retained the introductory formula to Levi's first dream-vision, the present text includes the awakening formula of his second revelation. *Contra* Kugler (1996a: 49–50; cf.

2008: 13), the phrase אף דן in 4Q213b 1 4 cannot be taken as referring to a single dream-vision structure of *ALD* (Perrin 2015a: 112 n. 67).

While notices of "awakening" are common in ancient dream-vision texts (e.g., Gen. 28:16; 42:4, 7; 1 Kgs 3:15; Jer. 31:26; *1 En.* 90:40; *Jub.* 14:17; 32:36; *4 Ezra* 5:14; *2 Bar.* 37:1; Mt. 1:24), aspects of the phrasing here in *ALD* bear striking similarity to several other texts in the Aramaic DSS and beyond. At least four Aramaic texts at Qumran reference emerging from a sleeping state in the awakening formula (4Q547 9 8; 1Q20 15 21; 19 17; 4Q530 2 ii + 6–12 4; Dan. 6:18 [19]). Drawnel (2004: 245) detected "unquestionable vocabulary contacts" between the awakening formula here in *ALD* and the *Book of Giants*. However, the parallels with *GenAp* are arguably the closest. See especially ואתעירת א[נֿ]אֿ נֿוֹחֿ מן שנתי ("Then] I Noah, I awoke] from my sleep"; 1Q20 15 21) and ואתֿעִירת בליליא מן שנתי ("Then I awoke in the night from my sleep"; 1Q20 19 17). This cluster of idioms seems to relate to a form of response regarding knowledge of the paternity or destiny of progeny (Perrin 2020b: 449–50).

The specific reference to Levi tucking away the revelation in his heart and not disclosing it to anyone in line 4 exhibits a tight parallel with the awakening formula of Noah's dream-vision in 1Q20 6 12: וטמרת רזא דן בלבבי ולכול אנוש לא אחֿויתה ("And I hid this mystery within my heart, and did not make it known to anyone"). The concluding formula of Dan. 7:28 also features the element of internalizing the revelation: אנה דניאל שגיא רעיוני יבהלנני וזיוי ישתנון עלי ומלתא בלבי נטרת ("As for me, Daniel, my thoughts were greatly alarming me and my face grew pale, but I kept the matter in my heart"). Compare also the Aramaic fragment 4Q561 11 9.

In the later Greek tradition, the concluding formulae of both Levi's revelations reference hiddenness in Levi's "heart." The form and phrasing of *T. Levi* 8:19 (cf. 6:2) are especially close to the phrasing of 4Q213b 1 4, suggesting we have recovered an early Aramaic *Vorlage* of the tradition: καὶ ἔκρυψα καίγε τοῦτο ἐν τῇ καρδίᾳ μου καὶ οὐκ ἀνήγγειλα αὐτό παντὶ ἀνθρώπῳ ἐπὶ τῆς γῆς ("And I hid this in my heart as well, and I did not report it to any human being on the earth").

The motif of retaining or reflecting on dream-vison contents in one's heart also occurs in Gen. 37:11; Add. Esth. A 11 (OG); *4 Ezra* 3:1; 9:38; 10:25; *2 En.* 1:3. Finally, the phrasing here also calls to mind Luke 2:19 (cf. 2:51), which references Mary's cherishing and reflecting on the angelic annunciation of Jesus's birth τῇ καρδίᾳ αὐτῆς ("in her heart"). For an argument on the indebtedness of Lukan special material here to the terminology of the Qumran Aramaic texts, see Perrin (2020b).

Line 4: *w]hen Jacob, my father, tithed.* For the textual variant here, see the comment on 1Q21 4. The developing traditions of Jacob's tithe at Bethel here and in *Jub.* 32:2 extend out of the reference to his vow in Gen. 28:22. The impulse of these early Jewish traditions is to extend the tradition so that Jacob's promise to tithe is fulfilled (Kugler 1996a: 90). Jacob's actions thereby embody the ideal of Num. 18:21–28, which specifies the receiving of tithes by the Levites (Kugler 1996a: 90). Note that 4Q213a 3–4 8 also referenced a מעשר ("tithe").

Jacob's tithe in *ALD* 9 is a key component of Levi's priestly inauguration on a this-worldly plain. This action complements the angelic endorsement of Levi's priesthood that occurred immediately prior in the dream-vision. In this respect, the *ALD* tradition may share a key understanding of the complementary and even continuous nature of the priestly line with an angelic priesthood. This perspective is developed more fully in *VA* (see the commentary on 4Q545 4). The concept of a tithe is associated with Levi's priestly dream-vision in the later Greek *T. Levi* 9:3.

Line 5: *And to me from his sons he gave*. This material provides a glimpse of an early interpretive tradition that the tithe and offering also came from Jacob's family, a detail present in *Jub.* 32:3. As a result of this collective tithe, "[a]ssigning the tithe to Levi becomes a sign of his election to the priesthood from among his brothers and the first step in his priestly ordination" (Drawnel 2004: 251).

Line 6: *to Go]d Most High*. The content of this line is limited but retains most characters of the divine reference, אל עליון. 4Q213a 3–4 8 mentions the giving of a tithe to א[ל ("God"). The use of this language in the context of Jacob's tithe suggests the scribe is connecting this tradition with another famous patriarchal tithe and priest in Genesis. Kugler (1996a: 90–91) commented that "[i]t appears that the author of our text [*ALD*] wished to depict Levi's relationship to Jacob as similar to the one that existed between Abram and Melchizedek, and to claim for Levi the sacerdotal role of the latter figure." From this perspective, it is significant that Melchizedek is referred to as כהן לאל עליון ("a priest of God Most High") in Gen. 14:18.

In the immediate context of the Aramaic priestly literature, Kugel's proposal takes on new significance. *Visions of Amram* presents an angelic endorsement of Aaron's priesthood, likely from a celestial Melchizedek (see Perrin 2015a: 166–70, with bibliography). Though the form is reconstructed (Puech 2001: 342), it is possible that *VA* also leveraged this association by referring to Aaron as a priest to אל עליון (4Q545 4 16). If the language used here in 4Q213b 1 8 is connecting with this particular theology of priesthood, it may point to a shared understanding between *ALD* and *VA* that claimed the ancestral priesthoods were in association with, or inaugurated in the heavens by, an angelic Melchizedek.

2.11. *Text and Commentary: 4QLevi^d (4Q214)*

This manuscript survives in four fragments. 4Q214 1 and 2 come from known sections of *ALD*. 4Q214 3 and 4 do not relate to content from the later witnesses. The latter fragment is too small for a full commentary, although it retains references to both "and men" (וגברי) and "the/his Lord" (מרה), the context of which are unknown (4Q214 4 1, 4). A fifth fragment (labelled 4Q214 5) was included in the lot. However, as Stone and Greenfield (1996: 51) observed, the fragment is clearly not from this or other *ALD* manuscripts at Qumran. The content of this fragment is particularly limited, with only two partially preserved *yod-nun* endings in lines 1 and 5, suggesting the language is indeed Aramaic.

2.11.1. *Samples of Sacrificial Terminology (4Q214 1)*

A sliver of a fragment containing Levi's instructions for priestly service of the wood offering. The content of the fragment relates to *ALD* 20–23; 25a–b and involves at least one variant reading of indeterminate length with the later witnesses. Overlap: 4Q214b 2–6 i.

```
[...]ṭ[...] 1
[...]ל̊[...] 2
[...]אע[...] 3
[...]אל̊י̊ן[...] 4
[...]ל̊[מ̊דבח̇...] 5
[...]ל̊אסק̊[...] 6
[...]לח̇o[...] 7
[...]ב̊[...] 8
```

1. [...]...[...]
2. [...]...[...]
3. [...]wo[od...]
4. [...]these[...]
5. [...]altar[...]
6. [...]to offer[...]
7. [...]...[...]
8. [...]...[...]

Textual, Scribal, and Material Notes

Primary images for transcription: PAM M43.242; B-366682; B-371436; B-366681.

Line 3:]אע[("wood") – The extant text here follows Drawnel (2004: 182), suggesting the original form was likely אעין, as in *ALD* 22 (MS A, Bodl. c 9 9; cf. τὰ ξύλα in MS E 18,2). Stone and Greenfield (1996: 44) read a partial form:]אס̊[.

Line 4: אל̊י̊ן ("these") – Read with Drawnel (2004: 182). Stone and Greenfield (1996: 45) read ג̊ליך ("your feet"). The form does not correspond with anything in the other witnesses.

Commentary

Lines 3–6: *wo[od][...]these[...]altar[...]to offer.* Stone and Greenfield (1996: 45) noted that "[a]lmost no words of this fragment are preserved in full," which makes both its content and context difficult. They observed that the fragment seems to align generally with the content of *ALD* 20–23, though a reconstruction based on the corresponding Cairo Genizah materials suggests that the Qumran text may have been "different at this point" (Stone and Greenfield 1996: 45). While assessing the full scope and shape of the passage is beyond what the fragment allows, the additional readings Drawnel recovered provide a few pegs for pinning this content to the larger section of *ALD* 20–23 and 25a–b.

The form אָלֵּין ("these"), however, suggests at least the presence of a variant reading when compared with the other witnesses. At most, the few phrases that have survived indicate 4Q214 1 contained content relating to the wood offering for priestly service. On this topic, see the comment on 4Q214b 5–6 i.

2.11.2. *Order of the Animal Sacrifice and Drink Offering (4Q214 2)*

Levi's instructions on the orderliness and details of the sacrificial process. This material represents content of *ALD* 26–30. Overlap: <u>4Q214b 2–6 i</u>, and possibly 1Q21 45.

1 [...]לְמִזרָ[ק] [...]
2 [...]וּרְ[גְלֵיךְ מִן] [...]
3 [...]מְלִיחַ[רֵ]אשָׁא הֹ[וי...]
4 [...]תַּרְבָּ[א ואל ותחזו]ο[...]
5 [...]צַוָּר[אָ וּבָתרהן ידיא] [...]
6 [...]וּבַת[רֹ]הֹן ירכתא ושדרתֹ[...]
7 [...]רְחִ[יעַ]ן עִם קרביא וכֻלֹהֹ[...]
8 [...]לְהוֹ[ן] כְּ[כ]מסתן *vacat* וּבָ[תר...]
9 [...]נֹתַ כלא חמר [...]
10 [...]וְ[לֶ]הוא עבדך בסֹ[דרך...]
BOTTOM MARGIN

1. [...]...[...]
2. [...and] your [f]eet fro[m...]
3. [...salt]ed. The head fi[rst...]
4. [...]...[...the fat]and do not let be seen...[...]
5. [...the nec]k and after them the forequarters
6. [...and aft]er them the thigh and the spine of[...]
7. [...was]hed with the entrails. And all of th[em...]
8. [...to the]m[ac]cordingly. *vacat* And af[ter...]
9. [...]...everything, wine [...]
10. [...and] your work will be in or[der...]

Textual, Scribal, and Material Notes

Primary images for transcription: PAM M43.242; B-366684; B-366683. I have accepted many of Drawnel's (2004: 132–33) minor reconstructions of partial forms. For differences, however, see the following notes.

Line 3: ראשא ("first") – The overlapping text of 4Q214b 2–3 8 reads likewise (cf. 1Q21 45; Perrin and Diggens 2020c). Stone and Greenfield (1996: 46) record a variant here with the Cairo Genizah text of *ALD* 27, which reads ואשא. As Drawnel (2004: 134) acknowledged, Charles (1908, 250 n. b) proposed such an emendation to the form ראשא here in view of the variant reading τὴν κεφαλὴν in the Greek text (MS E, Mt. Athos). The Qumran materials affirmed his hunch and demonstrate how the form and details of some aspects of the lost *Vorlage* of the Mt. Athos text are put in fresh perspective by the Qumran finds. In this particular fragment, the Qumran and Mt. Athos witnesses agree several times in content and syntactical details against the Cairo Genizah Aramaic materials.

Line 3: וֹ]הֿ וי ("of[fer") – Drawnel's (2004: 184) reading is accepted here, implying the text likely possessed the compound verb form הוי מהנסק ("offer") as in the Cairo Genizah text of *ALD* 27 (MS A, Bodl. d 9 4). Stone and Greenfield (1996: 46) here read [לֹ]קָֿ[דמין] ("first"), which corresponds with a phrase later in the discourse of *ALD* 27 but would introduce an unnecessary syntactical variant.

Line 5: וּבֹתרהן ידיא ("and after them the forequarters") – This phrase occurs in some variation across the witnesses to *ALD* 28. The Cairo Genizah (MS A, Bodl. d 9 7) text reads ובתר צוארה ידוהי ("and after the neck its forelegs"), where the Mt. Athos (MS E 18,2) text reads καὶ μετὰ τοῦτο τοὺς ὤμους ("and after this the shoulders"). This suggests the Greek translator's *Vorlage* was closer in content and form here to the Qumran text.

Line 6: [...] וּבתֿ[רֹהֿן ירכתא ושדרתֿ ("aft]er them the thigh and the spine of") – In this section of *ALD* 28, the Cairo Genizah text reads בתר ידיא ירכאתא עם שדרת ("after the forelegs the thigh with the spine"), where the Mt. Athos (MS E 18,2) manuscript reads καὶ μετὰ ταῦτα τὴν ὀσφὺν σὺν τῷ νώτῳ ("and after these the loin with the back"). In this respect, the presumed *Vorlage* of the Greek text shared details with the Aramaic forms of the phrasing of both the Qumran and Cairo Genizah texts.

Line 8: כ[מסתן ("ac]cordingly") – The Cairo Genizah text of *ALD* 29 (MS A, Bodl. d 9 12) reads כמסתהון ("as they require").

Line 10: וּ[לֹהוא עבדך ("[and] your work will be") – This initial word here is read with Drawnel (2004: 184). Stone and Greenfield (1996: 46) read וּהֹוא[("let follow"). This phrase also reveals some variation in the witnesses to *ALD* 30. The Cairo Genizah (MS A, Bodl. d 9 14–15) text reads ויהוון כֹן עובדיך ("and thus your actions will be"). The Mt. Athos (MS E 18,2) text reads καὶ ᾖ τὸ ἔργον σου ("And your deed will be"), which is again arguably closer in detail and form to the Aramaic phrasing of the Qumran fragment.

Commentary

Line 2: *your [f]eet fro[m.* This phrase comes from a section outlining the needs to cleanse one's hands and feet from blood spattered over the altar after slaughter but before offering a bull upon it. *Aramaic Levi Document* represents a tradition prescribing three phases of ablutions throughout the ritual process, with the present material relating to the final stage (cf. *ALD* 19, 21). This threefold model is found also in *Jub.* 21:16 and received later in *T. Levi* 9:11. At intervals, the Hebrew Scriptures reference the importance of ablutions for hands and feet before entering sacred space (Exod. 30:19, 21; 40:31), yet the specifics and sequence are unclear. In this way, *ALD* interprets this practice included in Mosaic tradition and retroactively applies it in an earlier ancestral discourse concerning the inaugural generation of priests.

As Drawnel (2004: 275) observed, in the larger context of *ALD*, specifications on this offering come alongside prescriptions for grain, libation, and frankincense offerings (*ALD* 30). He further noted some varieties of offering that are described in ancient priestly descriptions (e.g., Ezra 6:2–12; 11Q18 13, 28) and remarks that the scope of items included in the present context is linked to a purpose of *ALD*. "The [*Aramaic Levi*] *Document*'s choice of the burnt offering is probably motivated by pedagogical interests of the author who intends to teach priestly students not only the proper order of the sacrificial proceedings (*A.L.D.* 30), but metro-arithmetical calculations as well."

Lines 3–4: *salt]ed. The head fi[rst...][...]...[...the fat]and do not let be seen*. This and the following lines include the remains of the prescriptions and processes for the bovine offering. While most familiar from the prescriptions and processes of Leviticus 1, there is a robust and diverse set of ancient Jewish writings that reflect upon or project such a process. The content here in *ALD* is arguably one of the earlier participants in that tradition.

The reference to [מליח]ן ("salt") in line 2 indicates the addition of salt to all the items awaiting offering. By casting a wider comparative net on ancient traditions, we can already sense variety in the process and procedure. Leviticus 1 does not include salt for preservation, yet Lev. 2:13 makes the blanket statement "with all your offerings you shall offer salt" (cf. *Jub.* 21:11). It is not until Ezek. 43:22–24 (cf. Ezra 6:9) that salt is more directly associated with the bovine offering. By the mid-Second Temple period, several writers integrate salt into sacrificial descriptions, though not always in the same way. Though equally fragmentary, the Aramaic *New Jerusalem* seems to include salt at an early point in the preparation of the bull (11Q18 13 2), which suggests a shared priestly understanding and interpretation between the two works. The *Temple Scroll* specifies salt at two stages in the process, first upon the slaughtered flesh and second upon washing the entrails and legs (11Q19 34 9–11). In different ways, Josephus and *GenAp* portray or prescribe salting as the penultimate stage of the process of offering (*Ant.* 3.227; 1Q20 10 17), a practice later rabbinic literature affirms (*m. Tamid* 4:3).

In various ways, the above traditions could be understood as participating in what Anderson described as the "scripturalization of the cult." He wrote, "[n]o longer are we speaking of *development of cultic practice but rather of learned reflection on a developing canon of textual material*" (Anderson 1992: 883, emphasis original). This phenomenon is at once native to the development of priestly prescriptions in the Hebrew Scriptures and demanded by them in their early reception due to their often incomplete or ambiguous nature. Himmelfarb (2004: 105) remarked that "despite the profusion of details it offers, the priestly source of the Torah is certainly not a handbook for priests. Anyone attempting to perform a sacrifice on the basis of the laws in Leviticus and Numbers alone would be left wondering how to proceed at many points." By anchoring this instruction in a discourse delivered by Isaac and received by Levi, *ALD* claims an early and ancestral authority for this interpretation of the process. In this respect, then, we can begin to sense the importance of understanding *ALD*'s sacrificial presentations as developing primarily in orbit around traditions associated with authoritative ancestral figures and less in relation to a specific form of an antecedent scriptural text. As Feldman (2020: 345) recently reminded us, shared concerns of content between *ALD* and Leviticus, for example, "should not automatically mean that the texts are genetically related."

Lines 5–8: *and after them the forequarters[... and aft]er them the thigh and the spine off[...was]hed with the entrails. And all of th[em...to the]m[ac]cordingly.* These lines relate to the continued preparation of various aspects of the sacrificial animal. There are at least three ways *ALD* participates in the interpretation of cultic sequence.

First, while the fragmentary nature of the text makes it difficult to discern the referents and antecedents of this process, the general order of the process is instructive. A number of ancient and rabbinic texts are relevant here for context, including: Lev. 1:3–9; Ezek. 43:24; Ezra 6:2–12 [cf. ancient translations for added variety]; 1Q20 10 13–17; 11Q18 13; 11Q19 34 7–14; *Jub.* 6:1–3; *Ant.* 3.9.1; *m. Tamid* 4:1–3. Additional sections relevant to sacrificial elements and process in *ALD* include: 4Q214 2 1–9; 4Q214b 2–6 i 6–9; and *ALD* 25b–30. See also the complementary discussions and references in Greenfield, Eshel, and Stone (2004: 171–77) and Drawnel (2004: 269–79).

Second, there is a question of what pieces of the animal are included in the washing. *Aramaic Levi Document* is somewhat ambiguous here (cf. Greenfield, Stone, and Eshel 2004: 173–75). Nonetheless, it seems that the two hind legs and entrails are the only items that are washed (*ALD* 28). In this respect, Greenfield, Stone, and Eshel note that *ALD* follows the requirement of Lev. 1:9, which specifies the washing of innards and legs. Perhaps not surprisingly given the coherence with Aramaic *New Jerusalem* noted above, this text also refers to the washing of innards and legs (perhaps all four?) as in *ALD*. A broader representation of ancient texts, however, refers to the washing of the entire body of the sacrificial elements (2 Chron. 4:6; Ezek. 40:38; *m. Tamid* 4:2).

Third, the final extant phrase in *ALD* refers to the repeated salting of all elements of the animal. Thus, the text shares yet another similarity with *New Jerusalem*, which prescribes likewise immediately after the washing (11Q18 13 2). As Drawnel (2004: 278) noted, the topic of salt quantities for different animals is addressed in *ALD* 37–40a (cf. *T. Levi* 9:14).

Line 9: *and af]ter [...]... everything, wine.* This partial line comes from a portion of *ALD* 30 referencing the drink offering. The specifics of the amounts of flour, oil, and wine are described in Isaac's priestly instruction in *ALD* 42–45 and 52. *Aramaic Levi Document*'s treatment of these topics may be considered in light of references to the offering, integration, or provision of wine in various sacrificial references in the Hebrew Scriptures (e.g., Exod. 29:40–41; Lev. 23:13; Num. 15:1–10; 28:7–21; 1 Chron. 9:29; Ezek. 45:17). Drawnel (2004: 278) commented that "[i]t is interesting to notice that according to 1 Chron. 9:29 Levites are in charge of the fine flour, wine, oil, incense, and spices."

The Aramaic *New Jerusalem* is a helpful comparative, both for similarities and differences. First, while the present *ALD* fragment does not specify measurements, *ALD* 42–44 does so by updating the pre-exilic measurements of Num. 15:9–10 to post-exilic measurements (Drawnel 2004: 278–90; Schiffman 2005:

197). As far as we can tell from the fragmentary materials of 11Q18 13 4–5, *New Jerusalem* shares this metrological knowledge and uses post-exilic measurements for proportions of oil and wine (Perrin 2015a: 173). Second, where *New Jerusalem* refers to a receptacle of sorts for the wine (1Q18 13 5), *ALD* does not seem to share this practice (cf. *m. Sukkah* 4:9; *t. Sukkah* 3:24). On this point, *ALD* shares the understanding that the wine is poured over the entire offering as endorsed also by *Temple Scroll* (11Q19 34 13) and *Jub.* 7:3–5. In this way, the priestly traditions related to sacrificial processes in the Aramaic DSS exhibit both common patterns and variety.

In the context of the Aramaic DSS, *GenAp* would presumably be another comparison on the use of wine. However, in Noah's sacrifice upon leaving the ark (1Q20 10 16), wine is not mentioned, perhaps for narrative purposes as Noah had not yet planted his vineyard. Alternatively, perhaps Noah's private reserve ran dry after floating about for forty days and nights on history's rankest and dankest cruise ship.

Line 10: *[...and] your work will be in or[der.* The final partial line of the fragment comes from *ALD* 30, which emphasizes the orderliness of the entire sacrificial process. Levi's priestly duties are referred to here as עבדך ("your deed, activity, work"). While this word is very common in the Aramaic DSS, it is only here and in *VA* that it is applied to the activities and duties of a priest. In Amram's revelation relating to the Aaronic line, the angel states: א]חׄוה לכה רז עובדה ("I will tell you the mystery of his work"; 4Q545 4 16).

2.11.3. *The Accent on Glory (4Q214 3)*

A fragment of unknown placement in the compositional structure of *ALD*.

```
0 [...]ο ο[...]
1 ארו מן יקר בא○[...]
2 אנה די תמרון לי דׄ דׄ[...]
3 יקירין מןׄ נׄשיא [...]
4 ○לׄ[...]ο [...]
```

0. [...]...[...]
1. Look, more than glory in...[...]
2. I that you may say to me that ...[...]
3. more glorious than the women[...]
4. [...]...[...]...[...]

Textual, Scribal, and Material Notes
Primary images for transcription: PAM M43.242; B-366686; B-366685.

Line 0: The fragment includes a right intercolumnar margin with a rather straight vertical break at the edge of the fragment. This may suggest the material came from the beginning of a sheet.

While no full characters or forms can be recovered, the top of the fragment includes traces of the lower sections of lost content.

Line 1:]ο‎בא‎ ("in...") – There are ink traces of a character at the edge of this fragment for the now-lost world. Stone and Greenfield (1996: 49) do not venture a reconstruction. Drawnel (2004: 171) proposes בא‎]עא‎ ("in [the] count[ry").

Line 2: ‎די‎ ("that") – The relative particle is written above the line.

Line 4: There are visible ink strokes, perhaps on an angle, offset in the right intercolumnar margin. This may be text running over from a previous fragment or some other marginal note.

Commentary

Lines 1–3: *Look, more than glory in...[...]I that you may say to me that ...[...] more glorious than the women.* Stone and Greenfield (1996: 49; cf. Greenfield, Stone, and Eshel 2004: 223) noted that this fragment and the next "cannot be identified with any other material from *ALD* or *Testament of Levi* which has survived." Drawnel (2004: 32–34, 171) labeled this fragment as *ALD* 104 and placed it as the final fragment of his reconstruction. He indicated that the language here suggests a discourse from Levi to his children, perhaps also relating in some way to the rape of Dinah (Drawnel 2004: 348). Greenfield, Stone, and Eshel (2004: 223) noted that the word יקר ("honor, glory") also occurs in Jochebed's onomastic midrash as well as in Levi's wisdom poem (*ALD* 71; 88–91; 93–94; and 98).

It is possible that the language and topics here could also reflect a revelatory context. The particle ארו ("look!") is one of the more common idiomatic features of dream-visions in the Aramaic DSS (Perrin 2015a: 102–103, 118). As noted above, Levi's first dream-vision likely broached the Shechem incident in some way, which may be implied here. Finally, the first-person voice could be either ancestral discourse or revelatory disclosure.

2.12. Text and Commentary: 4QLevi^e (4Q214a)

Three fragments are preserved from this manuscript. Of these, a partial column of 4Q214a 2–3 ii is the only material not matched with known content from the later witness. In this case, the Aramaic material provides valuable insight into the continuation of Levi's wisdom discourse and visionary profile. For material description, see Stone and Greenfield (1996: 53–54)

2.12.1. *Species of Wood for Preparing the Altar (4Q214a 1)*

Though limited in content, the material likely comes from a context describing species of wood for use in burnt offerings, probably *ALD* 24–25. Overlap: 4Q214b 2–6 i.

1 ק̇תא̇ א̇ל̇ א̇]נון די[...]
2 עלמדבחא vacat ו̇כ̇[י...]
3 ל̇[ה]ל̇ד̇ל̇]קא

1. [...asph]althos. These are th[ose...]
2. upon the altar. *vacat* And wh[en...]
3. to bu[rn them...]

Textual, Scribal, and Material Notes

Primary images for transcription: PAM M41.945; PAM M43.260; B-371317.

Line 1: ד[ק̇ת̇א̇ ("asph]althos") – The form here is reconstructed on the basis of *ALD* 24 in the Cairo Genizah texts, which read דקתא (MS A, Bodl. c 9 19). Compare also the corresponding Mt. Athos reading, ἀσφάλαθον (MS E 18,2). Drawnel (2004: 185) proposed ה̇דסא ("myrtle"). On the problem of this reading, see the commentary below.

Line 1: א]נון ("those") – The edge of the fragment retains only a partial *aleph*, yet the form is restored on the basis of 4Q214b 2–3 5, which reads א̇נון. Similarly, the Cairo Genizah text reads אינון (MS A, Bodl. c 9 20)

Line 2: י̇]כ̇ו̇ ("And wh[en") – While the present fragment includes only the partially extant *vav* and *kaph*, these are instructive for confirming the general background of the Cairo Genizah text which is longer than the corresponding Greek text of *ALD* 24–25. As Drawnel (2004: 131) described, the translator or *Vorlage* of the Mt. Athos manuscript omitted text here due to homoioteleuton over paired forms of על מדבחה in this section.

Line 3: ל̇[ה]ל̇ד̇ל̇]קא ("to bu[rn them") – The reconstruction here is made on the basis of the corresponding Cairo Genizah text, which reads להדלקא (MS A, Bodl. c 9 23). Drawnel (2004: 186) also proposed that 4Q214 1 7 overlaps with the reading ל̇ה̇ד̇]לקא. This connection, however, is uncertain.

Commentary

Line 1: *asph]althos. These are th[ose.* The fragment here relates to a larger set of Qumran fragments (4Q214a 1; 4Q214b 2–3; 5–6 i) that attest to *ALD* 23–25 (MS A, Bodl. c 9 13–23). For discussion on the order and scope of species, see the comments on 4Q214b 5–6 i.

The ink traces in 4Q214a 1 1 provide only glimpses of the species list. The beginning of the fragmentary line reads only ות̇א. Based on the corresponding Cairo Genizah text (MS A, Bodl. c 9 19), Stone and Greenfield (1996: 54) reconstruct ד[ק̇ת̇א ("asphalthos"). This corresponds to the Greek reading ἀσπάλθον (MS E, Mt. Athos). Contextually, this makes sense as the next word א̇ל̇ likely comes at the start of *ALD* 25, the section immediately after the list.

Drawnel (2004: 185), however, suggests that the character cluster of the partial first word in 4Q214a 1 reads ה̇דסא, that is, the "myrtle" tree. He clarified that "the proposed reading is only a conjecture, which, however, corresponds to the actual remains." The only clear letter traces here are the remains of a pair of lower extensions of the final character, plausibly read as an *aleph*. While Drawnel's reading is ambitious and its coherence with the "actual remains" is overstated, the mere possibility of this reading introduces an intriguing new dynamic. In the Cairo Genizah *ALD* text, the myrtle is the eleventh or penultimate species of the list. Yet if it is presented in the final position in 4Q214a, there is perhaps a hint of a shorter or rearranged list of tree species in this manuscript. In the end, this possibility must remain in the realm of speculation. Sufficient text simply does not survive to verify the reading or confirm the order and items of the list in the present fragment.

2.12.2. *A Fragment of Yochebed's Birth Notice (4Q214a 2–3 i)*

A few phrases relating to the birth notice of Yochebed in the larger priestly genealogy of Levi's children and grandchildren. The fragment corresponds to some content of *ALD* 69–73.

1 [...]וֹכֹדִי
2 [...]עָֿלוהא
3 [...]שֿעא
4 ...]אֿ[ברת ושׁוית
5 [...]בֿשׁנת
6 [...ש]בֿיעא
7 [...]ooo

1. [...]...And when
2. [...]over him
3. [...]...
4. [daught]er and I named
5. [...]In the year
6. [seven]th
7. [...]...

Textual, Scribal, and Material Notes
Primary images for transcription: PAM M41.945; PAM M43.260; B-361399; B-371317; B-361398. 4Q214a 2–3 i and ii are known from two fragments that represent the remains of two columns on the same sheet, separated by an inter-columnar margin.

Line 3: שֿעא[("...") – Stone and Greenfield (1996: 56) read עי[as a partial form of either "seven]th" or "four]th." However, Drawnel (2004: 146, 191) is correct that the best reading here is שֿעא[, which may be the remnants of an attempted correction from שע[ת to ת[שׁיעיא. The corresponding Cairo Genizah (MS A, Cambr. c 7 17) text reads תליתאֿי ("third"), which may suggest a variant reading between the witnesses. The Qumran text, however, is too damaged to determine the content and degree of the difference.

Line 4: ב[רת‎ ("daught]er") – The form is reconstructed on the basis of the Cairo Genizah reading ברתא (MS A, Cambr. c 7 19).

Line 6: שב̊[יע̊א ("seven]th") – The number is restored in light of the Cairo Genizah text, which reads שביעיא (MS A, Cambr. c 7 19).

Line 7: ooo ("...") – Drawnel (2004: 190) proposed מ̊צ̊[ר]י̊ן ("Egyp]t") in light of the form מצרים in *ALD* 73 (MS A, Cambr. d 7 2). While possible, the reconstruction goes beyond what the available ink traces allow.

Commentary

Lines 1–6: *And when[...]over him[...]...[daught]er and I named[...]In the year [seven]th.* This fragment comes from a section in *ALD* where Levi reflects on the births of his children with Melcha (cf. *Jub.* 34:20; *T. Levi* 11:1). As Kugler (1996a: 117) observed, this section of *ALD* "establishes Levi's lineage and indicates how his seed became a priestly family." From the more complete *ALD* witnesses, we learn that Levi accounted for the details of four children—Gershom, Qahat, Merari, and Yochebed—which segue into birth notices of his grandchildren with special emphasis on Amram. The surviving material here in 4Q214a relates specifically to the birth notice of Yochebed. To provide some context for this section, a synoptic reading of these accounts reveals some common patterns and themes in the details provided in birth notices of Levi's offspring in *ALD*.

Table 2.1: Trends in Birth Notices in *Aramaic Levi Document*

	Gershom	Qahat	Merari	Yochebed	Amram
Maternity stated	"I took a wife for myself from the family of Abraham my father, Melcha, a daughter of Bathuel, son of Laban, brother of my mother. And she conceived by me, bore the first son..." (*ALD* 63).	"[And it happen]ed about the ti[me appropriate for women, and I was] wi[th h]er (i.e., Melcha), [and she concei]ved again [by me and bore me] another [son, and I call]ed his name [Qahat" (*ALD* 66).	"And once again I was wi[th] her (i.e., Melcha) and she bore me a third son, and I called his name Merari" (*ALD* 69).	"And again I was with her (i.e., Melcha), and she conceived and bore me a daughter" (*ALD* 71).	"I to[ok wives] from the daughters of my brothers at the moment corresponding to their ages, and sons w[ere b]orn to them" (*ALD* 73).

Future forecasted and/or onomastica	"and I called his name Gershom since I said: 'my seed will be sojourners in the land where I was born. We are sojourners as it (will be) in the land which is considered ours" (*ALD* 63). "And concerning the youth, I saw in my dream (or: vision) that he and his seed will be cast out of the high priesthood" (*ALD* 11:3; cf. *T. Levi* 11:2).³	"And I sa]w that to him [would belo]ng the congregation of all the [people and th]at to him would belong the high priesthood (he and his seed will be a supreme kingship, a priesthood) for [all Is]rael" (*ALD* 67; cf. *T. Levi* 11:5–6).	"for I was exceedingly bitter on his account, for when he was born he was dying, and I was very bitter on his account because he was about to die. And I besought and asked for mercy for him and it was in all bitterness" (*ALD* 69).	"and I gave her the name Yochebed, (for) I said: 'When she was born to me, for the glory she was born to me, for the glory of Israel'" (*ALD* 71).	"And I called the name of Amram, when Amram was born, for when he was born I said, 'This one will {exalt} <lead> the people <out> of the land of Egypt. [Th]us [his name] will be called: '<the> exalted [<people>'"" (*ALD* 76).

3. This line is known only in the Mt. Athos text and is rightly placed in this section by Greenfield, Stone, and Eshel (2004: 94–95), hence the retention of their versification here. See also Drawnel (2004: 140).

Birth chronology	"[I was thirty years old when he was born in my life,] [and he was born in the tenth month at sunse]t" (*ALD* 65).	"In the fou[r and th]irtieth year of my life he was born, in the first month of the [fir]st day of the mon[th] at sunris[e]" (*ALD* 68).	"In the fortieth year of my life she gave birth in the third month" (*ALD* 70).	"In the sixty-fourth year of my life she was born to me on the first day of the seventh month after that we were brou[ght] to Egypt, in the sixteen[th] year of our entry into the land of Egypt" (*ALD* 72).	"And Amram took a wife for himself, Yochebed, my daughter, while I was still living, in the ninety-fou[rth] year of my life...On the same day the [children] we[re bo]rn, he (i.e., Amram) and Yochebed, my daughter." (*ALD* 75, 77).

What is significant about the content of the present fragment is that it features the birth notice of a daughter among a larger list of sons. Yochebed is already connected with Amram in the Hebrew Scriptures (Exod. 6:20; Num. 26:59). The naming of Yochebed is derived via onomastics to underscore how her seed will bring "glory" to all Israel (*ALD* 71). Drawnel (2004: 311; cf. Greenfield, Stone, and Eshel 2004: 192) stated, "Yochebed's name is interpreted with recourse to the synonymous Hebrew (כבוד) and Aramaic (יקר) lexemes meaning 'glory,'" which fits with a pattern for the orientation toward Hebrew roots in the onomastica of *ALD*. The connection with glory in this case is likely due to Yochebed's association with the projected futures of her brother, Qahat. Qahat was said to hold superiority in both the high priesthood and royal domains. The fate of his son, Amram, includes the exaltation and leadership of Israel by his seed (i.e., Moses and Aaron).

The connection of Yochebed to this priestly line is solidified by virtue of her stated endogamous marriage to Amram. This aunt–nephew union establishes a clear and traceable line of the genealogy that includes wives/mothers of reputable priestly stock. What makes the present case of Yochebed's union so intriguing, however, is that the opening scene of *VA* is for a wedding celebration between Amram's daughter, Miriam, with Amram's brother, Uzziel (cf. 4Q543 1 a–c; 4Q545 1a i; 4Q546 1). That is, *VA* presents an uncle–niece marriage in order to focus on the endogamous relationship of a daughter in a key generation of the priestly lineage.

While the pattern of the relationship is inverse in *ALD* and *VA* (i.e., aunt–nephew and uncle–niece, respectively) both texts operate on a similar principle. At critical stages in the priestly genealogy, it is essential to ensure there are no loose threads that could imply exogamy or result in a compromise to the priestly line. In *ALD*, this concern already presented itself in the focus on the rape of Dinah. The present fragment now extends this ethic to emphasize the ongoing stability of the priestly line, including Yochebed's union. This, in turn, continues in *VA* via the tight priestly parameters established for Miriam's marriage in the next generation. In this way, the construct of the purity of the priestly line involves continuity, consistency, and coherence of paternal and maternal lines.

There are many traditions relating, or debating, the (dis)approved parameters for endogamous marriages in both the Hebrew Scriptures and DSS. Leviticus 18:12 and 20:20 are the most relevant here as they disallow aunt–nephew relations. Drawnel (2004: 312) wrote that "[t]he author of the composition [*ALD*] seems not to be aware of the conflict with the marital legislation caused by this union [between Yochebed and Amram]." However, it is more likely that the suite of Aramaic priestly literature could creatively avoid tension with the Mosaic prescription as their narratives are set in a world *before* Mosaic instruction existed. In this way, the writer of *ALD* developed this endogamous infrastructure for founding figures of the priesthood without the need to adhere to, or abide by, the legalities introduced in subsequent generations.

2.12.3. *Scribal Craft and a Revelatory Allusion in Levi's Wisdom Poem (4Q214a 2–3 ii)*

Another fragment of Levi's wisdom poem beyond previously known witnesses. The text here includes mention of scribal craft and reference to Levi's dream-visions. Overlap: 4Q213 1 ii–2; **4Q214b 8**.

1 וֹמְדִינה[...]
2 לא יִשְׁכְּחוּ[ן...]
3 טֻבָה oo[...]
4 מנה ̊ו[...]
5 וכען בני ספר ו[...]
6 חזית בחזוי ד[י...]
7 ל oooo oo[...]

1. and province[...]
2. they will not find[...]
3. her good things...[...]

4. from him and...[...]
5. And now, my sons, scribal craft and[...]
6. I saw in visions that[...]
7. ...[...]

Textual, Scribal, and Material Notes
Primary images for transcription: PAM M41.945; PAM M43.260; B-371317; B-361399; B-361398.

Line 1: וּמֹדִינה ("and province") – Stone and Greenfield (1996: 58) read וֹמדיתא ("and the country"), which would be a variant with the later Cairo Genizah text. However, וּמֹדִינה is more likely in view of the ink traces at the fringes of the fragment (Drawnel 2004: 199).

Line 2: לא ("not") – The Cairo Genizah texts here read ולא ("and not; MS A, Cambr. f 6 23).

Line 6: ד]י חזית בחזוין ("I saw in visions that") – Drawnel's (2004: 199) reading חזית בחזוין ד[י is confirmed in the latest digital infrared image plates (B-361399 [October 2012]). Stone and Greenfield (1996: 58) here read חֹזית ת∘∘חו ("I saw").

Commentary
Lines 1–4: *and province[...]they will not find[...] her good [things...]from him.* These lines refer to the hiddenness of wisdom within the impenetrable sapiential city as related in the better-preserved materials of 4Q213 1 i; 1 ii–2.

Line 5: *And now, my sons, scribal craft and.* This line includes both the common discourse marker for transitioning within an address to children and the first element of the common triad of characteristics Levi endorses in his wisdom poem. On these items, see the comment on the overlapping material in 4Q213 1 i 9.

Line 6: *I saw in visions that.* Drawnel's recovered reading here adds an important new dynamic to the poem. This is the second reference Levi makes to his dream-vision experiences. In the Mt. Athos text (MS E 18,2) of *ALD* 64, Levi indicates that he learned of Gershom's being cast out of the priesthood through an ὅραμα ("dream" or "vision"). While *VA* deployed a dream-vision to reveal the direction of the priesthood from Amram through Aaron, *ALD* 64 seems to use the opposite strategy to disqualify an ancestral line from the approved channels of the priesthood (Perrin 2015a: 163).

In Drawnel's reconstruction (2004: 166; cf. Greenfield, Stone, and Eshel 2004: 104) the reference to the dream-vision(s) comes before a statement from 4Q213 2 9, which reads]תֹּרתון אנון[("you will inherit them"). If the pronoun "them" refers to the triad of qualities known in the foregoing line, Levi may be referencing a revelatory experience in which he not only received a priestly blessing but also special knowledge of the inheritance reserved for his priestly progeny. If this interpretation is correct, the emphasis on scribal craft, instruction, and wisdom in this section are not simply ideals to pursue and protect. Rather, they may also be presented as qualities that are divinely disclosed and delivered as the unique legacy of the priesthood. The parallel text of 4Q213 1 ii–2 6 confirms this interpretation.

2.13. Text and Commentary: 4QLeviᶠ (4Q214b)

This sixth *ALD* manuscript from Qumran Cave Four is known by eight fragments. Of these, 4Q214b 1 is too meager to warrant full commentary and does not relate to any known content of *ALD* in the other witnesses. The partial phrase כֹּל לבִיך[("all for your heart") in line 2 of this fragment is intriguing yet lacks context. 4Q214b 7 is also quite fragmentary and is still not placed in the known structure or content of *ALD*. This fragment is, however, included in the commentary below given its potential terminological parallels with other *ALD* materials. All other fragments of 4Q214b are assigned to known passages. For a material description of the fragments, see Stone and Greenfield (1996: 61–62).

2.13.1. *Isaac's Instruction on Wood Species for Fueling the Altar (4Q214b 2–6 i)*

Isaac's instruction to Levi describing suitable wood species and preparations for animal sacrifice. The text below corresponds to *ALD* 22–27. Overlap: 4Q214 1–2 and 4Q214a 1. Compare also 1Q21 45.

1 [עעי...] מצלחין
2 [...וב[אד]י[ן] אסק [אנו̇ן] ארו [כדן חזית לאברהם
3 [... תרי ע[שר עעין א[מ]ר לי] די חזין ל[אסקא מנהון למדבחא
4 [...ל[סלק ואל[ן שמה[תהו]ן א[רזא ודפ[רנא וסוגדה
5 [...ב̇רות]א̇ ותככה[ועעא משחא ע[ר̇א אדסא ועעי
6 [...רקתא [אלן אנו̇ן די א[מר לי די חזין לאסקא מנהון [לתחות עלתא
7 [...וכדי אסק[ת [מן עעי[א אלן על מ̇דבחא ונו[ר]א...]
8 [...דמא] על כותלי מדבחא ותוב̇[...]
9 [...לאסקא [אבר[יה] מ[לי]חין רא[שא הוי...]

1. [...] splitting [woo]d
2. [...And t]he[n offer] thes[e, look,] just as I saw Abraham
3. [... twel]ve woods, he to[l]d me, [that are suitable to] offer of them on the altar
4. [...] rises up. And these are [the]ir names: ce[dar and jun]iper and almond
5. [...] cypress and *tkkh*[and oleaster, l]aurel, myrtle, and wood of
6. [...asphalthos.] These are those that [he] to[ld me that are suitable for offering of them] beneath the offering
7. [...] And when] you [have offered] from these [woods] upon the altar and [the] fi[re...]
8. [...blood] on the sides of the altar. And again [...]
9. [...to offer its] limb[s] sa[lt]ed. [The] he[ad...]

Textual, Scribal, and Material Notes

Primary images for transcription: PAM M41.945; PAM M43.260;B-361395; B-361397; B-361396; B-371317; B-361394. The fragments that comprise 4Q214b 2–3, 4, and 5–6 i form a partial column. My presentation of the text here is based on an independent analysis of images, both old and new, yet is heavily informed by Drawnel's (2004: 188) reconstruction, which offered several improvements to other editions. However, I include only minimal text from the Cairo Genizah witness given some variety among the texts at this point. My textual notes here relate only to the reading of extant materials in 4Q214b. For another reconstruction, see Stone and Greenfield (1996: 68).

Line 1: עֵ[י ("[wood]") – Drawnel (2004: 188) correctly infers the form based on the Cairo Genizah text אעין (MS A, Bodl. c 9 9).

Line 2: וּב[אָ]דִֿ[י]ן ("And t]he[n") – Read with Drawnel (2004: 188). Stone and Greenfield (1996: 66, 68) read traces of an *aleph* and *dalet* and reconstruct similarly.

Line 3: תְרי עֲ[שר עעין ("twel]ve woods") – This reconstruction comes from 4Q214b 2–3 2 and involves a variant reading. The Cairo Genizah text reads תריעשר מיני אעין ("twelve types of wood"; MS A, Bodl. c 9 13). The Mt. Athos text, however, has a shorter reading, ιβ′ ξύλα ("twelve woods"; MS E 18,2), now supported by the Qumran fragment.

Line 4: וֹאֵלֵּן ("And these") – The Qumran fragment again provides background for the shorter text of Mt. Athos, which reads καὶ ταῦτα ("And these"; MS E 18,2). The Cairo Genizah text has the fuller, formulaic ואלין אינון ("And these are those"; MS A, Bodl. c 9 15–16).

Line 7: עַֿל מֹדֿבֿחָֿא ("upon the altar") – The *lamed* of the preposition is visible on the upper edge of 4Q214b 2–3 (Drawnel 2004: 186). Stone and Greenfield (1996: 64) read לְמֹדֿבָֿחָֿ[א, yet the traces preceding this are better accounted for in Drawnel's reading.

Line 8: וּתוּבֿ ("And again") – The Cairo Genizah (MS A, Bodl. b 9 2) manuscript reads ועוד ("And again"). The Mt. Athos translation καὶ πάλιν ("And again"; MS E 18,2) could reasonably be based on either of these two Aramaic forms. Note that the adverbial form תובא occurs also in 4Q540 1 1–2.

Commentary

Lines 1–3: *splitting [woo]d[...And t]he[n offer] thes[e, look,] just as I saw Abraham[... twel]ve woods, he to[l]d me, [that are suitable to] offer of them on the altar.* Isaac's instructions to Levi regarding the procedures of sacrifice include the species of wood that are deemed acceptable for the burnt offering. Line 2 specifies that this teaching is anchored in the ancestral authority of Abraham. References to wood for sacrifice occurs regularly in Levitical teachings on priestly duties (Lev. 1:12, 17; 3:5; 4:12; 6:12). However, specific species of wood are mentioned only on occasion (Lev. 14:6, 49–52; Num. 19:6). The present text, then, represents one scribal strategy for providing order, infrastructure, and authority to a tradition for the provision of wood at the altar.

While rabbinic literature does not restrict wood deemed acceptable for offering (e.g., *m. Tamid* 2:3), several writings of the early to mid-Second Temple period engage this topic. To support the reinstatement of sacrifice in the Second Temple, Neh. 10:34 (cf. 13:31) references the casting of lots between the priests, Levites, and general population at fixed annual intervals "as it is written in the law." Williamson noted (2003: 336) that, despite this legitimizing statement, no organized scheme for facilitating this offering is mentioned in materials traditionally assigned to the Pentateuch. With our growing knowledge of the larger scope of pentateuchal traditions, however, it is clear other scribes found, or developed, an authoritative basis for this in Mosaic traditions.

Following the running text of Lev. 23:42–24:2b, 4QPentateuch^c (4Q365) 23 4–11 includes an eight-line plus related to materials for a festival of oil and likely prescriptions for a festival of wood. While those materials are increasingly fragmentary, it seems that the fragment established a basis for pairs of tribes bringing wood daily, presumably for a six-day event. As the text breaks away, לוי ("Levi") is one of the first tribes responsible for bringing wood to the festival, likely alongside Judah (4Q365 23 10). Though the topic is not exactly the same as in *ALD*, the scribal authority claiming and conferring strategy for establishing a rhythm of wood offering in cultic life went beyond a mere claim to a Mosaic authority as in Nehemiah. The scribe of 4Q365 grafted the "new" prescriptions into an existing foundation of Mosaic instruction. In similar form to 4QPentateuch^c, *Temple Scroll* also includes prescriptions for the contribution of wood to offerings. Though fragmentary, 11Q19 23 1–3 references the bringing of wood to accompany burnt offerings by pairs of tribes. The scribal innovation for securing an authoritative stance in this work, of course, is based in bold divine pseudepigraphy presenting prescriptions in the first-person voice of God.

Nehemiah, *ALD*, 4QPentateuch^c, and *Temple Scroll* engage different aspects of the necessity, process, or cycle for bringing wood for sacrifice. They do so using a variety of mechanisms for claiming an authoritative basis to their developing tradition. In the cases of Nehemiah, 4QPentateuch^c, and *Temple Scroll*, authority orbits around a Mosaic legislative gravitas. For these writings, Najman's words on ancient Jewish legal developments are insightful: "no law is authoritative unless it is appropriately connected to the Law of Moses—perhaps even pseudonymously attributed to Moses himself" (Najman 2000: 205). However, the priestly traditions of *ALD* reveal that Mosaic attribution was not the only way of innovating and extending legal traditions related to the cultic system. In the present fragment, the scribe of *ALD* sought to secure a more ancient ancestral basis in the instruction and example of figures such as Isaac, Abraham, and now Levi *before* the ascendancy of Moses (cf. Kugler 1996a: 109).

Lines 4–5: *[...] rises up. And these are [the]ir names: ce[dar and jun]iper and almond[...] cypress and tkkh[and oleaster, l]aurel, myrtle, and wood of.* For a more detailed discussion of these phrases as it relates to the literary form of *ALD*, see Perrin (2017a). The materials here include remnants of reasonably reconstructed partial list of eight species of trees. In most content and detail, this Qumran Aramaic fragment provides a background for the form of the text known in the later manuscript witnesses to *ALD* 23–25a, which feature a full list of twelve woods. The parallel tradition of *Jub.* 21:12–14 also includes a list of twelve acceptable woods for sacrifice, although in an alternate position to that of *ALD*, which presents the list of wood *before* the description of the bovine offering. *Testament of Levi* 9:12 receives the tradition of twelve trees yet does not list them.

For all the continuity across the *ALD* witnesses, however, the lists include at least one key difference regarding the eighth species referenced. In the eighth position, the Cairo Genizah text (MS A, Bodl. c 9 18) reads תאנתא ("fig"). The earlier Aramaic tradition represented at Qumran here reads תככה, which is both a *hapax legomenon* as well as an otherwise unknown species. At this point, the Mt. Athos text reads θεχαx (MS E, 18,2), an apparent transliteration of the term attested in 4Q214b.

Greenfield, Stone, and Eshel (2004: 167) note that the confusion over this term extended even to the analogous list in *Jub.* 21:12, where the Ethiopic "*tānaka* should be regarded as another corruption of this unknown tree name." Drawnel (2004: 130) looked to the analogies of *taqak* in modern Persian, to denote a cypress or pine-like tree, and *tkk* in modern Syriac, for a type of creeping melon plant or stem upon which melons and cucumber grow. From this, he ventured that "the fig in the Genizah manuscript is probably a misinterpretation of the word תככה that was not understood by the scribe" (Drawnel 2004: 130). This explanation is possible but the lack of semantic equivalents in known ancient languages—not least Aramaic—is problematic. Davila (2013: 137 n. e) noted only that "[t]he name of the tree in 4QLevi^f ar is unidentified and perhaps damaged." Cook (2015: 253) glossed the noun simply as a "species of tree." While some scribal error in the transmission of the text cannot be fully ruled out, Norin (2013: 124) suggested that the most likely explanation is the Cairo Genizah reading was an attempt to clarify or update an ambiguous text. This small variant thus indicates a degree of scribal interpretation in the transmission history of *ALD*, which resulted in the incremental evolution, perhaps even confusion, of the text. For discussion of additional variations in the tree lists revealed by the Qumran *ALD* fragments, see the comment on 4Q214a 1 1.

Line 6: *These are those that [he] to[ld me that are suitable for offering of them] beneath the offering.* This line includes a rejoinder to the Abrahamic authority claimed in line 2. In that instance, Isaac's instruction is based on what he witnessed in Abraham's priestly model, "just as I saw (חזית) Abraham." Now, Isaac refers to the oral instruction of Abraham: "[he] to[ld me" (א[מר לי; cf. MS A, Bodl. c 9 20). The pedagogical aspect of Abraham's teaching on this point is retained in *T. Levi* 9:12.

Lines 7–8: *And when] you [have offered] from these [woods] upon the altar and [the] fi[re...blood] on the sides of the altar. And again.* Isaac now instructs Levi on the appropriate cleansing of the altar by spattering blood upon its sides. Drawnel (2004: 276) observed that "[t]he [*Aramaic Levi*] *Document* does not imply that the fire is to be kindled. It only says that the blood sprinkling should begin when fire begins to kindle the wood." Feldman (2020: 357–58) here noted that "[t]here is no rationale given for this ritual action. It is worth recognizing, though, that the blood is kept off the top of the altar."

Line 9: *to offer its] limb[s] sa[lt]ed. [The] he[ad.* This line includes limited content from the opening description of the bovine offering. For more complete treatment of this topic in *ALD*, see the commentary on 4Q214 2 2–8.

2.13.2. *Oil Provisions and Animal Offerings (4Q214b 7)*

A fragment of limited content and unknown placement, perhaps relating to sacrificial prescriptions or visionary priestly inauguration. Potential overlap: 4Q213b 1.

1 [...]מִֿן כּוֹֿל בִּשְׂרָֿ[א...]
2 [...]מִֿשחא וֹ[...]

1. [...]than all fles[h...]
2. [...]oil and...[...]

Textual, Scribal, and Material Notes
Primary images for transcription: PAM M41.945; PAM M43.260; B-371317.

Line 2: מִֿשחא וֹ ("oil and") – This line is known only by ink traces at the lower reaches of the fragment. Stone and Greenfield (1996: 69) are rightfully cautious and transcribe שׁ̇ooo oo. Drawnel's (2004: 204) reading, preliminarily accepted here, is possible but not certain. The term here could mean either "measure" or "oil."

Commentary
Line 1: *than all fles[h.* Though its placement is unknown, line 1 includes a phrase also found in *ALD* 14 (MS A, Bodl. b 8 11), which reads מן כל בישרא ("greater than all flesh"). This may suggest an overlap. In that fragment, the reference is to the higher standard for judgment in purity for the Levitical line. Drawnel (2004: 204) proposed that the language may also recall Levi's priestly elevation (cf. *ALD* 6; *T. Levi* 8:4). Though possible, Drawnel's suggestion is difficult to understand in light of the reference to oil or a measurement in the next line.

Line 2: *oil and.* In the known materials, the mention of משח ("oil") occurs only at *ALD* 29 in the context of its mixing with fine flour for the offering (MS A, Bodl. d 9 11).

2.13.3. *Levi's Words on the Priceless Pursuit of Wisdom (4Q214b 8)*

Levi's discourse on the incomparability and invaluable nature of wisdom. Overlap: 4Q213 1 ii–2 and **4Q214a 2–3 ii**.

1 [...וְלֹא [אִ]יתִי כֹלֹ֑] מִחוּר נגדה[...]
2 [...מ]טמרא מנה ○[...]
3 [...]○חֹ○○○○[...]

1. [...and] there is [no] p[rice equal to it...]
2. [...] the [hid]ing place from it
3. [...]...[...]

Textual, Scribal, and Material Notes
Primary images for transcription: PAM M43.260; B-371317; B-361403; B-361402.

Line 2: מ]טמרא ("the [hid]ing place") – Stone and Greenfield (1996: 70) read מ]טמריא ("the[h]idden places"). Drawnel (2004: 201), however, is correct that the *yod* is absent.

Line 3:]○חֹ○○○○[("...") – The text here is unrecoverable. Stone and Greenfield (1996: 70) are appropriately cautious in reading]○○○○[. Drawnel (2004: 201) ventured מ]וֹסַֹר חֹכְֹ[מה ("instruct]ion wis[dom"). The only likely character here is a *khet*; all others are largely lost.

Commentary
Lines 1–2: *and] there is [no] p[rice equal to it...] the [hid]ing place from it.* This fragment is part of Levi's poem admonishing his children toward pursuing wisdom as an invaluable treasure. The form מ]טמרא in line 2 reveals a minor variant reading with the overlapping text of 4Q213 1 ii–2 6, which reads מטמרה ("to hide it"). For more complete discussion of this section, see the commentary on 4Q213 1 ii–2.

Chapter 3

WORDS OF QAHAT

3.1. *The Figure of Qahat in Texts and Traditions*

The Hebrew Scriptures mention Qahat/Kohath (קְהָת MT; Κααθ LXX) in Levitical genealogies (Gen. 46:11; Exod. 6:16; Num. 3:17; 4:2; 16:1; 26:57–58; 1 Chron. 6:1, 16, 38; 23:6), lists of his own lineage (Exod. 6:18; Num. 3:19, 27; 1 Chron. 6:2, 18, 22; 15:5; 23:12), descriptions of his clan's priestly duties (Num. 3:29; 4:4, 15; 7:9), and notations of priestly allotments of cities (Josh. 21:5, 20, 26; 1 Chron. 6:61, 66, 70). The Hebrew Scriptures also make several references to the Qahatites/Kohathites: Num. 3:27, 30; 4:18, 34, 37; 10:21; 26:57; Josh. 21:4, 10; 1 Chron. 6:18, 39; 9:32; 20:19; 29:12; 34:12. The Greek Scriptures also include additional references to Κααθ, where the Hebrew has adjectival forms: 2 Chron. 20:19; 29:12; 34:12. We have glimpses of Qahat's reimagined biography in *ALD*'s birth notice (*ALD* 66, 74; cf. *T. Levi* 11:4–6) and *VA*'s inclusion of Qahat as Amram's father-in-law returning to build ancestral tombs (4Q544 1 1 // 4Q546 2 3). Other Second Temple period literature at Qumran and beyond include scattered references to Qahat (4Q245 1 i 5; 4Q545 1a i 1; 11Q19 44 14; *Jub.* 44:14). Yet in all of these traditions, Qahat is a voiceless figure.

It is no secret that controversy and conversation increased around the identity and office of the priesthood in the mid- to late Second Temple period. In this turmoil, some Jewish scribes writing in Aramaic saw to it that Qahat was given a voice from the past with apparent words for the present. *Words of Qahat* is our earliest and only known example of a writing attributed to this priestly ancestor in antiquity. The resulting text is one that reimagines Qahat as an integral priestly ancestor in the early stages of the priestly line; a critical link in the reception and transmission of ancestral inheritance; a source for admonition and identity formation; and an anchor for developing an eschatological outlook.

3.2. *Publication History*

Words of Qahat is known by a single fragmentary manuscript discovered in Qumran Cave Four. As Milik (1972a: 97) preliminarily published the yet unknown Aramaic compositions from this cave, he presented four partial lines of

WQ (4Q542 1 ii 9–12) as an addendum to an article focusing on *VA*. In the years that followed, fragments of *WQ* were published piecemeal across various editions and studies. Eventually Puech (2001) prepared the "official" DJD edition. For editions and studies including presentations of *WQ*, see the following: Milik 1972a: 97; Beyer 1984: 210; Puech 1991: 33, 47, 49; Eisenman and Wise 1992: 149–50; Cook 1993: 205–206; Beyer 1994: 83–85; García Martínez and Tigchelaar 1998 2:1082–84; Puech 2001: 268–69, 279–81; Fitzmyer and Harrington 2002: 96; Beyer 2004: 115–17; and Parry and Tov [Puech] 2005: 566–68.

3.3. *Material Quality and Scribal Features*

Words of Qahat is now studied as three fragments (4Q542 1 i–ii, 2, 3) even though the photographs indicate the main fragment is comprised of three fragments of various sizes. While the material evidence is damaged, the surviving fragments permit some observations on the material and scribal character of the manuscript.

3.3.1. *Codicological Characteristics*

The largest fragment, 4Q542 1 i–ii, includes text spanning two columns. Since upper, lower, and intercolumnar margins are preserved, we can conclude that the scroll presented content in columns with thirteen lines of text. The inclusion of text inscribed down the intercolumnar margin and into the lower margin in 4Q542 3 i suggests that, in at least one instance, the material parameters of the manuscript were creatively utilized. This scribal intervention evidences either a correction or adaptation by the scribe or a later user. The smaller fragments, 4Q542 2 and 3, preserve the scroll's lower margins and the bottom portions of now-lost columns, hence the numbering of their lines up to thirteen. For precise measurements of lines and margins, see Puech (2001: 257–58). The rightmost edge of 4Q542 1 i also includes stitching holes indicating this content was attached to another sheet of now-lost content. Since the discourse of 4Q542 1 i 1 picks up mid-sentence, we may infer that the content that preceded 4Q541 1 i was indeed of material from *WQ*. It is unknown how much material was lost. As noted below and in the conclusion to the present volume, the physical size and configuration of the text on 4Q542 are so similar to 4Q547 that it is likely the two works or traditions were housed on the same scroll. This invites other questions of the potential literary relationship of the Amram and Qahat materials.

3.3.2. *Paleographical Profile*

Puech (2001: 264) described the hand of 4Q542 as archaic Hasmonean and dated the script to the range of 125–100 BCE.[1] He is also no doubt correct that this

---

1. Puech (2001 : 264) described the range as "dernier quart du deuxièmes s., ou au plus tard vers 100 avant J.-C."

scribe is the same that produced 4Q547, confirming further the material association of these items. At times the scribe used medial characters in final position (e.g., 4Q542 1 i 11; 2 11) and final characters in medial positions (e.g., 4Q542 1 ii 2; 2 5). For an in-depth description of the formation of characters in this hand, see Puech (2001: 262–64).

3.3.3. Scribal Interventions

There are several corrections in the fragments, some of which are in a hand noticeably different from the main hand of the manuscript (e.g., 4Q542 1 i 5). This suggests either the contribution of a second scribe or the use of a different writing implement by the first hand. Corrections are made throughout the manuscript in various ways, including: erasures (e.g., 4Q542 1 i 2), overwritten characters (e.g., 4Q542 1 ii 10), cancellation dots (e.g., 4Q542 1 ii), characters written above the line (e.g., 4Q542 1 ii 4), and, as noted above, the apparent addition of material in the margin (4Q542 3 i).

At 4Q542 1 ii 8–9, the manuscript includes a horizontal stroke between lines at a point that coincides with a shift in discourse. It is unknown if the marginal stroke is from the scribe(s) who produced the manuscript or from a later user. The only other occurrence of this type of marginalia in the Aramaic DSS is in a fragment of *ALD* (4Q213a 2 10–11).

3.4. Prominent Themes and Noteworthy Structures

Words of Qahat contains an intriguing blend of themes and topics that invite comparison with other items in the Aramaic DSS and broader literary heritage of ancient Judaism. Five of the more central emphases of *WQ* are introduced here, with more detailed discussion on each item included in the commentary below.

3.4.1. The First-Person Voice and Ancestral Attribution

While Qahat is not named in the extant materials, the phrases "my son, Amram" and "my father, Levi" (4Q542 1 ii 9, 11) confirm the work is presented as a first-person discourse of Qahat. The deployment of a first-person voice is a prominent compositional technique in the Aramaic DSS (Stuckenbruck 2011). This narrative style harnesses an authoritative perspective from the imagined past in order to have it strategically speak into a contemporary culture and setting. In this case, the attribution of the text to Qahat may be less about his inherent authority than about his authority by association with other more famed figures from the past (Uusimäki 2021).[2] Regardless of the reason for the selection of this voice and figure, *WQ* is pseudepigraphic in the technical sense.

---

2. Thanks to Elisa Uusimäki for sharing a prepublication version of this study, upon which my engagements are based in this volume.

In the extant text, Qahat's words are an address to his children, though the scope of this audience comes in and out of focus in the fragments. Earlier sections refer to a second-person plural audience of his general progeny (4Q542 1 i 1–ii 9), which narrows to Amram (4Q542 1 ii 9), and then seemingly expands again with a set of second- and third-person plural references (4Q542 1 ii 10–13). While the final section of this blended discourse is fragmentary, the later portions likely refer to the anticipated next generation of priestly progeny issued through Amram and his descendants. In this way, the work presents itself as words from the past with a trajectory into the Second Temple present of the audience.

The genealogical arc of *WQ*, however, also reaches backwards to the very foundations of the forefathers. While Qahat is mentioned only once in Genesis (Gen. 46:11), *WQ* establishes a direct and traceable link between him and the more famed figures of Abraham, Isaac, Jacob, and Levi (4Q542 1 i 7–8, 11). This association galvanizes Qahat as a reliable and authoritative figure whose resumé commences in Genesis. In effect, he is no longer a placeholder in a genealogy or name easily glossed over in a list—Qahat is reimagined as a foundational figure from a recreated priestly past.

3.4.2. *The Transmission of Inheritance from the Forefathers*

While the genealogical interest in *WQ* is, in part, to establish a traceable heritage of the priestly ancestors, it also illustrates how the ancestral inheritance was preserved and passed along through approved channels. Much like the actual genealogy of the family line, the tradition too has an imagined history through the generations. The text makes regular reference to the "inheritance" that was received by Qahat and is now transmitted to his children (4Q542 1 i 4–5, 12). The content of this inheritance, however, is not articulated in a single place. Rather, Qahat's admonitions seemingly consisted of at least four things: (1) the teachings and models of the ancestors (4Q542 1 i 7–12); (2) a set of virtues for right living (4Q542 1 i 12–13); (3) the institution of the priesthood inaugurated in the past (4Q542 1 i 13); and (4) writings given to Amram (4Q542 1 ii 9–13).

3.4.3. *Forming Priestly Identity and Maintaining Boundaries*

The exclusive quality of the inheritance is emphasized in a discussion on the necessity of its preservation and the perils of it falling outside the priestly lineage. In this way, the text uses both the priestly genealogy and its heritage as a means of constructing an "insider" identity in juxtaposition with "outsiders" deemed dangerous to the lineage and inheritance. *Words of Qahat* builds this boundary by using language cautioning against mixing with foreigners (4Q542 1 i 6–9). This focus on the bounds of marriage also takes on a particularly priestly application in *ALD* (16–17; 62; 73–78) and *VA* (4Q543 1a–c 5–7; 4Q544 1 8; 4Q545 1a i 4–8; 4Q546 1 3–4; 4Q547 1–2 7).

3.4.4. *Priestly Application of an Eschatological Outlook*

At various points, *WQ* includes terms and topics that forecast the role of the priestly lineage in the future (4Q542 1 ii 1–8; 2 11–12). In language bordering on dualism, and in view of the foregoing juxtaposition of insiders vs. outsiders, *WQ* presents an eschatological scene in which the priestly progeny are granted a role in judgment (4Q542 1 ii 5). While details are limited due to the fragmentary nature of the text, part of this description draws on relating to the domains of the guilty in Enochic tradition (4Q542 1 ii 6–7). In this way, the work in its original form may have had an apocalyptic outlook (Dimant 1994: 191; DiTommaso 2010: 473–76), contributing further to the representation of priestly apocalypses among the Qumran Aramaic texts (Perrin 2018a: 128–31).

3.4.5. *Patriarchal Discourse in Poetic Structure*

Much of *WQ*'s discourse proceeds in the form of Aramaic poetry. As Lee (2015: 280) commented, "[t]he poetry in the *Testament of Qahat* is one of the longest extant examples of Aramaic poetry within the Qumran library," which also exhibits "a certain affinity with the wisdom-poem in the *Aramaic Levi Document*." His analysis focused on the more complete section of the text (4Q542 1 i 1–ii 1) and deduced a number of features that indicate its poetic structure. These include: a stichometric division of at least seventeen units, parallelism of verbal and nominal phrases in paired cola, semantic and syntactical terseness, and verb gapping. This poetic structure, of course, invites larger questions of the genre(s) of *WQ*.

3.5. *Genre*

Genre analysis of any work preserved only by brittle bits "remains problematic" (Tervanotko 2014: 48). Without a fuller view of the composition, determinations of genre must rely on internal hints and insights from comparisons with other texts yet remain open-ended.

The largely poetic discourse is framed as paternal instruction from Qahat to his children and features a blend of encouragement, caution, and future-orientation. For these reasons, from an early time the work was considered a testament (Milik 1972a: 97). While it cannot be ruled out that *WQ* was indeed a testament in its original and complete form, the fragments that have come down to us lack some hallmarks of that genre. The biggest obstacle is that it is unclear if the discourse was delivered leading up to the death of Qahat, which is generally agreed to be an integral setting for testamentary literature (Reed 2014: 386). Without the deathbed setting, *WQ* seems to be drawing upon and contributing to a larger tradition for passing inherited knowledge, ancestral lore, or insights from special revelation in first-person narratives of the Aramaic DSS. (For examples in the broader collection, see the comments on 4Q542 1 i 13; 1 ii 9.) Many such features in *WQ* become "testamentary tropes" (Uusimäki 2021) or may be perceived as giving the impression of a "testamentary character" (Frey 2010: 361). Yet, at this point, these features are not unique to the emerging genre. Rather, this style of discourse extends to other writings of the so-called apocrypha and pseudepigrapha in the Hellenistic period (cf. Reed 2014: 390). In the context of the Aramaic DSS, these features have a strong association with apocalyptic literature with a priestly bent (Perrin 2018a).

It is also relevant that *VA*—arguably one of the closest counterparts to this Aramaic Qahat tradition—though clearly culminating in the death of Amram, does not introduce itself as a testament. Rather, the narrative is framed with a titular introduction emphasizing the focus of the following work, namely Amram's dream-vision.

The material and scribal association between 4Q542 and 4Q547 also invites questions of the potential relationship between *WQ* and *VA*. Machiela (2021a) advances the case that the Amram and Qahat materials were likely a single work, with the latter developed on the model of Isaac's priestly instruction to Levi in *ALD*. This would demand a reorientation of our thinking about these two works as a single priestly composition. This is a compelling possibility; however, it is not the only solution.

It is equally possible that 4Q542 and 4Q547 represent the remains of separate priestly pseudepigrapha housed on the same scroll. That is, they are materially conjoined yet literarily distinct. This form of serial pseudepigraphy is well attested in the Aramaic DSS—not least in *GenAp* and perhaps Danielic traditions—as well as finds support from other Hebrew writings that use physical space and/or section headings to frame units of text, for example, in the cases of 1QS, 1QSa, and 1QSb or the scrolls of pentateuchal or minor prophets materials at Qumran (Perrin 2021b). In this regard, it is perhaps most helpful to cease referring to *VA* and *WQ* as "texts" in favor of perceiving them as related "traditions" that collectively advance, address, and construct priestly ideas and identities in pseudepigraphic voices.

Based on a literary, thematic, or material association between *WQ* and *VA*, we might then ask: what is the core content of *WQ* that might guide our contemporary description or title of the text? Drawnel (2006, 73) argued that the didactic content is predominant over other sections, such as those forecasting the future of the priestly line. On this account, he argued that the modern title "*Admonitions of Qahat*" is a better descriptor of the text, since it "corresponds to its preserved literary form and educational character." I agree with this conclusion, though prefer "*Words of Qahat*," since this captures the pseudepigraphic quality that is common to the entire text. Ultimately, any determination on genre must remain open-ended. As Lee (2015: 253) concluded, "the extant text indicates only that it is an exhortation without providing any details about the narrative that comes before and after it." In view of this, Lange and Mittmann-Richert's (2002: 125) designation of the text as related to the figure of Qahat yet comprising a "text of mixed genre" is helpful.

3.6. Compositional Date and Social Setting

The paleographic date of 4Q542 (125–100 BCE) provides a general frame of reference for the production of the manuscript. Although, as with many proposals of the paleographical dates of Qumran manuscripts, the date range is likely too specific. A more moderate paleographical date is from the mid-second to mid-first centuries BCE. Even if the paleographical dates are taken with some flexibility, there is no reason to believe that the present manuscript is an autograph.

Radiocarbon analysis of material from 4Q542 dated the manuscript's leather in the range of 388–353 BCE (Bonani 1991: 30). The range of the Carbon-14 test is approximately two centuries off from Puech's paleographical dating. Van de Water noted (2000: 426; cf. Carmi 2000: 886) that "[t]he greatest discrepancy between the paleographic estimates and the Zurich radiocarbon ranges, however, appears in the dating of *4Q542*." The sprawling margin between the two dating methods suggests that the manuscript sample may have been contaminated by another element introduced in either the ancient or modern context (Bonani 1991: 30; Van de Water 2000: 427 n. 21; Gross 2013a: 1869; Drawnel 2006: 56).

Given that the traditions represented in the work indicate an active scribal engagement and reimagination of motifs, terms, and topics shared with a number of other mid-Second Temple period texts—not least a large network of items in the Aramaic DSS such as *ALD*, *VA*, and aspects of the early Aramaic Enoch materials—a compositional date in the early to mid-second century BCE is reasonable.

This timeframe also makes sense in view of the crescendo of critiques on the priesthood found in literature of this period. Cook (Wise, Abegg, and Cook 1993: 210) proposed that *WQ*'s concern over strangers was reminiscent of "the perspective taken by many on the Hellenizing party led by Menelaus." He later posited that this theme "may be an allusion to the religious crisis under the high priest Jason (174–171 B.C.E.)" (Wise, Abegg, and Cook 2005: 545). For Puech (2001: 261), the boundary-marking and judgment language suggests the ejection of legitimate Sadducean priests from the temple, which called to mind the exile of Onias III. Gross noted the obscurity of terms for outsiders in lines 4Q542 1 i 5–7. He proposed that such language fits with the crises of the early second century BCE, "more specifically being a polemic against Hellenizing Jews whom the author felt were denigrating the traditions of the priesthood" (Gross 2013a: 1870). *Words of Qahat*'s delineation of priestly insiders against outsiders no doubt relates to some social concern or crisis. However, the available text does not include any clear references allowing for certain connection with a specific individual, circumstance, group, or moment in the priestly controversies of this era. The only social setting we can be confident of is its place within the literary collection of a receiving community at Qumran. Its precise compositional setting remains unknown.

3.7. *Text and Commentary: 4Q542*

The commentary that follows covers all known fragments of *WQ* as represented by this Cave Four manuscript.

3.7.1. *The Preservation of Inheritance and Pursuit of Virtue (4Q542 1 i)*

The fragment picks up at the end of what must have been a longer benediction Qahat spoke over his children. This section highlights the privileged knowledge of the name of God and gives insight into his enduring nature and preservation of all things. The text transitions into a discourse on ancestral inheritance and tradition that is to be preserved and passed along within the priestly line. Doing so maintains the purity of this heritage from outsiders, honors the ancestors who bequeathed it, results in a virtuous life, and assures the vitality of the priesthood.

TOP MARGIN
1 ואל אלין לכול עלמין ונהר נהירה עליכון ויודענכון שמה רבא
2 ותנדעונה {וְתִנְֹנְֹדְֹעֹוֹנֹהֹ} די הוא אלה עלםיה ומרא כול סעבדיא ושליט
3 בכולא למעבד בהון כרעותה ויעבד לכון חדוא ושמחא לבניכון בדרי
4 קושוטˢ לעלמין וכען בני אזדהרו בירותתא די משˢלמא לכון
5 ודי יהבו לכון אבהתכון ואל תתנו ירותתכון לנכראין ואחסנותכון
6 לכילאין ותהון לשפלו{ן}ת̇ן ולנבלו בעיניהון ויבסרון עליכון ד̇י
7 להון תותבין לכון ולהון עליכון ראשין להן אחדו בממר יעק̇ב
8 אבוכון ואתקפו בדיני אברהם וˢצדקת לוי ודילי והוא קד̇י]שין ודכין
9 מן כול [ע]ר̇ב̇רוב ואחדין בקושטא ואזלין בישיר̇ותא ולאבלבב ולבב
10 להן בלבב דכא וברוח קשיטה וטבה ותנתנון לי ביניכון שם טבוחדוא
11 ללוי ושמח לי[ע]קוב ודיאצ לישחק ותשבוחא לאברהם די נטרתון
12 והילכתון ירות̇[תא...]ד̇י שבקו לכון אבהתכון קושטא וצדקתא וישירותא
13 ותמימותא ודִ̇כ̇[ותא וק]ו̇דשא וכה̇]ו̇]נתא ככל די פקדתון וככל די
BOTTOM MARGIN

1. and God of gods for all eternity, and may he shine his light upon you and make you know his great name
2. so that you may know him {so that you may know him}. For he is God of the ages, lord of all labors, and ruler
3. over all, making them according to his will. May he make for you joy and gladness for your descendants, in generations of
4. truth for eternity. And now, my sons, be careful with the inheritance that has been bequeathed to you
5. and that your ancestors gave to you. Neither give your inheritance to strangers nor your heritage
6. to assimilators lest you become debased and disgraced in their eyes and they despise you. For

7. they will become resident foreigners to you and become rulers over you. Therefore, cling to the command of Jacob
8. your ancestor. Hold fast to the judgments of Abraham and the upright practice of Levi and myself. Be ho[l]y and pure
9. from any [inter]mixture, clinging to the truth and walking in integrity— not with a divided heart,
10. but with a pure heart and with a true and good spirit. Then you will grant for me a good name among you, and joy
11. to Levi, gladness to J[a]cob, rejoicing to Isaac, and praise to Abraham because you kept
12. and preserved [the] inheritan[ce...] that your ancestors left for you: truth, upright practice, integrity,
13. perfection, pur[ity, ho]liness, and the pri[est]hood, according to everyv thing that I commanded you and according to everything that

Textual, Scribal, and Material Notes

Primary images for transcription: PAM M43.565; B-370775; B-370774.

Line 1: וינהר ("and may he shine") – The *yod* prefix of the verb is written supralinearly.

Line 2: ותנדעונה ("so that you may know him") – This initial verb seems to have been inadvertently written twice (i.e., dittography), with the second occurrence removed by an erasure. For most of the erased characters, the lower portions of the effaced letters are visible.

Line 2: עלמיה...סעבדיא ("world...labors") – The scribe of 4Q542 often uses final *mem* in medial positions.

Line 4: קושוטא ("truth") – The form here involves at least one correction. The addition of a supralinear *aleph* is clear on the fragment. Puech (2001: 270) indicated that the second *vav* is scratched out. The scribe preferred the spelling of this noun as קושט(א) (4Q542 1 i 9, 12; 1 ii 2, 8), suggesting that the present occurrence may have been a self-correction. Note, however, the presence of the form בקושוט in 4Q542 1 ii 1. Either our scribe was inconsistent in noun patterns or did not uniformly correct variant forms. On the potential linguistic significance of this correction for recovering noun patterns, see Cook (1993: 208–209).

Line 4: משׁהלמא ("has been bequeathed") – The original form here read משלמא, which seems to have been corrected towards מהשלמא via a supralinear *he*. Note, however, the position of the supralinear *he* is above the *sin* and *lamed*. In addition to the *he*, Puech (2001: 270) proposed an erased *aleph* above the *shin*, which would imply a staged linguistic correction of a *peal*, to *aphel*, to *haphel* form. This is possible but the evidence of an erasure or recoverable letter is scant. Eisenman and Wise (1992: 149) saw a supralinear *aleph*, which is incorrect. Cook (1993: 205), García Martínez and Tigchelaar (1998 2:1082), and Beyer (2004: 115) do not include an erased character above the *shin* but all agree on the supralinear *he* and the reading supported here.

Line 5: ואחסנותכון ("your heritage") – The form here is the result of at least one major correction. The character following the medial *nun* in the middle of the word was penned over an erased word or morpheme. The pronominal suffix is also inscribed in either a notably different hand and/or stylus with a narrower contact point with the manuscript surface. García Martínez and Tigchelaar (1998 2:1082) and Puech (2001: 270) read ואחסנותכון. Puech (2001: 270) proposed that the text originally read ואחסן לכון, which is possible but cannot be verified. Eisenman and Wise (1992: 149), Cook (1993: 205), and Beyer (2004: 115) all read ואהסנותכון. The digital image plates confirm the third character is a *khet*.

Line 6: לשפלו{ת̇} ("debased") – A larger than normal space at the end of this word and surface damage suggest an erasure. García-Martínez and Tigchelaar (1998: 1082) and Puech (2001: 270) proposed a *tav*, which, if retained, suggests a correction from a plural to singular. All others read לשפלו without an emendation (Eisenman and Wise 1992: 149; Cook 1993: 205; Beyer 2004: 115).

Line 7: תותבין ("resident foreigners") – There are a series of corrections built into this form. The clearest item is the *tav* in the middle of the word which is written over another character, giving it a strong and pronounced quality (see also 4Q542 1 ii 10). It seems that at least one character was erased, or partially so, in the process. Puech (2001: 268) suggested this may have been a *bet* or *he* in a sequence of corrections. This is possible but not certain. Eisenman and Wise (1992: 149), Cook (1993: 205), García Martínez and Tigchelaar (1998 2:1082), and Beyer (2004: 115) all agree on the reading supported here, with subtle differences on the certainty of both the *tav* and final *nun*.

Line 7: יַעֲקׂב ("Jacob") – The name was originally written with defective spelling and then *plene* with a supralinear *vav*.

Line 8: וּבְצדקת ("and the upright practice") – The preposition *bet* is written supralinearly.

Line 9: ולאבלבב ולבב ("not with a divided heart") – The negative particle is inscribed over an erasure. Puech (2001: 270) proposed that the scribe began to write the first two letters of בלבב and then undertook a series of corrections to remedy the form. For another correction involving לא, see 4Q542 1 ii 4. García Martínez and Tigchelaar (1998 2:1082) read the erasure as כל. Others did not acknowledge erased characters (Cook 1993: 206; Beyer 2004: 115).

Line 10: ביניכון ("among you") – The *kaph* in this form is irregular. It is perhaps an emended or corrected character (perhaps a *pe*; cf. the formation of the medial *pe* in 4Q542 1 ii 9).

Line 11: ודיאצ...ושמח ("gladness…rejoicing") – The forms on the manuscript are written without a final *aleph*. This is slightly irregular, not least due to the form ושמחא in 4Q542 1 i 3.

Line 13: וכהֻ[וּ]נתא ("and the pri[est]hood") – The form here is likely, but not certain given the available ink traces.

Line 13: פקדתון ("commanded you") – The form in the manuscript is missing the *kaph* of the verbal suffix.

Commentary

Line 1: *and God of gods*. This is the only certain occurrence of the title אל אלין in ancient Jewish Aramaic literature. Other proposals for reconstructions of similar Aramaic terminology are speculative due to lack of material and textual support (4Q202 1 iii 14 [Milik 1976: 171]; 4Q537 1 + 2 + 3 0 [Puech 2001: 175]).

The similar pairing אלה אלהין occurs in Dan. 2:47. The Hebrew Daniel tradition also includes the analogous phrase אל אלים at Dan. 11:36. These occurrences in the Danielic tradition are rendered in the Old Greek as θεὸς τῶν θεῶν. The Qumran Hebrew texts include the divine reference אל אלים seven times (1QM 14 16; 18 6; 4Q403 1 ii 26; 4Q405 4–5 2 [rec. 4Q403 1 i 34]; 4Q405 14–15 i 3; 4Q491 8–10 i 13; 4Q510 1 2), suggesting the Hebrew configuration was relatively common in the Second Temple period. In view of this, the phrasing of 4Q542 here is likely a Hebraism (Puech 2001: 272; Stadel 2008: 52; Muraoka 2011: 79).

The Aramaic scrolls include a diversity of names, epithets, or circumlocutions for the ancestral God of Israel. The most prevalent is אל עליון ("God Most High"), indicated by the concentration of uses in *GenAp* (1Q20 12 17, 21; 15 24; 20 12, 16; 21 2, 20; 22 15, 16 [×2], 21), *ALD* (3 [1Q21 1 3]; 9; 13; 30), and a few occurrences in more fragmentary materials (4Q552 6 10; 4Q558 88 1; cf. 4Q543 22 2). Muraoka (2011: 74 n. 346; cf. Schattner-Rieser 2004: 107) noted that this title too seems to have begun as a Hebraism but became "naturalised" in Aramaic. Two additional scribal approaches to divine names in the Aramaic DSS include the use of the tetrapuncta (i.e., four dots) to represent the name אלהא ("God") in an Aramaic *Tobit* manuscript (4Q196 17 i 5; 18 15) and the deployment of varied paleo-Hebrew script to pen the form אלהכה ("your God") in a *Pseudo-Daniel* text (4Q243 1 2). For comments on this final set of approaches, see Machiela (2013) and Perrin (2021c).

The term אל אלין should also be contextualized theologically, since the Qumran Aramaic texts include several scenes imagining the order and beings of the divine domain. Perhaps the most significant of these is a shared throne room scene occurring in *1 Enoch* 14, *Book of Giants*, and Daniel 7. The similarities and differences between these have been studied and explained in various ways (cf. Stuckenbruck 1997b; Trotter 2012; Penner 2014; Davis Bledsoe 2016). While textual or traditional relationships cannot be ruled out, Dimant (2017: 46) remarked that "[t]he similarities as well as divergences suggest a common tradition shared by all three throne visions but adapted differently by each one." For the present purposes, what is most relevant is how all of these works portray a view of an otherworldly throne room, populated with large numbers of divine attendants, over whom God is supreme (*1 En.* 14:22; 4Q530 2 ii + 6–12 17; Dan. 7:10). For these traditions, heaven was hardly a home to but one divine being. It seems the reference to the "God of gods" in 4Q542 shares this understanding: the ancestral deity of Israel is chief among a presumably larger population of unidentified but implied or angelic divine beings.

Line 1: *and may he shine his light upon you and make you know his great name*. This material recalls concepts found in the priestly blessing to all of Israel in Num. 6:25–27. *Words of Qahat*, however, reconfigures the terms, authority, and addressees of the blessing. In the Hebrew Scriptures, the divine blessing originates with Moses but is directed toward the Aaronides. In the Aramaic text, the terms are spoken as a blessing from a different priestly forefather, Qahat, and conferred upon his particularly priestly progeny. In this way, *WQ* represents an early reception and reorientation of the distinctive language of Numbers 6. For another likely redeployment of terms from the priestly blessing of Numbers 6, see *1 En.* 1:8.

This line also provides new Aramaic lexical data. Cook (1993, 207) noted that the form נהירה is the first attestation of this word spelled with a *yod* outside of Dan. 2:22. As Caquot observed (1995: 40), the mention of the שמה רבא ("great name") recalls a more diverse set of texts deploying that metonymy (e.g., Ezek. 36:23; 4Q504 1–2 iv 9–10; 1QM 11 2; *2 Bar.* 5:1).

Line 2: *so that you may know him*. The illumination and blessing results in a special knowledge of God for Qahat's progeny. This phrase follows on the similar form ויודענכון ("and make you know") a few words prior in line 1. Caquot (1995: 40) observed that the coordination of language referring to illumination and knowledge is also found in 1QSb 4 27 and *T. Levi* 4:3; 18:3.

While the extant materials of 4Q542 do not include a revelatory scene or encounter in the traditional sense, elsewhere in the Aramaic corpus the verbal root √ידע ("to know") is closely associated with dream-visions (e.g., 1Q20 2 22; 12 19–15 21; 4Q530 2 ii + 6–12 23–24). For discussion on this point, see Perrin (2015a: 132–35) and Fabry (2013: 79–93). This larger frame of reference suggests that the name and particular blessing of God is understood as privileged knowledge in *WQ*. Later in the fragment, it becomes clear that the inherited, ancestral traditions are also in some way understood as a unique and special channel of knowledge or revelation from the past. The access to this heritage for the insider group itself enables the ability to know the name of God and to receive this blessing. In this sense, revelation is not only something that comes from the otherworld beyond—it can be received, or retrieved, from a reimagined ancestral past. For a sketch of the larger framework of revelatory innovations in the DSS, see Najman (2019).

Line 2: *God of the ages*. This is the first of three items in lines 2–3 that articulate the theological characteristics of the "God of gods" referenced in line 1. If Milik's (1976: 142) reconstruction is accepted, the Aramaic Enoch materials include the term אלה עלמה ("the God of the ages") at 4Q201 1 i 5 (*1 En.* 1:4). *Genesis Apocryphon* (1Q20 19 8) may feature similar terminology, though the reading is not secure (Machiela with VanderKam 2018: 118). In view of the potential occurrence in *GenAp*, Fitzmyer (2004: 179) noted that other writings include analogous phrasing (Gen. 21:33 [LXX]; Isa. 40:28; *Jub.* 13:16; Rom. 16:26; *Ass. Mos.* 10:17). In the Aramaic scrolls, variations on the phrase מרא עלמ(י)א ("the Lord of eternity/the ages") are more common than these two configurations (1Q20 0 18; 21 2; 4Q202 1 iii 14; 4Q529 1 6–7, 11, 12).

Line 2: *lord of all labors*. Stadel (2008: 52) proposed this phrase as a probable Hebraism. While the Aramaic DSS routinely utilize the term מרא (e.g., "lord"), this is the only instance where the language implies divine lordship over human actions. If this is the case, *WQ* includes a degree of determinism, which invites comparison with a larger set of Qumran Hebrew texts typically brought into discussions on the foreordination and direction of human deeds. For example, 1QS 4 25–26 reads, "He foreknows the outworking of their deeds for all the ages [of eternity]." 1QH[a] 9 9–10 also states, "And in your wisdom […]eternity, and before you created them, you knew {all} their deeds for everlasting ages. And [without you no]thing is done, and nothing is known without your will."[3] Of course, a belief in determinism is also a hallmark of Josephus's articulation of Essene thought (*Ant.* 13.172; 18.18). The reference here in 4Q542, then, provides an important reference point for this outlook within the world of the Qumran Aramaic texts and beyond traditional outlines of Essene belief.

Other common occurrences of the form מרא in the Aramaic DSS refer to God's oversight of the ages (see above), the heavens and/or earth (e.g., 1Q20 7 7; 12 17; 20 13; 22 16, 21; Dan. 5:23), human domains of political figures (1Q20 20 25; 22 18 Dan. 2:47), or in reference to the patron deity of ancestors (1Q20 20 13–16; 4Q204 4 4; 4Q213a 1 10, 18; 2 6). Amram refers to the interpreting angel of light he encounters in a dream vision as מר(א)י ("my Lord"; 4Q544 2 13; cf. 4Q546 8 5), which suggests that the term could also extend to other divine beings.

Lines 2–3: *ruler over all, making them according to his will.* This final descriptor begins at the end of line 2 and continues into line 3. Here, it seems, the deterministic themes of the foregoing material are now paired with an emphasis on God's role in creating and preserving. The reference to God as שליט ("ruler") also occurs in *GenAp* (1Q20 20 13), immediately following the term מרא ("Lord"), as in 4Q542. Language of divine will also occurs in the Aramaic imperial dispatch of Ezra 7:18. In a deterministic framework, the language of divine rulership according to divine will also invites comparison with the section of the *Hodayot* cited above (1QH[a] 9 9–22).

Line 3: *joy and gladness.* Qahat asks that God grant these items to his descendants and their eternal generations thereafter. These terms tie the end of the blessing in with the material in 4Q542 1 i 10–11. That later content relates how right living according to ancestral axioms and examples will bring חדוא ללוי ("joy to Levi") and שמח לי[ע]קוב ("gladness to J[a]cob").

While the pairing of these terms does not occur elsewhere in the Qumran Aramaic texts, each occurs individually. A fragment of *VA* references חדוה ("joy") in what seems to be a context of paternal discourse (4Q543 16 2–4). The only other possible occurrence of the term שמחא ("gladness") is in the fragmentary text 4Q548 (1 ii–2 5). Though not likely an additional copy of the *VA*, the dualistic fragments of 4Q548 seem to come in a context of instruction or blessing. Finally, from a lexical perspective, the root √שׂמח in Aramaic is a definite Hebraism (Cook 1993, 208; Puech 2001: 273; Schattner-Rieser 2004: 106; Stadel 2008: 52; Muraoka 2011: 81; Cook 2015: 248).

Line 4: *in generations of truth for eternity.* This phrase at the end of line 3 and the beginning of line 4 marks the end of the benediction. 4Q542 1 ii 8 also

---

3. Translations of 1QH[a] are from Schuller and Newsom (2012).

references בֹּ[ד]רִי קושטא ("in the [gen]erations of truth") in a forecasted blessing or judgment. The parallel term דרי קושׁטׂא also occurs in Enochic tradition at 4Q204 5 ii 28 (*1 En.* 107:1) in a context referencing the elect arising in the eschatological age (Puech 2001: 273). *Visions of Amram* includes a variation on this phrase at 4Q547 9 7, לכול דרי עלמין בקׂו[שט](א) ("for all the eternal generations in tr[uth]"). That content comes in the context of the revelatory exaltation of Aaron and his lineage immediately before Amram awakens from his dream-vision.

Line 4: *And now, my sons.* This phrase marks a shift from benediction to paternal instruction and admonishment. A similar transition occurs at 4Q542 1 ii 9, וּבֹען לכה עמרם ברי ("And now, to you, Amram, my son"). In that setting, the phrase signals a still narrower address to Amram. Of most significance for the occurrence in in *WQ*, however, is the fact that *VA* likely also included a similar shift from patriarchal instruction directed at a singular son to a plural progeny (4Q546 16).

To add to this trend, Tobit's final admonishment adheres, to a similar model. First Tobit addresses his wider progeny in Tob. 14:8 (καὶ νῦν, παιδία, "And now, children"), then focuses in on instruction for his son, Tobias, in Tob. 14:9 (καὶ νῦν, σύ παιδίον, "And now, you child"). While this section of Tobit is not extant among the Qumran fragments, given their similarity in content and detail to the so-called "long" Greek version (Fitzmyer 2003: 9–10), it is likely that the Greek phrasing is based on an Aramaic pair of terms not unlike what we find here in *WQ* and perhaps analogous to the more fragmentary formations in *VA*.

The Aramaic DSS feature several occurrences of transitions into, or within, paternal instruction featuring configurations of the terms (וּ)כען ("[and] now") with either בר (1Q20 5 9; 4Q546 12 2; 4Q546 14 1) or בן (4Q546 14 4; perhaps 4Q212 1 ii 19 [*1 En.* 91:19]). To this list, we may add occurrences of such paired terminology in the *ALD* materials not extant at Qumran but available in the Cairo Genizah (15:11; 88:17). For discussion on these transitions and others, see the commentary on the discourse directed toward Amram in 4Q542 1 ii 9.

The apparent synonymous uses of בר and בן in such formulae in the Qumran Aramaic materials suggest that, while בן may have entered the Aramaic register via Hebrew, at this point it is naturalized in ancient Jewish literary Aramaic. The mingling of these forms is most evident in 4Q546 1, 4, which features both in close proximity. These early Aramaic formulae introducing paternal instruction in a pseudepigraphic discourse may also be considered in view of analogous terms in other testamentary literature or literary units featuring discourse delivered from parent to child (*Jub.* 7:34, 39; 20:6; 21:5; 25:3; *T. Reub.* 3:9; *T. Sim.* 3:1; 5:2; 7:1; *T. Levi* 10:1; 13:1, 5; 14:1; 19:1; *T. Jud.* 13:1; 14:1; 17:1; *T. Zeb.* 5:5; 10:1; *T. Dan* 2:1; 6:1; *T. Gad* 3:1; *2 En.* 2:2, 4; 36:4; 39:3, 8; 40:1; 47:1; 53:1; *LAB* 2:10).

Line 4: *be careful.* When inflected in the *ithpeel*, the verb √זהר means "to be careful" (Cook 2015, 70). *Words of Qahat* includes the only two occurrences of this verb in the Aramaic DSS. Both uses come in the context of paternal instruction (4Q542 1 i 4; ii 12). The Cairo Genizah *ALD* materials feature this verb in Jacob's warning to Levi to "beware" of impurity and sin (*ALD* 14:8) and of defilement due to promiscuity (*ALD* 16:14).

Line 4: *with the inheritance that has been bequeathed to you.* The theme of ancestral inheritance—its origins, safekeeping, transmission, and reception—is central to *WQ*. References to ירותה ("inheritance") occur in three places in the fragmentary text (4Q542 1 i 4, 5, 12). The reference to ירותה in 4Q542 1 i 4 emphasizes that this inheritance is something received from the ancestors via the genealogical channel of Amram. The *haphel* passive participle of the root √שׁלם may also carry the idea that the inheritance has reached its culmination or completion with the bequeathal of this heritage through the lines, or in the generations, of Levi, Qahat, and Amram.

As Puech (2001: 273) proposed, the Aramaic form here is a calque of the Hebrew יְרֻשָּׁ(ו)ה. Stadel (2008: 52) lists it as a probable Hebraism. The only other certain occurrence of this term elsewhere in the Aramaic DSS is in 1Q20 16 12, which references יְרוּתַת עָלְמִים ("an eternal inheritance") in the context of Noah's division of the land for his sons.

Line 5: *and that your ancestors gave to you.* Feldman (2019) notes both the expansion of the roster of figures understood as patriarchs and the roles they play in the literature of the Second Temple era (e.g., *4 Macc.* 7:19; 16:25; Heb. 7:4, 8–9; Sir. 44–50; Tob. 4:12). The use of the term אבהתכון ("your ancestors") here indicates that *WQ* is participating in this expansion, which becomes even more explicit in 4Q542 1 i 7–12 by integrating Levi and Qahat into the core of Abraham, Jacob, and Isaac.

This phrase connects the ancestral act of giving the inheritance from the past with the priestly progeny of the present. While Qahat is the immediate handler of this inheritance, the act of passing it along through a specific genealogical channel underscores the importance of a chain of ancestors involved in its ongoing transmission from the past, through the present, and into the future. This is made explicit in the following column at 4Q542 1 ii 11. There Qahat specifies the inscribed nature of the tradition that he received from Levi and is now passing on to Amram. As Reed (2014: 395) commented, "[t]he idiom of inheritance serves to invoke the transgenerational past and horizon of the ideal didactic tradition, whereby piety and knowledge are maintained in an unbroken line coterminous with lineage." On a related note, Feldman (2019: 479) observed that the close association between knowledge transmission within a patriarchal line is "particularly endorsed by the non-sectarian Aramaic texts from Qumran."

Line 5: *Neither give your inheritance to strangers nor your heritage to assimilators.* This phrase runs the rest of line 5 and into the first word of line 6. In this limited context, it seems our scribe is playing with synonyms and parallelism, some of which reveal a potential connection to themes and language in *ALD*. Such terminological play and interchanges in this section relate to *WQ*'s poetic nature.

First, whereas the previous sentence stated that the ancestors "gave" (יהבו) this unique inheritance, the present sentence uses a synonymous verb warning the current generation to not "give" (תתנו) it away. Second, the "inheritance" or "heritage" is described using parallel nouns with essentially the same meaning: ירותה and אחסנא. The latter is a *hapax legomenon* in the Aramaic DSS. Subsequent uses of this term in the Targumim refer to the inheritance of property (*Tg. CG* Gen. 48:4; *Tg. Neof.* Gen. 49:30; *Tg. Ps.-J.* Num. 34:11), yet that limited notion does not apply here. Third, the final set of terms is נכרי ("stranger, foreigner") and כילא ("assimilators"). These tandem terms describe and/or construct an "outsider" that could compromise the ancestral inheritance if it fell into their hands. This entity is not necessarily or exclusively strangers in the sense of foreigners. This final set of terms can also be studied for their uses elsewhere in Qumran writings.

The Cave Eleven Job translation rendered the Hebrew form זר ("stranger") with the Aramaic נכר]י at 11Q10 2 4 (Job 19:15). It is possible that this translated equivalent connects us, even in a tangential way, to a larger semantic field of the Aramaic term as it was understood in the mid-Second Temple period. In this light, it is intriguing that some occurrences of זר in Hebrew literature refer to a lay-person within the community at odds with or outside of the priestly lines of the ancestors (Lev. 22:10–12; Num. 3:10–38; 18:4–7; Sir. 45:18). Two Hebrew texts at Qumran are instructive for their use of זר and/or נכר in contexts that also warn about not abandoning one's inheritance to outsiders (4Q501 1 1; 4Q525 5 7–8).

The second term, כילא, implies an individual or group of mixed ethnicity. While Aramaic ancient lexical data is limited, this meaning is suggested by the later use of the root in *Tg. Ps.-J.* Lev. 19:19 to refer to blended linens. Cook (2013: 209–10) proposed that the term here is an "Aramaicization of כלאים, a technical term in the Pentateuch (Lev. 19:19, Deut. 22:9) for things of mixed origin" and that in the present text "it is a prohibition of mixed marriages, or marriage to wives of mixed blood, apparently originating in an allegorical exegesis of Lev. 19:19" (cf. Caquot 1995: 41). This interpretation makes good contextual sense given the reticence towards those in mixed marriages, or the dilution resulting from such unions in the Qumran Aramaic texts, in general, and in *ALD* and *VA*, in particular. In view of this concern, Reed (2014: 395) noted that *WQ* emphasizes "the threat of rupture" to the lineage and its lore. Finally, although the rendering "assimilators" adopted here is not perfect, it is preferable over the pejorative term "half breed," which carries unsettling racial connotations in post-colonial contexts.

While these larger contexts are helpful, the most relevant parallels to the terms and topics of 4Q542 here are found in Levi's wisdom discourse in *ALD*, which is fragmentary in both the Qumran and Cairo Genizah materials. In *ALD* 91, Levi describes how learning wisdom and scribal craft of the ancestors will make one *not* like a נכרי (4Q213 1 i 16 // MS A, Cambr. f 6 9]) or כילא]י (MS A, Cambr. f 6 10]). On the contrary, these proficiencies will elevate his progeny such that outsiders will "desire to learn" (צבין למאלף) from them (MS A, Cambr. f 6 11–12).

As other commentators noted (cf. Lee 2015: 253; Caquot 1995: 40), the shared use of this "rare word-pair" suggests some terminological or conceptual connection between the texts. *Aramaic Levi Document* and *WQ* seem to be drawing upon and/or contributing to a shared trope or tradition regarding how ancestral teaching or inheritance postures the priestly progeny with respect to outsiders. *ALD* states this positively: ancestral wisdom will elevate the status of the priestly progeny and may even attract the attention of the outsiders. As is made clear in the following section, *WQ* postures this negatively: giving away the ancestral inheritance to those deemed alien or other downgrades the purity of the ancestral inheritance and privilege of the priesthood.

Line 6: *lest you become debased and disgraced in their eyes and they despise you.* This line specifies the risks of compromising the priestly inheritance. The ramifications of a potential compromise, however, are primarily for the identity and position of the priestly progeny, not the implications for the inheritance itself. This unit continues to use paired terminology. Here the first outcome is stated as becoming שפלו ("debased") and נבלו ("disgraced"). Traditional glosses for these terms are "humble state" and "shameful state," respectively (Cook 2015: 242, 151). More specific to the present context, it seems the effect of compromising the inheritance is a dilution of the priestly line's uniqueness, a demotion of their social and cultural status, and a resulting disdain in the eyes of the outsider.

The term שפלו may also occur in 4Q213 4 8 in a fragmentary context, though the reading there is less secure (Greenfield and Stone 1996: 22; Drawnel 2004: 170; Cook 2015: 242). *Genesis Apocryphon* includes a more secure reading for this form in a fragmentary context likely including some discourse by and related to the fate of the giants (1Q20 0 7). The term נבלו is a *hapax legomenon* in the Aramaic DSS and, as Stadel (2008: 53) noted, is also a Hebraism.

The verb בסר ("to despise") in the second part of the clause is also a *hapax legomenon*. *Aramaic Levi Document* includes a related noun in a fragmentary section of Levi's wisdom poem describing the implications of scorning the wisdom of the ancestors. Where 4Q213 1 i 11 includes a tandem set of terms, לב[ס]רון ולשיטו ("to dis]dain and scorn"), the Cairo Genizah material retains only a single item, לבשרון ("to disdain") at *ALD* 89 (MS A, Cambr. e 6 21]). What is illuminating here is that the earlier *ALD* material from Qumran deploys a set of terms to express a single idea, which is also the case in 4Q542. This structural similarity is lost in the later *ALD* materials.

Lines 6–7: *For they will become resident foreigners to you.* The first word of this clause comes from the end of line 6. The particle די introduces a clause that indicates the outcomes of the despised state envisaged in the previous line. The effect is that failing to retain the integrity of the ancestral inheritance will not only impact the standing and status of the priestly line, it will also result in rendering the outsider an insider.

The outsiders—described in line 5 as נכרי ("stranger, foreigner") and כילא ("assimilator")—will now become תותב. Here too, the form is a *hapax legomenon* in the Aramaic DSS. Cook (2015: 252) proposed the gloss "resident foreigner," and observed that the term is used in a pejorative sense in Saying 30 of the Ahiqar text from Elephantine (see also Cook 1993: 210; cf. Puech 1991: 37; Caquot 1995: 42). While the Aramaic term here is not likely a Hebraism (Stadel 2008: 54), it is used in the Targumim to render both תושב (*Tg. Onq.* Exod. 12:45) and גר (*Tg. Neof.* Gen. 15:13). As indicated in a supplementary note in *HALOT* (2000: 4:1713), these two terms have "meanings which are close to each other," in the sense that the תותב is a גר "whose roots are in foreign (but Israelite) territory, and is a protégé of the tribe which is now resident there; or more exactly one who has found a lasting acceptance as an individual occupant." For a global study of the context and connotations of the term גר in the Qumran collection, see now Palmer (2018).

If any of this sense applies to *WQ*'s use of תותב, it reveals that by accessing the inheritance, the "stranger" and "assimilator" are no longer an outsider. Rather, by virtue of this mismanaged inheritance, they are grafted into the insider group. In effect, the warning is less against insiders abandoning the heritage and becoming outsiders, than a caution against the "other" permeating the bounds of the priestly line and thereby polluting the inheritance from the inside out. For a similar interpretation, see Lee (2015: 266–67), who perceived the poetic development of terminology for foreigners here as "a logical sequence" ending in this result.

Line 7: *and become rulers over you.* The final negative outcome of sharing the inheritance is a loss or restructuring of authority. While the available fragments of 4Q542 do not explicitly describe the political association of the priesthood, as Drawnel (2004: 80) commented, *WQ* "affirms that the transmission of priestly inheritances is related to the exercise of power" and that "the same stance may be inferred from the Wisdom poem where Joseph's teaching activity (*A.L.D.* 90) is related to his glorification and elevation to a royal status." This phrase, then, signals both the final aspect of the warning and a worst-case scenario: loss of inheritance will result in losing grip on the power vested in the institution of the priesthood.

Lines 7–8: *Therefore, cling to the command of Jacob your ancestor.* The final word of this sentence begins line 8. The phrase begins with the coordinating conjunction להן, which opens a section explicating what came before (Muraoka 2011: 93). This section also starts to articulate the specific patriarchal origins and nature of the inheritance. Whereas line 5 referred generically to אבהתכון ("your ancestors"), starting here characters within that cast of forefathers are named. This naming provides an authoritative basis for the ancestral tradition. These forefathers come exclusively from Genesis traditions.

The first named figure is יַעֲקֹב ("Jacob"). Qahat admonishes his descendants with a *peal* imperative, אחדו, "to cling," to his heritage. The form ממר here is singular, suggesting this is not referring to a larger set of "words" or "commands" of Jacob, but some foundational directive.

Line 8: *Hold fast to the judgments of Abraham* (ואתקפו בדיני אברהם). The *aphel* imperative from the root √תקף is parallel to the *peal* imperative of אחד in the previous line. This set of verbs is also found at the outset of Noah's first-person discourse on his upright character in *GenAp* (1Q20 6 6).

The reference to the דיני אברהם ("judgments of Abraham") introduces another tier of ancestral authority by enshrining Abraham as both an exemplary model and source for tradition. The meaning of the plural "judgments" is difficult discern. It may refer to instruction on sacrificial processes. It is significant that Abraham is the source of extensive ancestral instruction on priestly matters in *ALD* 11–61. The teaching there is issued through Isaac, but claims even deeper antiquarian origins in Noachic lore. Within this section, *ALD* 50 also includes a command to Isaac to continue the heritage of commanding his lineage in the ancestral teachings in *ALD* 50. Similarly, in *Jub.* 22:16–25, Isaac instructs Jacob to follow "the commandments of your father Abraham," which are summarized as keeping separate from the nations, maintaining purity, and not intermarrying with foreigners. This line of ancestral instruction associated with Abraham persists in *T. Levi* 9:5–14.

Line 8: *and the upright practice of Levi and myself.* Qahat's self-reference connects the ancestral tradition, inheritance, and admonishment with his progeny. *Words of Qahat* appears to be the oldest attestation of sacerdotal ordinances attached to Abraham and Jacob, then passed on to Levi and Qahat (Puech 2001: 274).

This clause assumes the foregoing verb. Here, however, the object is neither a command nor judgment remembered from the past. Rather, it is the first of several virtues that appear in the text (see lines 12–13). In the context of the Aramaic DSS, the term צדקה often refers to acts demonstrating personal piety. As Machiela (2017; cf. Newsom 145; Uusimäki 2021) observed, this term is associated with charity and charitable acts in several key Aramaic texts represented at Qumran (Dan. 4:27 [24], Tob. 14:2 [4Q198 1 1]; 4Q213 1 i 7), with particular reference at times to "almsgiving." In this sense, *WQ* endorses following the model of exemplary, pious lives of these priestly ancestors. For more detailed comment on this term, see the comment on 4Q542 1 i 12.

Lines 8–9: *Be ho[l]y and pure from any [inter]mixture.* This material is found at the end of line 8 and first two words of line 9. The notion of not intermingling resumes here from its first introduction in lines 5–6, which established the insider vs. outsider identity parameters and posture. The difference here is that the issue is no longer about maintaining distance from the "other" for sake of the ancestral inheritance, but for the vitality and integrity of the priestly line itself.

The descendants are called to be "holy" (קדיש) and "pure" (דכי), which seems to be defined in terms of remaining free from impurity brought by sexual or marital relations with an outsider. While the reading [ע]רֹבׄרוּב is uncertain and the meaning "intermixture" is inferred from later writings (e.g., *Tg. Neof.* Exod. 12:38), the initial pair of terms in this clause already point in this direction (cf. Puech 2001: 274–75). This is particularly evident with the term דכי, which functions in the Aramaic DSS predominantly in the sense of (im)purity brought about by illicit sexual or unapproved marital relations. Cook (1993: 211) emphasized that the content of this line underscores the "moral tone of the exhortation" against "illicit intermingling, intermarriage, assimilatory customs, or habits."

Tobit and *ALD* are again relevant to this topic. In an Aramaic Tobit manuscript (4Q196 6 9 [Tob. 3:14]), Sarah states in her prayer that she has remained דכיה אנה בגרמי מׄ[ן כ]ׄל טֻמׄאֹתׄ[גבר ("clean in my body fr[om an]y defilement of a [man])." She acknowledges that this pure state meant she has not brought a bad name upon her family. In *ALD* 18, Levi admonishes Jacob, כען דכי בבשרך מן כל טומאת כל גבר ("Now be pure in your flesh from every impurity of any man"; MS A, Bodl. b 8 22–23). This material follows on the heels of a larger section underscoring the avoidance of promiscuity. In view of this larger context, it is most certain that

WQ is participating in a similar discourse. See the comment on 4Q542 1 i 10 for a reference to "purity" as a virtue.

Line 9: *clinging to the truth and walking in integrity.* In line 7 above, the verb אחד ("to cling") was used with reference to the command of Jacob. The initial phrase ואחדין בקושטא here parallels Noah's remark בקושטא וֹאֹחֹדֹת ("I held to truthfulness") in *GenAp* (1Q20 6 6). In the Aramaic DSS, the virtue ישירו ("integrity") is referenced only in *WQ* (4Q542 1 i 9, 12) and closely paired with קושט in both instances. Stadel (2008, 55) proposes the term is a Hebraism.

Line 9: *not with a divided heart.* Literally, "and not with a heart and a heart" (ולאבלבב ולבב). The Hebrew Scriptures include a similar idiom at 1 Chron. 12:33 (34) to emphasize the Zebulunites's unwavering support of David's military efforts בלא לב ולב ("with an undivided heart" [NASB]). Negative deployments of this idiom occur in two Hebrew poetic texts. Psalm 12:2 (3) references those who speak flattery: בלב ולב ("with a double heart" [NASB]). Similarly, 1QH^a 12 15 speaks of adversaries whose plans are misguided, hypercritical, and deceitful for ידרשוכה בלב ולב ("they seek you with a divided heart"). The potential division of one's heart also invites questions over the relation of this Aramaic phrasing to larger ideas of so-called anthropological dualism as represented, for example, in the Hebrew "*Treatise of the Two Spirits*" (esp. 1QS 4 23–24). As indicated in the following line, Qahat admonishes his progeny away from this sort of inner bifurcation and toward a unity of identity and ethic, as represented by a pure heart.

Line 10: *but with a pure heart.* Taken with the previous phrase, the priestly lineage is to be unwavering in their commitment to carrying on the ancestral traditions of the priestly past and undistracted in their devotion to God within their privileged domain. Line 8 already issued a call for דכי ("purity") with respect to the priestly line. Here, however, it is associated with purity of heart, suggesting now the call is to a virtue in its own right. In addition to the terminological background of the first three virtuous items included so far in lines 8–9, Uusimäki (2021) observed a similar cluster of terms in 1 Kgs 3:6 with respect to David's character. Puech (2001: 275) noted that the motif of a pure heart calls to mind the statements of Ps. 73:13 and Prov. 20:9.

Line 10: *and with a true and good spirit.* This coordination of terms is unique to *WQ*. Here the reference is to the upright qualities of a human spirit. The "*Treatise of the Two Spirits*" describes how the spirit of truth enables a series of virtues and traits, one of which is טוב עולמים ("perpetual goodness"; 1QS 4 3). References to a רוח אמת ("spirit of truth") also occur in this context (1QS 4 21, 23; cf. 1QM 13 10; 4Q177 12–13 i 5).

Line 10: *Then you will grant for me a good name among you.* The phrase ותנתנון לי ביניכון שם טב is challenging for interpretation, yet its apparent sense is significant for the context. Grammatically, Qahat's descendants are the subject of the verb ותנתנון. The following *lamed* preposition with a first-person pronominal suffix indicates that their protecting and adhering to the ancestral inheritance, as described in the foregoing lines, results in something given to Qahat. What is granted? The assurance of a שם טב ("good name"). This name, however, is not only of benefit for the preceding generation (i.e., Qahat). There is a reciprocity that results: the name extends ביניכון ("among you"), that is, throughout the priestly descendants. This phrase, then, introduces a new concept regarding the dynamic and multi-directional quality of receiving and participating in the ancestral inheritance. By safeguarding the ancestral inheritance, aspiring to its exemplary models, and embracing its virtues, the present generation builds into the inheritance by upholding the priestly reputation in the present. This effectively connects the ancestral past with Qahat's lineage, which, in turn, positions his progeny to become like their priestly forefathers by protecting and passing it along to subsequent generations.

Attaining or preserving a "good name" occurs in several other texts and traditions, some represented among the Qumran Aramaic corpus. *Jews in the Persian Court* refers to the courtier Bagasraw's good reputation with the phrase שמה טבא ("his good name"; 4Q550 2 2), which is established, in part, on the reputation of his father Patireza. In at least eight places, the Targumim use a variation of the term ש(ו)ם טב (*Tg.* Prov. 22:1; *Tg.* Qoh. 6:3, 4; 9:8; 10:1; *Tg.* 1 Chron. 16:22; 17:8), but only once in a rendering of a similar underlying Hebrew set of terms (*Tg.* Qoh. 7:1). As Puech (2001: 275) noted, the phrase שם טב also occurs in one Aramaic inscription (*Nerab* 2:3).[4] Since the issue here is the reputation of the ancestral line, other references to the protection of the name of the "father(s)" are also of note (4Q196 6 10 [Tob. 3:15]; 4Q213a 3–4 3, 5).

Line 11: *and joy to Levi, gladness to J[a]cob, rejoicing to Isaac, and praise to Abraham.* The initial word of this phrase is found at the end of line 10. The multi-directionality of receiving and participating in the ancestral inheritance extends here with a series of statements on how the uprightness, adherence, and integrity of the priestly descendants results in esteem and favor for the forefathers. The previous statement began with the most immediate ancestor, Qahat, which now extends backwards through four successive ancestral generations: Levi, Jacob, Isaac, and Abraham.

This trajectory, now traced in reverse, constitutes central figures associated with priestly instruction and ordination in *ALD* (8, 11–13, 17, 22, 49–50). *Visions of Amram* seems to have also mapped the priestly genealogy as far back as Abraham, as implied in the phrase שביעי באנוש רעותֿ[ה ית]קרה ("seventh among men of [his] favor [he will be] called") spoken with regard to Aaron in 4Q545 4 18 (Puech 2001: 343; Perrin 2015a: 164). *Damascus Document* associated Abraham with מצות אל ("the commandments of God"), which were said to have been passed down to both Isaac and Jacob (*CD* 3 3–4).

The effect of four different terms here for honor given to the forefathers—חדוה ("joy"), שמחה ("gladness"), דיץ ("rejoicing"), and תשבחה ("praise")—is for poetic emphasis. Together they express the broad jubilation and honor granted to the priestly ancestors collectively. The first two terms echo the end of the

---

4. Primary texts and references for all Aramaic inscriptions are from Schwiderski (2004; 2008).

benediction above in 4Q542 1 i 3, requesting that God grant "joy" and "gladness" to Qahat's descendants. This parallel hints again that the effect of participating in the inheritance is to experience the same blessing received by the ancestors when the heritage is guarded and granted for future generations.

These four terms have varied representation in the Aramaic DSS. The third term, "rejoicing," is a *hapax legomenon* in the corpus. The final term, "praise," occurs elsewhere but only in contexts referring to the praise of God (1Q20 11 13; cf. 4Q212 1 ii 15 [*1 En.* 91:10?]) or the splendor of his works (4Q201 1 ii 10 // 4Q204 1 i 29 [*1 En.* 5:1]).

Some of these items also occur in the so-called Apocryphon of Levi fragments. 4Q541 24 ii 5 mentions maintaining לאבוכה שם חדוא ("a name of joy for your father") by appropriately revering the priestly vestments, in particular the head plate. If 4Q541, or even the ancestral reference in this fragment, is associated with Levi, then 4Q541 and 4Q542 share a concentration of themes and terms. For both works, the appropriate behavior—that is, the avoidance of certain actions—of the priestly descendants brings about "joy" for Levi. As noted above, 4Q541 articulates this in terms of his reputation, or שם ("name"), which echoes the themes of 4Q542 1 i 10. 4Q541 24 ii 6 states this will result in the increased knowledge and gladness for the lineage. In this way, 4Q541 and 4Q542 appear to share a common understanding of the dynamics of priestly blessing as moving both backwards and forwards for those within the genealogy.

Finally, this content invites a look into the later Greek testamentary literature. Puech (2001: 275) observed the similarity to *T. Levi* 18:14: τότε ἀγαλλιάσεται Ἀβραὰμ καὶ Ἰσαὰκ καὶ Ἰακώβ, κἀγὼ καρήσομαι καὶ πάντες οἱ ἅγιοι ἐνδύσονται εὐφροσύνην ("Then Abraham, Isaac, and Jacob will rejoice, and I [Levi] shall be glad, and all the saints shall be clothed in righteousness"). The close parallel in not only terminology but also the motif of extending blessing back upon the priestly forefathers suggests that the later Greek *T. Levi* is in some way receiving or reworking a tradition represented in *WQ*.

Line 12: *because you kept and preserved [the] inheritan[ce...] that your ancestors left for you.* The first two Aramaic words of this phrase are at the end of line 11. The set of three verbs in the clause locates the priestly descendants within the channel of tradition. Their role is of "keeping" (*peal* of √נטר) and "preserving" (*haphel* of √הלך) the inheritance "left" (*peal* of √שבק) by the ancestors. Later in 4Q542 1 ii 13, the second verb is connected with the idea of transmitting an imagined textual heritage through Amram's line. Cook (1993: 212) remarked that the sense is that "the priestly inheritance is being passed down without change or contamination from generation to generation." In his dictionary (Cook 2015: 64), the inflected form of הלך is entered as "you *passed on* the inheritance." Note, however, that the idea of preservation is more accurately captured by CAL, which lists the instance here under the general gloss "to be with constantly." The translation offered there is "you preserved and kept the inheritance that your fathers left you."

In view of this third and final reference to ירותה (cf. 4Q542 1 i 4–5), we may now step back and consider what this "inheritance" entails. In line 4, the inheritance was something given by the ancestors and received by the present generation. The emphasis there, however, was more on the protection and cautious handling of the inheritance than on the exact nature of the inheritance itself. Lines 7–10 provided a clearer view of the inheritance by connecting it with both named ancestors and virtues.

The phrase here in line 12 draws these threads together by connecting the ancestral past and admonishments in virtue directly to the priesthood. The list that follows consists of six virtues (truth, upright practice, integrity, perfection, purity, and holiness [see the comments on individual items below]) yet culminates with the institution of the priesthood as the seventh item. While Lee (2015: 271) noted that "it is difficult to know how to group these seven items," the position of the priesthood no doubt indicates that, for *WQ*, the institution is the pinnacle of the inheritance. The virtues that build up to this point both underscore the qualities of those ancestors who established the priesthood and highlight those qualities to which the lineage must aspire in order to ensure its vitality and continuity. *Words of Qahat* does not emphasize virtuous living as an end in and of itself. Rather, these items are significant for their provision of an ethical infrastructure for the priestly office and lineage.

Line 12: *truth*. With various spellings, the term קושט occurs several times in the Aramaic DSS. Six of these occur in 4Q542 (1 i 4, 9, 12; 1 ii 1, 2, 8). The term is used once in the Cave 11 Job translation (11Q10 7a 8 [Job 23:7]) to render the underlying Hebrew ישר ("upright"). Remaining uses in literary texts are diverse yet fit within emerging trends. To supplement my analysis here, see also the discussion by Stadel (2016: 516–20).

Genesis Apocryphon includes twenty two uses, with most occurrences in the earlier columns on the antediluvian age. Lamech's accusation and heated exchange with Emzera focuses on the "truth" of Noah's paternity (1Q20 2–7). Emzera recalls her sexual pleasure in the child's conception and states her fidelity and explanation are "in truth" (1Q20 2 10, 18). Unconvinced of her testimony, Lamech flees to his father Methuselah, who in turn seeks council from Enoch, to learn the "truth" of the matter (1Q20 2 19–22). Enoch's response too is anchored "in truth" (1Q20 5 9), which foreshadows a later scene of Abraham's Egyptian sojourn where "truth" is connected to an imagined tradition of Enochic lore (1Q20 19 25; cf. 4Q204 1 vi 9 [*1 En.* 14:1]). The *leitmotif* continues in the Noachic section of *GenAp*, where various references to "truth" define Noah's practice and character, ultimately presenting him as a patriarchal embodiment of this virtue (1Q20 6 1–6).

Though the section is fragmentary at Qumran, Levi commences his ethical discourse to his children in *ALD* 85 (MS A, Cambr. e 6 10–11 // 4Q213 1 i) by stating, ראש עוהדיכון יהוי קושטא ("Let the principle of all your actions be *truth*").

At least three compositions in the Aramaic DSS utilize the terminology of "paths of truth." In *ALD*, the phrase is found in the context of Levi's two-ways instruction (4Q213 4 5) and his prayer asking God to set him on the right path (4Q213a 1 12). The Qumran Aramaic materials of the Enochic *Apocalypse of Weeks* features the phrase in its description of the ninth week (4Q212 1 iv 22 [*1 En.* 91:14] and, as in *ALD*, in a two-ways discourse delivered to Enoch's children (4Q212 1 v 25 [*1 En.* 94:1]). The eternal kingdom forecasted in *Aramaic Apocalypse* also pairs these terms when articulating the nature of eternal divine rule (4Q246 1 ii 5).

At least two traditions deploy the term in the theme of a "plant of truth." This usage predominates in Enochic tradition with respect to Noah and a new humanity (*1 En.* 10:1–3, 16) and Abraham and Israel (*1 En.* 93:2–10). It also occurs once in *GenAp*, with respect to the division of the land for Shem (1Q20 14 13). Nickelsburg (2001: 444–45) noted that this righteous plant imagery emerges out of biblical metaphor and blossoms in other Second Temple period literatures (e.g., *Jub.* 1:16; 16:26; 21:24; 36:6; 1QS 8 5). When used in this idiom and application, the term serves the purposes of identity formation and maintenance understood with respect to either an ancestral past or present reality. As Tiller (1997) explored, this concept also relates to the terminology of an "eternal planting," which is found in a variety of texts (4Q418 81 i 11–13; 1QS 11 7–9; 1QH^a 14 18; 16 7).

In these ways, the mention of קושט here in 4Q542 connects the list of virtues with a larger network of concepts and associations in the Aramaic and Hebrew DSS. It has a noticeable function in redrawn portraits of model patriarchs or in imagined discourses delivered by them. Additionally, the term has some currency in two-ways instructions, admonishing right living or extending such an understanding into the eschatological future. Finally, it also functions in contexts where it contributes to a metaphor used to establish or affirm a group boundary. Fronting the mention to קושט in the list of virtues may suggest this item provides the foundation or point of departure for all subsequent items.

Line 12: *upright practice* (וצדקתא). Of the seven instances of the term צדקה in the Aramaic DSS, two occur in 4Q542 (1 i 8, 12). The Cave 11 Job translation (11Q10 26 3) utilizes the term for the analogous Hebrew form at Job 35:8. As indicated in the commentary on line 8 above, the usage in 4Q542 makes most sense if understood with respect to ethical and pious practices reflecting a lifestyle marked by charity. This is suggested by the word's associations with almsgiving in Tobit (rec. 4Q196 10 1, cf. Sinaiticus: τὴν δικαιοσύνην [Tob. 4:7]; 4Q198 1 1 [Tob. 14:2]) and mercy toward the poor in Daniel (Dan. 4:27). In view of the *ALD* parallel noted immediately above, it is significant that everlasting "justice" (4Q213 1 i 7: צדקת; MS A, Cambr. e 6 12: צדקה) follows Levi's reference to קושטא in *ALD* 85. The pairing of these items also seems to be present in 4Q541 13 3, though the reading is tenuous: ק̊וׄשׁט̊[וׄ]צׄ[דקק(ה). Finally, the dualistic fragments of 4Q548 1 ii–2 7 likely feature the term בני צ[דקתא ("sons of ri[ghteousness"), suggesting a different nuance than most other Aramaic texts attested at Qumran that is perhaps closer to the thought and terms traditionally associated with Qumran sectarianism (cf. 1QS 9 14; 1QM 1 8; 4Q259 3 10;

4Q496 3 7). For additional discussion of this term, see the entry by Zanella (2016: 383–94).

Line 12: *integrity*. See the comment on 4Q542 1 i 9 for discussion of ישירו used in the proximity of קושט.

Line 13: *perfection*. The Aramaic form תמימו here is a *hapax legomenon* in the Aramaic DSS. While Cook (2015: 255) listed "perfection" as the lexical gloss, CAL specifies the meaning here could be closer to "honesty" or "sincerity," which may in fact fit better within a section enumerating virtues. Puech (2001: 397) proposed that a second occurrence was penned by the first hand of 4Q548 2 6 (Puech = 1 ii–2 13) as תמימותא, which was later corrected to לֹנְעִֹימֹתא. While that fragment is particularly difficult to decipher, the reading לשֹמחֹ[ת ("for gladness") seems to be most likely with indeterminate text underlying what may have been a correction (Perrin and Hama 2017b: n.p.). The same form as is used here in *WQ* occurs in *Tg. Neof.* Gen. 20:5, when Abimelech confesses his innocence with Sarah to God in a dream. In the context of the Hebrew texts at Qumran, the concept of perfection (תמים) also took on both a present and eschatological significance (cf. Deasley 2000: 210–54; Brooke 2016: 103).

Line 13: *pur[ity*. While the related adjective occurred in 4Q542 1 i 8 and 10, the partially extant reading ודכֹ[ותא here is likely a nominal form. If this reading is correct, it is the only occurrence of the noun in the Aramaic DSS corpus. On this form, Uusimäki (2021) noted that "the integration of purity, holiness, and priesthood into ethical reflection seems like a novelty in comparison with biblical wisdom materials or lists of virtues" (Prov. 1:3–4; 6:16–19; Mic. 6:8; cf. Jer. 7:9; Hos. 4:2). In this way, the next set of three virtues seems to cluster together.

In the setting of the virtue list, the emphasis on purity is not on a state of being or mental posture, as implied by the uses in 4Q542 1 i 8, 10. Rather, it is something to aspire to in the highest ethical, moral, and spiritual sense. "Purity" here is presented as an almost philosophical ideal, endorsed and elevated through a patriarchal discourse. This invites comparison with the ideal of purity in the Qumran Hebrew texts, which is constructed largely through exegesis and, in most instances, emphasizes cultic and communal purity (e.g., 1QS 4 3–6).

Line 13: *and ho]liness*. The reading וקֹ[דשא includes the sixth virtue listed, the penultimate item before the pinnacle item of the ancestral inheritance: the priesthood. The Aramaic Leviticus fragments of Cave 4 feature the expected correlate by rendering the Hebrew הקדש with the Aramaic קדשא (4Q156 2 4 [Lev. 16:20]). While the noun functions elsewhere in the Aramaic DSS to describe the holy character of other nouns—a "tithe" (4Q213a 3 18), divine "words" (4Q212 1 v 16 [*1 En.* 93:11]), the eschatological "city" (4Q196 17 ii 8 [Tob. 13:20]), or the holy "place" (4Q156 2 4 [Lev. 16:20])—this is the only occurrence of the noun in the sense of a virtue or ideal to be attained by a human being.

Line 13: *and the pri[est]hood*. The reading וכהֹ[ו]נתא represents the culmination of the ancestral inheritance. The mention of the priesthood as the seventh item in the list is a structural mechanism to underscore its importance. While the Aramaic DSS are not short on scenes, narratives, or descriptions of priestly topics (e.g., genealogies, sacrificial processes and places, etc.), this is the only certain reference to the "priesthood" as an earthly institution in the entire corpus. The form בהנות עלמא ("eternal priesthood") occurs alone on a broken line of an already small fragment of *ALD* (4Q213a 5 i 3). Greenfield and Stone (1996: 35) noted the reference there is likely of a "Levitical character," not least due to its use of a phrase also found in Exod. 40:15 and Num. 25:13. As Stadel (2008: 57–58) observed, the occurrence here in *WQ* is a Hebraism. This reference to the priesthood should also be considered in light of the revelation regarding the elevated status and ongoing nature of Aaron's priesthood in *VA* (4Q547 9 6–7).

Line 13: *according to everything that I commanded you and according to everything that I have taught you in truth from now on.* The sentence here begins in the final line of column i and continues onto the opening line of column ii. The sections are consecutive and unbroken. The list of virtues and the institution that make up the ancestral inheritance resolve on a didactic note. In short, the only sure way to retain the integrity and vitality of the inheritance for future generations is to heed the entirety of ancestral teachings.

The discourse uses tandem verbs to underscore the instructional quality: פקד ("to command") and אלף ("to teach"). This pair of verbs occurs in a similar setting in Isaac's instruction to Levi in *ALD* 13 (MS A, Bodl. b 8 7). Individually, these verbs also function in various contexts of ancestral instruction across ancient Jewish Aramaic literature.

The first of this pair of verbs (פקד) is used twice more in the context of Qahat's specific instruction and admonishment to Amram later in the text (4Q542 1 ii 9–10). Fathers instructing—or literally "commanding" (פקד)—their children in wisdom is a common motif in the Qumran Aramaic texts. As noted below in the commentary on 4Q542 1 ii 10, the motif of command and fulfillment for ancestral teachings seems to have been a driving force for the generation and connectedness of the Aramaic Levi, Qahat, and Amram materials (*ALD* 13 [MS A, Bodl. b 8 7]; 82, 84 [MS A, Cambr. e 6, 9]; 49–50 [Mt. Athos MS E 18,2]; 4Q542 1 i 13; 1 ii 9; 4Q543 1 a–c 2 // 4Q545 1a i 2, 11; 4Q546 14 4). As each generation received the tradition, the priestly forefather admonished their progeny to pass it along, which is actualized in the next priestly work, and ancestor, in the chain of tradition (see also Perrin 2021a). Note also the injunctions for instruction using this verbiage in the book of Tobit (4Q196 11 2 [Tob. 5:1]; 14 i 8 [Tob. 6:16]; 18 16 [Tob. 14:3]; 4Q197 4 ii 12 [Tob. 6:16]; 4Q198 1 2 [Tob. 14:3]). Generational transmission of knowledge is equally pervasive in the Enochic tradition (*1 En.* 83:1; 85:2; 91:1; 93:2; 94:1; 106:1).

The second verb (אלף) has a more diverse usage in the Aramaic DSS, with at least one explicit, though fragmentary, occurrence indicating paternal instruction: אלף בניכה ("teach your children"; 4Q569 1–2 9). In these ways, while teaching and instruction are not explicitly an element of the ancestral inheritance, they are implied in *WQ* as part of this profile. Such a role is requisite for retaining and transmitting the heritage.

3. Words of Qahat

Finally, Qahat's instruction is claimed as utterly reliable in that it is anchored בקושוט ("in truth"). On this term in the context of *WQ* and the wider Aramaic DSS, see the comment on 4Q542 1 i 12.

3.7.2. Address to Amram and an Eschatological Outlook (4Q542 1 ii)

Qahat's discourse continues, first with content addressed to all his descendants, then directly to Amram. For the broader audience, he emphasizes the certainty of ancestral teaching and the blessings that result if they are heeded, and forecasts judgment awaiting the guilty. In his words to Amram, Qahat underscores receiving and transmitting ancestral booklore inherited from Levi.

TOP MARGIN
1 אלפֿתכון בקושוט מן כען ועֿד כוֹל[...]
2 כֹּוֹל ממר קושטא יאתא עליכֿ]ון[...]
3 ברכת עלמא ישכונן עליכון ולהוֹ]ן[...]
4 קאם לכול דריעלמין ולאיעוד תבֿ]...[
5 מן יסורכון ותקומון למדן דין עֿ[ל...]
6 ולמחזיא חובת כול חיבי עלמין הב[ו]ס[...]
7 ובאֿרֿעֿא ובתהומֿ[י]א ובכול חלליא לבלמֿ[...]
8 בֿ[ד]רֿי קושטא ויעדון כול בני רשעֿ]א[...]
9 וֿבֿען לכה עמרם ברי אנא מפקֿ]ד...[
10 וֿ[ב]נֿיכֿ]אֿ{ה וֿ}לֿ{בניהון אנא מפקד ○[...]
11 ויהבו ללוי אבי ולוי אבי לי [...]
12 כֹּול כתבי בשהדו די תזדהרון בהוֹן]...[
13 לכון בהון זכו רבה באתהילכותהון עמכון [...]
BOTTOM MARGIN

1. I have taught you in truth from now on. All[...]
2. every true word will come to fruition for y[ou...]
3. everlasting blessings will rest upon you and [they] wi[ll...]
4. enduring for eternal generations. No longer will...[...]
5. from your suffering and you will stand to hand down judgment up[on...]
6. and to see the guilt of all the eternally guilty...[...]
7. and on the earth and in the depths and in all the caverns...[...]
8. in the [gen]erations of truth but all [the] sons of wickedne[ss] will pass away[...]
9. And now, to you, Amram, my son, I comma[nd...]
10. and your [des]cendants and their [des]cendants, I command[...]
11. and they gave to Levi, my father, and my father Levi to me[...]
12. all my writings as a testimony with which you should be careful[...]
13. to you. There is great merit when they are preserved with you. [...]

Textual, Scribal, and Material Observations

Primary images for transcription: PAM M43.565; B-370775; B-370774.

Line 2: יאתא ("will come to fruition") – The eventual reading here involved at least one previous correction. A dot of ink above the *aleph* is either the remnants of an erasure or possibly of a previous cancellation dot. Cancellation dots above and below a character occur in the *lamed* of the form ולבניהון in 4Q542 1 ii 10. Puech (2001: 270) proposed a series of corrections here, but the characters and sequence are not certain. Cook (1993: 206) and García Martínez and Tigchelaar (1998 2:1082) read יאׄתא. Beyer (2004: 115) presented a shorter reading of יתא.

Line 4: דריעלמין ("eternal generations") – The set of nouns in this construct chain are written without space between them (cf. 4Q542 1 i 10).

Line 4: ולאׄעוד ("and no longer") – The supralinear *aleph* completes the negative particle in this form. For another correction involving לא, see 4Q542 1 i 9.

Line 5: יסורכון ("your suffering") – The upper portions of the fourth character are effaced, making both *dalet* (García Martínez and Tigchelaar 1998 2:1082; Puech 2001: 270, 277; Beyer 2004: 115) and *resh* (Puech 1991: 33; Beyer 1994: 83; Cook 1993: 206; 2015: 104) possible. Even in high-resolution digital images, the reading is indeterminate. Contextually, the reading יסור ("suffering") makes more sense than יסוד ("foundation") and is adopted on that basis here. Note also that at the end of the line there is an ink trace of an unknown character, likely an *ayin*.

Line 7: ובאׄרׄעׄא ("and on the earth") – There is an unfortunate lacuna that makes reading the middle characters of the form difficult. Editions generally fall into two categories, with varying degrees of certainty and minor reconstruction. Some read remnants of the form ובאישא ("in the fire"; Puech 1991: 33; Eisenman and Wise 1992: 149; Cook 1993: 206; Beyer 1994: 83; García Martínez and Tigchelaar 1998 2:1082), while others perceived what was originally ובארעא (Puech 2001: 269; Beyer 2004: 117). The ink traces and available space make either reading possible. However, the reading accepted here fits with the geographical/cosmological terms featured on the line.

Line 7: ובתהומׄאׄ[י] ("and in the depths") – The scribal correction is peculiar. As Puech (2001: 270) observed, there is a supralinear *yod* written in the first hand with a second *yod* inscribed next to it by a second hand. The first instance is either slightly faded and effaced on the fragment or partially erased. All others recognize a single supralinear *yod* (Eisenman and Wise 1992: 149; Cook 1993: 206; García Martínez and Tigchelaar 1998 2:1082; Beyer 2004: 115). In any case, the size and nature of the correction makes it challenging to know if the emendation was from *vav* to *yod* or vice versa.

Line 7: לבלמׄ[– The end of line includes this character cluster just before the text breaks away. The final letter, while only partially extant, is most likely a medial *mem*, not a *bet*, as in Eisenman and Wise's לבלב (1992: 149) or Beyer's לבלבּ]לה (2004: 115–16). Cook (1993: 207) originally read לבלד]ה, but later adjusted to לבלחׄ]ודיהון (2015: 35). The question is if these four letters are a complete form or are the remnants of a lost word or phrase. Since the scribe does not consistently use medial or final *mems* in their expected positions (4Q542 1 i 2, 11; 2 5, 11), it is entirely possible that this is a complete form. In this case, the reading would be a *lamed* preposition attached to a *pael* infinitive construct of the verb בלם ("to muzzle"; see Puech 2001: 272; Cook 2015: 35). Given that the text is fragmentary at this point and that this would be a *hapax legomenon* in the Aramaic DSS, I do not include this rendering in the translation above.

Lines 8–9: There is a horizontal stroke in between these lines, flush with the right edge of text. It is uncertain if this is in the primary or secondary hand, or that of a later user. In terms of content, line 9 begins a new discourse spoken directly from Qahat to his son, Amram. Tov (2004: 180) noted that, "when occurring between two lines, section markers usually mark the end of the preceding section, and not the beginning of a new one." A Qumran fragment of *ALD* (4Q213a 2 10–11) includes a horizontal stroke with a downward hook penned between two lines of text that is offset into the rightmost margin. There too, the mark coincides with a narrative shift from the conclusion of Levi's prayer to the continued narrative description of his movement to visit Jacob, initiated with the adverb באדין. See also an additional marginal marking in the *ALD* fragments at 4Q213 1 ii–2 10–11. A fragment of the *Book of Giants* (4Q532 1 ii 6–7) includes an interlinear horizontal stroke. In that instance the mark is placed in the right intercolumnar margin and seems to be inscribed with a different writing implement, perhaps suggesting a later scribe or user.

Line 10: ה̇{א}נ̇יכ[ב]ו̇ ("and your [des]cendants") – This fragmentary form involves several uncertain and debated characters. The initial *vav* of the form is read as partially extant by most (Milik 1972a: 97; Eisenman and Wise 1992: 149; García Martínez and Tigchelaar 1998 2:1082; Puech 2001: 269; Fitzmyer and Harrington 2002: 96; Beyer 2004: 115). Cook (1993: 206) read only כה[...]. The presence of the medial *nun* is debated. Puech (2001: 269) and Beyer (2004: 115) read it with varying degrees of certainty, while all others place it within square brackets. The final character seems to have originally been penned as an *aleph*, which was then overwritten and morphed into a *he*. For a similar correction, see 4Q542 1 i 7. Eisenman and Wise (1992: 149) read *aleph*. All others include a final *he* (Milik 1972a: 97; Cook 1993: 206; García Martínez and Tigchelaar 1998 2:1082; Fitzmyer and Harrington 2002: 96; Beyer 2004: 115).

Line 10: ו{ל}בניהון ("and their descendants") – Tov (2004: 191) noted 1Q20 22 27 is the only certain occurrence of dots used above and below a character in the Aramaic corpus. However, the *lamed* has cancellation dots above and below. This seems to be a grammatical correction as the noun here is most naturally an indirect object.

Line 13: באתהילכותהון ("when they are preserved") – The pronominal suffix is written in a distinctively narrower script. This suggests either intervention by a second scribe, use of a differently stylized implement, or cramping of text due to space limitations. For a similar script and intervention, see 4Q542 1 i 5. While most read a *yod* in the middle of the form, Eisenman and Wise (1992: 149) and Cook (1993: 206) read *vav*: באתהולכותהון.

Commentary

Line 1: *I have taught you in truth from now on. All.* See the comment on 4Q542 1 i 13 for this phrasing that began at the end of the previous column.

Line 2: *every true word will come to fruition for y[ou.* This line extends the concept and phrasing of 4Q542 1 i 13–ii 1. There Qahat's instruction and command were anchored in truth; Qahat described the words he spoke over his lineage as a "true word" coming to realization. This material and section, then, evidences a slight shift in focus. Whereas the material following the benediction focused on the inheritance, its nature, and the need to safeguard it, the content of 4Q542 1 ii 2–8 is forward looking and articulates the anticipated blessing upon future generations in juxtaposition with the fate of the guilty and wicked. The Aramaic phrasing of 4Q198 1 6 (Tob. 14:4) also uses the *peal* of אתי in a similar sense, there referring to the assured fulfillment of God's utterances delivered through the prophets.

Line 3: *everlasting blessings will rest upon you and [they] wi[ll.* The past inheritance makes a future impact in the form of an everlasting blessing upon Qahat's descendants. The phrase ברכת עלמא ("everlasting blessings") is unique in the Aramaic DSS. This language suggests that *WQ* understands the trajectory of the inheritance in covenantal terms originating in the past, extending to the present, and projected into the future (cf. Num. 25:13; Mal. 2:5–8). It is, however, also possible that the phrase means "blessings of eternity," with a more eschatological tone. This would then juxtapose with eschatological judgment language in the following lines. For eternal priesthood language in *ALD*, see the comment on 4Q213a 5 i–ii 3.

Line 4: *enduring for eternal generations. No longer will.* While the antecedents of this line are lost in the fragmentary text, it seems that the eternality of the blessing is underscored and extended to all future generations of the priestly line flowing through Qahat. The use of the *peal* form of קום in the sense of "enduring" occurs also in Dan. 2:44, with reference to the longevity and sustainability of God's eternal kingdom.

This line exhibits close verbal parallels with at least three other Aramaic texts represented at Qumran. *Visions of Amram* (4Q547 9 7) features the same phrase, לכול דרי עלמין ("for all generations of eternity"), in a similar setting explaining the generational and everlasting quality of the priestly line. In that context the phrase refers to the heritage of Amram to Aaron and his descendants. *Words of Qahat* and *VA*, therefore, deploy the idiom to advance a shared theme.

Analogous idioms occur in contexts in the Aramaic DSS. The Aramaic Enoch fragments include the same phrase in two places. 4Q212 1 iv 18 [*1 En.* 91:13]) reads לבֹול דֹרי עלמין ("for all generations of eternity"), as a descriptor of the lasting eschatological temple. 4Q212 1 ii 17 (*1 En.* 91:17) reads כל דרי עלמי[ן] ("all the generations of etern[ity") in the introduction to the Epistle. The Qumran *ALD* fragments (4Q213a 3–4 7) reference לכל דרי עלמׄא ("for all the generations of eternity") seemingly in the context of the defilement of the ancestral name and reputation. The Qumran Tobit fragments (4Q196 17 ii 15 [Tob. 13:12]) feature a similar idiom, לד[רי עלמא ("[for] everlasting [gener]ations"), to refer to the enduring quality of the name of God.

While *WQ* and *VA* exhibit the closest terminological and thematic parallels of this cluster of uses, what is common to all is the deployment of the idiom to articulate the everlasting sustainability of an institution, office, or identity marker in a future age (i.e., the priestly line, an ancestral or divine reputation, or the temple). This example is instructive in that it shows how the scribes of the Aramaic DSS often drew upon and contributed to a common fund of idioms, which suggests some cogency to the cluster of texts and/or perhaps proximity of compositional environment. It also reveals how the application of an idiom to support a particular theme likely suggests a closer degree of relation between pairs or small sets of texts.

Line 5: *from your suffering.* The tone and direction of the future-oriented outlook of *WQ* shifts to an acknowledgment or expectation of suffering for the priestly line. If the reading here is correct, Cook (2015: 104) proposed the glosses "chastisement, correction" for the noun יסור. For this meaning, see later uses in *Tg.* Jon. 28:22; Jer. 30:14). See the textual note above for the alternate proposals of this form for יסוד ("foundation").

The nature of this forecasted adversity is unclear in the text's damaged state. In the narrative setting, these words are spoken by Qahat over his children, yet the generational language of the previous line suggests the message is meant to transcend generations. In this way, the material likely offers a word of encouragement to a priestly audience in the mid-Second Temple period undergoing some form of struggle. The rhetoric of *WQ* offers an authoritative voice of assurance that this suffering is neither unexpected nor without an anticipated resolution. On possible social settings, see the preliminary remarks in the introduction to the composition.

Line 5: *and you will stand to hand down judgment up[on.* As with the origins of the suffering, here too the fragmentary text fails to offer a full view of those who stand in judgment. Nonetheless, the available terminology indicates the likely eschatological outlook of the fragment, suggesting some priestly role within it.

It is tempting to see a hint at resurrection here in the verb קום (i.e., *arising* to have a role in some eschatological judgment). Puech (2001: 277) suggested that the notion of resurrection might be present here as part of his proposal that the concept is already operative in "cercles hassidéens." In the nearest comparative context, however, resurrection does not seem to be part of the eschatological or apocalyptic outlook of the Qumran Aramaic texts. While some perceived a hint at resurrection in the use of this term in *Pseudo-Daniel* (4Q245 2 4; Milik 1956: 414; García-Martínez 1992: 141; Puech 1993: 572), others have shown this is unlikely the case (Collins and Flint 1996: 163; Hobbins 2001: 416). On the evolution of a thought related to resurrection in the DSS, see Elledge (2017: 150–74).

There is some precedent, however, for the use of this verb to signal the emergence of an eschatological group with a judicial function. *Aramaic Apocalypse*

(4Q246 1 ii 4–6) includes the statement עד יקום עם אל ("until the people of God arise"), which is followed by a statement of this group's judicial role in that ידי[ן] ארעא בקשט ("they will judge the land justly"). In view of this, it is more likely that this section of *WQ* is referring to an eschatological role of the priestly descendants. This is suggested further by the concentration of terms that align with this concept in the following lines.

Line 6: *and to see the guilt of all the eternally guilty.* The theme of guilt connects with the idea of judgment from the previous line. The exact syntactical relation of the fragmentary material in lines 5–6 is unclear, yet it seems the sinners throughout the ages are the object of judgement. The choice of the verb למחזיא ("to see") here is also intriguing in view of terminology and themes reminiscent of abodes of the guilty in Enochic tradition in line 7. Here the reference to viewing the guilty from all eternity suggests a final judgment where the priestly progeny exercise their role of judges while viewing the throngs of wrongdoers.

The emphasis on the "guilt" (noun: חובה) of the "guilty" (adjective: חיב) underscores this context of judgment and continues *WQ*'s tendency for paralleling or compounding terms for poetic emphasis. The adjective here is best understood in the sense of "guilty" rather than with relation to "sin." At least two other works in the Aramaic DSS reference the nouns חובה ("guilt, obligation") and חטא ("sin") in close proximity, indicating a degree of differentiation (4Q537 1 ii + 2 16; 4Q537 6 1)

Line 7: *and on the earth and in the depths and in all the caverns.* The application of this language is unclear in the text due to its increasingly fragmentary nature. In the context of an eschatological judgment indicated in the previous lines, references to תהומיא ("the depths") and חלליא ("the caverns") likely connote domains or holding places of the guilty. As Stuckenbruck (2011: 311) observed, *WQ* draws upon Enochic themes relating to post-mortem chambers in the *Book of Watchers*. While the Aramaic is lacking at Qumran for this section of *1 Enoch*, the description of the "Mountain of the Dead" in *1 En.* 22:1–14 repeatedly references "hollow" and "deep" places in the rocky crags that are reserved for sinners awaiting judgment.

The noun תהום has a limited usage in the Aramaic DSS. The Cave 11 Job translation includes the phrase רחם תהומא ("womb of the abyss") at 11Q10 30 6 (Job 38:8). However, the form in question does not align directly with anything in known Hebrew texts of Job; rather, it seems to have emerged as the translator was attempting to balance the imagery of the passage. *Aramaic Apocalypse* also includes the term in compositional Aramaic, yet the word comes at the very end of a line in an incomplete construct form (4Q246 1 ii 9). The broader semantic field of the corresponding Hebrew term includes associations with metaphorical or imagined depictions of the netherworld (1QH^a 11 18, 32–33; 4Q372 2 3; 4Q416 1 12; 11Q11 4 7) as well as cosmological descriptions or references to the flood (e.g., 4Q252 1 5; 4Q370 1 i 4). The Hebrew Scriptures include similar such uses (e.g., Gen. 7:11; Ezek. 31:15; Amos 7:4; Jon. 2:5) as well as a diversity of occurrences referring to the creation or function of waterways (e.g., Gen. 1:2;

Exod. 15:5; Isa. 51:10; Ps. 104:6; Prov. 8:27–28). In view of this, the form here in *WQ* is a Hebrew loan word (Stadel 2008: 58; Muraoka 2011: 81).

With Cook (2015: 85), I take the form חלליא as derived from חלל ("cavern") rather than חלה ("valley"), as Puech proposed (2001: 277). The noun חלל is a *hapax legomenon* here in the Aramaic DSS and the Qumran collection as a whole. It is also absent in the Hebrew Scriptures. The idea of an "empty space," however, is known from Babylonian Aramaic. See, for example, *b. Šabb.* 77b, which refers to כל חללי עלמא ("all the empty spaces of the world").

Line 8: *in the [gen]erations of truth*. While the reading of the construct noun בֿ[ד]רִי is not certain, as Puech (2001: 278) observed, it is more plausible than reconstructing בבני ("in/with the sons of"). Furthermore, the new digital images do not support that reading. With this, compare the terminology of 4Q542 1 ii 4 (cf. 4Q547 9 7). The eschatological tone of these terms is suggested by the Aramaic Enochic traditions' reference to דרי קושׁטא (4Q204 5 ii 28 [*1 En.* 107:1]). In that context, the phrase occurs at the end of Enoch's discourse commenting on the expectation of the end of evil and ascendancy of the righteous in the eschatological future.

Line 8: *but all [the] the sons of wickedne[ss] will pass away*. This phrase is in juxtaposition with the reference to generations of truth in the previous line. Together, they bring the eschatologically oriented section of the discourse to Qahat's progeny to a close with a statement on the ultimate resolution of evil. The terms of reference in the available text focus on a section of society deemed בני רשע]א ("[the] sons of wickedne[ss]"). Recall that the previous column developed an image or outline of an outsider group when cautioning against intermingling and emphasizing the protection of inheritance. This phrase should be read in light of the recent reference to the comprehensive guilty collective that transcends all ages. No doubt the outsider group in view in 4Q542 1 i is also part of this larger cohort.

The pairing בני רשע]א ("[the] sons of wickedne[ss]") is unique in the Aramaic DSS. While Collins and Flint (1996: 144; cf. Milik 1956: 414) reconstructed the form בני רש[עׄאׄ ("the [sons of wicked]ness") at 4Q243 24 1, the material evidence of *Pseudo-Daniel* is highly fragmentary at that point and cannot support the reading. Though its remains are tattered, 4Q548 1 ii–2 8 refers to בני שקר ("sons of lies") in the context of other binary terms, specifically light and darkness. That same fragment also references the "removal" (*ithpeel* אדה) of the sons of darkness, which reveals another tier of similarity to *WQ* with its reference to the "passing away" (*peal* אדה) of the sons of wickedness (cf. 4Q541 9 i 4). This opens the question of the function of binaries or permutations of dualism in the Aramaic DSS and the degree to which the juxtaposition of truth and wickedness in an eschatological scene of judgment in *WQ* presents such a worldview.

Line 9: *And now, to you, Amram, my son, I comma[nd*. If there was any question of the pseudepigraphic voice dominating this text, the reference here to Amram, paired with the mention of Levi in 4Q542 1 ii 11, confirms this tradition is attributed to Qahat. This phrase also marks the next major transition in the discourse of *WQ*, which is complemented by a marginal stroke in between lines 8–9 (see the textual note above). Qahat now addresses Amram specifically in a scene of generational transmission of teaching and lore.

The opening conjunction and adverbial particle וכען functions regularly in the Aramaic DSS to shift within or between narrative scenes or sections (e.g., 1Q20 0 12; 4Q204 5 ii 29; 4Q213a 3 12; 4Q537 1 + 2 + 3 3; 4Q542 1 i 4). At least four texts use the marker in the context of paternal instruction to a child. The Aramaic Enoch materials include the phrase וכען לכון אנה אמר בֹנֹי ("And now, to you I say, my sons") at 4Q212 1 v 24 (*1 En.* 94:1). *Genesis Apocryphon* uses a similar formulation in Enoch's disclosure to Lamech: וכען לכ{א} אנה אמרֹ ברי ("And now to you, I say, my son"; 1Q20 5 9). Amram's own discourse to his children includes the partial phrases וכען בני שמעו דֹי ("And now, my sons, hear what") and וכען ברי אֹ[נה ("And now, my son, I") at 4Q546 14 1 and 14 4. While more fragmentary than the others, 4Q213 1 i 9 also fronts the form וכען after a *vacat* in a larger section of Levi's instruction on wisdom and scribalism. It is possible that a similar phrase occurred in the *Apocryphon of Joseph* (4Q539 2–3 2), though it must be inferred and reconstructed.

For references to other Aramaic DSS that frame the transmission of knowledge to the next generation using the verb פקד ("to command"), see the comment on 4Q542 1 i 13 and the next line.

Line 10: *and your [des]cendants and their descendants, I command.* The motif of the ongoing transmission of ancestral tradition is described again with the verb פקד ("to command"). This language seems to connect with a larger theme in the Aramaic Levi, Qahat, and Amram traditions, which may also be a key to understanding their potential relationship.

In a general way, *ALD* 88 issues a call for the ongoing instruction of future priestly generations (cf. *ALD* 88; 4Q213 1 i 9–10). *Aramaic Levi Document* 49–50 is explicit about how Levi's commanding his sons is based on the model of instruction and admonishment of Abraham. The present text contributes to this theme by demonstrating how Qahat embodied the instructional model his father Levi exemplified, now commanding his own son, Amram, to ensure the continuation of the tradition. *Words of Qahat* is tracing the themes of ancestral instruction and lore forward to the extent that it seems to present itself as "the next link in the chain of transmission" (Reed 2014: 394–95). Picking up on the same idea, Feldman (2019: 478) proposed that the "body of patriarchal knowledge" imagined in these texts may provide "an alternative to what later becomes known as the rabbinic chain of tradition."

Eventually, in his own tale, Amram picks up this mantle and "commands" his progeny on his dying day (4Q543 1a–c 2 // 4Q545 1a i 2, 11). In the context of *WQ*, however, 4Q542 1 ii 10 is technically an unfulfilled command, an open-ended aspect of the tradition, even an inviting exegetical departure point for generating a tradition concerned with the next generation. There is already a trend in the Aramaic DSS for generating fresh compositions and redrawn patriarchal profiles out of perceived gaps or hints to something more in the Hebrew

Scriptures. Perhaps the simplest example of this is Enoch's expansive biography that is rooted in the suggestive phrasing of Gen. 5:22–24 (Dimant 1983). Machiela (2009: 102) noted that the creation of Noah's dream-vision in *GenAp* (1Q20 11 15–12 1) was likewise exegetically generated based on ambiguous phrasing in Gen. 9:21. The spark for the scribal imagination of Levi's profile as a dreamer in *ALD* seems also to have been based on creative exegesis of terms in Mal. 2:5–6 and 1 Sam. 2:27 (Perrin 2015a: 149–56).

In view of this trend in the Aramaic DSS and the immediate interest in the transgenerational transmission of teaching, it is possible that what we have uncovered the hints of what occasioned the evolution of the Aramaic Levi, Qahat, and Amram texts. At a literary level, we might say that these share the theme of ancestral instruction. What I suggest here, however, is that this is not only a literary theme but the compositional mechanism that enabled the growth of the tradition. Each generation models ancestral instruction and commands that this practice continue among their progeny. These commands for the next generation are technically unfulfilled, providing the scribal cue for the innovation of the next text, oriented around the next patriarch, answering this call and actualizing the command for the next generation. If this is the case, then the interface between these two texts is some of our strongest evidence indicating the Aramaic Amram tradition is to be read as a counterpart to, or in coordination with, the Aramaic Qahat materials, and the Qahat text functions as a follow-up to the Levi Document.

Line 11: *and they gave to Levi, my father, and my father Levi to me.* Though fragmentary in content, the concept of a chain of traditions passed on from one generation to the next is clear. Qahat received the traditions from his father Levi, who in turn received them from generations past. This opens the questions of both who passed this heritage on to Levi and what constituted the ancestral heritage. While the antecedent of the plural verb יהבו ("they gave") is lost, ancestral references of the previous column suggest the lost antecedent was almost certainly a collective reference, such as אבהתכון ("your fathers") as in 4Q542 1 i 5. This class would no doubt include Abraham, Jacob, and Isaac, who are named in the context of the ancestral inheritance in 4Q542 1 i 7–8, 11. It is also possible that the antecedent was simply אבהתכון ("your fathers"), in view of an analogous understanding and reference in 4Q545 1 i 5. Such an association suggests that the ancestral inheritance of virtues and the priesthood associated with the forefathers in the previous column is also the object of the chain of transmission here. However, while Amram is no doubt heir to this inheritance as much as all others in the general audience addressed up to 4Q542 1 ii 9, the following line suggests he was also the recipient of a unique aspect of the ancestral heritage in the form of real or imagined scribal knowledge and artefacts. With this, compare Levi's reception, preservation, and continued transmission of ancestral lore in *Jub.* 45:15.

Line 12: *all my writings as a testimony with which you should be careful.* The connection between Levi and Qahat in the previous line related to the transmission of something. Qahat's reference to כול כתבי ("all my writings") here strongly suggests that lines 11–12 imagine a genealogy that is not only about a family tree, but a lineage of inscribed tradition. This tradition originated in the deep ancestral past and was safeguarded and handed down through a particular branch of the priestly genealogy. While this is the only certain place in ancient Jewish literature where Qahat is associated with booklore, both his father, Levi, and son, Amram, are associated with procuring or producing texts in the Aramaic DSS (*ALD* 57–59; 4Q543 1a–c 1; 4Q547 9 8).

The present fragment, then, both situates Qahat in this network of ancestral lore that draws a close association between priestly figures and scribal craft and emphasizes the safeguarding of such ancestral traditions. Puech (2001: 279) commented that the association between priesthood and instruction has its basis in Deut. 33:10; Mal. 2:7 (cf. Sir. 47:17; Lev. 10:10–11; 2 Chron. 15:3; 17:7–9; 19:4–11; 35:3; Ezra 7:10–11). On the broader topic of texts and textuality, see the comment on 4Q213 1 ii–2 12.

While some infer that the content of these imagined writings related to priestly instructions (Lee 2015: 279), all the extant text confirms is that this inherited lore somehow functions as a "testimony" (שהדו). The determinative form of this Aramaic word is famously included in the sole Aramaic phrase in Gen. 31:47, which references יגר שהדותא ("Jegar-Sahadutha"). As in the Hebrew Scriptures, the noun is a *hapax legomenon* in the Aramaic DSS. The related masculine noun שהד ("witness") is used in the Aramaic Enoch tradition at 4Q212 1 iv 12 (*1 En.* 93:10) with reference to "witnesses of righteousness" at the end of the apocalyptic age. Unfortunately, due to the fragmentary context of the present line it is unclear how the ancestral writings are understood as a testimony.

One of the interpretive challenges of this fragment, however, is the addressee of the plural verb. 4Q542 1 ii 9 marked a clear transition and address to Amram. Yet Qahat's call to תזדהרון ("be careful") with this inherited anthology is technically a plural. This echoes his earlier admonishment in 4Q542 1 i 4 for all his descendants to אזדהרו ("be careful") with their inheritance. Note also, that this second-person plural address persists in the next line. Given the emphasis placed on Amram in this section as the next figurehead of the priesthood, it seems most likely that Qahat is here addressing a plural audience that is forward looking and encompasses the next generation of priestly progeny flowing through Amram. It is this group that is tasked with receiving and keeping the scribal heritage of the priestly past.

Line 13: *to you. There is great merit when they are preserved with you.* The concept of safeguarding the tradition as bringing honor to the priestly ancestors is extended here as a benefit to the future lineage. In a way, the preservation of this inheritance ensures the persistence of the priestly line. As Amram and his seed transfer this intellectual heritage to generations ahead, they are agents in this process yet also attain זכו רבה ("great merit") for their participation and preservation. In this way, they become part of the heritage and receive honor by the ongoing preservation of the inheritance by priestly generations to come. The idea of preservation—with the inflected form of the verb הלך as in 4Q542 1 i 12—forms an important connection with earlier content of the address. That is, part of the merit of this lineage is in their commitment to preserving the intellectual and textual lore along *with* them through the generations.

Finally, while Stadel (2008: 58–59) took זכו as a Hebraism, Cook (2015: 71) commented that "the root is well-established in Aramaic." In ancient Jewish literary Aramaic, Dan. 6:23 uses the term to emphasize Daniel's "innocence" before God.

3.7.3. *Fragmentary Forecasts of Judgment and Juxtaposition of Light and Dark (4Q542 2)*

This fragmentary bit of text likely continues Qahat's discourse. The language touches on eschatological judgment and binaries of light and darkness.

5 [...]ל̇ס̇קרא י̇[...]
6 [...]ל̇ס̇ בנוהי̇[...]
7 [...]ל̇ס̇ באנושא ובח̇י̇[...]
8 [...]ל̇רצא [...]
9 [...]מרש̇ל̇[...]
11 [...]ל̇ס̇יהון ו[...]
11 [...]ה̇ש̇וך ולח̇[שוכא...]
12 [...]ונהיר להן [...]
13 ואנא רוז̇נ̇[א...]
Bottom Margin

5. [...to] call/read [ ]
6. [...]... his sons[...]
7. [...]... in humanity and in living[...]
8. [...]... [...]
9. [...]...[...]
10. [...up]on them and...[...]
11. [...]darkness and to dark[ness...]
12. [...]and light for them [...]
13. and I, [the] prince[...]

Textual, Scribal, and Material Notes

Primary images for transcription: PAM M43.565; B-359480; B-359479.

Line 8: ל̇רצא – This character cluster is the remnants of a full word. Eisenman and Wise (1992: 149) read רצא/ד, with both the *dalet* and the *resh* as possibilities.

Line 9: מרש̇ל̇ – Here too, only a partial word has survived. Eisenman and Wise (1992: 149) read the shorter מרש and do not include a final *aleph*. Puech (2001: 280) included a possible *aleph* as the fourth character.

Line 10: ו יהון[עֿל ○ – ("up]on them and...") – Puech (2001: 280) reconstructed the last word as וֿ]לֿ. This is possible, but the traces of a second character are too small and faint to venture a guess.

Line 11: ולח]שוכא ("and to dar[kness") – The character formation and ink density for the three extant characters of this form indicate a correction. Puech (2001: 280) suggested the extant letters originally read ומם, which is possible but difficult to recover on the fragment. I accept Puech's proposal here tentatively, based mostly on the context of the previous word and light vs. darkness theme implied by the following line.

Commentary

Line 5–6: *to] call/read...[...]...his sons.* Both the content and context of this fragment are limited, allowing for only preliminary observations. The phrases and forms here suggest the material relates to a scene of paternal instruction, plausibly of Qahat's instructions to the broader audience of his immediate offspring. Note, however, the third person suffix on the form בנוהי ("his sons"). If the verb in line 1 is understood in the sense of "to call," this fragment may be part of a narrative description of the gathering of Qahat's children prior to his address to them. The verb features in this way in similar settings in the Aramaic DSS (1Q20 12 16; 4Q545 1a i 9; *ALD* 82 [MS A, Cambr. e 6 5]). Alternatively, if it is understood in the sense of "to read," it may relate to the topic of ancestral writings, which is a key theme of 4Q542 1 ii 11–13. Compare also the uses of the verb in this sense in *GenAp* (1Q20 19 25).

Line 7: *in humanity and in living.* In view of the language of light and darkness later in the fragment, it is possible that these forms relate to a depiction or explanation of judgment upon humanity. However, without greater context, this is a conjecture.

Line 8–9: *[...]...[...]...[...].* These lines include only partial words, the meanings of which are unknown. They read: [...]○מרש[...] ○רצא[...]. Since the character cluster ○רצא is followed by a space, this is most certainly the end of a word. As Puech (2001: 280) noted several possible forms could have been here: פרצא ("the breach"), קרצא ("the portion, piece"), כרצא ("the slander"), or חרצא ("the kidneys"). Of these potential forms, only the final term occurs in the Aramaic DSS, within a description of the sacrificial process in *ALD* 28 (חרצא, 4Q214 2 6; [MS A, Bodl. d 9 9]). A reference to sacrificial terminology here in 4Q542, however, seems difficult given the dualistic language of the following lines.

If the second reading is understood as a full form, it may be a *peal* infinitive or *haphel* participle of the root רשא (Puech 2001: 280). If the form is related to the root רשי, it may also have some association with authorizing or permitting something (cf. 4Q546 2 1).

Line 10: *up]on them and.* This language is at first reminiscent of earlier statements of benediction or blessing upon Qahat's progeny in 4Q5421 i 1; 1 ii 3. However, the third person plural suffix on the first form, עֿל[יהון, suggests a group that is not the same as the immediate progeny. If the seemingly dichotomous language of light and dark in lines 11–12 are any indicator, the "them" here could refer to a positive outcome of some eschatological or judgment scenario for the priestly progeny (cf. 4Q542 2 12). Alternatively, it may also relate to the negative fate of the outsider, perhaps the group introduced in 4Q542 1 ii 6–8. Final answers lie beyond the fringes of the available fragmentary text.

Lines 11–12: *darkness and to...[...]and light for them.* The extant forms and phrases of these lines suggest a binary or dichotomy of some sort. Yet this could also be more perceived than actual, given that light and dark language are essentially all that has survived here. In the context of *WQ*, the concept of illumination has already been applied to the priestly lineage (4Q542 1 i 1). The dividing line is largely between an insider priestly group and an outsider that is guilty, wicked, and brings the risk of diluting the priestly inheritance.

Line 13: *and I, the prince.* While the form רוזן]א is highly fragmentary, the reading is relatively clear. Its meaning in context, however, is far murkier. The noun רוזן occurs only here and in the *Book of Giants* (4Q530 2 ii + 6–12 2). The occurrence there is in Gilgamesh's words of the divine judgment awaiting the giants and the cursing of רוזניא ("the princes"). Stuckenbruck (1997a, 107) commented that the reference is open to interpretation: the noun may refer to human rulers or indicate a tradition that distinguished between factions of the giants.

The first-person pronoun, ואנא, suggests that the previous content was framed as a discourse delivered by Qahat. It cannot be ruled out, however, that the voice here is of another source of authority. For the occurrence in *WQ*, we would then have multiple interpretive options for identifying this authority.

First, if the "I" speaker here is Qahat the form רוזן may be a self-referent indicating some political association and connotations of his priestly line. This is an intriguing possibility in view of the Levi traditions that underscore the political-religious domains of the priestly office (1Q21 1 2; 4Q213 1 ii–2 15).

Second, the form may not be a self-reference, but a word spoken by Qahat against some singular tyrant or ruler. This would introduce an interesting political dynamic to the likely eschatologically oriented judgment sections of *WQ*.

Third, if the "I" here is not Qahat but some otherworldly revealer, the form רוזן could also be either a positive self-referent for the authority and position of an angel or, similar to the second option, a word spoken against a human ruler. Note that in both *ALD* (4Q213a 2 18) and *VA* (4Q543 10 1; 4Q544 1 12; 2 15–16; 3 1) we hear the voice of angelic revealers also in the first-person. If this is the case, then the present reference in *WQ* may shed new light on the perennial interpretive problem of *VA* related to the names of the angels of light and darkness (4Q544 2–3). Could it be that *WQ* here contributes to this tradition with a reference to one of the figures as a prince of some description? In the end, none of these avenues of interpretation can be travelled further than the fragment allows.

3.7.4. *A Warning against Promiscuity (4Q542 3 i–ii)*

A fragment referencing the motif of promiscuity featuring a unique style of vertical, marginal scribal intervention.

Col. i ? [...]ֹל שורשֽׁ [...]
Col. ii 11 [...]בה יקרו אָבֿנָיא אֹ[...]
Col. ii 12 [...]ץֹ[...] להון מנ זנותא שגי מן די[...]
Col. ii 13 לחדה די לא אי תאי לה כול בֿ[...]
BOTTOM MARGIN

Col. i ?. [...]... its root[...]
Col. ii 11. [...]in it, the stones were heavy ...[...]
Col. ii 12. [...]... they will be from/out of much fornication after [...]
Col. ii 13. much, for he does not have any...[...]

Textual, Scribal, and Material Notes
Primary images for transcription: PAM M43.565; B-359482; B-359481.

Column i, line ?: ֹל שורשֽׁ[...] ("...its root") – This phrase, and more content now lost, is written vertically down what seems to be an intercolumnar margin. The form is also subject to a correction, in the form of a supralinear insertion of the *he*. The resulting text goes down into the bottom margin of the fragment. It is unknown how much content was included in this position, what line it began on, or why it was added to the manuscript in this way. The script is noticeably smaller, yet this may simply be a symptom of writing in a cramped space. Not enough text of the insertion has survived to gauge whether it was penned by the scribe of the manuscript or another user. As Tov (2004: 227) observed, only in "rare cases" was added content inscribed vertically. While he noted occurrences of this style of insertion in the larger Qumran collection, 4Q542 3 i–ii is the only certain instance of this type of scribal intervention in the Aramaic DSS. With varying degrees of certainty, all read an initial *vav* at the beginning of the first partial form, save for Eisenman and Wise (1992: 150), who read only a *lamed*.

Col. ii 12: להון ("they will be") – Puech (2001: 281) reconstructed slight ink traces at the front of the line as a verb, דֿ[בֿ]דֿ[י] ("to lead"), which, though possible, cannot be confirmed.

Col. ii line 13: אי תאי ("he does") – There is a noticeable space between the two clusters of characters that comprise the existential particle, איתי ("there is, are"). This is also the only instance of this fuller spelling of the adverbial particle in the Aramaic DSS. Beyer (2004: 117) proposed emending the form to לא איתיא. Muraoka (2011: 26 n. 174) deemed this unlikely, asking, "could one just ignore the BA form vocalised אִיתַי?"

Commentary

Col. i, line ?: *its root*. It is impossible to determine the meaning of this form penned in the margin. The term שרש ("root") occurs at least five times in the Aramaic DSS, with a special concentration of uses in symbolic dream-vision episodes that feature images of trees or gardens under threat of destruction as in *GenAp* (1Q20 19 15–16) and the *Book of Giants* (4Q530 2 ii + 6–12 8; 6Q8 2 1).

Col. ii, line 11: *in it, the stones were heavy*. The reference to heavy stones does not remind of any specific image or phrase from other ancient texts. If, however, the verb יקר is taken in the sense of "to be precious," the present text may refer to "precious stones." This could conceivably call to mind the extravagant architectural descriptions of an eschatological city as in Tobit 13 or *New Jerusalem*, though neither text refers explicitly to "precious stones." Arguably, the closest use of similar terminology is found in the Hebrew section of the book of Daniel, which references אבן יקרה ("precious stones") at Dan. 11:38 among the list of elaborate gifts given to idols. The similar Hebrew phrase אבני חפץ ("precious stones") occurs also in the *War Scroll* (1QM 5 9, 14; 12 12–13) and *Beatitudes* (4Q525 2 iii 3).

Col. ii, line 12: *they will be from/out of much fornication after*. While the meaning of this full phrase is not easily discerned, the reference to זנו ("fornication") connects *WQ* into an important theme of caution against promiscuity in the Levi tradition. In *ALD* 16, Isaac's instruction to Levi underscores the avoidance of promiscuity. For discussion on this motif and potential association between the Qahat and Levi traditions, see the comments on 4Q213a 1 13.

Col. ii, line 12: *much, for he does not have any*. Without further context, the meaning of this partial sentence is unknown. Puech (2001: 282) drew attention to the use of a similar cluster of forms in the Qumran *ALD* fragments (4Q213 1–2 ii 4 // 4Q214b 8 1).

Chapter 4

VISIONS OF AMRAM

4.1. *The Figure of Amram in Texts and Traditions*

Perhaps not unlike Qahat, Amram is a priestly ancestor famous only by association. If Qahat's claim to fame in the Hebrew Scriptures was he was a son of Levi and head of a clan, Amram's prominent position in the priestly genealogy is secured by the priestly status of his son: Aaron. As an individual figure Amram features primarily in the Hebrew Scripture in lists and genealogies (Exod. 6:18; Num. 3:19; 26:58; 1 Chron. 6:2–3; 6:18; 23:12–13; 24:20). The parallel traditions of Exod. 6:20 and Num. 26:9 provide the only detail of his largely unwritten biography by specifying his marriage to Jochebed, the daughter of Levi. As described below, the accent on Amram's endogamous marriage within the priestly line is amplified in *VA*. In this way, Amram's profile in the Hebrew Scriptures provided a near blank pseudepigraphic canvas to redraw the portrait of an ancestor of priestly significance in ancient Jewish Aramaic traditions.

Amram features moderately in writings of the mid-Second Temple period. As noted in the preceding chapters on *ALD* and *WQ*, Amram's role and position is already evolving in Aramaic writings represented among the DSS. *Jubilees* 46:6–47:1 includes a tradition of geopolitical tensions between Egypt and Canaan, aspects of which derived from a shared common tradition with *VA*. *Jubilees* 47:9 indicates that Moses's scribal learning originated with instruction from Amram *before* the former entered into the ranks of the Egyptian court. As described at intervals in the commentary below, Amram's association with scribal craft is key also to *VA*. *Liber Antiquitatum Biblicarum* 9:3–14 develops an intriguing blend of Amram traditions, including his words regarding the strategy to save Moses from the Egyptian infanticide as well as a covenantal promise from God for securing his eternal priestly line. This passage also features Miriam's dream-vision of Moses's ascendancy, a report that Amram and Yochebed did not believe. Amram features in the writings of Josephus (*Ant.* 2.10–223), which too link Amram with visionary revelation regarding the risks on Moses's life and the future of the nation in Egypt. Philo once references Amram, here too for his marriage to Yochebed and their parentage of Moses (*On the Preliminary Studies* 24.131). Later literatures of various collections also include passing reference to Amram for his genealogical position with primary orientation around Moses's birth (e.g., *3 En.* 1:3; 49:5; *Dem.* 2:19).

None of the above Amram allusions or episodes, however, were as ambitious as *VA* discovered in Qumran Cave Four. This text transitions Amram from a figure making cameos in other narratives and tales to the leading actor in a full feature tradition oriented entirely around him. Here he is not overshadowed by the arguably more famous ancestors with whom he is typically associated. *VA* creates a new and dynamic image of Amram that is anchored in the past yet enhances his profile with authoritative claims of revelatory experiences and scribal prowess as well as didactic performances and exemplary models for preserving the present priestly identity. The early formation of this tradition and its attestation in at least five copies at Qumran indicate a surge of interest in Amram in the mid-second century BCE in the context of the emerging constellation of Aramaic priestly literature represented at Qumran.

4.2. *Publication History*

The earliest acknowledgment of the *VA* fragments is found in a report of the content of Starky's lot of fragments (Starky 1956: 66; Puech 2001: 283). The content of the fragments remained unknown until Milik's (1972a) preliminary publication of select fragments. As noted below, the scope of fragments to be included under the heading of *VA* is of some debate. Eventually, Puech (2001: 283–406) completed the publication of the materials, presenting 4Q543–548 as copies of the same work (4QVisions of Amram^{a-f}), with the less certain manuscripts of 4Q549 published alongside with a title reflecting its ambiguity unknown relation (4QVisions of Amram^g?).

Over the years, several other editions of varying completeness have been published that remain valuable for the study of *VA*. These include: Kobelski 1981: 24–28, 35; Beyer 1984: 210–14; Eisenman and Wise 1992: 151–56; García Martínez 1992: 177–79; Beyer 1994: 85–92; García Martínez and Tigchelaar 1998 2:1084–97; Puech 2001: 268–69, 279–81; Fitzmyer and Harrington 2002: 90–96; Beyer 2004: 117–25; Parry and Tov [Puech] 2005: 413–443. Most recently, Duke (2010, 9–42) undertook a fresh and independent transcription of the *VA* fragments, presented in an eclectic edition. While his readings are at times helpful, unfortunately the organization of the text is at times less so. As such, in the commentary below I do not undertake a synthesis or integration of the fragments but present them in manuscript order and sequence indicating overlaps when present.

4.3. *Material Quality and Scribal Features*

Visions of Amram is represented by multiple manuscripts with textual overlap in several cases. In the sections that follow I categorize the relevant manuscripts for consideration and highlight aspects of their physical characteristics.

4.3.1. *Codicological Characteristics*

The scope of manuscripts representing *VA* is challenging to discern. The publication history and ongoing study of the materials often involves a broader cluster of texts of varying degrees of relation. To capture the quantity and quality of these, I propose three categories: (1) manuscripts that are *certain* to represent *VA* evidenced by textual overlap, (2) manuscripts that *possibly* represent *VA* despite the lack of textual overlap, and (3) manuscripts that may be *associated* with *VA* via tradition or theme. Note that these descriptions fall on a spectrum of certainty. The latter two groups are included here to capture the scope and context of materials that may be relevant to ongoing study. Given these ambiguities, however, I include only the certain *VA* manuscripts in the commentary that follows.

Certain manuscripts. This category includes five texts from Cave Four that exhibit definite overlap with each other: 4Q543–4Q547. Three of these fragments include components of the ancient title of the work indicating that we can be confident our manuscripts retain the beginning of *VA* (4Q543 1 a–c 1–4; 4Q545 1a i 1–4; 4Q546 1). One of the fragments carrying the ancient title also comes at the beginning of a sheet with stitching still retained at the rightmost margins (4Q543 1a). This invites questions of what preceded this sheet. Another work? A separate pseudepigraphic unit? A handle sheet? The material relationship between 4Q542 and 4Q547 also demands rethinking the compositional or codicological association of these traditions (see next).

Possible manuscripts. As highlighted in the introduction to *WQ*, Puech's recognition of the paleographic coherence of 4Q542 and 4Q547 along with Machiela's observation of material similarity of the two manuscripts indicates these Amram and Qahat traditions are in some way related. Codicologically, this opens up new questions of their textual or traditional relationship. Scribally and codicologically, then, 4Q542 is in some proximity to one certain *VA* manuscript. For discussion of whether 4Q542–4Q547 is a manuscript of *VA* or of a priestly pseudepigraphic collection, see the introduction to *WQ*.

Associated manuscripts. This category includes three main groups of fragments also found in Cave Four (4Q548; 4Q549; 4Q580). Duke (2010: 35–42; cf. Trehudic 2010) noted that the apparently different narrative voice in the dualistic fragments of 4Q548 and varying concern for Miriam's marriage in 4Q549 disqualifies these two manuscripts for consideration as manuscripts of *VA*. 4Q580 adds another intriguing, though vexing, codicological dynamic to the equation of our associated manuscripts. While this manuscript has escaped close analysis beyond its presentation in the DJD edition (Puech 2009: 415–30), a preliminary evaluation of its size, shape, and scribal profile suggests it was part of the same manuscript as 4Q548.

It is important, however, to underscore that these manuscripts may be associated with *VA* in terms of their topics of interest. That is, compositionally they are likely separate but conceptually they draw upon and extend some similar notions. For example, 4Q548 is steeped in dualistic language, at times even using terms once thought to be distinctive to Qumran Hebrew writings (Perrin and Hama

2017b). Though equally fragmentary as 4Q548, 4Q580 too features language of darkness, destruction, and truth, suggesting it may also have leveraged a light vs. dark dichotomy or binary. While the dichotomies and binaries of 4Q548 and 4Q580 cannot be read onto those of *VA*, and vice versa, together they represent early and ambitious impressions of dualism in the Aramaic priestly literature of the mid-Second Temple period. Similarly, despite some differences between the Miriam traditions of 4Q549 and the certain *VA* fragments, these may be jointly considered insofar as they represent key formations of traditions in the orbit of the figure of Miriam, a figure of prominence in the retrospective evaluation of priestly genealogies.

4.3.2. Paleographical Profile

Detailed paleographical analyses of the manuscripts suggests that 4Q543, 4Q544, and 4Q547 were produced in the mid- to late second century BCE, with the possibility that 4Q545 and 4Q546 were inscribed slightly later in the first half of the first century BCE (Puech 2001: 285). The scribe of 4Q547 also appears to have been responsible for producing 4Q542 (Puech 2001, 259: 377). For detailed paleographic descriptions of the individual *VA* manuscripts, see Puech 2001: 291, 320–21, 332–33, 353, 377).

4.3.3. Scribal Interventions

Given its representation in at least five different manuscripts, the number and scope of scribal features are too numerous to document here. While the Cave Four *VA* manuscripts are both well-prepared and well-executed in most regards, some samples here capture the scribal characteristics of the texts as well as some features which may reflect interaction by later users.

There are instances of the remnants of inter-sheet stitching or string holes in some fragments (e.g., 4Q543 1 a; 4Q544 1; 4Q547 1–2), some of which coincided with inked guide dots for directing the horizontal lines of text (4Q546 14). 4Q547 5 retains both the remnants of the leftmost stitching for a sheet as well as the stitching of an ancient repair to the ripped manuscript. There are relatively few instances of interlinear corrections or revisions, but some occur either for correction of the text as produced or received (e.g., 4Q547 1–2 7; 3 4–5; 6 2; 8 4). Such insertions at times also include cancellation dots or erasure, though the material evidence does not always permit a clear sense of the corrected text or sequence or revision. In the commentary below, I selectively detail these and other cases of scribal interventions. For more comprehensive descriptions, see the individual manuscript introductions and commentary by Puech (2001).

4.4. Prominent Themes and Noteworthy Structures

Despite its representation by at least five fragmentary manuscripts, the full scope and structure of *VA* are unknown. Regardless of these blind spots in the material evidence, the narrative and ideological infrastructure of *VA* include a rich blend themes and topics. I touch here on those that represent core characteristics of the work, with discussion of several others integrated into the commentary below.

4.4.1. *Amram: Seer, Scribe, Priest, and Patriarch*

As with the Levi and Qahat traditions, *VA* is built around a priestly pseudepigraphic persona. This time, of course, the voice is that of Amram, a liminal figure in the priestly past of Pentateuchal traditions that is now amplified using a strategic set of authority-claiming mechanisms. As noted above, Amram is an essential, though overlooked, individual in the priestly genealogy. The scribe of *VA* leveraged his place as a priestly-patriarch in the development of a new tradition that cultivated a more robust persona.

The most ambitious features of this development relate to the construction of Amram's identity as a seer and scribe. Both of these items are evident from the very opening lines of the work, which title the composition as both a visionary account and copy of a written record (4Q543 1 a–c 1 // 4Q545 1a i 1). As the narrative progresses, it is evident that Amram's revelatory account is indeed central to the narrative structure and ideological edifice of the work as a whole. Fragmentary as it is, Amram's dream-vision touches on several key topics, including: the dichotomized and dualistic structure of the world, revelation and/or recollection of priestly activities, the mysterious nature of the priestly duties of Aaron, and some features related to Sinai tradition (e.g., 4Q545 4 16; 4Q547 9 4). Upon awakening, Amram promptly inscribed the account to ensure its preservation and transmission (4Q548 9 8). This mechanism, therefore, forms a sort of linkage with the opening of the work—the very writing in the reader's hands or striking the hearer's ears purports to be a copy of this more ancient and authoritative work rooted in visionary revelation.

This complex of pseudepigraphic mechanisms is reminiscent of several other ancestral or exilic figures that are redrawn or presented as seer-scribes in the Qumran Aramaic corpus, not least Enoch in both *1 Enoch* and *Book of Giants*, Abraham in *GenAp*, Levi in *ALD*, or Daniel in the book of his namesake and possibly the *Pseudo-Daniel* materials.

4.4.2. *Extending the Roles of Amram's Offspring: Aaron, Moses, and Miriam*

Visions of Amram's interest in developing ancestral profiles extends beyond the figure of Amram to include treatments or cameos of his three children. In various ways, the character (re)formations also contribute to select narrative scenes and theological structures of *VA*. They also evidence how scribes of this period amplified the roles of ancestral figures.

As a figure of priestly prominence in the next generation, it is perhaps not surprising that Aaron is referred to by name up to three times in *VA* (4Q545 1a i 8; 4Q545 11 1; and perhaps 4Q546 12 3). Most intriguing are the allusive and suggestive references to him in fragmentary sections of Amram's dream-vision.

Drawing upon the language and terms of Levi's priestly profile in *ALD*, it seems that *VA* presents Aaron as a figure who is the head of an eternal priestly line. This line is not only traced back through a line of seven ancestors—likely Abraham, Isaac, Jacob, Levi, Qahat, Amram, and Aaron—it is presented as in alignment and continuity with the otherworldly priesthood (4Q545 4 18; cf. 4Q546 8 2). As I argue below, this is the most natural meaning of the reference to the רז ("mystery") of Aaron's work in 4Q545 4 16. These horizontal and vertical axes of the priesthood in *VA*, therefore, capture both the antiquity and otherworldly character and associations of the priestly generations that issue from Amram.

Moses's role in *VA* is arguably of less priestly consequence than Aaron. Nonetheless, his references dovetail this Aramaic priestly tradition with Mosaic tradition in a way that is not typical in the Aramaic DSS. In general, the Aramaic texts tend to treat ancestral narratives in a pre-Sinai world or exilic experience (Dimant 2006: 464–65; 2007: 203; Ben Dov 2009; 2017 Tigchelaar 2010; García Martínez 2014). In one key instance early in the narrative, *VA* reveals what it claims as the likely original name of Moses: מלאכיה ("Malakiya"; 4Q545 1a i 8; cf. 4Q543 2a–b). In this way, *VA*, an Aramaic text, rewrites a critical element of Moses backstory by giving him, or arguably recovering, his Hebrew name. In addition to this recovered onomastic of Moses's claimed original name, *VA* references the figure by his traditional name, מושה, in 4Q545 4 15. These Moses references should also be considered in the context of fragmentary materials that seem to look ahead to the exodus and possibly the wilderness experience (4Q543 16; 4Q547 9 4).

Miriam also plays a significant role in *VA*. As described below, her marriage to Uzziel champions the ideal of endogamous marriage as exemplified by ancestors in the priestly line. While Miriam's role in the narrative of *VA* is largely concentrated in the opening scene of her marriage celebration, like Aaron, she is also associated with the concept of the רז in 4Q546 12 6, the meaning of which is not easily recovered from the frustratingly fragmentary materials.

4.4.3. *Embodying and Advocating Endogamous Marriages*

As was the case in both *ALD* and *WQ*, *VA*'s accent on endogamous marriage has a clear focus on preserving the purity of the priestly line and insulating its generations and their inheritance from outsiders. The opening scene of *VA* places this emphasis on center stage as it details a marriage celebration between Miriam and Uzziel (4Q545 1a i 5), *not* Hur as Josephus would have it (*Ant.* 3.2.4). This particular example of idealized endogamy is intriguing for at least two reasons. First, it demonstrates a positive endorsement of uncle–niece marriage, an apparent item of halakhic tension among texts of the Qumran community (see the comment on 4Q543 1 a–c 5–7 below). Second, it connects *VA*'s endogamous rhetoric to that of *ALD*, which also went to great efforts to encircle matriarchs into the endogamous infrastructure of the priestly ancestral tales (see *ALD* commentary on 4Q214a 2–3 i).

Amram also plays a key role in *VA*'s advancing endogamy. This is most evident in his stated fidelity to his wife, Yochebed, during his sojourns to build the ancestral tombs in Hebron. When the borders are closed or compromised due to the regional wars between Egypt and Canaan, Amram lived as a refugee but emphasized that he did not take another wife (4Q544 1 8; 4Q547 1–2 6–8 cf. 4Q543 4 4). This instance also hints to the reader/hearer the importance of maintaining identity boundaries through endogamous unions even while in culturally foreign spaces. While *VA* does not include patriarchal discourses underscoring the essential of endogamy, it achieves this emphasis by providing models of endogamy in the lives of exemplary figures from the past.

4.4.4. *Otherworldly Beings and a Multi-Dimensional Dualism*

Whether or not "dualism" is the right—or too blunt of a—word to describe the dichotomies presented in Amram's dream-vision, it is evident that dichotomies and binaries are a feature of *VA*'s outlook. The extent and directions of the splits in *VA*, however, suggest that this text provides an essential space for articulating and reevaluation an early expression of dualism in ancient Judaism.

For *VA*, dualism is explicitly linked to the presentation of two oppositional celestial beings met in the very opening scenes of Amram's dream-vision. The descriptions and domains of both leverage the natural binary of light and dark (esp. 4Q543 5–9 5; 4Q544 1 13–14; 2 14–16). The scope of their rules, however, is not limited to a horizontal reach of two spaces on a plane: for *VA* the domains of the dichotomized rule extend also vertically (4Q544 2 16). A key feature of this constructed reality for *VA* is the beings directing each course. While the extent of the names of these figures is lost in *VA*, 4Q544 2 13 specifies at least one went by the moniker מלכי רשע ("Melchiresha"), which *may* imply their counterpart was known as מלכי צדק ("Melchizedek"). It also seems that *VA* ascribed at least three names to each figure (4Q544 3 2), indicating the text is important both for the early naming of malevolent or benevolent otherworldly beings and their convergence of identities. If that inference is accepted, the conspicuous name of the light being would be of consequence not only for the dualistic structure of *VA* but also for its priestly rhetoric (see the commentary on 4Q544 2, 3; 4Q545 4).

One of the implications, or perhaps open questions, regarding dualism in *VA* pertains to what "type" of dualism is implied in the work. While an overly rigid categorization of dualisms is not necessarily helpful, *VA* does apply or detect binaries in the oversight and structure of the cosmos. The issue of what this means for humanity, however, is debated. While some of discern a type of "free choice" dualism in *VA*, particularly in Amram's dream-vision, this is an overreading of the text and cannot guide our interpretation of this aspect of *VA*'s theology (see the comment on 4Q544 1 11–12). At most, we can say that *VA* is certainly concerned with retaining the integrity of the priestly line against outsiders—a binary or boundary in itself—and that part of this rhetoric is framed within an understanding of a dichotomized reality under the oversight of celestial beings. Whether one's place in these bifurcated domains is hard-wired or a matter of choice extends beyond what the fragments allow.

4.5. Genre

Unlike most texts discovered among the Qumran caves, *VA* benefits from three manuscripts which retain the internal title of the work (4Q543 1 a-c 1–4; 4Q545 1a i 1–4; 4Q546 1). The most relevant section of this title are the opening words retained in 4Q543 and 4Q545, which may be jointly reconstructed as: פרשגן כתב מלי חזות עמרם בר] קהת בר לוי ("A copy of 'The Writing of the Words of the Vision(s) of Amram, son of [Qahat, son of Levi'"). The ensuing lines of the narrative frame add important chronological details regarding the time and setting of the first-person discourse that follows. This content serves several functions: from securing a pseudepigraphic voice, to claiming ancestral authority, to establishing a priestly perspective, to anchoring the work in both revelation and writtenness. The question here, however, is what this title tells us about the intended or perceived genre of the work.

The affinity with, or association between, *VA* and the testamentary genre is as early as Starky's initial announcement of the materials (Starky 1956, 66). By Milik's (1972a) preliminary publication, this association had become a title for the emerging fragments, then known as "Testament de 'Amram." Drawing on his foundational work on establishing the formal features defining the Greek patriarchal testaments, von Nordheim (1980: 115–18) also accepted the classification of *VA* as a testament. In the earliest independent study of the fragments following Milik's first impressions, Kobelski affirmed this genre characterization concluding, "[i]ndeed, the content of the introductory passage of 4Q'Amram, which can be compositely read from fragments of MSS a, c, and d, indicates that the work is in the same literary category as the *Testaments of the Twelve Patriarchs*, and is in fact the *Testament of 'Amram*" (Kobelski 1981: 24). Extending on the scholarship of von Nordheim, Frey re-assessed items in the Qumran library which may be testaments or relevant for understanding the pre-history of the later developed genre. With respect to *VA*, he concluded "with regard to formal criteria, the *Visions of Amram* might be the work from the Qumran library for which the genre 'testament' is most appropriate, although in its title the work is called 'words of the vision of Amram…,' not '(words of the) testament'" (Frey 2008: 361). The assessment of the testamentary genre or character of *VA* is accepted in several other studies (e.g., Lange and Mittman Richart 2002; de Jonge 2003: 122; Dimant 2008: 28–35; Duke 2010: 122; Goldman 2020: 101–102).

Several scholars, however, have interrogated the assumption that *VA* is a testament. Drawnel (2010b) critiqued that there are major differences between *VA* and the Greek testamentary literature, suggesting that this classification is inadequate and anachronistic for *VA*. As noted in the genre discussion of *WQ* in the previous chapter, Drawnel highlighted that *VA* likely comes from a common literary background as the Levi and Qahat traditions. The essential testamentary setting of a deathbed discourse is also unclear in *VA*. Note also that while 4Q543 1 a–c 3–4 locate the narrative in the 136th year of Amram's life, the year of his death, it is not clear that this is a deathbed discourse (contra Milik 1972a; Kobelski 1981; Philonenko 1993; Goldman 2020; Høgenhaven 2020). It is near the end of his life but not his dying day.

In view of these emerging tensions with a primary association with the testament genre, it is worth considering other features of the composition indicative of its literary character. Beyer (1984: 210) was first among these, emphasizing the work is a "priesterliche Apokalypse," although his title of the texts still retains a testamentary quality ("Die Abschiedsrede Amrams"). In his description of the general characteristics and scope of apocalypses in ancient Judaism, Stone (1984: 394–95) highlighted *VA* as an exemplar of the emerging apocalyptic literature. In view of the larger trend for Aramaic writings that advance priestly interests and identities through otherworldly revelation, I extended the apocalyptic genre characterization to *VA* as a representative of what may be termed a "priestly apocalypse" (Perrin 2018).

There is no denying there are what appear to be testamentary qualities to *VA*. However, there are several problems with this genre assessment as *the* defining characterization of the work.

First, it is necessarily anachronistic and determines the definition of this genre largely upon the later Greek testamentary literature. If the lesson of *ALD* and the *Testament of Levi* has taught us anything it is that these earlier Aramaic priestly traditions should inform how we think about and characterize the later Greek ancestral texts, not the reverse.

Second, not only is the term "testament" absent in *VA*'s title, characterizations of the work as a testament steamroll what the work tells us it is: a priestly pseudepigraph oriented around a vision. While visionary revelation can and does play a role in later testamentary literature—*T. Levi* 2:5–5:7; 8 and *T. Naph.* 5:1–7:1 are cases in point—the association between apocalyptic literature and revelatory episodes is far stronger and more pervasive. As such, the visionary claims and content of *VA* should bend our genre descriptions toward the apocalyptic and away from the testamentary.

Third, while ambiguities remain regarding the narrative shape and structure of *VA*, the extant materials are comprised of several different units: a marriage feast, scenes of instructions, a travel narrative, and a dream-vision episode. Even if *VA* does represent characteristics of a testament, this diversity suggests it cannot only be characterized as such. As was the case with the Levi and Qahat materials, the common denominator to all of the elements presented in *VA* is their orientation around the figure of Amram. In this case, then, descriptions of *VA* should underscore its essential priestly-pseudepigraphic quality and prioritize what the work tells us what it is from the very first line: a visionary text.

4.6. *Compositional Date and Social Setting*

The compositional date of *VA* is technically uncertain. Yet we may triangulate a plausible range in light of the paleographical dates of the manuscripts and the compositions literary and theological affinity with other ancient Jewish works. The production of the manuscripts in the second half of the second century BCE provides a *terminus ante quem* for the composition. There is no reason to believe that any of the five certain *VA* manuscripts are autographs. If anything, the existence of the work in this number suggests a considerable degree of interest in the Amram tradition by this time. If Puech's paleographical conclusions about 4Q545 and 4Q546 are correct, this Cave Four collection also evidences continued copying of *VA* into the first century BCE.

In view of the thematic and textual affinities *VA* exhibits with the Aramaic Levi and Qahat texts, it is clear that the Amram materials draw upon and contribute to a fund of priestly traditions created and converging in late third to mid-second century BCE.

Beyond the pale of these Aramaic traditions, *VA* and *Jub.* 46:9–47:1 exhibit striking similarities in their knowledge of the Egypt–Canaan wars. Not surprisingly, the direction of influence, or none at all, remains a point of debate. Some detect *Jubilees*' indebtedness to the Aramaic Amram traditions (Puech 2001: 285–87; Halpern-Amaru 2005; Drawnel 2010: 326–27). Others determined that *VA* and *Jubilees* are of no certain relationship on this point and the pair are independently drawing upon a shared tradition (Duke 2010: 98–100; VanderKam 2010). The latter position seems most likely. Once this argument for intertextuality has evaporated, *Jubilees* is of help for dating only insofar as it attests only to another independent interaction with the Egypt–Canaan war traditions in the mid-second century BCE.

So where does this leave us? In view of the paleographical and traditional considerations, Jones (2019: 4–5) summarized the general consensus on dating *VA*: "A lack of any concrete historical referents make the *Visions of Amram* difficult to date with much certainty, though there is a relative agreement among scholars that it was authored at some point during the third to early second century BCE…during the early Hellenistic period, likely prior to the Maccabean revolt." At present, this general range accounts for the available evidence without overstepping it.

The social location of *VA* is likewise unknown. Nonetheless, previous scholarship attests to a variety of potential plotted points for its production. The common denominator to most proposals is the reasonable inference that the detailed priestly knowledge and rhetoric of *VA* suggests the scribes who created it were of some priestly pedigree. Their place, proximity, and perspective on the Jerusalem establishment, however, is where we find variation among scholarly proposals.

Duke (2010: 85–88) argued that the geographical interest in Hebron as well as the language regarding what he perceived as multi-colored clothing for the angel of darkness in 4Q543 5–9 5 // 4Q544 1 13 suggests *VA* was penned by a group of disenfranchised priests, likely at Hebron critiquing the opulence of the Jerusalem establishment. While inventive, this conclusion overreads both narrative geography and visionary symbolism as indicative of social location. Jurgens (2014) perceived *VA* as fitting within a larger context of priests disillusioned with the Jerusalem priesthood, though he too was critical of the specificity of Duke's argumentation. Jones (2019) recently reoriented the question by suggesting that *VA* is not necessarily a piece of an anti-Jerusalem priestly propaganda; rather he proposed that the text could have originated *within* the Jerusalem establishment, though Jones was cautious to conclude the idea is not definitive.

The potential intersection between sectarian and priestly identities has also resulted in proposals related to the Qumran community and/or its parent movement. Newsom (1990) briefly suggested the work was of Qumran sectarian origin. Pearse (2004) proposed that the most likely context for *VA* is some non-sectarian group in the late second century BCE, but that the dualistic nature of the work was of appeal to the Qumran community. Clustering *ALD*, *WQ*, and *VA* together, Frey (2010: 268–69) proposed the group of writings originated as early as the third century BCE in some priestly context beyond the sectarian community.

While many of the preceding proposals have their merits, none has been accepted as more than possibilities. Like the *ALD* and *WQ* texts, it is unquestionable that *VA* was produced by some priestly group—where, when, and by what type of priests is unknown. Yet when it comes to specific priestly locations, I share the sentiment of Walsh that "the brevity and fragmentary condition of the text means that specific proposals for the scribal context of the document need to be considered tentatively" (Walsh 2019: 121). Also, as was the case with the Aramaic Levi and Qahat materials considered in previous chapters, the Qumran social location is significant. While the production of the manuscripts there is possible but not certain, their presence at Qumran secures the community as a locus of reception. In that respect, the constellation of Aramaic Levi, Qahat, and Amram materials do benefit from a secure social location in terms of their early reception in a known community off the northwest shores of the Dead Sea. Perhaps modern scholarship's obsession with origins has overlooked the significance of this space as a social location for the use of *VA* and the suite of Aramaic priestly literature.

4.7. *Text and Commentary: 4QVisions of Amram^a (4Q543)*

There are several fragments of 4Q543 that are too small to warrant full commentary (4Q543 10–14, 17–46). Despite their limits and lack of context, some include terms or phrases that either relate to topics treated in more complete fragments or hint at content in the larger, now-lost, narrative structure of *VA*. The more notable items include the following:

1. The phrase "I am ruler" (אנה שליט) in 4Q543 10 1 likely comes from revelatory disclosure in Amram's dream-vision.
2. The mention of "Egy[pt" (מצר[ין) in 4Q543 11 1 refers to either narrative movement or the Egypt–Canaan war, a theme perhaps echoed in the mention of "the armies" (חֿיליא) in 4Q543 24 1.
3. Several fragments retain verbal phrases indicating lost first-person discourse, presumably delivered by the patriarch in some instructional setting (cf. 4Q543 12 1; 17 3; 20 1).

4. 4Q543 17 1 includes a likely chronological reference to "the years" (שׁנִיא).
5. In what appears to be some second/third-person discussion, 4Q543 18 2 references לך לבב ("to you a heart").
6. The sole surviving full form "Most High" (עליון) on 4Q543 22 2 indicates the presence of a divine title that is common in a small cluster of the Aramaic DSS (see the commentary to 4Q542 1 i 1).
7. The phrase "he sa[id], 'Oil'" (א[מֹר שמן) at 4Q543 25 2 may indicate some discussion, or instruction, of sacrificial processes, akin to *ALD*.
8. The likely form "daughter" (ברת) at 4Q543 26 1 likely relates to the Miriam tradition of *VA*.
9. Two fragments include verbs related to "weeping" (למבכין) at 4Q543 17 2; and בכה at 4Q543 19 1).
10. 4Q543 14 2 may include the phrase "[your] names" (שׁמֹהתֹ[ך) and possibly overlap with the disclosure of angelic names known in 4Q544 3, but the fragment is too small and damaged to be certain (cf. 4Q543 19 3).
11. The plural verb discourse markers "t]o me and they answered" (ע[לי וענו) in 4Q543 32 1 as well as "and] they [s]aid" ((וא[מרו) in 4Q543 33 1 likely relate to responses from the otherworldly figures of Amram's dream-vision.
12. The phrase "Behold, [he] knew" (אֹרוּ יֹדֹ[ע) in 4Q543 40 1 could also fit naturally within a dream-vision setting.

In these ways, while the commentary that follows explores fragments carrying more extant text, the preceding summaries are a healthy reminder that our knowledge of the content, scope, and shape of 4Q543 is partial and incomplete.

4.7.1. *Pseudepigraphic Title and Miriam's Marriage Celebration (4Q543 1a–c)*

This is the first of three *VA* fragments including the internal title, which frames the pseudepigraphic perspective and establishes narrative context. The opening scene features a marriage celebration for Miriam and Uzziel followed by Amram's instruction to his children. Overlaps: 4Q545 1a i; **4Q546 1**.

1 פַּרְשֶׁגֶן כתב מלי הזוֹת עַֹמְרם בר[קהת בר לוי כול]
2 אחוי לבֲנוהי ודי פקד אֹנון בֹ...[בשׁנת]
3 וֹתלתין ושת היא שֹׁנֹתאֹ דיֹ[מותה...∘∘ת מאה]
4 וֹחמשין וֹתֹרחתיׁ לֹגֹ[לות ישר]אֹל למֹ[צריׁ]ן[...עבד]
5 עַלוהי ושלֹח וקרא לעוזיאל אֹ[חוהי זעירֹ[א ואסב]
6 לה למרים [ברתה לאֲנתה ברת תֹ[לֹתין ש]נֹין ועבד משתותה]
7 שֹׁבֹ[עה יומין ואכל ואשתי במ]ֹשׁתותהֹ[וחדי אדין כדי]
8 [אשתציו יומי משתותא שׁ]לֹחֹ[קרא לאהרון לברה]
9 [כמא בר שנין...לה קרי לי ברי למלאכיה אחיכון]
10 [מן בית...דתה לעליה קרא לה]

1. A copy of "The Writing of the Words of the Vision(s) of Amram, son of [Qahat, son of Levi." All that]
2. he told to his sons and that he commanded them on...[...]
3. and thirty-sixth [year,] which was the year of [his death...one hundred]
4. and fifty-second [*year*] of the e[xile of Isra]el to E[gyp]t. [...he crossed over]
5. toward him. And he sen[t and called Uzziel] his younge[r b]rother. [And he took]
6. for himself Miriam, [his daughter, as a wife. She was th]irty ye[ars old. And he made her wedding feast for]
7. ...[seven days. And he ate and drank at] her [we]dding feast[and rejoiced. Then when]
8. [the days of the wedding feast were completed, he s]ent[a summons to Aaron, his son]
9. [who was *x* years old...to him, "Call for me my son, Malakiya, your brothers]
10. [from the house of...over him, call him]

Textual, Scribal, and Material Notes
Primary images for transcription: PAM M43.577; B-361881; B-361880.

4Q543 1 presents an inviting and confounding codicological challenge in that the rightmost edge retains stitching to now-lost material. While it is possible that this fragment was preceded by written content—as Puech (2001: 259) proposed with respect to a copy of the *WQ*—it is equally possible that a blank handle sheet came before. On strictly material grounds, therefore, we cannot know if this copy of *VA* was part of a larger collection of content. For the comparative context of consolidated traditions housed on the same scroll in the context of the Aramaic DSS and wider Qumran library, see Perrin (2021: 58–63). See also the opening material remarks on 4Q545 1a i for codicological impressions of that fragment that also retains the beginnings of *VA* in another manuscript.

Line 4: וחמשין ("and fifty") – Though relatively few semantic textual variants exist among the scant overlapping manuscripts in the Qumran Aramaic scrolls (Perrin and Diggens 2020c), this form varies in each of the three manuscripts in play: וחמשין (4Q543 1a–c 4), חמשין (4Q545 1a i), and המשׁות (4Q546 1 2). For transcription differences in the editions for the last form, see the textual notes to 4Q546 1 2.

Line 5: ושׁל[ח ("he se[nt") – The verb is partially extant here but also evident in 4Q546 1 3. While Puech (2001: 334) included the verb in the reconstruction of 4Q545 1a i 4 in round brackets, it is possible the reading there extended beyond a reasonable reconstruction of the line and involved a variant text (Duke 2010: 12). However, without a fuller knowledge of 4Q545, this remains but a possibility.

Lines 5–6: ואסב] לה למרים ברתה לאנתה] ("And he took] for himself Miriam, his daughter, as a wife") – I accept Puech's (2001: 292) minor reconstruction of the verb ואסב made on the basis of a partially extant *bet* in 4Q545 1a i 5 (cf. Beyer 1994: 86; Beyer 2004: 118; Duke 2010: 12). As noted below, this idiom also reflects common phrasing elsewhere in the Aramaic DSS for a marriage. Note also that the antecedent to this verb is Uzziel, not Amram who has been the implied subject of verbs to this point and resumes immediately with the reference to ברתה ("his daughter") reconstructed in this line based on the overlapping text of 4Q545 1a i 5.

Lines 8–10: Save for the partially extant verb שׁלֹח ("he s]ent[") in line 8, the materials here are reconstructed predominantly from 4Q545 1 a i 7–9. Due to several missing brackets in the DJD edition, Puech (2001: 292) inadvertently gives the impression of extant text in the present fragment. Since the text is not technically extant for these lines, I reserve the commentary here for 4Q545.

Commentary

Lines 1–4: *A copy of "The Writing of the Words of the Vision(s) of Amram, son of [Qahat, son of Levi."* As noted above, this is one of three fragments in the *VA* manuscripts that retain aspects of the composition's ancient title. The form and functions of this title may be considered from a number of perspectives, both internal and external to *VA*.

Internally, the title achieves a number of aims related to the literary form and structure of *VA* as well as the scribal strategies for claiming authority to the work as a whole. The title introduces both the persona of Amram as well as prepares the reader for hearing his life and times reported in the first-person voice. Along similar lines, Jurgens (2014: 9) remarked that "unlike third-person narrated accounts of the exceptional experiences of significant figures, the first-person perspective of the Vision of Amram creates the effect that the reader is not simply reading a biography of the patriarch, but is reading the first-hand experiences and words of Amram himself, asserting the sacred and esoteric nature of the text and its contents and affirming its authoritative value." As a figure, Amram is introduced for his place in the priestly genealogy: he is a son of Qahat and grandson of Levi. As was the case in both *ALD* and *WQ*, the integrity and direction of the priestly ancestry is a core concern.

As noted in the introduction to *VA*, Amram is at best a placeholder in priestly genealogies in the Hebrew Scriptures. He is essentially a nobody but becomes a somebody by virtue of his association with his more famous forebears. As such, the scribe of *VA* overlaid his nascent authority as a priestly figure with other qualities in the opening lines to communicate that Amram's first-person voice was worth hearing. Amram's scribal authority is flagged at the very outset as the text is introduced as a פרשגן כתב associated with Amram, terms which Popović (2017: 317) also noted function paratextually to secure an authoritative and pseudepigraphic perspective. Amram's first impression in *VA*, therefore, is both scribal and priestly.

This is compounded with his additional association with visionary revelation. The accounts that follow are not only claimed to originate in antiquarian ancestral lore, their contents are inextricably bound to Amram's report, that is his מלי, derived predominantly from הֹזוֹת. This is scribal mastery: four words in, at the top of a sheet, and the creator of *VA* has already redrawn a flat character from the Hebrew Scriptures as an integral priest, accomplished writer, and apocalyptic seer.

These associations and authority-claiming strategies are also anchored into a clever substructure of the work of *VA*, which is not altogether clear to a reader/hearer until later in the narrative. In 4Q547 9 8, Amram relates: ואנה אתעירת מן שנת עיני וחזוא כתב[ת ("Then I woke up from the sleep of my eyes and inscribed the vision"). This mechanism essentially connects the title of the work with a purported writing inscribed by Amram himself within the narrative. This compounds the claimed authoritative status of the work as a whole: the complex of pseudepigraphic mechanisms not only presents Amram as an authoritative figure but the very work of *VA* as an authoritative artefact of his handiwork.

Externally, both the details and aims of *VA*'s title find new meaning. Several other writings among the Aramaic DSS also feature titles as a paratextual feature, often deploying similar terms (Perrin 2013). For example, the introduction of an ancestral work or visionary unit as a פרשגן is also a feature of *GenAp* (1Q20 5 29) and *Book of Giants* (4Q203 8 3–5). *1 Enoch* 14:1 does likewise: however, the Aramaic for this section is not extant among the Qumran fragments. The form also occurs in the purported imperial documents and dispatches in Ezra (Ezra 5:6; 7:11; cf. Ep. Jer. 6:1; cf. the analogous Hebrew term פתשגן in Esth. 3:14; 4:8; 8:13). In later testamentary literature, von Nordheim (1980: 117) proposed that the Aramaic פרשגן was likely behind the Greek formulae framing sections of the *Testaments of the Twelve Patriarchs* as "A Copy (ἀντίγραφον) of the Testament of X" (*T. Reub.* 1:1; *T. Zeb.* 1:1; *T. Naph.* 1:1; *T. Gad* 1:1; *T. Asher* 1:1; *T. Jos.* 1:1; cf. Frey 2010: 360–61 for comparison of other aspects of introductory formulae).

The introduction of a work, or unit within a work, as a כתב finds even broader representation in other literatures. Among the Aramaic texts, this feature occurs again in *GenAp* (1Q20 5 29) and *Book of Giants* (4Q203 8 3–5; cf. *1 En.* 14:1). More significant for *VA*, however, is that both *Words of Michael* and Tobit pair this claim to textuality with language of capturing the veritable "words," מלי, of the lead persona of the text. *Words of Michael* launches its bold angelic pseudepigraph with the following fragmentary title: מלי כתבא די אמר מיכאל למׂלאכיא עֹ[ד ("The words of the writing that Michael said to the angels conc[erning"; 4Q529 1 1). While the Aramaic of Tobit's title and early narrative are not extant at Qumran, it is significant that the Greek frames the works as: Βίβλος λόγων Τωβιθ ("The book of the words of Tobit"). A reasonable retroversion of this into Aramaic suggests that the *Vorlage* here likely read כתב מלי טובי, which is also reminiscent of the Syriac tradition of Tobit, ܟܬܒܐ ܕܡܠܘܗܝ ܕܛܘܒܝܐ. Though the textual nature of the title is not present in the *Prayer of Nabonidus*, that work too commences with the claim to hold the maddened king's verbal report (4Q242 1–3 1).

From the above examples, the cast of characters associated with such words and textual artefacts are diverse, including: antediluvian ancestors and monsters, priestly patriarchs, named angels, insane heads of empire, and Jewish exiles. Yet despite this diversity, the form and function of these titles align with some common patterns for constructing multi-tiered authority-claiming and conferring strategies.

Lines 2–4: *All that] he told to his sons and that he commanded them on... [...]and thirty-sixth [year,] which was the year of [his death...one hundred] and fifty-second [year] of the e[xile of Isra]el to E[gyp]t.* This material is part of the title of *VA* yet serves a different purpose than the initial elements of line 1. If that content was about introducing an authoritative pseudepigraphic persona, this material provides key details of the literary context for the narrative that follows. This involves at least two types of information.

Admonition: we are informed that Amram's words were delivered in a discourse to his immediate progeny, particularly his sons. Perhaps ironically, the opening scene of the work in the lines that follow center on Miriam, his daughter! Regardless, this context-setting element of the title underscores that Amram's words were also discursive and directed at his offspring. The emphasis on this instruction as commanding, √פקד, is also noteworthy as this verb functions across the Aramaic Levi, Qahat, and Amram materials to express the ongoing instruction of inherited lore through the priestly generations. In this respect, Drawnel's (2006: 72) recognition of the thoroughly didactic quality of the three writings is relevant.

Chronology: lines 3–4 set the narrative on a timeline along two axes. The first is in terms of Amram's lifetime. Note, however, that while the narrative is framed as occurring in the year of Amram's death, *VA* is *not* presented as a deathbed discourse. Rather, as we learn from 4Q545 1 a i 3, the discourse was delivered in the 136th year of Amram's passing—it does not follow that it was his dying day. Second, the narrative is clocked in light of the patriarchal sojourns to Egypt. The terminology is intriguing as this residency turned slavery in North Africa is described in *VA* using the term גלו ("exile") with the collective captive group understood as ישראל ("Israel"; cf. 4Q545 1a i 4). The only other extant occurrence of the term גלו in the Qumran Aramaic corpus occurs in the so-called *Pseudo-Daniel* fragment of 4Q244 12 4, in the context of a review and reflection on the causes of the Babylonian exile. As such, the reference in *VA* is unique insofar as it understands the captivity of Egypt in the ancestral past as an "exile," of sorts, and one that involved the nascent nation. Finally, the form of the chronological marker here in *VA* also invites comparison with similar phrasing in the Hebrew *Apocryphon of Jeremiah*, which seems to utilize the form at the outset of a narrative unit relating to a letter dispatched from Jeremiah in Egypt to the exiles in Babylon (4Q389 1 6).

These two aspects of the title for setting time and place of the narrative are also relatively common features of other titles represented in the Qumran Aramaic texts or inferred from later witnesses. Compare, for example, the framing content at the outset of Tob. 1:1–2; *1 En.* 14:1; *Book of Giants* (4Q203 8 3–5), *Words of*

Michael (4Q529), and *Prayer of Nabonidus* (4Q242 1–3 1–3). Therefore, as was the case with the phrases of line 1, the function of the content from the title in lines 2–4 fits within a larger complex of titular materials that take shape in the Second Temple period.

Lines 4–5: *he crossed over] toward him. And he sen[t and called Uzziel] his younge[r b]rother.* The opening scene of the narrative begins with Amram apparently moving towards something or someone to summon his sibling Uzziel. Aspects of this line are drawn from the extant material for the title to narrative transition in 4Q545 1a i 4–5. The Hebrew Scriptures record Uzziel primarily for his place in genealogies as a son of Qahat or member of that clan (Exod. 6:18, 22; Num. 3:19). His children, however, ascend to important roles in some critical passages for early priestly identities. After flames engulf Nadab and Abihu, Moses summons Uzziel's sons, Mishael and Elzaphan, to remove their toasty corpses from the camp (Lev. 10:4). Numbers 3:30 names Uzziel's son, Elizaphan, as the head of the ancestral house of the Qahatites. In these ways, while Uzziel is a flat character in the Hebrew Scriptures, his progeny is significant in the ongoing history of the priestly patriarchs. It may be that the important profile of Uzziel's offspring in early priestly traditions is what presented him as an ideal figure to integrate into narratives about priestly identity and genealogy. This is a topic which, of course, is established in *VA* largely on account of Uzziel's marriage to Miriam in the following lines.

Lines 5–7: *[And he took] for himself Miriam, [his daughter, as a wife. She was th]irty ye[ars old. And he made her wedding feast for]...[seven days. And he ate and drank at] her [we]dding feast[and rejoiced.* The opening narrative of *VA* centers on the figure of Miriam as it relates to her marriage to Uzziel. This celebration, however, has a strong didactic accent as it aims to establish priestly identity, which is a shared emphasis with *ALD* and *WQ* (Goldman 2013: 239–40). Amram's assurance of an endogamous marriage and Miriam's embodying that ideal are presented as a celebration in the narrative but, at a higher level, they present Miriam as the personification of an ideal. Later in the narrative, Amram will also embody endogamy in his testimony of fidelity to Yochebed despite their separation (4Q543 4 4; 4Q544 1 8; 4Q547 1–2 7). In this regard, the integrity of the priestly line in this Aramaic literature often refers to, or even rewrites, scenes where daughters and mothers within the genealogy are significant (e.g., Dinah, Yochebed, Miriam).

In addition to the above-noted ideological infrastructure of priestly endogamy, the nature of the marriage relationship presented in the opening scene of *VA* invites consideration from philological, legal, and tradition-historical perspectives.

First, the structure of the Aramaic phrase ואסב לה למריע ברתה לאנתה, which seems rather rigid, reflects a fairly stable idiom for securing a spouse in Aramaic literature of the period. Other variations on the "(not) taking a wife for oneself" idiom occur in *ALD* 62; 73; 1Q20 6 7–10; 20 9, 27, 34; 4Q197 4 i 19 (Tob. 6:12; cf. Tob 1:9; 4:12); and 4Q544 1 8. In this respect, it is significant that this Aramaic literature not only exhibits a common focus on endogamous unions but seemingly shares a formal linguistic structure for expressing that interest.

Second, Miriam's résumé begins with roles in the Hebrew Scriptures (Exod. 15:20–21; Num. 12:1–15; 20:1; 26:59; Deut. 24:8–9; 1 Chron. 5:29; Mic. 6:4) yet extends into several Second Temple period writings. Several scholars have amassed Miriam texts and traditions that indicate a larger reach and reception of her profile: 4Q365 6b 5–6; 6a ii + 6 c 1–7 (cf. Exod. 15:20–21); 4Q377 2 i 9; *Ant.* 2.212–15, 221, 226; 3.54, 105; 4.78; *Agr.* 80–81; *Contempl.* 87; *Leg.* 1.76; 2.66–67; 3.103; *Dem.* 3; *Ezek. Trag.* 18–26; *Jub.* 47:4; *LAB* 9:10; 20:8 (cf. White Crawford 1992; Brooke 1994; Puech 2001: 365; Feldman 2013; Tervanotko 2016). This list indicates that Miriam's profile in *VA* is part of a larger emerging portfolio, of which the Qumran finds are the earliest entries. While fragmentary and of questionable relationship to *VA* (see the introduction above), 4Q549 provides another glimpse into the formation of Miriam traditions in the Aramaic DSS. In that text, Miriam seems to be referenced in the context of her genealogical association with the priestly line, specifically for her parentage of Sithri (4Q549 2 9) and presumably also Mishael and Elizaphan, as these three are recorded as the sons of Uzziel in the Hebrew Scriptures (Exod. 6:22).

Beyond Qumran, the most significant tradition of consequence for *VA* is found in Josephus, who also references a Miriam marriage tradition. The difference there is her union is not to Uzziel but to Hur (*Ant.* 3.2.4). As such, we see roughly contemporary and competing traditions around Miriam's marriage already in the Second Temple period. Incidentally, Hur is also mentioned in the fragmentary text of 4Q549 2 1, 9. The question is: Who is Hur? Exodus 17:10–12; 24:14 acknowledge a Levite named Hur upholding the arms of Moses in battle against Amalek. Exodus 31:2 references a Hur, a Judahite craftsmen of the tabernacle. To add even more complexity to later traditions, the Talmud later asserts Miriam's union to Caleb (*b. Sotah* 11b–12a; cf. 1 Chron. 2:19). In this way, not unlike the Dinah as a wife of Job tradition (*B. Bat.* 15b; *Gen. Rab.* 19:12), it seems some later exegetes were in the business of retroactive matchmaking for the ancient unbetrothed in Jewish memory. Regardless of who Hur is, for a text like *VA* the association of liminal priestly significance was likely unsatisfactory for a core family member of the early priestly line. As such, an imagined, arranged wedding between Miriam and Uzziel advanced endogamy, thereby ensuring the integrity of the early generations of the priestly line.

Third, the opening scene of *VA* invites a cultural conversation around the legal parameters of approved, or disapproved, relationships with extended family. *Visions of Amram* presents an uncle–niece marriage here for the preservation of the priestly line. This is not to say the celebratory scene is necessarily a full endorsement of the practice—yet it does imply that such a union was acceptable, even promoted, so long as it served to preserve the priestly lineage (cf. Tervanotko 2015b). The uncle–niece marriage, however, does present a potential tension with views represented among the sectarian literature of Qumran. At least three texts in the collection prohibit uncle–niece marriage (CD 5 7–11; *Temple Scroll* [11Q19] 66 15–17; 4Q251 17 2–3). The last text of this list in fact critiques a group who deems the practice acceptable. If we are correct in mirror reading this in light of latter rabbinic literature, we learn that the rabbis permitted the practice, which may suggest there is a heritage to earlier perspectives in Pharisaic Judaism (*b. Yebam.* 62b; *b. Giṭ.* 83a; *b. Sanh.* 76b). This diversity of opinion, of course, develops out of Lev. 18:7–20, which is sufficiently ambiguous on the matter of uncle–niece unions. As Duke concluded, considering *VA* in the context of other writings on this matter "clearly demonstrates that 1) these types of [uncle–niece] marriages were happening and 2) these types of marriages were frowned upon by some groups soon after *VA* was written" (Duke 2010: 65).

In the context of such legal developments in these writings and groups, *VA* makes an important contribution insofar as it points to an apparent variety of perspectives among groups of the Second Temple period and reminds us that we should not expect or insist upon uniformity throughout the Qumran collection. As White Crawford (2003: 39) also noted, it is possible that the given position in one writing was permitted without the awareness of other perspectives or prohibitions from other traditions. While we have the luxury of laying all these materials out before us in a neat, comparative synopsis, we cannot assume ancient scribes or communities had the same access or awareness of the same scope of traditions.

Lines 8–10: *the days of the wedding feast were completed, he s]ent[a summons to Aaron, his son who was x years old…to him, "Call for me my son, Malakiya, your brothers from the house of…over him, call him].* Since these lines are heavily reconstructed based on overlap, for discussion of their content see the commentary on 4Q545 1a i 8–9.

4.7.2. *Amram's Instruction and Onomastics of Moses's Hebrew Name (4Q543 2a–b)*

Elements of Amram's initial instruction following Miriam and Uzziel's wedding feast. The topics include wisdom and justice as well as onomastics of Moses's Hebrew name. Overlap: 4Q545 1a i.

1 [...]ממרך ונתן לך [...]
2 [...]דֹרֹי עלמין ונתן לך חכמה [...]
3 [...]ׂ[...]ׂ[...]י[הוסף לךְׂ[...]
4 [...]אל תהוה ומלאך אל תתקרה [...]
5 [...]תעבר בארעא דא ודין ׂמון ׂ[...]
6 [...]יהך לה שמך לכל מ[...]ׂ[...]
7 [...]כל דרי עלמ[י]ן.[...]
8 [...]בה תעבד[...]
9 [...]ׂתׂשר [...]

1 [...] your command. And he gave you [...]
2 [...]...eternal generations and he gave you wisdom [...]
3 [...]...[...]...[he] added to you[...]
4 [...] of God you will be. And the messenger of God you will be called [...]
5 [...] you will do in this land, and judgment…[...]

6 [...]...to him your name for all...[...]
7 [...]all etern[al] generations[...]
8 [...]in it you will do[...]
9 [...]...[...]

Textual, Scribal, and Material Notes
Primary images for transcription: PAM M43.577; B-361889; B-361888; B-361891; B-361890; B-361887; B-361886.

Line 1: ממרך ("your command") – Note the morphological variant with the overlapping form מֹמרכה in 4Q545 1 a 14.

Line 2: דֹרִֹי ("generations") – Puech's (2001: 294; cf. Beyer 2004: 118) reading is possible but this section of the manuscript is heavily effaced with but a few ink strokes. Note the parallel phrase also in line 7. Beyer (1994: 86) and García Martínez and Tigchelaar (1998 2:1084) do not venture any reading of these traces. Duke's (2010: 14) composite text is wrong here as it reads דֹרִי, yet does not include forms of "eternal," which is clear on 4Q543 2a–b 2 (עלמין) and plausible on 4Q545 1 a 15 (על[מֹיִן).

Line 4: אל ("of God") – Puech (2001: 294–95) here reconstructs [בחיר] אל ("l'élu de] Dieu"). With this, compare the phrasing in 4Q534 1 i 10 (בחיר אלהא) and 1QpHab 10 13 (בחירי אל). Duke (2010: 14–15) reads [ידיד] אל ("friend] of God"), which is made on the basis of a parallel phrase in *ALD* 83b. While Puech (2001: 295) rightly noted that whatever the head noun is here it parallels the phrase מלאך אל ("the messenger of God") later in the line. Without a more complete knowledge of this text we cannot conjecture what was lost.

Line 7: כֹל דרי ("all generations") – The *kaf* on the first form is certainly debatable, even on the new infrared images (B-361891). Regardless, the reading here is plausible and taken with Puech (2001: 295) and the partial reconstruction reading of Duke (2010:14). Early proposals of the potential reading לדרי, taking the extant text together, remain a possibility (Beyer 1994: 86; García Martínez and Tigchelaar 1998 2:1084).

Line 9: תֹשֹׁר° ("...") – The first two characters of this form are uncertain, but the *tav* seems likely (Puech 2001: 295). Duke (2010: 14) proposes the form יֹת[חשב ("it will] be reckoned"). Earlier proposals of reconstructing the form ישר[אל] here, therefore, overread the text (Beyer 1994: 86; García Martínez and Tigchelaar 1998 2:1084).

Commentary
Lines 1–8: *your command. And he gave you [...]...eternal generations and he gave you wisdom [...]...[...]...[he] added to you[...] of God you will be. And the messenger of God you will be called [...]you will do in this land, and judgment... [...]...to him your name for all...[...]all etern[al] generations[...]in it you will do.* The fragmentary material comes from Amram's discourse to Aaron, Moses, and perhaps others, in his initial discourse to his children following the marriage

celebration between Miriam and Uzziel. This narrative flow is evident from the minor overlaps and sequence of 4Q545 1a i. The nature, topics, and scope of the discourse are unknown. It is possible, however, to recover some hints. Given that the pronominal suffixes on both prepositions and verbs are second person, singular forms—save for the sole third person suffix in line 6—this material is undoubtedly spoken over or about an individual.

As noted in the commentary to 4Q545 1a i 9, Beyer and Duke are correct that Amram referred to Moses by his Hebrew name, מלאכיה, when gathering his children for a moment of instruction. With that association in view, line 4 of the present fragment provides something of an etymological exposition on that name. Høgenhaven (2020: 127; cf. Duke 2010: 16) added that the reference to בארעא דא in line 5 further affirms this connection, since, in the present narrative context, that geographical referent must refer to Egypt (cf. 4Q545 1a–b ii 11). The reference to דן, therefore, suggests that Amram's opening discourse likely projected the ascendency of Moses, which will result in "judgment" upon the Egyptians in the delivery of the people. Puech (2001: 295–96) proposed that the individual in view was Aaron, but this seems less likely in this immediate context (cf. Duke 1010: 15–16; Goldman 2020: 107; Høgenhaven 2020: 127). In this respect, *VA* finds parallel traditions in *LAB* 9:10, in which Miriam received a dream-vision forecasting Moses's rise, as well as *Ant.* 2.215–17, in which Amram is associated with revelation regarding Moses salvation from the slaughter of the innocents in Egypt.

The references to דרי עלמין in lines 2 and 7 have a larger usage in *VA* and the wider Qumran Aramaic corpus. The language of eternal generations occurs also in 4Q547 9 7, in the context of a reference to activities on Mount Sinai, which may hint at a Mosaic association, as it likely in the present fragment (cf. 4Q545 4 17). The phase occurs also in 4Q212 1 ii 17; and 1 iv 18. Variations on the similar expression דרי עלמא occur at 4Q196 17 ii 15 (Tob. 13:11); 4Q201 1v 4; 4Q213a 3 17; and 4Q542 1 ii 4. While these phrases are not unique to the priestly Aramaic literature, it seems they hold a particular currency in the register of Levi, Qahat, and Amram traditions.

4.7.3. *Reference to Egypt and Travels Outside the Land (4Q543 3)*

This small fragment includes content related to Amram's building of ancestral tombs and the war with Egypt. Given the small size of the present fragment, a material reconstruction is not terribly helpful. Overlap: **4Q545 1a–b ii**; 4Q546 2.

1 [...]וֹשׁבקוֹנֹיַ[...]
2 [...]מן ארעֹ[א...]
3 [...]לֹ[מ]צֹרוֹיֹן[...]

1 [...]and [they] left [me...]
2 [...]from [the] land[...]
3 [...]against E[gy]pt[..]

Textual, Scribal, and Material Notes
Primary images for transcription: PAM M43.577; B-361893; B-361892.

Commentary
Lines 1–3: *and [they] left [me...]from [the] land[...]against E[gy]pt*. In this small fragment, Amram confirms his isolation in Egypt. From the context recovered from the overlapping fragments indicated above, we learn that this refers to his sojourn to Canaan to build tombs, after which his father, Qahat, returned to Egypt. The geographical references in lines 2–3 also confirm this narrative movement known more fully from 4Q545 1a–b ii and 4Q546 2.

4.7.4. *Amram's Fidelity to Yochebed (4Q543 4)*

Amram preserves his marriage to Yochebed in war-torn Canaan. Given the small size of the fragment here, I do not undertake reconstructions. For fuller context, see the better-preserved overlapping fragments, including: **4Q544 1** and 4Q547 1–2.

1 אלכן ○[...]
2 ובכל דן[יוכבד אנתתי...]
3 מטרתי[...]
4 נסבת [...]
Bottom Margin

1. Therefore…[…]
2. Now, through all this, [Yochebed, my wife…]
3. my watch […]
4. I [*did not*] take […]

Textual, Scribal, and Material Notes
Primary images for transcription: PAM M43.577; B-361899; B-361898.

Line 1: אלכן ("Therefore") – As Beyer (1994: 86; 2004: 119) noted, the form is to be understood as על כן (cf. 11Q10 37 8 [Job 42:6], so Puech 2001: 297).

Line 2: [יוכבד אנתתי] ("Yochebed, my wife") – While the Aramaic is lost here, I accept Puech's (2001: 297) reconstruction of the phrase based on the parallel reading יוכבד]אֹנֹתתי in 4Q544 1 7 (cf. 4Q547 1–2 6–7).

Lines 4: נסבת ("I take") – The idiom for taking a wife in marriage here is known only by the verb נסבת at the outset of line 4. Based on fuller readings of this phrase in 4Q544 1 8 and 4Q547 12 7, it is likely that the idiom here read: ואנה אנתה אחרי לי לא נסבת ("But, another wife I did not take").

Commentary
Line 3: *my watch*. This fragment adds little new information beyond what is known from the overlapping materials indicated above. The form, however, does

not benefit from overlap and the lexical form מטרה is a *hapax legomenon* in the Qumran Aramaic texts. The gloss here is from Cook (2015: 135). CAL proposes the meaning "safekeeping" with respect to usage at Qumran, but does not specify the instance here in *VA*.

4.7.5. *A Visionary Tableau of Light and Dark Beings (4Q543 5–9)*

This fragment includes the opening discussion and description of Amram's revelatory encounter with light and dark otherworldly beings, including a description of the physical features. Overlap: **4Q544 1** and <u>4Q547 2</u>.

1 [...אנו̇[אנת̇]ן̇...]
2 [...א̇נ̇]חנא...]
3 [...ושליטי̇]ן̇ על̇[...]ל̇י̇ ב̇מ̇[ן̇...]
4 [...ו̇]נ̇טלת עינ̇י והזית והד מ̇[נהון...]
5 [...ו̇]כ̇ל לב[ושה צב]ע̇נין ו̇ח̇ש̇ך̇ חשוך[...]
6 [...] *vacat* ואחרנא חזית וה]א
7 [...וא̇]נ̇פ̇ו̇הי חעכן ומכסה ב[...]
8 [...] לחדה̇[...ע̇]ל עינוהי̇[...]
9 [...]ל̇[...]

1. [...]...yo[u...]
2. [...] "W[e...]
3. [...and rul]e over[...]to me, "Whi[ch...]
4. [...And] I lifted[...]my eyes and saw. And one of [them...]
5. [...and] all [his dy]ed cloth[ing] and pitch darkness[...]
6. [...] *vacat* Then I saw another, and beh[old...]
7. [...But] its [f]ace was smiling and he was covered with[...]
8. [...] very much[...and ab]ove his eyes [...]
9. [...]...[...]

Textual, Scribal, and Material Notes

Primary images for transcription: PAM M43.577; B-361895; B-361894; B-361815; B-361814; B-361807; B-361806; B-361813; B-361812; B-361797; B-361796; B-361817; B-361816. The bulk of the material presented above is from 4Q543 5. There are no physical joins with the other fragments, which add partial detail. I tentatively accept Puech's configuration of the fragments yet undertake only minor reconstructions below for the sense of immediate context of forms.

Lines 3–5: My rendering of several aspects of these lines departs from Puech (2001: 298). Since most items pertain to reconstructions made on the basis of revised transcriptions of 4Q544 1–2 12–13, I reserve discussion of such readings for commentary on those fragments.

Line 7: There is a minor textual variant here with 4Q544 1 13, which reads the form הַעֲבֵן. For discussion on the origins of this variation and the meaning of the root in context, see the textual note to 4Q544 1 13.

Commentary
Lines 1–3: *yo[u...] "W[e...and rul]e over[...]to me, "Whi[ch...]*. These fragmentary forms are the remains of the initial question and answer between Amram and the debating figures in the opening scene of his dream-vision. For discussion of this feature, see the commentary to the more complete text of 4Q544 1 11–12.

Line 4: *And] I lifted[...]my eyes and saw. And one of [them*. The phrase [ו]נטלת עיני והזית indicates narrative movement within dream-vision, here signaling Amram's shifting focus to different elements of the symbolic tableau. Amram's focus first falls on the dark figure, signaled by the above phrase and specifier והד מ[נהון]. He then shifted his eyes toward his light counterpart, marked by the phrase ואחרנא חזית וה[א] ("Then I saw another, and beh[old") in line 6. In this case, variations on this idiom occur in other Aramaic revelatory episodes (Perrin 2015a: 105). Compare, for example, when God tells Abram to ושקול עיניך וחזי ("Lift up your eyes and look") in GenAp (1Q20 21 9) or when Enoch relates נטלת] לשבני עיני לתרעי ה'[יכל שמיא ("I lifted] my eyelids to the gates of the te[mple of heaven"; 4Q204 1 vi 3–4 [*1 En.* 13:8]; cf. *1 En.* 62:1; 87:2; 89:2). These expressions, however, seem to also have an earlier heritage in the visionary cycle of Zechariah 1–6, which routinely features variations on the Hebrew phrase אשא את עיני ואראה ("I lifted up my eyes and saw"; Zech. 1:18 [2:1]; 2:1 [5]; 5:1, 9; 6:1) or other occurrences scattered throughout the Hebrew Scriptures (Gen. 18:2; 31:10, 12; Josh. 5:13; Ezek. 8:5; Dan. 8:3; 10:5; and perhaps 4Q364 4 b–e ii 22).

Line 5: *and] all [his dy]ed cloth[ing] and pitch darkness*. These descriptors relate to the portrayal of the dark angel in the otherworldly pair. See the comment to 4Q544 1 13 for additional context and content related to the description of this figure.

Lines 6–8: *Then I saw another, and beh[old...But] its [f]ace was smiling and he was covered with[...]very much[...and ab]ove his eyes*. This line includes both another phrase connoting Amram's shifting gaze, ואחרנא הזית, now toward the light angel, as well as accentuates his focus on the sight with the particle of presentation, והא. With the spotlight cast on this figure, Amram remarks that the figure's face was "smiling" (see the comment on 4Q544 1 14). The present fragment, however, extends beyond this with partial phrases in line 8 that indicate Amram's description also includes something over the figure's eyes.

Given the fragmentary context of these lines it is unclear what feature is described here. The feature is not likely the eyes themselves but seems to be something ע[ל ("ab]ove") the eyes. Jurgens (2014: 37–39) proposed a lost reference to a diadem, which he argues builds into the depiction of a priestly Melchizedek. If the angelic form is patterned on the human one, there is another viable option: hair. In this respect, it is significant that several Aramaic texts of the period describe miraculous figures or deity with glowing white hair. The

Enochic birth of Noah tradition indicates that the newborn's hair was both "white as wool" and "whiter than snow" (*1 En.* 106:2, 10; cf. 4Q534 1 i 2). The Ancient of Days of Dan. 7:9 famously also had hair כעמר נקא ("like pure wool"). That text also indicates לבושה כתלג חור ("his clothing was white as snow").

Given that *VA* already described the dark figure's clothing and was shown to have depicted him in terms tightly paralleled to Dan. 7:7 (cf. *1 En.* 14:20), it is entirely possible that the light figure was also portrayed as having fair garments. *3 Enoch* 28:7 also references the Holy One's snow-white hair and dazzling robes. The *Apocalypse of Abraham* 11:2 also describes the body, face, and snow-like hair of the archangel Michael with a revelatory encounter. Revelation 1:14 also describes the wool and snow-white hair of Jesus at the outset of the apocalypse. In light of both contemporary and later traditions portraying positive otherworldly beings as having white or shining hair, it is plausible that *VA* presented a similar image—although, as is routinely the proviso in Qumran studies, the fragmentary evidence does not allow certainty on the matter.

4.7.6. *Words from Qahat or an Angel for Safe Passage Home (4Q543 15)*

A discourse or discussion on the return to one's people, perhaps relating to the assurance of Amram's sojourn back to Canaan after the geopolitical unrest with Egypt.

Top Margin
1 [...]תתוב לעמֶדָ[...]
2 [...]לכלהון[...]להוא [...]
3 [...]בכל שנאיׂן ○[...]○[...]
4 [...]○ן [...]

1. [...] you will return to your people [...]
2. [...] to all of them [...] it will be [...]
3. [...] with all enemies...[...]
4. [...]...[...]

Textual, Scribal, and Material Notes
Primary images for transcription: PAM 43.578; B-361775; B-361774.

Line 3: שנאיׂן ("enemies") – Puech (2001: 302) reads the remains of an additional two forms at the end of line, אׂן ל̇[י ("là o[ù"). The available ink traces are too small to say anything definitive of the lost text (cf. Beyer 2004: 124; Duke 2010: 146). García-Martínez and Tigchelaar (1998: 1086) read שנאיא.

Commentary
Lines 1–3: *you will return to your people [...] to all of them [...] it will be [...] with all enemies*. Without a more complete context for the fragment, or benefit of overlap with another *VA* manuscript, it is difficult to discern the context of the

broken discourse here. The phrasing of line 1 indicates a context of one individual speaking words over another that anticipate the addressee's return to his people (cf. 4Q543 16 2; 4Q546 14 2). Given what we know of the dialogue partners within other *VA* fragments, as well as geographical movements in the narrative that might compromise a return to Egypt (4Q544 1 3–8), this fragment likely contains words spoken to Amram while in Canaan. The reference to enemies in line 3 also makes sense in such a context, likely referring to the warring peoples disrupting Amram's travel plans. If this is the case, then only two first-person speakers present themselves: Qahat, offering his departing words, or the *angelus interpres*, speaking a word of certainty for Amram's safe return. Either option adds new dynamics to *VA* that are yet unrecognized. If the speaker is Qahat, these would be the only certain words spoken by Amram's father in the known *VA* fragments. If the speaker is the *angelus interpres*, the fragment would extend our knowledge of the topics covered in Amram's dream-vision to include assurance of his imminent return and safe passage home.

4.7.7. Ancestral Words: Sacrifice, Virtue, and the Exodus? (4Q543 16)

Instruction from father to son including language that may touch on a variety of topics such as sacrificial processes, attaining joy for the ancestors, and an outlook to the exodus.

1 [...]ה̇[...]ר̇[לדכר] [...]
2 [...]תעבד לעמך וחדוה
3 va[cat] אדין כאלין [...]
4 עדבך א̊[נ]ה̇ ברי
5 [...] מלכא[...]ל̇[...]

1. [...]your[...] for a ram/male [...]
2. [...] you will make for your people and joy
3. [*vac*]*at* Then like these [...]
4. [...] your lot. I, my son, [...]
5. [...] the king[...]...[...]

Textual, Scribal, and Material Notes
Primary images for transcription: PAM 43.578; B-361773; B-361772; B-371305.
    Line 4: עדבך א̊[נ]ה̇ ברי ("your lot. I, my son") – García-Martínez and Tigchelaar (1998 2:1086) read עדבך לך ברי. However, what they perceived as the upper extension of a *lamed* in the PAM plates is now confirmed as a hole in the fragment in the new images (B-361773; B-361772).

Commentary
Line 1: *your[...] for a ram/male*. This fragment contains several intriguing forms and phrases, yet, once again, the lack of context only allows for possible interpretations of their meaning. If the form דכר refers to an animal, it may relate to

priestly prescriptions, perhaps around sacrifices. In the Aramaic DSS, the form is also known in the symbolic universe of the Enochic *Animal Apocalypse* (4Q205 2 i 26 [*1 En.* 89:12]) as well as in a scene of a celebratory feast in Tobit (4Q197 4 iii 11 [Tob. 7:9]). If the reference is to "male," the Aramaic corpus includes fewer comparative options (cf. 4Q531 2 + 3 9; 4Q560 1 i 3, 5).

Line 2: *you will make for your people and joy.* Other references to עמך ("your people") in *VA* include 4Q543 15 1 and 4Q546 14 2. Whereas it is possible that the occurrence in the previous fragment was in the context of a dream-vision, the same is not true here as the ensuing lines confirm a this-worldly context of patriarchal instruction. The reference to חדוה ("joy") here fits within a larger context of priestly applications of the form, often related to bringing joy to the ancestors or their names (4Q542 1 i 3, 10–11; 4Q541 24 ii 5; cf. *ALD* 12 [MS A, Bodl. a VII l.5]).

Lines 3–4: vac]at *Then like these [...] your lot. I, my son.* The *vacat* and discourse marker here confirm a new section or unit framed as patriarchal instruction. Both the subject and addressee are unknown, but the known context of *VA* permits few options. If these are the first-person words of Amram, his words are presumably spoken to Aaron or Moses, to whom he gave direction in the opening instructional scene (4Q543 2a–b; 4Q545 1a i 8–9). Given that Qahat is also present in the narrative—and perhaps even the speaker in 4Q543 15—it may be that these words are from his first-person voice spoken over Amram. If the latter, then 4Q543 15 and 16 open up a space for an increasing patriarchal profile for Qahat in the narrative of *VA*.

Line 5: *the king.* While I would like to claim this as an ancient prophecy of Elvis, sadly this is not the case. Here too we have interpretive possibilities without certainty. Since the form here is definite, it is likely referring to a specific royal figure (cf. 1Q20 20 8; 4Q196 2 1 [Tob. 1:19]); 4Q244 1–3 1; 4Q318 8 7). It seems less likely that the language here relates to the royal associations of the priesthood as initiated in *ALD* (1Q21 1 2; 4Q213 1 ii–2 15). In the context of an imminent exodus from Egypt, and a narrative already establishing Moses's ascendancy (4Q543 2a–b; 4Q545 1a i 7–9; 4 15), it is possible that this form relates in some way to an expectation of the tensions with Pharaoh. If that is the case, then the highly fragmentary references to מפתין ("miracles") near the toponym מצרין ("Egypt") in 4Q546 10 1–2 may be relevant to outlining an exodus tradition with *VA*. The non-ciphered reference to הר סיני ("Mount Sinai") in the final scene of Amram's dream-vision at 4Q547 9 4 confirms that the exodus from Egypt was indeed part of the visionary unit and narrative outlook of *VA*. Of course, whether or not the present fragment contributes to this aspect of *VA*, depends on which father and son combination is in view here.

4.8. Text and Commentary: 4QVisions of Amram^b (4Q544)

All known fragments of 4Q544 include a sufficient amount of text for commentary below.

4.8.1. *Ancestral Tombs, Amram's Endogamy, and Dream-Vision Onset (4Q544 1)*

A sequence of key scenes in *VA* including: the building of the ancestral tombs; the geopolitical tensions between Egypt, Canaan, and Philistia; Amram's fidelity to Yochebed while sojourning; and the introduction to his dream-vision. Overlap: **4Q543 3, 4, 5–9**; 4Q545 1a–b ii; 4Q546 2; 4Q547 1–2.

TOP MARGIN

1 קהת תמן למקם ולמעמרא ולמבֿ[נא...שגיאין מן בני דדי כחדא...]
2 גבר ומן עבדתנא שגי לחדא עד יֿ[...מתין...שנת רישי ברשוֿ...שמועת קרב מבהלה...לארע...וסלקת למקבר...]
3 לעובע ולה בנו קבריֿאֿ דיֿ[אֿ]בֿהֿתֿהֿוֿן וֿשבקֿ(ו)ני אבי קהת...ולמבנה ולמסב להון כל צרכיהון מן ארע כנען[...]
4 עד אנחנא בנין *vacat* וקרבא הוא ביֿן[פלשת למצרין...]
5 ואחידו גֿ[בולי] מצרין ולא איתי אפשר[...תֿאֿתֿהֿ...]
6 שנין ארבעין וחדא ולא הוינא יכלין לֿ[מתב למצרין...]
7 בין מצרין לכנען ולפלשת וֿ[בכוֿ]ל דֿ[ן יוכבד אֿנֿ]תֿתי...
8 לא הוֿת *vacat* וֿאֿנה אנתה אחֿ[רי לי לא וֿ]נֿשֿבֿת וֿנשיֿ[ן...]
9 כולא די אֿתוב למצריֿן בשלֿם ואחזה אנפי אנתתי [...וחזיֿתֿ]
10 בֿחזוֿיֿ חזוא דֿי חלמא *vacat* והא תריץ דאנין עלי ואמרין [...דֿילוהֿי]
11 וֿאֿחדיֿן עלי תגר רב ושאלת אנון אנתון מן די כדן משֿל[...לי אנחנא]
12 [...]לֿטין ושליטין על כֿול בני אדם ואמרו לי במֿן מננא [...]אֿנֿתֿ[ה בעה...] ונטלת עיני והזית
13 [...והדֿ] מנהון חזוה דחֿ[י]לֿ[ואימ]תֿן[וכל]לֿבֿוֿשֿה צבענין וֿחֿשֿיֿךֿ חשוֿךֿ[...]
14 [...]ואחרנא חזית[ ]וֿהֿאֿ[...] בחזוה ואנפויה העכֿן[...]○[...]

1. Qahat there to rise, settle, and bui[ld graves...many from the sons of my uncle together...]

2. a man and from our servants, a great many, until...[...the dead...my first year with authority...a report of war was alarming...to the land... So I went up to bury...]

3. hastily. But they did not build the graves of their [f]athers. [And my father, Qahat, left me...and to build and to take for themselves all their needs from the land of Canaan...]

4. while we were building. *vacat* But there was war between [Philistia against Egypt...]

5. And the b[orders of] Egypt were shut down and it was not possible[... she may come...]

6. forty-one years. We were not able to [return to Egypt...]

7. between Egypt, Canaan, and Philistia. Now, [through al]l th[is, Yochebed, my wife...]

8. she was not. *vacat* But I did [not] take anot[her] wife [to myself.] And wome[n...]

9. everything that I may return to Egypt safely. And I beheld the face of my wife…[…And I saw]

10. in my vision, the vision of the dream. *vacat* Behold! Two beings were disputing above/over me and speaking […]

11. And they were locked in a great dispute about me. So I asked them, "Who are you thus…[…to me, "We…]

12. […]…and rule over all humanity." And they said to me, "Which of us are yo[u seeking?"… And I lifted my eyes and saw]

13. […]the appearance [of one] of them was dre[ad]ful [and terrify]ing[… And all] his dyed clothing and pitch darkness[…]

14. […Then I saw another,] and behold[…]in his appearance. But his face was smiling …[…]

Textual, Scribal, and Material Notes

Primary images for transcription: PAM M43.571; B-370881; B-370880.

Line 1: קהת ("Qahat") – The scribe seems the have spelled the name with a *he* rather than the expected *khet*. García-Martínez and Tigchelaar (1998, 2: 1086) amend accordingly.

Line 3: ולה ("and not") – The negation is penned with a *he* not an *aleph* as we might expect and is found in the overlapping text of 4Q545 1a–b ii 17. See also García-Martínez and Tigchelaar (1998 2:1086).

Line 4: עד אנחנה בנין ("while we were building") – On the recommendation of Muraoka (2011: 227; "whilst we were building"), I take עד here as signaling that the report reached Amram during his company's construction of the ancestral tombs.

Line 5: ג[בולי] מצרין ("the b[orders of] Egypt") – Though only the *gimel* of the head noun is extant due to an effaced section of the fragment, I accept Puech's (2001: 322; so also Duke 2010: 16) minor reconstruction on the basis of narrative sense and material space. García-Martínez and Tigchelaar (1998: 1086) read ג[בו]ל ("b[ord]er"), but there are no remains of a *lamed*. Beyer's readings evolved throughout his editions from תֹ[רעי] מצרין ("Und die Tore Ägyptens"; 1994: 86) to ג[שרי] מצרין ("Und die [Brücken nach] Ägyptyen"; 2004: 119–20).

Line 7: [יוכבד] ("Yochebed") – The name "Yochebed" can be reasonably restored on the basis of 4Q547 1–2 6. Puech (2001: 322) proposed following with the אׄ[נתתי] ("ma] fem[me"). The ink traces, however, are both distant and faint for this reading.

Line 8: נֹסבֹת [לא] לי [רי אחֹ[רי אנתה אחֹ]נה[ו] ("[But], I [did not] take [for myself] anot[her wife]) – Elements of this phrase are reconstructed without benefit of overlap but are proposed on the basis of this idiom elsewhere in the Aramaic DSS. For similar readings, see Beyer (1994: 86; 2004: 199), Puech (2001: 322), and Duke (2010: 17), who did not reconstruct the negative particle. At the end of the line Puech also reads a partial form, נׄשׄ[ין] ("Cependent, des femme[s"), which is possible, but the text is highly fragmentary.

Line 10: והא תרין דאנין ("Look! Two beings") – My rendering here is informed by Muraoka's (2011: 202) observation that the cardinal number is substantive, supplying the implicit reference—only here, it is not "two (people)" as he avers, but two otherworldly figures, engaged in some action of judging.

Lines 11–12: ...]מש ("...") – With Milik (1972a: 79) and Duke (2010: 19) I do not venture a reconstruction here. Most editions infer from the answer Amram receives in the following line that the complete form here reads a variation of מש]לטין (Kobelski 1981: 26; Beyer 1984: 211; García Martínez and Tigchelaar 1998 2:1088; Fitzmyer and Harrington 2002: 92). That is, Amram's initial inquiry regarded the rulership of the angels in debate. This is plausible. However, it is not extant in the text. To compound the potential for over-, or even, misinterpretation of this line, starting with Milik (1972a: 79–80) many scholars imposed the verb בחר in the lacuna (Fitzmyer and Harrington 2002: 92; cf. Vermes 1995: 312). Kobelski (1981: 26–27; cf. García Martínez and Tigchelaar 1998 2:1088) amplified this assumption by extending the reconstruction to yet another verb, resulting in the question: במן מננא אנת]ה בחר לאשתלטה ("By which of us do yo[u choose to be ruled?"). Puech (2001: 379–80; cf. Wise, Abegg, and Cook 2005: 549) rightfully critiqued the verb בחר, proposing instead the form בָּעֵה as more appropriate. However, he retained the secondarily reconstructed verb, apparently influenced by Kobelski and García Martínez and Tigchelaar. This meant the question remained one of ultimatum and allegiance: במן מננא אַנְתֹ]ה בעה לאשתלטה ("Par lequel d'entre nous [veux-]tu [être dominé"). In contrast to these overly ambitious readings, I align with the more cautious proposals of scholars who do not venture beyond what the fragmentary material allows (Beyer 1994: 211–12; Duke 2010: 20; Maier 1995: 720). For additional critiques of past readings and a digitally informed perspective on the material evidence, see Perrin (2014: 110–12).

Line 12:]לטין ("...") – Duke's (2010: 149) reading]ל טין is similarly reserved but mistaken in the space between forms. Despite minor disagreements on the extant characters here, the beginning of the form has been reconstructed in numerous ways. These include: מהש]לטין (Milik 1972a: 79; Fitzmyer and Harrington 2002: 92); מש]לטין (Beyer 1984: 211; 1994: 87; García-Martínez and Tigchelaar (1998 2:1088); משת]לטין (Eisenman and Wise 1992: 154; Kobelski 1981: 26); ש]לֹיטין (Puech 2001: 322).

Line 13: דֹחִ[י]לֹ[וא]ימ[תן ("dre[ad]ful [and terrify]ing") – The reading is based on my analysis of the material evidence at the Israel Antiquities Authority, now published in Perrin (2014). This stretch of text has been subject to a history of reconstructions and reinterpretations, which have significant implications for interpretation (see below). Here too, Milik's early impressions have resulted in a long history of over-interpretation of the text. He proposed the reading דֹחִ[י] ל [כפ]תן ("terrifiant comme celui d'un dragon"; Milik 1972a: 79–80). Milik's reading of the first form is correct and accepted here.

The same cannot be said of the second form. While the visual of a dark angel in dragon- or serpent-like form is exciting, it introduces an otherwise unknown descriptor into the text (see the comment on line 14) as well as does so with a lexically rare form only known from later Aramaic. Despite these shortcomings, the reading has been accepted by several scholars, with variations in their preferred renderings (Kobelski 1981: 26–27; Fitzmyer and Harrington 2002: 92). Puech (2001: 322–24) took the text even further into this snake-laden territory by rereading the phrase as חֹשֵׁל [כפ]תָן ("avait mué [comme un ser]pent"), which obscures the imagery further. The first form is both unlikely in the material evidence as well as suffers a lexical deficit in contemporary Aramaic literature, which does not feature the form in the sense of "molting" implied here (cf. Dan. 2:40; for additional references, see Perrin 2014: 113–14 n. 28). Cook (2015: 52) also remarked that the meaning claimed by Puech is "implausible." Unfortunately, Goldman (2010: 427) accepted the reading without question and found a comparison with the horrifying faces of Death, three of which are snake-like, in *T. Abr.* 17:12–16. These, of course, evaporate upon interrogation of the reading.

Beyer (1984: 212) proposed the reading דח[י]ל כמו[תן] ("furchtbar [wie eine] Seuche"), thus likening the figure's foreboding visage to a plague (cf. García Martínez and Tigchelaar 1998 2:1088). Based on an independent evaluation of the manuscript evidence at the IAA and a digital reconstruction (Perrin 2014: 115–16), however, another reading emerges. Following the hunch of Cook (2012; see now Cook 2015: 52), I confirmed the viability of the reading דְּחִ[י]ל וְאִימָ[תָן], which, as seen below, has significant implications for interpretation as well as contextualization of the imagery in light of Danielic tradition.

Line 14: הָעֵכֶן ("smiling") – This form too has been subject to debate and misinterpretation, complicated further by a minor textual variant with the overlapping reading חעכון in 4Q543 5–9 7. Milik (1972a: 82) understood the form to be a reference to a "viper," thus connecting the visual to his already serpentine portrayal of the figure of darkness in the previous line (cf. Kobelski 1981: 32). García Martínez (1985: 111–14), however, rightfully noted that, judging from the phrase ואחרנא חזית וה]א ("Then I saw another, and beh[old]") in 4Q543 5–9 6, the form in question must be with reference to the light angel. That is, Amram has shifted his gaze in a lost portion of the text. In view of this contextual clue, he also argued compellingly that the form here derives from the root √האך, meaning "to laugh, smile." García Martínez (1985: 113; cf. Greenfield and Sokoloff 1992: 82; Puech 2010: 299, 328) argued that origins of the form are in the proto-Semitic root *ḍḥk*, and that the *khet* in 4Q543 and *he* in 4Q544 likely derive from confusion over the metathesis that occurs in the resultant Aramaic root, from √עחק to √חעק. As such, this results in an entirely different perspective on this element of *VA*'s vivid portrayal of the angelic figures in Amram's revelation.

Line 15: לחדה ומעל עינוהי ("very much and over his eyes") – This content is hardly legible on the fragment, save for a few ink traces of the upper reaches of lost characters. In this regard, the reconstruction is made largely on the basis of the overlapping text of 4Q543 5–9 8. Given its highly tentative nature, I include it here as only possible (cf. Puech 2010: 323). (For other variations, see Fitzmyer and Harrington 2002: 92; Duke 2004: 20.)

Commentary

Lines 1–2: *Qahat there to rise, settle, and bui[ld graves...many from the sons of my uncle together...] a man and from our servants, a great many, until.* Line 1 opens with the first recoverable reference to Qahat within the narrative. Prior to this, Qahat was only mentioned in the title of *VA* (4Q545 1a i 1). Here, however, he emerges as a figure in the travel itinerary. In this way, *VA* also contributes to the emerging complex of Qahat traditions, known more fully in the pseudepigraphic tradition of *WQ*. The reconstructed text drawn from 4Q545 1a–b ii indicates that this group also included a larger number of cousins. While it is unclear in the present text which uncle is in view here, the biblical genealogies leave us with only two options: Gershon or Merari (Gen. 46:11; Exod. 6:16; Num. 3:17; 26:57; 1 Chron. 23:6; cf. *Jub.* 44:14; and the remarks by VanderKam 2010: 152). In this respect, the group travelling to Canaan to build the tombs has a thoroughly priestly and Levitical profile (Goldman 2013: 236–37).

In the present fragment, Amram, Qahat, and their Levitical cousins comprise the contingent of travelers that accompany Amram to reside temporarily in Canaan for the purposes of building ancestral tombs. Behind this reference is the literary tradition, and logical situation, of an increasing number of deceased family members in Egypt as time wore on, including decorated ones, such as Jacob, whose dying instructions were for an internment at Machpelah (Gen. 50:1–13; *Jub.* 45:15). In *VA*, Hebron is the likely location of this ancestral burial site. The only other references to חברון in the Aramaic DSS are found in the Abram travel narratives of *GenAp* (1Q20 21 10–22; 22 3). In *Ant.* 2.199–200, Josephus also references the transport and burial of the deceased from Egypt to Hebron; however, Amram is not referenced there.

While founding ancestral tombs recalls Abraham motifs in the Hebrew Scriptures, Goldman (2013: 242) is no doubt correct that the concern for burial of the dead here in *VA* hearkens to a common theme with the book of Tobit (cf. Tob. 1:18–20; 2:3–8; 14:12). Both texts feature the families of pious Jews living outside the land who go to great lengths—even risking their personal safety—to ensure the appropriate internment of deceased family members. In the present fragment, both Amram and Qahat are associated with this activity. The tradition of founding ancestral tombs is also known in *Jub.* 46:6–10. For comment on the tripled verbs indicating Amram's narrative movement here, see the discussion on 4Q545 1a–b ii 11–13.

Lines 3–4: *hastily. But they did not build the graves of their [f]athers. [And my father, Qahat, left me...and to build and to take for themselves all their needs from the land of Canaan...]while we were building.* The content here clarifies that the nature of the expedition was to construct ancestral tombs back in the land, a task which was apparently not complete before the disruption of warfare between Canaan and Egypt (see next). The extent of the incompletion, however, is not altogether clear. The phrase א[בהתהון] (cf. 4Q545 1a–b ii 17; 4Q546 2 3) suggests that Amram is referring to how some of the members of the group did not complete tombs for *their* fathers.

Recall from 4Q545 1a–b ii 14 that this group included many of Amram's Levite cousins. While the literary context is limited by the fragmentary nature of the text, it is plausible that that group is the most natural and recent antecedent here. If that is the case, *VA* indicates that Amram pressed ahead in building the tombs while others abandoned the task. Not unlike Tobit, Amram persisted in ensuring proper burials of kin in the face of great personal risk.

The reconstructed text, drawn primarily here from 4Q546 2 3, also indicates that Qahat left Amram onsite in Canaan to return to Egypt. Both 4Q545 1a–b ii 18 and 4Q546 2 4 indicate that the construction of the tombs at Hebron was enabled by drawing upon the resources of the area.

Lines 4–7: *But there was war between [Philistia against Egypt...]And the b[orders of] Egypt were shut down and it was not possible[...she may come...] forty-one years. We were not able to [return to Egypt...]between Egypt, Canaan, and Philistia.* The construction of the ancestral tombs at Hebron is disrupted by regional warfare. At the literary level, this serves to underscore the depth of Amram's commitment to ensuring appropriate internments for deceased family members. As noted above, this draws a tight parallel between the characteristics and convictions of Amram and Tobit. It also contributes to an authentic setting of the scene in a pseudepigraphic narrative by creating a plot and casting foes from the remembered past. Høgenhaven (2020: 122) observed,

> The notion of the Philistines as playing an important role on the stage of international politics would also seem, from the vantage point of the author of *VA*, to reflect the ideas of a distant past, suitable for the situation in which the Amram narrative is set. The geographical language of *VA*, in other words, seems to be chosen to support the general perspective reflected in the composition, which presents itself as a tale coming out of the distant past, and situates its narrative between the patriarchal period and the exodus from Egypt.

From a tradition-historical perspective, *VA* here shares common ground with *Jubilees* 46, which also alludes to the Egypt–Canaan war in the context of the burial of the fathers. That tradition also includes the conspicuous reference, "Many returned to Egypt but a few of them remained on the mountain of Hebron. Your father Amram remained with them" (*Jub.* 46:10). It is unclear if this similarity betrays a source relationship between *VA* and *Jubilees*. Puech (2001: 285) concluded that the author of *Jubilees* used *VA* in its formation of this tradition. VanderKam (2010: 143; cf. 2018: 95) averred that "[t]here is no clear indication that either writer used the work of the other; rather the war in question seems to have been a motif that was available to both when they composed their works and that each adopted and adapted independently." Even with some distance between the traditions, VanderKam (2010: 153–56) tallied a number of similarities between the traditions, which, of course, *VA* and *Jubilees* develop in their own directions. These include: references to the phases of the conflict as well as its chronology, specifically the forty-one years in Canaan (cf. 4Q546 2 1). VanderKam (2010: 157–58) balanced these similarities with differences including the absence of reference to Joseph's bones in *VA* as well as *VA*'s emphasis on Amram's endogamy (see next).

In these lines, then, *VA* draws upon and contributes to a surprisingly broader network of traditions in the (re)formation of Amram's life and times as it relates to his treatment of the dead and sojourns in the land.

Lines 7–9: *Now, [through al]l th[is, Yochebed, my wife...]she was not.* vacat *But I did [not] take anot[her] wife [to myself.] And wome[n...]everything that I may return to Egypt safely. And I beheld the face of my wife.* Amram's fidelity to Yochebed in the face of danger, distance, and a long duration of separation are no mere romantic flare for narrative effect—the statement here underscores his commitment to maintaining an endogamous marriage at all costs. This contributes to the wider complex of identity maintenance achieved in part through endogamy as initiated already in the opening scene of *VA*. On this point, Goldman (2013: 238) highlighted that, while the war tradition of *Jubilees* 46 used the geopolitical unrest to explain the delay of Joseph's internment, for *VA* it served "to accentuate his [Amram's] faithfulness to his wife Jochebed by refusing to entertain the possibility of marrying a Canaanite woman during the forty-one years he is detained in Canaan."

From another perspective, however, re-presenting patriarchs as examples of endogamy occurs in several of the Aramaic DSS. Regarding Amram, *ALD* 62, 75 already established his union to Yochebed and presented the link as a key element of the ongoing genealogy of the ancestors. Even ancestors who are not priests are presented as embodiments of endogamy in the Qumran Aramaic literature. For example, while Noah's wife is technically unnamed in the Hebrew Scriptures, *GenAp* (1Q20 6 7) indicates her name was "Emzera," whom Fitzmyer (2004: 147) observed is a cousin on Noah's father's side according to *Jub.* 4:33. This tradition is also significant for Tob. 4:12, which champions Noah as a model of endogamy alongside the patriarchs of Abraham, Isaac, and Jacob.

Line 10–11: *And I saw] in my vision, the vision of the dream.* vacat *Behold! Two beings were disputing above/over me and speaking [...] And they were locked in a great dispute about me.* This material signals the next major narrative shift in *VA* toward what is, judging by the work's internal title, the central element of the composition: Amram's dream-vision. The topics and scope of the dream-vision are not fully known as they are strewn across several fragments. Regardless, the framing material found here in the introduction to the revelatory episode provides some key perspectives on its form and content.

Context: Høgenhaven (2020: 123) noted that, while the geographical setting is not explicit in preserved text, "the geographical scheme of the text indicates that the vision was indeed set in Canaan." At a narrative level, Amram's received this revelation, then, while sojourning but after both the construction of the ancestral tombs and his abandonment by his father and companions. Note that the foregoing lines underscore his commitment to endogamy until he is reunited to Yochebed, not that he has returned. This geographical and narrative context, however, do not answer the chronological question of when the dream-vision occurs. In line 6 we learned that Amram resided in Canaan for forty-one years while the borders to Egypt were shut. It is unknown when in this time Amram received the revelation.

Formula: Amram's dream-vision is introduced by a brief but noteworthy formula. He opens the account remarking that וחזית בחזוי חזוא די חלמא, with the initial verb reconstructed at the end of line 10 in light of the overlap with 4Q547 1–2 9. Internally, the formula here exhibits a slight variant with the reading there, which announces the episode with the phrase וֹ]חזית בחזות, immediately after which the fragment disintegrates. In a general sense, this formula reflects a pattern for framing revelations in the Aramaic DSS (e.g., 1Q20 22 27; 21 8; 4Q213a 2 15; Dan. 4:2; 7:1). In a particular sense, *VA*'s turn of phrase here shares key elements with Dan. 4:9 (6), in which Nebuchadnezzar demands Daniel to relate חזוי חלמי די חזית ("the visions of my dream that I saw"; Perrin 2015a: 101–102).

This formal feature is here complemented with a material philological one as a *vacat* intervenes between the introductory formula and the actual descriptive content of the account. While blank spaces serve a variety of purposes in the DSS collection and are also subject to scribal preference or perception of narrative shifts, there are several instances where either dream-vision units or sub-sections are bracketed by *vacats* (4Q112 3 ii, 4–6 18; 4Q543 5–9 6; 4Q553 3 + 2ii + 4 1–7; 4Q554 1 i 17). Drawing attention to new elements or information within a dream-vision using the particle (ו)הא is one of the most ubiquitous features of the revelatory encounters of the Aramaic texts (Perrin 2015a: 102–103). This feature, of course, has clear antecedents in the Hebrew Scriptures in dream-vision reports, apocalypses, and prophetic visions (Dehandschutter 1974: 53; Collins 1993: 162; Fitzmyer 2004: 184)

Tableau: While Amram's dream-vision will include dialogue with an *angelus interpres*, the revelation is clearly visual in nature and opens with a scene of two figures in dispute over Amram. This suggests that *VA*'s revelation falls within the category of "symbolic dreams" rather than "message dreams" as established by Oppenheim (1956; cf. Artemidorus, *Oneir* 1.1–2; 4.1), a typology that is equally applicable to the ancient Jewish dream-vision literatures of the Second Temple period (Flannery-Dailey 2004: 114–31).

The language used to describe this initial scene is both intriguing and challenging. Amram beholds two figures actively debating one another, and apparently he seems to be the subject of the dispute. The debate, however, cannot be about which figure is the recipient of Amram's body on his deathbed or after he has departed (contra Milik 1972; Berger 1973; Kobelski 1981: 24; Philonenko 1993). The narrative of *VA* is *not* framed as a deathbed account and the dream-vision unit is also set at period in Amram's life well in advance of his death. As such, an angelic contest over his body would be confusing and premature (Goldman 2010: 428; Perrin 2015a: 68 n. 70). This interpretation seems to be influenced by other traditions unrelated to *VA* (cf. Jude 9; *T. Abr.* 13:9–14 [rec. A]; *Vis. Paul* 14–17; *Ques. Ezra.* 1:14–15 [rec. A]; and *Deut. Rab.* 11:10).

The language of a תגר רב may provide a better angle of interpretation. While the verb תגר is a *hapax legomenon* in the Aramaic DSS, its occurrence in legal and contractual items from Muraba'at and Naḥal Ḥever suggests a judicial setting involving a legal dispute (Puech 2001: 325). Drawing on the earlier work of Greenfield and Sokoloff (1992: 92), Cook (2015: 250) provides the gloss of "to contend, bring a claim." This meaning applies also in later Aramaic (*Hev/Se* 9 9; *Sam. Tg. Gen.* 13:7; *b. Yev.* 100a; *Tg.* Job 31:35; *Tg.* Ps. 35:1). As such, the more helpful interpretive framework is not testamentary disputes over the corpses of the pious but angelic courtroom disputes, which Bauckham (1983: 65–66) traced to origins in priestly applications such as Zechariah 3.

Lines 11–12: *So I asked them, "Who are you thus...[...to me, "We...]...and rule over all humanity." And they said to me, "Which of us are yo[u seeking?"* The initial visual scene of debate now gives way to dialogue with Amram. These lines include one question from Amram with parts of a pair of answers retained in the extant text. It is possible, however, that the back and forth between Amram and the angels means that there is a lost question or comment from our pseudepigraphic seer. The questions and answers that ensue orient around the topic of what is traditionally referred to as dualism. This theme permeates different aspects of the revelatory encounter, but these lines hold both problems and prospects for the nature and scope of this theology in *VA*.

Amram interjects with a partially extant question in line 11 (see the textual note above). Though incomplete, this feature of Amram's dream-vision shares a rare element with the Aramaic *Four Kingdoms* text from Cave Four. In both visionary texts the seer interrogates the symbolic items directly, which in turn interpret themselves in *media res*. Typically in dream-vision literature of the period, and particularly in examples in the Aramaic DSS, dream-vision revelations and interpretations are bracketed out from one another with a separate interpretive authority unlocking the meaning of a witnessed scene or sequence within the revelation or upon awakening. Additionally, Machiela (2021b) observed that the phrasing of the questions in both texts is also similar. Compare: ושאלת אנון אנתון מן די כדן (4Q544 1 11) and ושאלתה ואמרת לה מן (4Q553 3 + 2ii + 4 5).

The figure that Amram questions here later transitions into the role of an *angelus interpres* of sorts; however, the plural verbs and pronouns in the responses that follow immediately indicate that the symbols respond in unison. Their initial response claims the universality of their rule over כול בני אדם. The language here is distinctly a Hebraism (Stadel 2008: 61) and occurs here in 4Q544 1 12 in the Qumran Aramaic texts. References to בני אדם are abundant in the Hebrew DSS corpus, yet none are preceded by כול as here in *VA*. See: 1QS 11 6, 15, 20 [sg.]; 1QH^a 9 29, 36; 12 31 [sg.], 33; 13 13, 17; 14 14; 18 30 [sg.]; 19 9; 4Q181 1 1; 4Q184 4 4 [sg.]; 4Q185 1–2 i 9; 4Q223–224 1 i 2 [*Jub.* 32:18)]; 2 iv 3 [*Jub.* 37:18]; 4Q227 2 3; 4Q258 13 2; 4Q264 1 2; 4Q381 76–77 2; 4Q382 40 1 [sg.]; 4Q385 2 5 [sg.]; 4Q386 1 i 4; 1 ii 2 [both sg.]; 4Q392 1 4, 6; 4Q408 1 1; 4Q413 1–2 2; 4Q418 55 11 [sg.]; 4Q423 4 3; 8 2; 4Q434 1 ii 2; 4Q511 26 3; 4Q577 7 4; 11Q5 24 15). There is, of course, a still larger representation of uses in the Hebrew Scriptures that is too extensive to report here. In this context of *VA*, the phrase may imply a blended type of cosmological-anthropological dualism involving the oversight of angelic rulers over all humanity (so Pearse 2004: 35). However, as we see elsewhere in the *VA* fragments, the binary building blocks of this outlook resist that sort of oversimplification.

The angels have comprehensive oversight in scope, yet they also claim a multi-dimensional rule over domains of reality, perhaps even with a created order or structure (4Q544 2 15–16; 4Q547 4 i 4). Similarly, if we consider *VA* expressions in light of those in *WQ*, we should recall the language of adherence to pure living, "not with a divided heart" (4Q542 1 i 9). In these ways, the binaries of the Amram and Qahat traditions caution against rushed conclusions about categorizing theologies too quickly.

The question Amram poses, however, has been understood variously in the history of research, in part due to inherited, or even uninterrogated, assumptions about the text and some key readings.[1] Often, interpreters perceive the answer to Amram's question as being an ultimatum between the light and dark sides in an almost Star Wars-esque type of free choice dualism. This is evident in interpretations by Duke (2010: 80), Flannery-Dailey (2004: 203, 258 n. 23), Goldman (2010: 424; 2013: 244), Popović (2010: 155 n. 17), and Dimant (forthcoming). Hultgren (2007: 321), however, offered a more reserved and cautious interpretation, remarking that after the celestial interlocutors claim rulership over humanity, "they (apparently) ask Amram, 'Which of us do you [choose to rule over you]?'" Though I disagree with the reconstruction here (see above), the slight semantic qualifier that the figures *apparently* ask Amram a loaded question related to dualisms or dichotomies is a helpful point of departure for exploring other options.

As seen in the textual note to line 11 above, the notion of free choice dualism in the dialogue with the symbolic actor turned *angelus interpres* is more a symptom of Milik's first impressions of *VA* and the subsequent acceptance of the reconstruction of the verb בחר ("to choose") in the lacuna. This, of course, *would* imply a choice. However, the reconstruction is inferential and not based on any extant overlapping text or a reasonable reconstruction based on ink traces—contra Dimant's (forthcoming) recent claims to the contrary. As such, the notion of a free choice type of dualism is entirely absent in *VA*. Here we only learn that the two beings in debate apparently relate to other aspects of the binary-built worldview of *VA*, elements of which we learn more about from other fragments such as 4Q544 2. In this regard, an early though often unrecognized critique by Davidson (1992: 266) is the most helpful perspective on the interpretive limits evident by the fragmentary forms related to the angel's response in 4Q544 1 12: "the reading is conjecture, firm conclusions should not be drawn from it."

---

1. The following two commentary sections are primarily abbreviated forms of the more detailed analyses and conclusions of Perrin 2014, with some updates in light of recent scholarship.

Lines 12–13: *And I lifted my eyes and saw...]the appearance [of one] of them was dre[ad]ful [and terrify]ing[...And all] his dyed clothing and pitch darkness.* For comment on the reconstructed phrase ונטלת עיני והזית marking the shift in Amram's focus toward the dark figure, see the comment on the extant materials in 4Q543 5–9 4. As in that overlapping fragment, the description here highlights the foreboding visage and clothing of the dark figure.

The first describes the figure as דֹחִ[י]לֹ[] ואימ[תן] (see above on this new reading). This newly recovered phrase not only adds detail to the internal images of *VA*, it results in a new external context for reconsidering the forms and phrases of Amram's dream-vision. As I argued elsewhere (Perrin 2014), the phrase closely parallels a key descriptor of the fourth beast in Dan. 7:7, who is likewise said to be דחילה ואימתני ("dreadful and terrifying"), which also comports with the description of the Kittim in *Tg.* Hab. 1:7 as אימתנין ודחילין ("terrifying and dreadful"). The Aramaic form of *1 En.* 89:30 now known at Qumran also expresses the awe-inspiring visual of the Lord of the sheep, stating וחזיה תקיף ורב ודֹ[חיל] ("and his appearance was strong and great and dr[eadful"; 4Q205 2 ii 29). In these ways, the phrasing of *VA* fits with what appears to be a larger complex of idioms for capturing either the frightful visage of otherworldly negative forces or the fantastic qualities of otherworldly positive figures.

The second element of the description relates the utter darkness of the figure's garments, which apparently reflect the shadowy nature of his domain. Though a *hapax legomenon* in the Qumran Aramaic texts, the word צבען likely indicates "dyed material" (Cook 2015: 198). This meaning is inferred from later Aramaic texts and dialects (cf. *Tg. Neb.* Ezek. 16:10; Pesh. Judg. 5:30; *Ginza Rab.* 229:2) but seems plausible here. The following hendiadys וחשיך חשוך may relate to the clothing or some other element of the figure's presence or portrayal. Either way, the form underscores the being is associated with utter darkness. Duke (2010: 85–87) proposed that the dyed clothing descriptor here may be a veiled critique of an alternate priestly group. While inventive, this proposal is forced and moves too quickly from fragmentary revelatory symbolism to an overly specific social location.

Line 14: *Then I saw another,] and behold[...]in his appearance. But his face was smiling.* As noted in the commentary of the more complete phrase in 4Q543 5–9 6, this material is introduced by a phrase marking narrative movement and an exclamatory particle drawing attention to the new symbol in the tableau. We saw above in the detailed textual comment that García Martínez (1985) provided a breakthrough re-reading of this line (cf. 4Q543 5–9 6) as relating to the form and face of the light figure. The result is a stark juxtaposition in the description of the two figures: the first is dreadful and cloaked in utter darkness, the latter's face is smiling upon Amram. 4Q543 5–9 8 also includes partial phrases of other aspects of this figure's face, see the comment on that fragment for details. In the following fragment we learn that this grinning angel is also associated with a domain of light, thus completing the light/dark contrast introduced already here.

3.8.2. *The Multi-Dimensional Domain and Naming of Melchiresha (4Q544 2)*

Dialogue between Amram and the *angelus interpres*. Surviving content relates to dichotomies, domains, and names of the light and dark figures.

11 [...מ]שׁ֯לט עליך [...]
12 [...]דֿן מן הוא ואמר לי הדן מ֯[...]
13 [...]וּ֯מלכי רשע *vacat* ואמרת מראי מא מא שׁל֯[טן...]
14 [...]ֹכה וכל עבדהֿ חֿ[ש]ׁיֿך ובחשוכא הוא דֿ[...]
15 [...]הֿ חזה והוא משלט על כול חשוכה ואנהֿ[...]
16 [...מ]עֿ֯ליא עד ארעיא אנה שליט על כול נהׄירא וב[...]○[...]
Воттом Margin

11. [...r]ules over you[...]
12. [...]this from him." And he said to me, "This one...[...]
13. [...] and Melchiresha." *vacat* And I said, "My lord, what is...[...]
14. [...]...and all his work is da[r]k and in the darkness he...[...]
15. [...]...see. Now, he is given authority over all the darkness. But I[...]
16. [...from] the heights to the depths. I am ruler over all light and in...[...]

Textual, Scribal, and Material Notes

Primary images for transcription: PAM M43.571; B-363265; B-363264.

Line 12: הדן ("this one") – While it seems most likely that the discourse here pertains to the question and answer of the otherworldly being's name, reconstructing the dialogue on inference is unhelpful. For proposals, see Milik (1972a: 79), Kobelski (1981: 27), Eisenman and Wise (1992: 154), García Martínez and Tigchelaar (1998 2:1088), and Puech (2001: 327). Duke (2010: 21) records a variant reading with the form הא דן (4Q543 10 2[?]). However, the overlap with that unplaced fragment is uncertain.

Line 13: מא של[טן ("what is the d[ominion") – The final form at the edge of the fragment is uncertain. However, given the nature of the discussion to this point and in the following lines, it seems likely that Amram's question pertained to the domain of the rule of darkness. For reconstructions along these lines, see Kobelski (1981: 27), García Martínez and Tigchelaar (1998 2:1088), and Puech (2001: 326).

Line 15 משלט ("he is given authority") – With Cook (2015: 235), I take this form as an *ophal* verb (cf. 4Q544 3 1).

Line 16 מ[עֿליא ("from] the heights") – Puech (2001: 326) transcribed מ[צֿליא ("les s]auvés") here—clearly informed by Kobelski (1981: 27), who first read the form צליא, but is not cited in the DJD edition. The latest digital images, however, confirm that the reading עליא is undoubtedly correct. For earlier variations on this reading, see: Milik (1972a: 79); Beyer (1984: 212); Eisenmann and Wise (1992: 154); García Martínez and Tigchelaar (1998 2:1088); Fitzmyer and Harrington

(2002: 94). Similarly, see the minor reconstructions by Duke (2010: 21) מ]עליא and Cook (2015: 25) מ]עֳליׇא. Fitzmyer and Harrington (2002: 95) understood the form as referring to the "Most High." Generally, that divine reference in the Aramaic DSS is in the form עליון (cf. 4Q543 22 2 and the commentary on 4Q542 1 i 1). In the present context of describing the reach and range of the domains of the otherworldly figures, the form here most likely refers to an upper portion of the land or cosmos. In this light, my rendering of the complete phrase מ]עֳלׅיׅא עד ארעיא above is informed by Cook's (2015: 25; cf. Eisenman and Wise 1992: 156; Duke 2010: 22) lexical gloss and translation.

Commentary
Line 11: *r]ules over you.* These words are no doubt spoke by the light angel, now serving as the *angelus interpres* dialoguing with Amram for the remainder of the dream-vision. Recall that the opening words to Amram's questions were a plural response from both angels (4Q544 1 11–12; 4Q547 1–2 12). Though there is no textual overlap here with other *VA* fragments, the form מ]שׁׅלׅט ("r]ules") suggests we are still in the context of the discourse over the nature of the rulership of both angels, which seems to have been the first topic covered in the dream-vision (4Q544 1 12).

Lines 12–13: *this from him." And he said to me, "This one...[...] and Melchiresha."* vacat *And I said, "My lord, what is.* The partial dialogue here between the angel and Amram seems to center around a key element of *VA*'s angelology, dualisms, and cosmology: the names of the angels giving oversight to their respective domains. It is unclear whether Amram is asked for this information—we only have the end of an unknown question in line 12—or if the *angelus interpres* offered up the names as part of another revelatory explanation. As seen in the commentary to the following fragment, 4Q544 3, it seems this disclosure involved the threefold naming of the angels of light and darkness, which has resulted in much speculation regarding the names in question.

The present fragment contains the only extant and, therefore, certain angelic name in the *VA* fragments. Here we learn that the dark and foreboding figure went by the moniker "Melchiresha." Given the penchant for onomastics of human figures in the Aramaic priestly literature, it is no doubt significant that the etymology of this name is "king of wickedness." The naming of Melchiresha in *VA* should also be considered in the immediate context of trends for assigning both names and specific roles to otherworldly beings in ancient Judaism, an expansive topic which I outline here by introducing the roster of angels, demons, and giant bastards in the Qumran Aramaic corpus

While the Hebrew Scriptures exhibit a variety of views of the population or vacancy of celestial beings in the heavens, Jewish literature of the mid-Second Temple period notably expands the names and roles of benevolent and malevolent otherworldly beings. While colloquially we might call these "angels" and "demons," those terms are increasingly problematized for the anachronism and lack of specificity when studying such early materials. Research in this area has seen advances in several directions in light of the DSS (Eshel 1999; Fröhlich 2001; Lichtenberger 2004; Reynolds 2013; Stuckenbruck 2014). For the present purposes, outlining the cultural and conceptual context in the Aramaic literature represented at Qumran is essential for understanding *VA*'s specificity for named figures and forces at work just beyond the pale of visible reality.

The most significant contributor to this is the early Enoch literature, which notably contains at least two strands of traditions for assigning fault to the wayward watchers for illicit revelation. The first orients around Shemihazah, the latter Azazel, but both understand the far-reaching implications of the blending of human and divine as relating to the acts and disclosures of two named figures. The roster of angelic consorts is extended further in these early traditions to also include several other named figures in *1 En.* 6:7, including: Shemihazah, Arteqoph, Remashel, Kokabel, Armumahel, Ramel, Daniel, Ziqel, Baraqel, Asael, Hermani, Maratel, Ananel, Setawel, Samshiel, Sahriel, Tummiel, Turiel, Yamiel, and Yehadiel. According to *1 En.* 6:8, these named figures are said to be leaders of groups of ten figures which only multiplies the fallen forces in the Enochic universe. *1 Enoch* also contributes to the positive side of named benevolent beings as Enoch routinely finds himself in the care of Uriel in the course of his visionary tours (e.g., *1 En.* 21:5; 33:3; 72:1; 80:1; cf. *4 Ezra* 4:1; 5:20; 10:28). Along this axis too, there are other named positive angelic figures in the Enochic universe, such as Michael, Sariel, Raphael, and Gabriel, among others (e.g. *1 En.* 9:1; 10:11; 20:5; 24:6; 40:9; 54:6; 60:4–5; 68:2–4; 69:14; 71:3). In a way, *1 En.* 71:8–9 (cf. *1 En.* 1:9; 6:6) sums up well the explosion of divine beings in the resultant Enochic imagination:

> And I saw angels that could not be counted, thousands of thousands and ten thousand times ten thousand; they were surrounding that house. And Michael and Raphael and Gabriel and Phanuel, and the holy angels who (are in) the heights of heaven, were going in and out of that house. And there came out of that house Michael and Raphael and Gabriel and Phanuel and many holy angels without number.

Though the identity of the seer is technically unknown, it is likely that Enoch is the best candidate for the figure referenced in the *Words of Michael* (4Q529, 4Q571; cf. 6Q23; Milik 1976 91; Puech 2009: 399–400; cf. Hamidovic 2013 for the early Jewish context of Michael traditions). This text, then, not only adds to the scope of Enochic angelologies and visionary tours, it does so in the bold first-person voice as an angelic pseudepigraph. In this text, Michael speaks and references other figures, including Gabriel (4Q529 1 1–4). The roles of Michael and Gabriel, of course, also invites comparison with the emerging Hebrew traditions of Daniel. There Michael is presented as a lead celestial figure associated with both inscribed revelation and divine protection against empire (Dan. 10:13, 21; 12:1). In this regard, the motif of divine protecting angels in the Aramaic DSS could be contextualized further still in light of analogous developments in the Hebrew literature of Qumran (Walsh 2019). Gabriel also makes cameos in

Danielic tradition (Dan. 8:16; 9:21), which is perhaps significant considering that this pairing is evident in *Words of Michael*.

Though Enoch figures in the *Book of Giants*, the work as it is represented at Qumran is not technically an Enochic pseudepigraph (for discussion of the Qumran manuscripts, see Stuckenbruck 1997: 41). Rather, it engages with and extends the watchers myth to imagine the plight and projected judgment on the giants. This text adds a new dynamic to the otherworldly cast of characters in the Aramaic texts. These materials include named giants, such as the brothers, ההיה ("Hahya") and אוהיא ("'Ohaya"; 1Q23 29 1; 4Q203 4 3; 7a 5; 4Q530 15 2; 4Q531 22 9; 46 1; 6Q8 1 2, 4), the sons of the fallen watcher Shemihazah. Most significantly, these figures experience a set of foreboding dream-visions affirming the imminent destruction of their bodies in the flood and guaranteed eschatological judgment of their spirits in the eschaton (4Q530 2 ii + 6–12; 4Q531 22 9; Perrin 2015a: 50–51, with bibliography). Another named figure, מהוי ("Mahaway"), the son of the fallen watcher ברקאל ("Barakel") apparently also has the ability to soar to visit Enoch on the outer reaches of the inhabited world to seek out an interpretation of another revelation (6Q8 1 3–5; cf. 4Q530 7 ii; 4Q531 7 2). In this regard, Gabriel's ability for flight in Dan. 9:21 LXX also takes on new significance in light of the capabilities portrayed in the *Book of Giants*. Most intriguing, however, is the naming of גלגלמיס ("Gilgamesh") as one of the giants (4Q530 2 ii + 6–12 2). This is apparently a not-so-subtle cultural jab from Judaean scribes writing in Aramaic that the epic hero of the ancient Near East was nothing more than the egregious outcome of a human-angelic sexcapade gone awry. In the Aramaic *Book of Giants*, Gilgamesh is also among a greater cast of gargantuan compatriots, including the named figure חובבס ("Hobabis"; 4Q530 2 ii + 6–12 2). (On the ancient Near Eastern and Hellenistic contexts of these figures as it relates to their presentation in the *Book of Giants*, see Goff 2009; Lemaire 2010; Fröhlich 2012; and Cooley 2014.) Judging from the fragmentary list of figures found in 4Q531 7 1–4, the *Book of Giants*' *dramatis personae* of watchers and giants was expansive, including but not limited to: אחירם ("Ahiram"), ענאל ("Anael"), ברקאל ("Barakel"), נעמאל ("Naamel"), and רזאל ("Raziel"), and עמיאל ("Ammiel").

The book of Tobit also contributes to this world, not least with the narrative roles and theological realities associated with Raphael. Despite concealing his identity for the better part of the narrative, Raphael is presented as a protector preserving the righteous (e.g., Tob. 5:16), a revealer of knowledge (e.g., Tob. 6:8–9, 16–18), and an opponent besting and even binding adversarial malevolent figures (e.g., Tob. 8:3). Tobit also contributes to the flip side of this angelic universe with the key role accorded to Asael, the demon stalking Sarai's bridal chamber, who is eventually exorcized by Tobias's apotropaic ritual and pursued to Egypt by Raphael. In these regards, like *VA* and Daniel, Tobit also benefits from the larger conceptual framework now provided by the Aramaic DSS.

For all the named benevolent and malevolent figures of this Aramaic literature, there are additional examples of texts that accord unnamed spiritual entities roles. Stuckenbruck (2014: 125–31) extended the scope of unnamed yet acknowledged existence of figures in the DSS by terms such as שׂד ("demon"; e.g., 4Q196 14 i 5, 12; 4Q197 4 i 13; ii 9, 13; 4Q243 13 2 // 4Q244 12 2 [plural]), רוח ("spirit"; e.g., 1Q20 20 16, 17, 20, 26, 28; 4Q197 4 i 13; 4Q538 1–2 4; 4Q560 1 ii 5, 6), מלאך ("messenger"; e.g., 1Q20 15 14; 4Q213a 2 18; 4Q529 1 1; 4Q543 1a–b 4; 4Q545 1a i 9; 11Q10 30 5), and עיר ("watcher"; e.g., 1Q20 2 16; 7 2; 4Q202 1 iv 6; 4Q203 7a 7; 4Q204 1 vi 8; 4Q532 2 7). Note that all of these references, save for one in 4Q560, occur in literary contexts. As its modern title suggests, 4QExorcism deals in an apotropaism, evidenced in part by the incantation: ואנה רוח מומה ("I adjure you, spirit"; 4Q560 1 ii 6). (For discussion of the possible maladies instigated by this malevolent spirit, see the discussions in Penney and Wise 1994; Naveh 1998; Puech 2009: 299.) As noted in the commentary on 4Q213a 1 17, it is significant that *ALD* also participates in an evolving understanding of שׂד as a class of demonic beings en route to becoming a chief being. Furthermore, the roster of revelatory texts in the Aramaic materials that feature unnamed interpreting angels should also be included here.

In these ways, the scribes of the Aramaic DSS both extend and amplify the imagined world of what later become known as "angels" and "demons" well beyond the roster and roles of earlier literatures. This is collectively true of the corpus as a whole as well as seen here in individual texts and emerging clusters of traditions. For the instance of interest in *VA*, the naming of Melchiresha is undoubtedly part of this larger trend and scribal effort.

Lines 14–15: *and all his work is da[r]k and in the darkness he…[…]…see. Now, he is given authority over all the darkness. But I.* The phrases in these fragmentary lines provide important detail into *VA*'s understanding of the respective domains of the light and dark figures, which was already hinted at in the opening dialogue of Amram's encounter (4Q544 1 11–12). As noted above, it is plausible that Amram inquired along these lines. Given the emphatic and threefold reference to terminology related to darkness, √חשׁך, it is clear that darkness is the defining metaphor for understanding the nature of this figure and his rule. Though the three references achieve this emphasis together, they may also be considered separately for their nuance and context in light of other contemporary Aramaic texts.

The first phrase וכל עבדהּ חֹ[שׁ]יֹך ("and all his work is dark") indicates that for *VA*, Melchiresha is not only the ruler of darkness but is actively engaged within this domain. In this regard, it is relevant that *Genesis Apocryphon* (1Q20 6 11) understands the wayward actions of the watchers as שמין בעובד בני ("the conduct of sons of heaven"). With this usage, compare also the phrase עובד שׁ[מיא ("the activity of the heavens") in 4Q204 1 i 18 (*1 En.* 2:1).

The second partial phrase ובחשוכא הוא ("and in the darkness he") is less intelligible given the broken context of the line. Given the preceding content, we may infer this included some additional comment on the nature of the deeds of Melchiresha within this dark domain. While it is possible this line indicated that this figure pulled, swayed, or led others into this dark realm, this cannot be assumed and is not evident in the extant text. The phrasing הֹשׁוֹכ ולח]שׁוכא ("darkness and to dark[ness") in *WQ* at 4Q542 2 11 may be of some relevance here.

That fragment, however, is even more limited than the present one, with multiple interpretive options for the first-person speaker.

The third item, והוא משלט על כול חשוכה ואנה ("Now, he is given authority over all the darkness. But I"), includes both a final and full phrase relating to the domain of the dark figure as well as what appears to be the opening of a new phrase now juxtaposing that reality and rule with those of the light figure. The use of the *pael* participle משלט ("he is given authority") introduces an essential concept here: the figure is made to rule, and his authority is granted, perhaps even mandated. In this respect, *VA* touches on a classic theological conundrum of dualistic expressions in that it seems to maintain an overarching authority and oversight by God. That is, there are two ways, domains, even appositional forces and figures, yet one supreme figure allowing this infrastructure to exist. The final phrase ואנה ("But I") no doubt signals the switch to the description of the domain of the light figure, parts of which survive in the following line.

This brings to mind a number of texts from the mid- to late Second Temple period that wrestle with the question of the origins and outcomes of evil as it relates to a universe increasingly populated with benevolent and malevolent forces. (For contributions and bibliography on this much larger area, see especially Davies 2002; Stuckenbruck 2004; 2009; Segal 2007; Frölich 2013; Brand 2013; and Wright 2015.) Within the Qumran collections, the end portion of the "*Treatise on the Two Spirits*" (1QS 4 16–20) specifies that God has appointed the spirits of light and darkness until the resolution of evil in the end of the age. Jubilees, of course, advocates that the initial dispatch of angels from on high was to help humanity—it was only after these turned rogue that their revelation and promiscuity hurt the human race and resulted in spiritual forces for evil (*Jub.* 4:15, 21–22; 5:1–6; 8:3; 10:1–13; 11:4–5). Enochic thought squarely placed fault on the errant watchers from the moment of abandoning their heavenly post under the leadership of wayward angels turned illicit revealers of hidden knowledge and fathers of human-angelic hybrids. This is not to reduce *VA*, 1QS, *Jubilees*, and Enochic thought to the same concept—the brief summaries here risk masking the complex dynamics of each text in question as well as the fragmentary knowledge we have of *VA* on this point. It is, however, to highlight that *VA* provides a second early and Aramaic engagement with this issue alongside the Aramaic Enoch materials. If some or all of these ideas circulated or inspired authors or communities, such as those responsible for *Jubilees* and 1QS, then the topic of the intersection of ideas on the origins of evil as it relates to dualistic domains in this network of writings deserves further study.

Line 16: *from] the heights to the depths. I am ruler over all light and in.* As noted above, the discourse marker ואנה at the end of fragmentary line 15 confirms that the content here relates to the domain of the light figure, the first-person speaker now functioning as the *angelus interpres*. These phrases offer at least two main insights into the ideology behind the imagery of *VA*'s dualism.

First, the language of עליא ("heights") and ארעי ("depths"; cf. 11Q18 1 2) hints at the cosmological scope of *VA*'s dualism. That is, it is not only about the domains of these figures, but also about the dimensions over which they rule. Reducing

VA's dualism to a two-dimensional light vs. dark divide flattens this multi-dimensional element. The language here also calls to mind the still more fragmentary reference to עֻ[מֹקָא ("the de]pth") in 4Q547 4 i 4. Though the terms do not precisely align, the concept of a dimensional universe and a description of its upper and lower reaches calls to mind Enoch's visionary tour that included various references or viewing of the upper heavens and lower reaches of the earthly realm or abyss (*1 En.* 18:8–12; cf. 4Q204 1 viii; *1 En.* 25:7–27; cf. 4Q205 1 xii). Many have noted the increasing cosmological complexification that begins in apocalyptic writings of this period (Himmelfarb 1993; Yarbro Collins 1996; Alexander 2011; Bremmer 2014). *Visions of Amram*'s contribution to this development is its overlaying such a cosmological representation with a dualistic reality for priestly identity. That is, it is not only the understanding of the world as dimensional that matters but defining those dimensions in light of a dualistic worldview that is important for *VA*. More recently, Høgenhaven (2020: 126) considered the spatiality and structure of "transcendent world" envisaged in Amram's revelation and noted that "[d]arkness and light become the two areas of dominion, ruled over by the angelic princes of evil and good," which can also be considered in the larger context of the geographical and narrative landscape of the work." In these ways, *VA*'s imagined world of bifurcated domains should be considered from both a cosmological perspective as well as its compositional context.

Second, the phrase אנה שליט על כול נהירא ("I am ruler over all light and in") provides the first clear evidence that *VA* is dealing in a light/dark dichotomy. Previous sections and fragments of the dream-vision were emphatic about the dark and foreboding nature of the other angel and his rule, yet language of light was yet nascent. In this light—pun intended—*VA* employs the surface metaphors of light and darkness to capture the character and qualities of the two opposing domains and dimensions under the rule of the two figures. In the present line, as was the case with the dark figure, we learn that the light angel likewise exercises dominion over his respective domain. In the context of the Qumran Aramaic corpus, the juxtaposition of light and darkness finds its fullest, though fragmentary, expression in 4Q548–4Q580, which uses the metaphors to refer to domains and lots of light and darkness in a way much more familiar from the Hebrew sectarian literature.

4.8.3. *The Lost Three Names of the Dark Angel (4Q544 3)*

Additional dialogue between Amram and the light being within his dream-vision, now revealing three names of his dark counterpart.

Top Margin
1 [...]רא אשלטת ושאלתֹהֹ[...]
2 [...]ֹֹ לִיֹ תֹלתה שמה[ן...]

1. [...]...I have been given authority." And I asked him[...]
2. [...]...to me, "Three name[s...]

Textual, Scribal, and Material Notes

Primary images for transcription: PAM M43.571; B-363263; B-363262.

Puech (2001: 328) proposed minor overlaps with 4Q543 14 and 4Q546 4. These, however, are uncertain and not included here.

Line 1: אשלטת ("I have been given authority") – As with the inflected form in 4Q544 2 15, I take this form and an *ophal* verb (so Cook 2015: 235).

Line 2: תלתה ("three") – Several earlier editions read a prefixed *daleth* on this form (Milik 1972a: 79; Kobelski 1981: 27; Eisenman and Wise 1992: 94; Fitzmyer and Harrington 2002: 94). However, the latest digital images confirm that the ink stroke in question is from the initial *tav* that is split due to a crack in the leather.

Commentary

Line 1: *I have been given authority." And I asked him*. This line, once again, contains partial content of dialogue as well as discourse markers of the ongoing conversation between Amram and his angelic guide. The first phrase relates to the light figure's claims over the nature and scope of his rule. As was noted above with respect to the granting of authority to a certain domain for the dark figure (4Q544 2 15), the light figure here too indicates his authority is given to him, or he has been made to rule (*ophal* of שלט). This further affirms that the dominions of both figures within the dichotomies and multi-dimensional model of *VA* are not ultimate but permitted by a higher power.

The content of Amram's follow up question later in the line is lost in the broken text. However, given that the following line includes revelation of the celestial beings' names, it is possible that Amram inquired about this information. In this way, the Aramaic *Four Kingdoms'* (4Q552, 4Q553, 4Q553a) dream-vision provides an intriguing counterpart, as the dialogue there between symbols and seer related to the names of the kingdoms represented by the trees.

Line 2: *to me, "Three name[s*. The few extant forms in this line have generated a great deal of interest and debate. The partially extant form לי ("to me") confirms that the following words are spoken to Amram by the *angelus interpres* in response to the lost question from line 1. Milik (cf. Milik 1972a: 85–86; Milik 1972b) astutely noted that in light of the revealed name Melchiresha in 4Q544 2 13, the present fragment likely relates to the disclosure of three names of the light figure. Given the plausibility of a parallel here, he also suggested that dream-vision included the revelation of three names for each of the figures and that the most natural antonym for the light figure's first name was Melchizedek. While Dimant (2012: 366) is correct that we cannot scaffold too lofty an interpretation over the assumption that the light figure was named Melchizedek, the majority of scholars accept this name as viable, if not plausible (Kobelski 1981: 27; García Martínez 1985; 1992: 177; Davidson 1992: 264–68; Davila 2000: 165; Puech 2001: 327–29; Wise, Abegg, and Cook 2005: 549; Mason 2008: 167–69; Mason 2012; Jurgens 2014: 27–28; Perrin 2015a: 166–67). If the *angelus interpres* did take the name Melchizedek then *VA* represents an important piece in the ongoing formation of the celestial-priestly understanding of this figure in ancient Judaism that includes a number of key texts, such as Ps. 110:4; *Songs of the Sabbath Sacrifice* (4Q401 11 3); 11QMelchizedek; and Hebrews 7 (for recent bibliography on each, see Perrin 2015a: 167–68). As seen in the commentary to 4Q545 4 16–19, this plausible priestly identification of the angelic revealer has significant implications for the priestly rhetoric of the work. As Walsh observed, this identification would also indicate that "Israel's priestly line has privileged angelic guardianship in Melchizedek" (Walsh 2019: 121).

Any number of other names could fill the slots of the lost titles for the figures in *VA*; however, such imaginative reconstructions are ultimately unhelpful (see the bibliography in preceding paragraph for proposals). What is significant, and can be reasonably inferred from the fragment in question, is that *VA* is apparently clustering multiple names of malevolent or benevolent beings and associating them with single entities. Recall here that *ALD* (4Q213a 1 17) also contributed to another aspect of this development by understanding שטן as a class of beings, not a single figure. In this way, this Aramaic priestly literature advances our understanding of efforts for both broadening and refining the personae and portfolios of angelic or demonic beings.

Finally, as seen in the commentary to 4Q545 4 19, the identification of the *angelus interpres* as Melchizedek has significant implications for the priestly identity and ideology of *VA* as it relates to the endorsement of Aaron's line and establishing continuity between the earthly and heavenly priesthoods. If Amram's dream-vision did feature revelation from an angelic priest, a celestial Melchizedek, then the priestly nature of the revelation later in the episode takes on new significance.

4.9. Text and Commentary: 4QVisions of Amram^c (4Q545)

There are several fragments of 4Q545 that do not include enough content for a full commentary (4Q545 2, 3, 5, 8, 10–12). Nonetheless, to capture something of their content and hints at unknown aspects of the work, I summarize key themes here.

1. The form בקשט לעלם ("with/in truth forever") occurs in 4Q545 2 2, which recalls similar phrases or terms in 4Q546 5 2; 4Q546 12 2; 4Q547 6 4; 9 6–7.
2. The language of something that יניר ("will shine") in 4Q545 3 3 reminds of the priestly blessing language of *WQ* (4Q542 1 i 1) and perhaps the language of illumination in the *Dualistic Fragments* (4Q548 1 ii–2 10–16).
3. The reference to כרסא ("throne") in 4Q545 5 3 suggests some sort of royalty language or divine throne room scene.
4. It is possible that 4Q545 5 and 9 join (see the comment on fragment 9 below).

5. 4Q545 8 1–3 include the phrases ליסוד ("for a foundation") and במלי ("with a word").
6. The phrase בני ("sons of") in 4Q545 11 1 may indicate a genealogical or geographical reference. Puech (2001, 349) partially reconstructs a name sequence of "Aaron" and "Amram" in this line, which is not certain.
7. The phrase בעדן ("in a time") at 4Q545 12 1 suggests some chronological marker, either in narrative structure or speculation.

Though none of these items adds significant detail to our developing understanding of *VA*, they provide glimpses of aspects of the text now lost.

4.9.1. *Pseudepigraphic Title, Miriam's Marriage, and Moses's Hebrew Name (4Q545 1a i)*

Another fragment including the narrative frame and initial episodes of *VA*, specifically the marriage celebration between Miriam and Uzziel and Amram's gathering his children (including Moses referenced by his Hebrew name) for instruction. Overlaps: <u>4Q543 1a–c</u>; <u>4Q543 2a–b</u>; **4Q546 1**.

TOP MARGIN

1 <u>פרשגן</u> כתב מלי הזו[ןׄ]ת עמרם בׄרׄ קהׄת בׄרׄ לוׄי כוׄ]ל...[
2 דׄי] אחוי ל[בׄנוֹ]והי ודי פקד [אנת ביוםׄ]○[...]בׄשנת [...]○
3 מׄאה ותלתין ושתׄ היׄ[אׄ ש]ׄנתא די מותהׄ]○[...]○○ת מאהׄ[...]
4 <u>המשין ותרתין לגל[ו]אׄ</u>ת[יׄ]שראל למצרין [...]○<u>עֹבדׄ עלוׄ]הי ושלח</u>[...]
5 וקרא לעוזיאל אחוהי זעיראׄ[ואס[בׄ לה לׄמׄרׄ]יׄ]םׄ ברתהׄ[...]
6 ל<u>אנתה</u> ברת תלתין שניׄן ועבד משתותה שבׄעׄהׄ[יומׄ]ןׄ
7 ואכל ואשתי במשתותה וחדי אדין כדי אשתציו
8 יׄ]וׄמי משתותא שלחׄ קרא לאהרון לברה בׄ[מׄ]אׄ בר שנין
9 [...]○[...]לׄהׄ קרי לׄיׄ בׄרי למלאכיה אחיוׄכׄןׄ מן בית
10 [...]דׄתה לעליה קרא לה
11 [...]○○ אׄנה
12 [...]○ אבוהי
13 [...] מן
14 [...]מׄמרכה
15]ונתן לךׄ...עלׄ]מׄיׄן
16]ונתן לך חכמהׄ...יׄ]הוֹסף
17]לךׄ...אל תהוה ומׄ]לׄאׄךׄ אל
18]תתקרה...תעבד בארעׄ]אׄ דא
19]וׄדׄיׄן...לׄ]הׄ שמד לוׄ]בׄ]ל

BOTTOM MARGIN

1. A cop[y of "The Writing of the Words of the Vision](s) of Amram, son of Qahat, son of Levi." Al[l...]
2. that [he told to his] son[s and that he commanded] them on the day...[...]

3. in the one hundred and thirty-sixth year, whic[h] was the year of his death...[...]one hundred[...]

4. fifty-second [*year*] of the ex[i]le of [I]srael to Egypt...[...] he crossed over toward [him. And he sent...]

5. and called Uzziel his younger brother. [And he too]k for himself Mir[i]am, his daughter[...]

6. as a wife. She was thirty years old. And he made her wedding feast for seven [da]ys[...]

7. And he ate and drank at her wedding feast and rejoiced. Then when the days

8. of the wedding feast were completed, he sent a summons to Aaron, his son, who was [...] years

9. [...]...[...]to him, "Call for me my son, to Malakiya, your brothers from the house of

10. [...]...over him, call him

11. [...]...I

12. [...]...his father

13. [...]...from

14. [...]your command

15. [And he gave you...eter]nal

16. [And he gave you wisdom...he]added

17. [to you...of God you will be. And] the [me]ssenger of God

18. [you will be called...you will do in] this the [land]

19. [and judgment...to] him your name for a[l]l

Textual, Scribal, and Material Notes

Primary images for transcription: PAM M41.941; B-370771; B-370770. This fragment includes two partial columns, the first of which retains the very beginning of *VA* as signaled by the title of the text. This is preceded by a margin significantly larger than the intercolumnar margins. Compare also a similar situation in 4Q543 1a–c, which has a jagged edge suggesting stitching. As with that manuscript, for 4Q545 it is technically unknown what may have preceded this material, although it seems clear that this is the beginning of a roll.

4Q543 2a–b 7–9 includes additional phrases of Amram's discourse, which would have extended beyond 4Q545 1a i 19 and presumably fit within the fragmentary opening lines of the next column. Puech (2001: 337) represents these as three partial lines at the top of 4Q545 1a–b ii 1–3. The extant text of column ii of the present fragment, however, begins at line 9 (see next).

Commentary

Lines 1–4: *A cop[y of "The Writing of the Words of the Vision](s) of Amram, son of Qahat, son of Levi." Al[l...]that [he told to his] son[s and that he commanded] them on the day...[...]in the one hundred and thirty-sixth year, whic[h] was the year of his death...[...]one hundred[...] fifty-second [year] of the ex[i]le of [I]srael to Egypt.* For discussion of the title of *VA*, see the commentary on 4Q543 1a–c 1–4.

Lines 4–5: *he crossed over toward [him. And he sent...]and called Uzziel his younger brother.* This material seems to be the remnants of the opening of the narrative proper following the title of *VA*. For commentary on these materials, see 4Q543 1a–c 4–5.

Lines 5–6: *[And he too]k for himself Mir[i]am, his daughter[...] as a wife. She was thirty years old. And he made her wedding feast for seven [da]ys.* The content here relates to the celebration of an endogamous marriage between Miriam and her uncle, Uzziel. For discussion of the philological, tradition-historical, and legal contexts of this material, see the commentary to 4Q543 1a–c 5–7.

Lines 7–9: *And he ate and drank at her wedding feast and rejoiced. Then when the days of the wedding feast were completed, he sent a summons to Aaron, his son, who was [...] years [...]...[...]to him, "Call for me my son, to Malakiya, your brothers from the house of.* Lines 8–9 include the last details of the marriage celebration for Miriam and Uzziel, thus drawing to a close the first scene of the narrative of *VA*. Though the content is increasingly fragmentary, the ensuing materials seem to refocus now on Miriam's siblings gathered for instruction: first Aaron, then Moses.

Aaron is mentioned by name, אהרון, in line 8 where Amram apparently sends word to retrieve him. The end of the line is broken but seems to have also indicated the age of Aaron. Other references to Aaron in *VA* include 4Q545 11 1 and perhaps 4Q546 12 3. Though not mentioned by name, it is likely that Aaron is implied in the angelic endorsement of the priesthood in Amram's revelation (see the commentary on 4Q545 4 18; cf. 4Q546 8 2). In this way, *VA* contributes to the early reception and reformation of Aaron's priestly persona. This profile expands modestly in other fragmentary items of the Aramaic DSS. Aaron is also mentioned in 4Q549, seemingly in the context of an endogamy-oriented priestly genealogy. Aaron's genealogical-chronological profile seems also to have been part of the Hebrew-Aramaic(?) lists of 4Q559 3 4; 4 1.

Line 9 apparently references Moses by what is rightly taken as *VA*'s presentation of his yet unknown Hebrew name: מלאכיה. Beyer (2004: 118–19) first observed the connection of this form with Moses, but did not comment on its import or significance, a task later taken up by Duke (2007; cf. 2010 12–13; 69–79) who, independent of Beyer's earlier work, also made the connection with Moses. Other editions rendered the form as reference to angel (Beyer 1994: 87) or messenger (Puech 2001: 335) with some association with a son of Amram. Duke (2007: 34) observed that the "forced etymology" of Moses's "perfectly common Egyptian name" in Exod. 2:10 seemed unnecessary for the writer of *VA*. At the very least, it was an opportunity to derive new meaning from an unresolved detail in the antecedent tradition. Note also that *VA* refers to Moses by his traditional name מושה in 4Q545 4 15. Apart from *VA*, the only other Aramaic texts at Qumran to reference Moses by name are the Aramaic *Four Kingdoms* (4Q553 1 i 2) and Tobit, which does so with reference to booklore (4Q197 4 ii 6 [Tob. 6:12]).

Duke (2007: 41–43) noted that the choice of the name מלאכיה is intriguing both for its representation in the DSS corpus as a name (4Q321; cf. Ostraca 97) as well as the antecedent traditions for associated prophets with the term מלאך in the Hebrew Scriptures (Hag. 1:13; Isa. 44:26; 2 Chron. 36:15), which takes on a significant prophetic-priestly aspect in Mal. 2:7. He also noted how 4Q377 2 ii 10–11 likened Moses to a "heavenly messenger"; although, as Goldman (2020: 107 n. 20) noted, the potential Mosaic association of that reference is debated. As such, Duke (2007: 43) concluded that *VA* contributes to reimaging Moses not only by name but in his roles—the resultant persona is one with shades of the prophetic, priestly, and even heavenly messenger qualities. Capitalizing on the latter element of that profile, Goldman (2020: 104–105) commented that the attribution of this name to Moses in *VA* "can thus possibly be traced to an exegetical tradition identifying the angel of God mentioned in the exodus account with Moses" (cf. Exod. 23:20; Num. 20:16; and later *Exod. Rab.* 32:2; *Lev. Rab.* 1:1; *Num. Rab.* 16:1). For discussion of how *VA* advances the aforementioned facets of Moses's profile, see the comments on 4Q543 2a–b.

In short, Duke's study focused on *what* the name means—its onomastic elements. The question remains, however, *why* rename Moses, or at least reimagine his Hebrew name, in a text that is set in orbit around ancestors primarily associated with priestly beginnings? In this regard, we would be wise to recall the onomastic efforts of *ALD*. In the commentary to 4Q214a 2–3 i 1–6, we saw that onomastics was a key element of birth notices of significant characters. Names were distilled down or expounded upon to project characteristics or outlooks that would define a figure's future. It is significant that *VA* seems to deploy a similar strategy here. The name of Moses is provided in Hebrew, as Beyer noted and Duke established, but the reason for doing so seems to be part of a larger effort in these two Aramaic priestly writings to develop meaning out of the names of ancestors with reference to claimed or provided Hebrew antecedents. That is, this is not only a shared motif or parallel interest in onomastics—it is the shared scribal strategy for recourse to Hebrew in compositional Aramaic texts that is significant. This suggests both these priestly works align in a strategic, and rather unique, approach to reimagining the profile of founding figures in Aramaic by renaming or reverse-engineering their names in Hebrew.

Lines 10–13: *over him, call him [...]...I [...]...his father[...]...from*. The content is limited here and does not benefit from overlap with another *VA* fragment. The surviving materials appears to be a blend of first-person discourse and third-person referents. Given that the preceding line concerned the summons of Moses, it is plausible that the forms לעליה קרא לה in line 10 also refers to Moses. With Amram having just gathered his two sons, it is likely that the אנה of line 11 is from a word spoken by Amram and, therefore, is the remnant of some opening discourse. It is impossible to discern who אבוהי refers to in this context. Given the first-person context of the early scenes of *VA*, this cannot be referring to Qahat and so must be another pointing to another character's father.

Lines 14–19: *your command [...And he gave you...eter]nal. [...And he gave you wisdom...he]added [...to you...of God you will be. And] the [me]ssenger of God [...you will be called...you will do in] this the [land...and judgment...to] him your name for a[l]l*. Since this content is reconstructed almost exclusively from 4Q543 2a–b, see the commentary on that fragment for discussion.

4.9.2. Founding the Ancestral Tombs and Rumors of the Egypt–Canaan–Philistia War (4Q545 1a–b ii)

Amram builds ancestral tombs and a reference to the war between Canaan and Egypt. Overlaps: **4Q543 3**; 4Q544 1; 4Q546 2; 4Q547 1–2.

9 וֹצׁ[...]
10 [...]ה̇○[...]
11 באַרעָא דא וְסלקת לְמ̇[קבר...]
12 למקבר אבהתנא וסלקתׁ[... קחת תמן]
13 לׁמׁקׁם ולעמרה וׁלמבנא קׁ[...]
14 שגיאין מן בני דדׁי כחד[א...גבר ומן]
15 עַבידתנאַ ש[ג̇יאין לח̇ן̇]דא עד̇...[...]רון מתין[...]
16 שמועת קרב מ̇בהלה תא[○...]ת̇נא לארע מ[...]
17 לעובע ולא בֿ[נו קב]ריא די אׁבָהַ̇]ת̇]הֿןׁ וׁשַׁבָׁקוןׁ[נִי אבי קהת...]
18 ולמבנה ולמסב לה̇ן̇ון כׁ[ל]ׁ[צרכיהון מ]ן̇[ארע כנען[...עד]
19 אנחנה בנין וקרְ[בא הוא בין]פלשׁת למצרין ונצ[○...]
BOTTOM MARGIN

9. and...[...]
10. [...]...[...]
11. in this land. And I went up to b[ury...Qahat there...]
12. to bury our fathers. And I went up [...]
13. to rise, settle, and build [...]
14. many from the sons of my uncle together[...a man and from...]
15. our servants...a [g]reat ma[ny, until...]...dead[...]
16. report of war was alarming...[...]to *the* land ...[...]
17. hastily. But [they] did not b[uild] the [gr]aves of their fathe[rs]. And they left [me, my father, Qahat,...]
18. and to build and to take for them[selves a]ll [their needs fr]om the land of Canaan[...while]
19. we were building. But [there was] wa[r between] Philistia against Egypt ...[...]

Textual, Scribal, and Material Notes

Primary images for transcription: PAM M43.566; B-370771; B-370770; B-359460; B-359459. See the notes section of the previous fragment for a comment on the likely inclusion of forms from 4Q543 2a–b 7–9 at the opening of this column.

Line 16: לארע ("to *the* land") – The form on the manuscript is without the definite article.

Line 19: ונצ◦ ("...") – The original, complete form cannot be recovered from the fringes of the fragment. Puech (2001: 338–39) proposed ונצחׄו] ("fu[rent] vainqueur[s"). García Martínez and Tigchelaar (1998 2:1090–91) read ונצחׄ]ין ("and was winning"). Duke (2010: 16–17) read ונצחׄ[("And they won ["). Beyer (1994: 86–87; 2004: 119–20) suggested ונצח [מלך פלשת על מלכ מצרין ("Und es siegte [der König von Philistäa über den König von Ägypten").

Commentary

The commentary on this fragment is best read in tandem with the other major fragment for this section, 4Q544 1. To avoid redundancy, my discussion here is more selective and largely treats items of interest found only on this fragment as they lack extant overlap with the 4Q544 1 or the other smaller overlapping fragments noted above.

Lines 11–13: *in this land. I went up to b[ury...Qahat there...] to bury our fathers. I went up [...] to rise, settle, and build.* The formulation באר׳עֹאׄ דא ("in this land") occurs also in 4Q543 2a–b 5, there in the context of what appears to be a forward-looking word regarding Moses's future and perhaps the deliverance of Israelites. The locution in *VA*, therefore, seems to be a natural way to reference Egypt within the narrative. Line 12 indicates explicitly that the central aim of the sojourn is to bury the forefathers, which is also evident in a more fragmentary passage of 4Q544 1 1–3. Note also the tripling of verbs here to indicate the actions and intents of Amram's travels to Canaan—קום ("to rise"), עמר ("to settle"), and בנה ("to build")—which gives the narrative a sense of a patriarchal sojourn in the land. In a rather tangential way, Amram's sojourns may be considered in light of Abram's survey of the land in Canaan as related in detail in *GenAp* (1Q20 21 8–19). That text also features chains of verbs to describe Abram's movement into the land (1Q20 21 13–14; cf. Gen. 13:14–17), and incidentally a sojourn disrupted by regional warfare.

Lines 14–15: *many from the sons of my uncle together[...a man and from...] our servants...a [g]reat ma[ny, until...]...dead.* For discussion of the priestly make-up of the group, see the commentary on 4Q544 1 1–2. The contribution of the present text is the specification in line 15 that the group included a larger number of Levitical cousins.

Line 16–19: *report of war was alarming...[...]to the land ...[...] hastily. But [they] did not b[uild] the [gr]aves of their fathe[rs]. And they left [me, my father, Qahat,...] and to build and to take for them[selves a]ll [their needs fr]om the land of Canaan[...while] we were building. But [there was] wa[r between]*

Philistia against Egypt. The disruption of the travels due to the regional war is a motif discussed in greater detail by VanderKam (2010), Goldman (2013), and Høgenhaven (2020). For treatment of this aspect of *VA*'s narrative, see the commentary on 4Q544 1 3–7.

4.9.3. *An Angelic Writing on Moses's Ascendancy and the "Mystery" of the Priestly Work (4Q545 4)*

Revelation regarding a written forecast of Moses's rise and role in the exodus as well as the "mystery" of the priestly work, position, and progeny of Aaron.

13 [...]ooo[...]
14 [...]ע̇ ואחוה לכה שׁמׂ[...]
15 [...]כּתׂבּ בארעׂא לה מושה ואף על[...]
16 [...]oוה לכה רז עובדהׂ כּהׂן קדיש הוא[לאל עליון...]
17 קד̇[י]ש להוה לה כל זרעה בכול דרי o[...]
18 שבועי באנוש רעותׂ[ה ית]קרה ויתאמׂ[ר...]
19 יתבׂחר לכּהׂן עלמיׂן[...] *vacat*
BOTTOM MARGIN

13. [...]...[...]
14. [...]... and I will tell you...[...]
15. [...]wrote/will write in the land for him, Moses. And also concerning[...]
16. [...]...to you the mystery of his work: he is a holy priest[to God most high...]
17. All his descendants will be h[o]ly to him throughout generations of ... [...]
18. seventh among men, of [his] will [he will be] called. And it will be said [...]
19. he shall be chosen as a priest forever [...] *vacat*

Textual, Scribal, and Material Notes
Primary images for transcription: PAM M43.566; B-359468; B-359467.
Line 14:]שׁמׂ ("...") – The partial form here has been reconstructed variously. Compare שמׂהׂ[ת]ךְ (Puech 2001: 342), שמ]ועת (Beyer 2004: 123), שמ]הת[García Martínez and Tigchelaar (1998 2:1090).
Line 16: עובדהׂ כּהׂן קדיש ("his work: a holy priest") – The reading comes at an admittedly challenging area of the fragment. For similar proposals, see Puech (2001: 343) and Duke (2010: 22). García Martínez and Tigchelaar (1998 2:1090) read the forms as עובדה דין ("his service: He is a holy judge"), which, though intriguing, are unlikely given the ink traces evident on the most recent images. The introduction of judicial language here would also seem to disrupt the predominant priestly tone of the fragment. Beyer also initially read (1994: 90)

עובדה דִּין ("Ein heiliger Richter ist er"), but later adjusted his reading עובדה כהן (Beyer 2004: 123).

Line 16: לאל עליון ("To God Most High") – The reconstructed form here is drawn from Puech (2001: 342; cf. Drawnel 2004: 181; Greenfield, Stone, and Eshel 2004: 155). Though this phrase lacks textual support in another *VA* manuscript, I accept the reading here based on sense and the implicit rhetoric of the text. For another occurrence of this phrase in a priestly context in *ALD*, see 4Q213b 1 6.

Commentary

Lines 14–15: *and I will tell you...[...]wrote/will write in the land for him, Moses. And also concerning.* The phrase ואחוה לכה ("and I will tell you") is a discourse marker of revelatory speech from the *angelus interpres*. The exact topic of the revelation is lost in this line. However, judging from the contents of line 15 and 16 it pertains to the roles of Moses and Aaron, with a particular focus on the priestly progeny of the latter (see the commentary on line 16 below). The explicit naming of Moses in the dream-vision here—by his traditional name מושה, not his Hebrew name מלאכיה as in 4Q545 1a i 9 (cf. 4Q543 2a–b 4)—is intriguing and calls to mind also the reference to אהרון ("Aaron") in another fragment of the revelatory episode (4Q546 8 2). It is unknown if these revelations of names were related to other lost symbolic elements of the dream-vision or were simply part of the discussion or disclosure offered up by the angel, perhaps with recourse to a written record.

The phrase כתב בארעא לה ("wrote/will write in the land for him") also invites speculation over what might have been lost in this fragment. Given the fragmentary opening of this line, linguistically, the verb כתב could be taken *peal* perfect, indicating a simple past, or reconstructed variously as a prefix form, indicating a future sense and outlook (cf. Puech 2001: 343). My rendering above aligns with Høgenhaven (2020: 128), who also emphasized the ambiguity of the fragmentary form.

The question then becomes: *who* is associated with this writtenness motif and *what* is written about them? On both points, the fragmentary text does not permit firm answers. Amram has a clear association with scribal activity in the known fragments of *VA* (see especially commentary on 4Q547 9 8). Here, however, the activity or outcome of writtenness are associated with Moses in some way. Given that the present fragment fits *within* the revelation, the most natural perspective is that the angel is referring to some written record that included a forecast of activities associated with Moses. Adopting a similar position, Høgenhaven (2020: 129) commented that "[t]he fragment seems to be part of the description of his [Amram's] vision, and the speaker, accordingly, must be the angelic figure addressing Amram." Also recognizing this visionary context, Puech (2001: 343) suggested the angel here referred to an ancestral writing of some sort that prospected the futures of both Moses and

Aaron. Given that there are hints of exodus traditions in other *VA* fragments (4Q543 16) and that the final scene of Amram's revelation already points to places and institutions in the wilderness wanderings—particularly Mount Sinai and tabernacle appointment (4Q547 9 2–5)—it is highly likely that Amram's dream-vision here included learning of the imminent exodus and deliverance from Egypt. The present fragment introduces the possibility that this preview was revealed in some form of imagined, inscribed media. Since the narrative context is within a dream-vision, it seems most likely that this revelation was disclosed via an otherworldly book or tablet (cf. 4Q546 20 2), which made special mention of the appointment of Moses (cf. 4Q543 2a–b; 4Q545 1a i 7–9; 4 15).

Lines 16–19: *to you the mystery of his work: he is a holy priest [to God Most High...] All his descendants will be h[o]ly to him throughout generations of... [...] seventh among men, of [his] will [he will be] called. And it will be said [...] he shall be chosen as a priest forever*. The phrase ואף על ("and also concerning") at the end of line 15 likely indicates the shift in discourse about Moses to Aaron. Though Aaron is not mentioned by name in the following lines, the individual described is clearly of priestly significance in this early generation and for its ongoing heritage. As seen below, there is no question from the suggestive language of these lines that Aaron is the best candidate. While the priestly rhetoric of these lines finds an authoritative anchor in the figure of Aaron, it uses his persona and position to extend a complex identity of the priesthood along two axes: a horizontal one for the ancestral heritage and a vertical one for an otherworldly association.

Ancestral associations: The recurring use of third-person pronouns and referents in these lines confirm that the *angelus interpres* is not speaking of Amram here. Similarly, it is clear from line 17 that the figure in view will have an ongoing progeny of priests. The clearest confirmation that the individual in view is Aaron, however, is found in the phrase of line 18. There we learn that this individual has a genealogical position of seventh in this early ancestral heritage. In their editions, both Beyer (1984: 213) and Puech (2001: 343) perceived that Aaron is the seventh individual in view here. Their genealogical sequences of seven, however, differed. Beyer proposed: Noah, Abraham, Isaac, Jacob, Levi, Qahat, and Aaron. Puech retraced the generation as follows: Abraham, Isaac, Jacob, Levi, Qahat, Amram, and Aaron. Given that the work under consideration is the *Visions of Amram*, it is unclear why Amram would be left out of the genealogy, as Beyer averred. As such, Puech's genealogical estimation is more likely.

As noted in my previous work (Perrin 2015a: 165), the following lines seem to describe Aaron's priestly role in terms inspired by, or even drawn from, those of *ALD*. This is best seen by comparison of phrases from the present fragment of *VA* with items from relevant sections of *ALD* in the Greek witness.

Table 4.1. *VA*'s Casting Aaron as a Priest in the Mold of *ALD*'s Presentation of Levi

Description of Levi in *ALD*	Descriptions of Aaron in VA
"you are a holy priest of the Lord (Mt. Athos: ἱερεὺς σὺ ἅγιος κυρίου)" (*ALD* 48).	"A holy priest is he[to God Most High (כֹּהֵן קדיש הוא] לאל עליון)" (4Q545 4 16).
"your seed shall be blessed upon the earth for all generations of eternity (Mt. Athos: πάσας τὰς γενεὰς τῶν αἰώνων)" (*ALD* 61). Cf. also "and all your seed will be priests (Mt. Athos: καὶ ἱερεῖς ἔσονται πᾶν τὸ σπέρμα σου)" (*ALD* 49).	"all his descendants will be ho[l]y to him throughout generations of …" (קד[י]ש להוה לה כל זרעה בכול דרי)" (4Q545 4 17).
"you were elected for the holy priesthood (Mt. Athos: ἐξελέχθης εἰς ἱερωσύνην ἁγίαν)" (*ALD* 51). Cf. "for all the generations of eternity (לכל דרי עלמא)" and "eternal priesthood (כהנות עלמא)" are also featured in *4QLevi*[b] (4Q213a 3–4 7; 5 i 3).	"he shall be chosen as a priest forever (יתבחר לכהן לעלמי[ן])" (4Q545 5 19).

Angel (2010: 133) already perceived that the terminology of *VA* is "reminiscent of the priestly ordination traditions in *ALD*, *T. Levi* and *Jubilees* 30–32." It is clear that the scribes of this tradition have now evolved a once-flat priestly character into a dynamic figure, whose authoritative position and moment of ordination reflects that of several other contemporary and later traditions. In this way, it seems that part of the goal of *VA* here was to present Aaron as a priest in the mold of his priestly ancestor, with much of its understanding of that mold coming from the Aramaic Levi tradition. The language applied to Aaron above also underscores his foundational identity extending down through the generations: this is an endorsement of both his priestly role and the priesthood issuing from him. In short, for *VA* Aaron is not only in the *line* of the priestly ancestors—his characterization in that role is also *like* them.

Otherworldly alignment: The narrative context of the dream-vision here, and the likely identity of the *angelus interpres* as a celestial Melchizedek, elevate the nature of this rhetoric. As noted in the commentary to 4Q544 3 2, there is a growing orbit of authority around this figure as an otherworldly figure of priestly significance. While the reconstruction of the phrase לאל עליון in 4Q545 4 16 is speculative, it is possible that such language was included here to make an implicit association between the earthly and otherworldly priesthoods explicit (for analogous language in other texts, see Puech 2001: 343; Greenfield, Stone, and Eshel 2004: 155). As previously noted in the commentary to 4Q213b 1 6, *ALD* already established a precedent for applying this conspicuous language to the earthly priesthood of the ancestors. For additional comment on the prevalence of this divine epithet in the Qumran Aramaic texts, see the comment on 4Q542 1 i 1. Even if that phrase was absent, or could not be assumed, it is difficult to sidestep the significance of Amram receiving an otherworldly endorsement of Aaron's eternal priesthood from an angelic figure who was, presumably, the head of the heavenly order itself (Perrin 2015a: 169). Jurgens (2014: 33) concluded along similar lines:

> [i]f we are to surmise that the figure opposing the ominous Melchiresha is none other than Melchizedek the priestly king, then it follows that we should interpret the vision *in light of* this identification. It seems extremely unlikely that a figure such as Melchizedek, who was nearly exclusively known as a priestly figure, would appear in a dream-vision bearing no connection to this background.

Beyond this suite of ancient Jewish priestly literature, it is also noteworthy that Amram's line received a covenantal endorsement for eternal service from God in *LAB* 9:7–8. In that text, the promise and position are the reward for Amram's strategizing to save Moses from infanticide in Egypt.

This, then, raises the question of the implications of such an endorsement from on high. The answer, it seems, comes in the opening phrase of line 16. The *angelus interpres* here specifies that he will reveal to Amram the רז עובדה ("the mystery of his [i.e., Aaron's] work"). (For brief evaluations of the quality and application of רז in some of the Aramaic texts, see Bockmuehl 1990: 54; Puech 2001: 139–40, 167; Goff 2003: 48; Thomas 2009; 2010; Machiela 2010: 211; cf. Brown 1968; Gladd 2008; and Tervanotko 2016: 135–38.) As I noted previously (Perrin 2015a: 169 n. 31), the term רז occurs a total of 118 times in the Hebrew DSS with an additional twenty-seven uses occurring in the Aramaic DSS, including those in Daniel: Dan. 2:18, 19, 27, 28, 29, 30, 47; 4:9 (6); 1Q20 1 2, 3, 7; 5 21, 25, 6 12; 14 19, 20; 4Q201 1 iv 5; 4Q203 9 3; 4Q204 5 ii 26; 4Q534 1 i 7, 8 (×2); 4Q536 2 i + 3 8, 9, 12; 4Q545 4 16; 4Q546 12 4. The final occurrence in this list, of course, is of great significance as it occurs also in *VA* and is applied to another foundational ancestor: Miriam. For discussion on the open-questions and significance of that fragment, see the commentary below.

As seen above, the concept of רז in the DSS has been the subject of extensive study. However, the precise meaning in context here is less studied. Thomas (2009: 210; cf. 2010) understood that Amram's linkage to רז was due to his genealogical association with the more authoritative priestly forebears of Levi and Aaron. This, however, is hardly mysterious; on the contrary, it is entirely obvious! In view of the wider Qumran Aramaic texts, Thomas (2009: 235) also suggested that the רז seems to be associated with knowledge of teaching and transmission of sacerdotal duties. This is perhaps closer to the mark as it seems that רז would dovetail with some form of insider knowledge. However, the term is not linked with understandings of priestly *tasks* elsewhere in the Aramaic DSS. As such, that assumption cannot guide our interpretation here. Puech (2001: 343) inched closer toward an appropriate interpretive compass when he noted that the רז here seems to be the priesthood itself, although he did not press further to tease out the implications of this recognition.

It seems that the mysterious nature of Aaron's priestly role and that of his progeny is that their angelic endorsement and eternally mandated role place their actions and identity in continuity with the otherworldly priesthood (Perrin 2015a: 166–70). In this respect, *VA* participates in a similar discourse of earthly-heavenly priestly conceptions. As Aschim (2000: 780; cf. Collins 2010b: 87–88) noted with respect to *ALD*, that tradition aimed to "establish a connection between the earthly cult, performed by Levi and his descendants, and the heavenly cult, performed by angels." While the final known scene of Amram's revelation did include some description or depiction of a sacrificial act and site, it does not seem that the רז עובדה here refers to the specifics of sacrificial process. Rather, it is arguably the symbolic nature of those acts that are of greater significance: their earthly affect enabled by human priests is occasioned by a tight association with otherworldly agents in the celestial priesthood. In this respect, the theology of *VA* (and to some extent *ALD*) provide an early exemplar for the association of human and angelic enjoinment that may have been highly attractive to the Qumran group or even formative to their liturgical thought. In view of such traditions, Newman (2018: 118) remarked:

> A hallmark of the sectarian perspective is the understanding that the purified, perfected community members were worshipping in the company of the angels. While the degree to which such angelic communion affected the ontological status of the worshippers has been debated, what is clear is that angels and heavenly worship were thought to be accessible within the Yaḥad. This marks a clear difference from the worldview of Sirach or Baruch, where no such mediating angels are mentioned. The Songs of the Sabbath Sacrifice reflect such angelic intimacy, as does a composition reconstructed in the Hodayot that is connected to the Maskil (1QH^a 25 34–27 3?), also known as the Self-Glorification Hymn.

In view of this larger framework for the intersections and elevation of the sectarian community and angelic hosts in liturgy, priestly Aramaic texts such as *ALD* and *VA* may have provided a formative framework for developing that signature sectarian thought.

4.9.4. *Glimpses of Revelation Regarding a Demonic Threat (4Q545 6)*

A small fragment likely in the context of revelation regarding some demonic figure. This context is inferred from a minor overlap with 4Q547, which allows for only modest reconstructing with confidence. Overlap: <u>4Q547 3</u>.

1 (17) [...]וֹלֹא תהוֹה[...]
2 (18) [...]ooקֹדֹמיתא תהא [...]
3 (19) [...] על <u>נפשה תכמון בין</u>[<u>תרתיהון</u>...]
BOTTOM MARGIN

1. (17) [...]and you will not be[...]
2. (18) [...]...she/it will be first [...]
3. (19) [...] for its life you shall lie in wait between[their two

Textual, Scribal, and Material Notes
Primary images for transcription: PAM M41.512; B-359470; B-359469.

Line 2: ○○ ("...") – It is possible that the initial ink traces here read עם (Beyer 1994: 90; García Martínez and Tigchelaar 1998 2:1090). Beyer (2004: 122) read מֿ[ן. Duke (2010: 26) read only ֯[. The line, however, is both fragmentary and faint at this point.

Commentary
Lines 1–3 (17–19): *and you will not be[...]...she/it will be first [...] for its life you shall lie in wait between[their two.* There is modest, but largely uninstructive, overlap with 4Q547 3. For comment on the partial forms and potential context of this material, see the commentary on that fragment. As noted in the commentary to 4Q547 3, the concept of pairs and demonology is evident in this section. The verb כמן is a *hapax legomenon* in the Qumran Aramaic writings (cf. Cook 2015: 114). CAL provides several examples of uses related to setting an ambush (e.g., *Tg. Onq.* Gen. 27:42; *Tg. J.* 1 Sam. 23:9; *Tg.* Job 38:40). Given the pronominal suffix on נפשה in line 3, the word spoken here seems to regard danger toward another figure's life (i.e., not Amram). If the reference to שד in 4Q547 3 1 is at all helpful, the present fragment may relate to the dangers of demonic influence or threat.

4.9.5. *Dialogue with the* Angelus Interpres *in Amram's Dream-Vision (4Q545 7)*

First-person dialogue, perhaps within Amram's dream-vision.

1 [...] ואמרת בדן אנה רבֿהֿ[...]
2 [...] למרגז עלי ולדחליתֿ[...]
BOTTOM MARGIN?

1. [...] Then I said in response to this, "I am great [...]
2. to be angry at me and to frighten [...]

Textual, Scribal, and Material Notes
Primary images for transcription: PAM M43.566; B-359458; B-359457.

Line 1: רבֿהֿ ("I am great") – Read here with Puech (2001: 346) and Beyer (2004: 124). Duke (2010: 21) read רבֿ[.

Commentary

Lines 1–2: *Then I said in response to this, "I am great [...]to be angry at me and to frighten.* The opening discourse marker here confirms that we are once again in the context of a dialogue with a first-person speaker. In view of the confirmed *VA* fragments, it is only Amram who speaks in this form of address, so presumably this fragment retains aspects of a lost discourse. The form בדן (lit., "in this," i.e., "in response") also suggests that his statement here is in reply to something, or someone, else. As such, it is likely that this material comes from the back-and-forth discussion with the *angelus interpres*.

The content of line 2 also hints at this as the paired forms indicating Amram's fright (√רגז, "to be angry"; √דחל "to fear"; cf. 1Q20 19 18; 4Q544 1 13; 4Q530 2 ii + 6–12 20; Dan. 4:5 [2]; 7:7) are common responses to revelations in the Qumran Aramaic dream-vision accounts (Perrin 2015a: 110–14) and indeed among the emotional responses to revelatory accounts in broader ancient Near Eastern, Hellenistic, and biblical literature (Oppenheim 1956: 191; Bar 2001: 35–43, 70–77; Flannery Dailey 2004: 23, 51, 63, 88).

4.9.6. *A Chronological Framework and Future Forecast (4Q545 9)*

A fragment clustering chronological references in what seems like a context of instruction, reflection, or admonition.

1 [...] ◦ [...]
2 [...] וֹמן רוחֹ [...]
3 [...]הֹ ולכול שנא
4 [...]בֹרה על רֹ/בֹ
5 [...]וֹמני עדניהוֹן
6 [...]◦ *vacat* [...]
7 [...] לֹ[...]◦[...]◦מ◦[...]

1. [...] and also [...]
2. [...] and from a spirit [...]
3. [...] and for every year...[...]
4. [...]his son over...[...]
5. [...] and from me are their times
6. [...] *vacat* [...]
7. [...] for [...] ... [...] ... [...]

Textual, Scribal, and Material Notes

Primary images for transcription: PAM M43.566; B-359464; B-359463. It is possible that 4Q545 5 provides four fragmentary lines of text preceding the materials of 4Q545 9. The fragments were already arranged in this way on PAM M43.566 and continue to be preserved in this way in more recent image plates of

B-359464 and B-359463. Unfortunately, a definite physical join is not present. The possibility of the connect rests on the "fit" of the fragments, although there is definite coloration difference in the fragments which may indicate their origins in different sections of the original scroll or the effects of aging and deterioration after their discovery. Given these uncertainties, I do not present the texts here jointly. For brief comment on the limited content of 4Q545 9, see the introduction to 4Q545 on small fragments not included in the commentary proper.

Line 1: ○ ("…") – The only remains of text here are the lower reaches of at least one character. This is possibly a final *kaph, nun, pe*, or *tsade*. Puech (2001: 347) reads וֹאף, which is possible but too ambitious.

Line 4: עֹל בֹ̇/רֹ̇ ("") – The first form is evident on the manuscript but what follows is less certain due to damage. The latest photos retain the upper portion of a lost letter, likely a *bet* or *resh*. It seems also that there is a space between these words. Other readings of these characters include: עלי̇הֹ[ן] (Puech 2001: 347) and עלי̊ו○[…] (Duke 2010: 32).

Commentary

Lines 2–5: *and from a spirit [...] and for every year…[...]his son over…[...] and from me are their times.* Unfortunately, having no more than two complete forms per line on this fragment limits our understanding of this material in context. Regardless, some of the surviving terms hint at possible topics. These, however, could conceivably fit within either Amram's revelation or some narrative scene of paternal discourse.

The form רוח ("a spirit") in line 2 may relate to the larger framework of angelology and demonology developed more fully in other fragments of Amram's dream-vision. Here it is relevant that other Aramaic texts reference malevolent beings using the form רוח (1Q20 20 26–28; 4Q197 4 i 13 [Tob. 6:8]; 4Q560 1 ii 6). See also the contextual comment on 4Q544 2 13.

The phrase ולכול שנא ("and for every year") in line 3 indicates the fragment has some sort of chronological element. This theme is also evident by the phrase וֹמני עדניהוֹן ("and from me are their times") in line 5. At the outset of *VA*, the context-setting element of the work's title also established a chronological framework (4Q543 1a–c 2–4; 4Q545 1a i 3; 4Q546 1 1–2).

The reference to בֹרה ("his son") suggests some context of paternal instruction and, presumably, genealogical reference to priestly offspring. In the known context of *VA*, Amram's dream-vision has a transgenerational view of the priestly line in view, with particular reference to Aaron (4Q545 11 1; cf. 4Q545 4 18; 4Q546 12 3). Given the third-person suffix here, it is also relevant that this form also featured earlier in the narrative with reference to Aaron when Amram was gathering his children (4Q545 1a i 8).

4.10. Text and Commentary: 4QVisions of Amram^d (4Q546)

Several fragments of 4Q546 are not included in the commentary below (4Q546 3, 6, 7, 9–11, 13, 15–19, 21–25). In several cases, these fragments are of reasonable size but their reasonably legible text is limited due to surface damage on the manuscript. Some of these, however, include terms and phrases that are noteworthy even if their full context is unknown. Relevant forms and phrases include the items described here:

1. The fragmentary references to חזית ("I saw") in the context of בֿנֿיֿ עַֿמה ("sons of his people") in 4Q546 3 3–4 likely indicates the ongoing association of revelatory knowledge with the priestly lineage.
2. The verb תטבע ("will sink") in 4Q546 6 2 also occurs in the image of drowning animals in the *Animal Apocalypse* (*1 En.* 89:5 [4Q206 4 i 19]).
3. 4Q546 7 includes a potential reference to the מי די[נא ("waters of judge[ment") as well as מוֹעֵ[דא ("[the] appoint[ed time") which may suggest an image of eschatological judgment channeling the motifs of the deluge.
4. 4Q546 9 has several complete forms—including שׁמה ("his name," line 3), עִּדעִֿדן ("at that time," line 5) and מהילכין ("walking about," line 6)— but none of which benefit from enough context to determine their sense or setting. This fragment also includes an unusual large medial *mem* at the lower edge of the column or fragment, suggesting a scribal correction or marginal marking. For a recent interpretation of this fragment, see Goldman 2020: 110–12 (cf. also Puech 2001: 361–62).
5. 4Q546 10 1–2 mentions מצרין ("Egypt") in the vicinity of the form מפתין ("miracles")—the latter is both a *hapax legomenon* and Hebraism (Stadel 2008: 61; cf. Duke 2010: 16)—suggesting some tradition related to the plagues and/or exodus. For brief comment on this likely context, see also: Puech 2001: 363; Goldman 2020 112–13; and Høgenhaven 2020: 127–28. It is possible that 4Q546 11 includes additional such content, but the fragment is so damaged that hints in this direction would require a more generous reading than the fragment affords.
6. 4Q546 13 3 may include a reference to "Moses," though the reading is far from certain (cf. 4Q543 2a–b 4; 4Q545 4 15).
7. Despite retaining ink traces and partial forms from likely two columns, 4Q546 15 offers up little in terms of complete forms. Of these, the reference to וכוֹל דֿרין ("and all generations") in 4Q546 15 ii 2 hints further at the genealogical and/or future orientation of *VA*'s discourses.
8. 4Q546 18 1–2 includes both fraternal and priestly language with the forms אחֿ ("brother") and כהנֿא ("the priest") in close proximity.

Many of these items confirm that *VA*'s ancestral traditions, revelatory scenes, and geographical elements extended beyond what is known from the larger fragments.

4.10.1. *Pseudepigraphic Title and Miriam's Marriage Celebration (4Q546 1)*

This is the third fragment including elements of the title and opening scene of *VA*. Overlap: <u>4Q543 1a–c</u>; **4Q545 1a i**.

1 [...]ooo[...]
2 [...]מא̇[ת ח̇משוּ̇ת] וּתר[תֿ̇י̇ן...]
3 [...] עֿ̇ל̇וֿ̇ה̇[י] וֿ̇שֿ̇ל̇ח̇[...]
4 [...]לא[נתֿ̇ה̇ בֿ̇]רתה[...]תֿ̇[ ]תֿ̇[...]o[...]

1. [...]...[...]
2. [...hund]red and fifty-[sec]on[d...]
3. [...] toward hi[m.] And he sent[...]
4. [...his] da[ghter as a w]ife[...]...[...]...[...]

Textual, Scribal, and Material Notes
Primary images for transcription: PAM M43.586; B-363301; B-363300. Given the small size of this fragment, my reconstructions are reserved. For more complete representations of the text, see the larger overlapping fragments listed above.

Line 2: חמֿשוּ̇ת ("fifty") – My reading differs from other editions but the form is quite clear on the new infrared images. Compare: וחמשיןֿ (Puech 2001: 353; cf. Beyer 1984: 210; 2004: 118), וחמשין (García Martínez and Tigchelaar 1998 2:1090), and וחמשין (Duke 2010: 12).

Commentary
Line 2: *hund]red and fifty-[sec]on[d.* For discussion of the features of the title of *VA* and the opening scenes of Miriam's union to Uzziel, see the commentary on 4Q543 1a–c 1–4.

4.10.2. *Amram's Sojourn to Build Tombs and the Departure of Qahat (4Q546 2)*

Another fragment relating Amram's sojourn to build ancestral tombs and reference to the Egypt–Canaan–Philistia war. Overlap: **4Q543 3**; <u>4Q545 1a–b ii</u>.

1 [...]שֿ̇נת רישי ברשוֿ[...]
2 o[...]o <u>וסלקת למקבֿ</u>[ר...]
3 אֿבֿ[התהוֿ]ןֿ ושבקני אבי קהֿ[ת...]
4 <u>ולמסב להוֿן</u> כל צרכיהון מן [...]o
BOTTOM MARGIN

1. [...] my first year with...[...]
2. ...[...]... And I went up to bur[y...]
3. [their] fath[er]s. And my father, Qah[at], left me[...]
4. and to take for themselves all their needs from ...[...]

Textual, Scribal, and Material Notes
Primary images for transcription: PAM M43.586; B-363303; B-363302. As was the case with 4Q543 3, while there are minor overlaps with other *VA* fragments, given the size of 4Q546, I do not undertake reconstructions here. For more complete representations and reconstructions, see the fuller fragments of 4Q544 1 and 4Q545 1a–b ii.

Line 3: וֹשׁבקני ("and he left me") – The reading here is clear on the new digital images. Earlier proponents of this reading include García Martínez and Tigchelaar (1998 2:1090). The form is a third-person, masculine, singular *peal* perfect with a first-person, common, singular pronominal suffix. Though the context is limited, this suggests Qahat is the subject of the verb. Puech (2001: 354) read the plural ושבקוני, as did Duke ושבקוני (2010: 16). Beyer initially read ושבקני (1994: 86) ut then shifted to the plural reading of ושבקוני in his later edition (2004: 119).

Commentary
Lines 1–4: *my first year with...[...]...[...]... So I went up to bur[y...their] fath[er]s. And my father, Qah[at], left me[...] and to take for themselves all their needs from.* The minor overlaps with both 4Q543 and 4Q545 noted above secure a narrative context for this fragment in the travel narratives of *VA*. For discussion of this section of *VA*, see the commentary on the larger fragment of 4Q545 1a–b ii. Though small in size, the present fragment does include important phrases and perspective on the founding of ancestral internment sites in Hebron that have not survived in the overlapping materials. Most significantly, the phrase שׁנת רישׁי ("my first year") indicates that this material was framed chronologically in some way. Elsewhere, Amram relates his solitary stay in Canaan lasted forty-one years (4Q544 1 6).

4.10.3. *Dialogue with the* Angelus Interpres *on the Dominions of Dualism (4Q546 4)*

Dialogue with the *angelus interpres*, perhaps relating to the content or context of 4Q544 2.

1 [...]o אָמֹר o[...]
2 [...]אָ[...]לֹא שׁליט וֹאנה ה̇[...]oo[...]
3 [...]oo[...]oלתֹהֹ אָמֹרת לֹהֹ ומא o[...]
4 [...]oooo[...]

1. [...] He said [...]
2. [...]... and I am ruler, not [...]...[...]
3. [...]...[...]...I said to him, "And what...[...]
4. [...]...[...]

Textual, Scribal, and Material Notes
Primary images for transcription: PAM M43.586; B-363305; B-363304.

Line 3: אָמְרת לֹהּ ומאָ ("I said to him, 'And what'") – Given the damage to the fragment, it is not possible to confirm overlap with 4Q544 2 with confidence. However, if overlaps are entertained, then line 3 would involve an internal textual variant with 4Q544 2 13, which reads: ואמרת מראי מא ("And I said, 'My Lord, what'").

Commentary
Line 2: *and I am ruler, not.* The fragment is devoid of context and does not benefit from certain textual overlap with any other known *VA* materials (see note above). Nonetheless, the blend of third-person and first-person discourse markers make it certain that the present fragment retains lost dialogue between Amram and the *angelus interpres*. The only hint of the topic of this question and answer is the form וֹאנה שליט ("and I am ruler") in line 2, which are unquestionably words spoken by the light figure. As seen in the commentary on 4Q543 5–9 and 4Q544 1–2, references to the domains and dimensions of the rule of each figure occur relatively early in the dream-vision's symbolic representation and celestial disclosures. This suggests that the current fragment relates in some way to the self-revelation of the nature and scope of the light figure's rule that begins in 4Q544 2 15.

4.10.4. *The Lot of the Righteous and Rulership in the Created Order (4Q546 5)*

A small fragment that touches on dualities and dimensions of rule, perhaps relating to the lot of righteous or truthful ones and a hint of creation language.

1 [...] שׁ[ל]טֹנה וֹ[...]
2 [...]אָ קָשׁיטיא ○[...]
3 [...] בְּרֹאָ[...]

1. [...]do[m]inion and...[...]
2. [...] also the righteous ... [...]
3. [...] he created [...]

Textual, Scribal, and Material Notes
Primary images for transcription: PAM M43.586; B-363319; B-363318.

Line 1: שׁ[ל]טֹנה ("do[m]inion") – I tentatively accept the reading (Puech 2001: 357), though with necessary diacritics. Duke (2010: 33) is the only other edition on offer at this point, reading only טֹנה[...]. The extant characters are only partially known and, more problematic, what many take as a partial *sin/shin* is too distant from the other characters or reconstructed *lamed*. This may suggest the stroke is from the previous word. It is possible, therefore, that the reading is in fact פּתֹח ○ ("...he opened"). See also the same verb at 4Q546 14 3.

Commentary
Lines 1–3: *do[m]inion and...[...] also the righteous ... [...] he created.* Given the presence of yet another reference to rulership language, here שׁ[ל]טֹנה ("do[m]inion"), this fragment likely comes from the section of Amram's dream-vision relating to the nature and scope of the dominion of the light and dark figures (cf. 4Q544 1–2; 4Q546 4). The reference to קשׁיטיא ("the righteous," or perhaps "truth") in line 2 may indicate that for *VA* these domains also included lots of humanity, which seems to be the case in 4Q548 1 ii–2 7–8. Given the nature of the fragment at this point, however, this proposal is speculative. Two-ways motifs featuring forms of קשׁוט also occur in *GenAp* (1Q20 6 2–6), and it seems likely the Aramaic *Vorlage* of Tob. 1:3 (cf. G¹ and G^II ἀληθείας ["truth"]; Syr. ܩܘܫܬܐ). Finally, it is possible that the contentious verb בּרא ("he created") in line 3 adds yet another element implied in the earlier comment on 4Q544 2 15 namely that *VA* explores the question of the origins of evil within the framework of divine oversight of God. The verb here may hint that *VA* framed this in some way within a creation theology. Given the brittle and broken text at this point, this too is speculative.

4.10.5. *The Naming of Aaron within Amram's Dream-Vision (4Q546 8)*

Fragmentary dialogue perhaps in the context of the dream-vision, here referencing Aaron by name.

1 [...] פּרֹקתּה שׁמֹהּ [...]
2 [...]אֹהרון ארו אנ[ה...]
3 [...]○דֹה יתוֹבּ[...]ל[...]
4 [...]תּקרא לה [...]
5 [...]אֹרוֹ א[...]

1. [...] you redeemed his name [...]
2. [...] Aaron. Behold, I[...]
3. [...]...he will return...[...]...[...]
4. [...] you called him [...]
5. [...] behold ...[...]

Textual, Scribal, and Material Notes

Primary images for transcription: PAM M43.586; B-363315; B-363314.

Line 1: פְּרַקְתָּה ("you redeemed") – I accept the reading also found in several other editions (Puech 2001: 360). The reading בְּרִקְתָּה ("lightning") is also possible based on the ink traces (cf. Duke 2010: 154). Even with the limited context here, however, it is unclear how that meaning would relate to a word spoken over, or about, Aaron.

Line 5: אֲרוּ ("behold") – The partial remains of the *aleph* here could also be read as a medial *mem*. Similarly, the final *vav* could be a *yod*. As such, the reading מָרִי ("my lord") should also be considered. See below for commentary on how either option would fit within a revelatory context.

Commentary

Lines 1–5: *you redeemed his name [...] Aaron. Behold, I[...]...he will return... [...]...[...] you called him [...] behold.* Since we cannot verify a narrative context on account of material overlap with another fragment, internal formal features are our only option. These too are in short supply. However, the repeated particle ארו in lines 2 and 5 fit most naturally within a revelatory context. For the avalanche of data that points in this direction from analogous settings in the Qumran Aramaic texts, see Perrin (2015a: 102–103). The phrases of lines 1, 2, and 4 all relate to either the name of a priestly figure—אַהֲרוֹן ("Aaron")—or some aspect of naming. Elsewhere in the dream-vision Aaron is alluded to in lofty terms establishing his place in the historic priestly genealogy and aligning his position in light of the heavenly priesthood (4Q545 4 18). Similarly, Levi, his sons, and seemingly also Aaron are in view in the final section of the dream-vision presented in 4Q547 8–9. It is uncertain if the redemption (√פרק) and calling (√קרא) in lines 1 and 4 are in reference to Aaron or another figure. Preserving a good name of the priestly forefathers is also a motif in *ALD* (4Q213a 3–4 13–16) and *WQ* (4Q542 1 i 10). Goldman (2020: 109) conjectured that the verb of line 4 hints that "in this passage Amram is informed of Moses's future role in the exodus" and that this indicates "Amram received revelation of his son's Hebrew name and his role as Israel's deliverer." While this remains an intriguing possibility in view of *VA*'s provision of Moses's Hebrew name in 4Q545 1a i 9, it goes beyond the bounds of what is certain from the present fragment.

4.10.6. *The Mystery of Miriam (4Q546 12)*

Ancestral discourse or angelic revelation with a likely reference to the "mystery" of Miriam.

1 [...] בְּנִין [...]לׄ[...]לׄ[...]עָלַם לחׄ[...]ooׄ[...]
2 [...] עָלְמִין [...]oׄ[...]לְקָרְבֹ הוּא[...]ooׄ[...]
3 [...] ל עליה בשלם oׄ[...]ooׄ[...]oׄ לחׄוֹהׄ[...]oׄ[...]
4 [...]oׄ וֹרוֹ מרים עׄבׄדׄ להׄ[...]לׄ[...]
5 [...]מׄ[...]oׄ[...]

1. [...]sons[...]...[...] ...forever...[...]...[...]
2. [...]ages[...]...[...]to approach him[...]...[...]
3. [...]...upon it in peace...[...]...[...]...he will be[...]...[...]
4. [...]and the mystery of Miriam he made for her[...]...[...]
5. [...] ... [...]

Textual, Scribal, and Material Notes
Primary images for transcription: PAM M43.586; B-363321; B-363320.
Line 1: בְּנִין ("sons") – The reading is tenuous, but I follow Puech (2001: 364) as the ink traces align with this contextually appropriate reading.
Line 2: לְקִרְב ("to approach") – The reading here recovers a likely *lamed* in the digital infrared images. Puech read and reconstructed the participle [מ]קְרִב (Puech 2001: 364). Duke (2010: 32) read]ב הוא.
Line 3: ̊ן̊ ("...") – Both old and new images are faint here, rendering more full transcriptions too ambitious. Here Puech (2001: 364) perceived a reference to Aaron, לְאַהֲ[רן]. More reservedly, I follow Duke's (2010: 32) minimal transcription of but a final *nun*.

Commentary
Line 4: *and the mystery of Miriam he made for her.* This fragment invites more questions than it answers, with most of them oriented around this remarkable phrase in line 4 regarding the רז̊ מרים ("mystery of Miriam"). The narrative context of this fragment is unknown. Although, if we had to venture a guess between the two plausible options of either ancestral discourse or angelic disclosure, the latter seems more likely to be the case.

As seen already in the commentary to 4Q545 4 16, the *angelus interpres* spoke of the רז עובדה ("mystery of his work") with respect to Aaron's priestly position and association with the celestial priesthood. It was also evident in that fragment that the angelic revelation began with information related to Moses and then shifted to Aaron. Given this sequence and the treatment of the רז already in that context, it is likely that the angelic revelation then proceeded to comment on the next sibling in the sequence: Miriam.

At this point in the narrative of *VA*, Miriam needs no introduction (see the commentary on 4Q543 1a–c). As noted in the commentary to 4Q214a 2–3 i 1–6, *ALD* already established a focus on women figures in the priestly genealogies. As such, both the narrative interests of *VA* and genealogical aims of the Aramaic priestly literature provided a space for developing Miriam's profile. Of course, this re-presentation and reformation of Miriam in *VA* fits within a cluster of emerging Miriam traditions from ancient Judaism (for the scope and selective treatment of traditions relevant to *VA*, see the commentary on 4Q543 1a–c 5–7).

As was the case with Aaron's mystery in 4Q545 4 16, the question of the meaning of רז here is challenging. Due to the small size of the fragment in questions here, most scholarly proposals are sufficiently open-ended. Puech (2001: 365) noted that in *LAB* 9:10 Miriam is associated with otherworldly revelation regarding Moses's illustrious future and that both *LAB* and *VA* seem to use the reference to Miriam as a הנביאה ("the prophetess") in Exod. 15:20 as their departure point for developing her profile.Thomas remarked generally that the suite of priestly literature often underscores priestly teaching and craft (Thomas 2010: 424), but did not indicate the exact bearing of that insight here. Tervanotko stated that "it is important to recognize that apart from individuals, certain families are connected with *raz*. In this case, several members of a single family have access to *raz*" and proposed that in *VA* this reference may relate to revelation regarding the future prophetic role or status of Miriam (Tervanotko 2016: 136–37). Elsewhere I argued that the dream-vision profiles of ancestors developed in the Aramaic texts were occasioned in some cases by a trend for the prophetization of the patriarchs (Perrin 2015a: 139–43). In view of Miriam's established prophetic status in the Hebrew Scriptures, it is likely that the *VA* Miriam also fits within this trend for ascribing or amplifying the prophetic credentials of ancestral figures. In this instance, therefore, *VA* makes an important contribution to this trend as it pertains to a woman character.

This may answer the question of *why* Miriam's character was developed—as a prophetess she *should* be associated with otherworldly knowledge. However, it does not answer the question of *what* constituted this רז in the imagination of *VA*. In the immediate context of *VA*, רז clearly has priestly associations and connotations when associated with ancestors (cf. 4Q545 4 16). As such, the meaning here likely has some connection to that concept. The implications of this idea as it relates to Miriam as a woman within the priestly line are unclear. Recall that it was the priestly acts of Aaron and his sons that were mysterious insofar as they aligned with a celestial priesthood. Since Miriam does not have a priestly performative profile, the mystery of Miriam may in some way relate to her genealogical position in the structure of *VA* (cf. 4Q547 9 10).

4.10.7. *Paternal Instruction to a Single Son and Collective Audience (4Q546 14)*

Paternal instruction focused on single son and then a collective progeny.

TOP MARGIN
1 וּכְעַן בְּרִי ○[...]
2 לְעָמְדָ[...]תֹּנִדְ[עַ]○[...]○ר̊○○[...]
3 אַל פְּתַח בֵּיתָךְ עַ[...]○○[...]
4 וּכְעַן בְּנֵי שָׁמְעוּ דִּי̊ [...]
5 חֲזִית[...]○[...]
6 [...]
7 [...]

1. But now, my son...[...]
2. to your people. You will kno[w...]...[...]...[...]
3. do not open your house...[...]
4. But now, my sons, hear what [...]
5. I saw...[...]
6. [...]
7. [...]

Textual, Scribal, and Material Notes
Primary images for transcription: PAM M43.586; B-363297; B-363296. The fragment includes both a top margin and generous right column from the beginning of a sheet, which still retains strands of the stitching. The column also features guide dots for the spacing of lines.

Line 2: תֻנֹד[ע ("You will know") – This reading is informed by Puech's transcription (2001: 367), a reading also accepted by Duke (2010: 27).

Line 3: בִּיתָךְ ("your house") – There is a crack in the fragment mid-form that compromises the reading in the latest digital images. The earlier PAM plates, however, retain more ink traces unobscured by the material edges of the leather to confirm the reading. For similar transcriptions, see Puech (2001: 367) and Duke (2010: 27).

Commentary
Lines 1–6: *But now, my son...[...] to your people. You will kno[w...]...[...]... [...] do not open your house...[...] But now, my sons, hear what [...] I saw.* The first-person voice here with specific reference to both a singular son (line 1) and a plural progeny (line 4, note the plural imperative שמעו) confirm the fragment comes from a scene of patriarchal instruction. On the trend for these Aramaic ancestral addresses to shift from singular to plural audiences, see the commentary on 4Q542 1 i 4. Note also that in the present fragment, the references to offspring in close proximity vacillate from use of בר and בן. The question, then, becomes: whose first-person voice are we hearing in this fragment? It is possible that the form חזית ("I saw") in line 5 is a reflection upon the revelation of a dream-vision, in which case Amram would be the most natural candidate for this address as in the opening scenes of *VA*. Note, however, that elsewhere I detected potential words that could be spoken by Qahat in smaller fragments (4Q543 15, 16). As such, we cannot rule out another patriarchal figure here is taking up the mantle of the first-person voice.

4.10.8. *A Tablet for Ancestral Instruction or Otherworldly Revelation (4Q546 20)*

A small fragment referencing a "tablet," presumably either in the context of ancestral instruction or otherworldly revelation.

4. *Visions of Amram*

[...]ο ה○○[...] 1
[...]בּלֹוחאָ[...] 2

1. [...] ... [...]
2. [...] with the tablet [...]

Textual, Scribal, and Material Notes

Primary images for transcription: PAM M43.586; B-363335; B-363334. Judging from what appears to be a dot at the right edge of lines 2, and perhaps for a lost line 3, it seems that the fragment comes from the right edge of the column as the present manuscript features such guide dots on sheets (see 4Q546 14). The fragment also has a rather large uninscribed space at the bottom, suggesting either a lower margin or *vacat* at the beginning of a lost line of text.

Line 1: ה○○ ("...") – Puech (2001: 371) read מֹלֹּה ("a word"). This is possible but not certain given the fragmentary nature of the text at this point. Duke (2010: 34) reads לה[.

Commentary:

Line 2: *In the tablet.* The phrase בּלֹוחאָ is the only recoverable form in this fragment. Though fleeting, it is potentially significant for how we understand the revelatory discourse of the narrative and the authority claiming strategies of the composition. Elsewhere *VA* associates Amram with both scribal skill and revelatory experiences. However, these are only with references to inscribed writings using reflections of the root כתב (4Q547 9 8). The inclusion of the tablet motif, even in lack of context, suggests that aspects of the revelation and authority ascribed to Amram encompassed learning from otherworldly media. The tablet also adds a yet unrecognized aspect of the edifice of authority bound up in Amram's persona as a seer of otherworldly inscribed media. As noted in the commentary to 4Q545 4 14–15, it is possible that this otherworldly record revealed the imminent exodus and ascendancy of Moses.

This reference may also be contextualized more broadly. Tablets occur in several other Aramaic texts represented at Qumran (1Q23 31 3; 2Q26 1 1–3; 4Q203 7b ii 2; 8 3; 4Q537 1 + 2 + 3 3–5) as well as other texts emerging in, or informed by, Second Temple period thought (e.g., *1 En.* 81:1–2; 93:2; 103:2; 106:19; *3 En.* 26:12; *Sib. Or.* 3:257; *4 Ezra* 14:24; *T. Levi* 5:4; *Artap.* 3:26; *Eup.* 4:5; *Hist. Rech.* 8:1; 16:14; *Liv. Pro.* 2:14; *Ps.-Philo* 12:5, 10; 19:7; 22:5; 26:12–13, 15; 54:1, 5; *Jub.* 1:0, 29; 3:10, 31; 4:5, 32; 5:13; 6:17). Heavenly writings, though not technically tablets, register also in Danielic literature (Dan. 7:10; 10:21; 12:1; 4Q243 6) as well as Hebrew writings among the Dead Sea Scrolls (1QH^a 9 25–26; 4Q180 1 3; 4Q504 1–2 vi 14 [recto]). The notion of divine ledgers for authority claiming and conferring, of course, has a deeper heritage in the Hebrew Scriptures and reach in other ancient Near Eastern texts (see Eppel 1937; Paul 1973; García Martínez 1997; Ravid 1999; Perrin 2015a: 194 n. 12).

4.11. Text and Commentary: 4QVisions of Amram^e (4Q547)

As with the other manuscripts, 4Q547 includes several fragments too small for a full commentary (4Q547 4, 6, 7). These include words or phrases worth noting:

1. The reading עֻ[מֹ]קָא ("the de]pth") in 4Q547 4 i 4 is far from certain yet may reflect the idea of dimensions of dualities for the light and dark figures of Amram's dream-vision (cf. 4Q544 2 15–16).
2. 4Q547 6 2 includes sacrificial language, specifically the verb אקטרין ("he will burn sacrifices"). This form also appears to have cancellation dots above the final two characters.

The following more complete fragments include items both overlapping with other *VA* manuscripts as well as providing insight into yet unknown aspects of its literary contours and theological outlooks.

4.11.1. *Amram Builds Tombs and Asserts His Commitment to Endogamy (4Q547 1–2)*

A set of fragments with limited content of Amram's founding tombs, sojourn, statement of endogamy, and opening of the dream-vision. Overlap: **4Q543 4, 5–9**; 4Q544 1; 4Q545 1a–b ii.

TOP MARGIN
1 [...שְׁמַ]וֹעַת קְרָב
2 [...]
3 [...]
4 [...]תֵאתֹה
5 [...לְ]מֹתֹב למצרין
6 [...וּ]בְכוֹל דַן יוכבד
7 [אנתתי...אַ]נְתָה אֹחרי
8 [...]אֲתוֹב למצרִין
9 [...וּ]חֹזית בחזות
10 [...]דילוהי ואחדין
11 [...]רִין ל' אנחנא
12 [...]אַנֶ[תָה בֹּעָה
13 [...]וֹחֹשִׁיךֹ
BOTTOM MARGIN

1. [...a r]eport of war
2. [...]
3. [...]
4. [...]she may come
5. [...]to return to Egypt
6. [...] through all this, Yochebed,

7. [my wife…]another [w]ife
8. […]I may return to Egypt
9. […]I saw in the vision
10. […]And they were locked
11. […]…to me, "We
12. […y]ou seeking?"
13. […]and pitch

Textual, Scribal, and Material Notes

Primary images for transcription: PAM M43.567; B-295533; B-294989; B-295539; B-294995. This set of fragments is notoriously difficult to read. The ink is faint and at times challenging to read even in infrared images. The leather is distorted, resulting in some shrinkage of the fragment. Depending on one's configuration and reconstruction of lost texts, there are at least two lines missing between the fragments (lines 2–3). While we can gain some insight into the lost content of this literary unit from overlaps listed above, even these reconstructions result in gaps of unknown text (cf. Puech 2001: 379; Duke 2010: 16–17; Beyer 2004: 119; 1994: 86–87). The above modest reconstruction integrates overlapping text when available, with the aim of contextualizing the materials of the present fragment rather than a full reconstruction of the literary unit. For fuller context, see the more complete overlapping fragments indicated above.

Line 12: בעה ("you seeking") – The form is faint on the manuscript, making any reading tentative. I tentatively accept Puech's (2001: 379) reading but note that in the new infrared images, it is possible the form reads דעא. The problem with this reading is that it does not relate directly to an Aramaic lexeme, unless we take it as an alternate and unattested representation of דעה ("knowledge"), which would be speculative.

Commentary

Lines 1–13: *a r]eport of war […]she may come […]to return to Egypt […] through all this, Yochebed [my wife…]another [w]ife […]I may return to Egypt […]I saw in the vision […]And they were locked […]…to me, "We […y]ou seeking?" […]and pitch.* The decay pattern of this fragment means we have only sets of forms or phrases at the beginning of several lines that relate to multiple elements of *VA*'s narrative. Line 1 includes the notation of the regional conflict that kept Amram in Canaan. As seen in lines 4–8, this conflict is presented in part to underscore Amram's fidelity to Yochebed and the practice of endogamous marriage even in such uncertain times. Finally, lines 9–12 include elements of the introductory formula of Amram's dream-vision, the opening scene of angelic debate, and Amram's interjection that results in dialogue with the figures. For additional comment on the war tradition, endogamous rhetoric, and dream-vision formula, see the discussion of the fuller fragment 4Q544 1.

4.11.2. *Revelation and Warnings against Demonic Influence (4Q547 3)*

Continued discourse and revelation regarding the direction of a demonic figure. Minor overlaps exist with 4Q545 yet given the fragmentary nature of both texts and uncertainty of narrative context I undertake only minor reconstructions. Overlap: 4Q545 6.

1 [...] ○[...שד תדבר וכדי תופֿעֿ...[וֿלא תהוה]
2 [...] ○[... קדמיתא לתניאניתא [קֿדֿמֿיֿתֿאֿ תהא]
3 [...] עֿלֿ[נֿפֿשה תכמון בין תרתיהוֿןֿ...]
4 [...]○[...]רֿהי לֿהֿי בחשׁבוניה וֿ[...]
5 [...] הֿיֿלֿהֿ חברא ורבֿרֿ[ב...]
6 [...] ○[...] ל[ה] זֿ[...]○ חברא
7 [...]○[...]

1. [...]...you will guide a demon. When you shine[...and not to be]
2. [...]...the first to the second [and with the first you shall be
3. [...for] its life you shall lie in wait between their two
4. [...]...Therefore, by his reckonings and...[...]
5. [...]having been made strong, the conjurer and the grea[t...]
6. [...]...the conjurer. The[re]fore...[...]
7. [...]...[...]

Textual, Scribal, and Material Notes
Primary images for transcription: PAM M43.567; B-295538; B-294994. The more recent digital images offer enhanced views of the content of most of the fragment (B-295538; B-294994). However, its scope is best appreciated in PAM M43.567. These include the lower two and half lines of text, which are lost or represented elsewhere in the modern collection.

Line 1: There is a horizontal stroke prior to and partially extending below to the first word of the line (שד, "demon"). Beyer (1994: 90; 2004: 122) transcribes a final *nun*, which is incorrect. While this could be the base stroke of a *bet* or medial *kaf*, the mark seems too long for such character formations. As such, it is possible that the line is a mark by a scribe or user. Similar occurrences of scribal lines or hooks occur at 4Q213 1 ii–2 10–11; 4Q213b 2 10–11; and 4Q542 1 ii 8–9. However, in all of those cases the markings are in the intercolumnar margins.

Line 1: תופֿעֿ ("you shine") – I follow the reading of Puech (2001: 381; cf. Beyer 2004: 122) here, though the proposed *ayin* is known by but a dot of ink at the edge of the fragment. Most other editions reconstruct this character to complete the reading (Beyer 1994: 90; García Martínez and Tigchelaar 1998 2:1092; Duke 2010: 26).

Commentary

Line 1: *you will guide a demon. When you shine[...and not to be.* Neither 4Q547 3 nor the minor overlaps in 4Q545 6 provide sufficient context to determine their narrative location. The topics and terms included here in lines 1–3 seem to relate to either the ongoing revelation within Amram's dream-vision or perhaps his reflection and expounding upon it for an audience upon awakening. This association is suggested by the forms שד ("demon") and תופַע ("you shine"; √יפע, see Cook 2015: 105), which likely pair with the topic of the otherworldly forces and figures at work in the dichotomized conceptual universe advanced in the dream-vision episode.

As seen in the commentary above to 4Q544 2–3, there are no shortage of demonic and angelic agents in the Aramaic DSS. References to שד ("demon"), however, are in relatively short supply. The vast majority of occurrences are found in the Aramaic Tobit fragments (4Q196 14 i 5, 12 [Tob. 6:15, 18]; 4Q197 4 i 13 [Tob. 6:8]; 4 ii 9, 13 [Tob. 6:15, 16]), with an additional plural occurrence found in a citation of Ps. 106:37 in the so-called *Pseudo-Daniel* materials (4Q243 13 2 // 4Q244 12 2), and a fragmentary reference in an unidentified Aramaic text (4Q564 1 ii 2). Given the disagreement in person and number with the following verb תדבר, it is clear that שד here is not the subject. As such, the present fragment does not refer to the leading, guidance, or influence of a demonic figure or force.

Lines 2–3: *the first to the second [and with the first you shall be[...for] its life you shall lie in wait between their two.* The several partial phrases here are not easily interpreted without greater context. One motif that is evident in these lines, however, is something framed as pairs. This may relate to the dichotomized or dualistic concepts of Amram's dream-vision.

Lines 4–6: *Therefore, by his reckonings and...[...]having been made strong, the conjurer and the grea[t...]...the conjurer. The[re]fore.* As with the foregoing lines, these provide more suggestive hints than certain conclusions about the context and meaning of the surviving materials. The pair of להן forms in lines 4 and 6 provide some pegs suggesting the sequence of discourse. The noun חשבון occurs in a variety of contexts in the Aramaic DSS, from chronological structures (1Q20 6 9; 4Q530 2 i + 3 4) to human or divine plans (4Q534 1 i 9–10) to measurements (4Q554 2 i 16). The meaning here in *VA* is unknown. The tandem occurrences of חבר are equally intriguing. With Puech (2001: 381) and Cook (2015: 74), I take this form to likely refer to some sort of "conjurer." The occurrence here is a *hapax legomenon* in the Aramaic DSS and the lexical data in later literature are equally limited, with a single occurrence with this meaning known in *Tg. Neof.* Deut. 18:11 (cf. *Pesh.* Ps. 58:6). Given the material damage and lexical deficit, venturing a guess of the import and interpretation of the occurrence in *VA* is inadvisable.

4.11.3. *A Noah Reference (4Q547 5)*

A not easily contextualized fragment with a certain reference to Noah, suggesting reference to or retrospection on a flood or watchers tradition.

Top Margin
1 [...]ורבנה
2 [...ב]קרב כדן
3 [...ב]תרה נוח
4 [...]א

1. [...] and our greatness
2. [...]approached/offered thus
3. [...a]fter him Noah
4. [...]...

Textual, Scribal, and Material Notes
Primary images for transcription: PAM M43.567; B-295531; B-294987. The fragment appears to come from the top of a column. The significant margin and hanging stitching at the left edge confirm that the content here comes from the end of a sheet. In addition to this vertical seam and strand, there is an angular sewn seam on the fragment that preserves what appears to be an ancient repair. For data on evidence of ancient repairs to manuscripts, see Tov (2004: 20–21; 116–17). Unfortunately, the stitch did not hold the materials that are now lost to decay and the ages.

Commentary
Lines 1–3: *and our greatness [...]approaches/offered thus [...a]fter him Noah.* Of the handful of forms extant here, the most intriguing element is the proper name נוח ("Noah") in line 3. This suggests that in some way an antediluvian tradition or ancestral allusion was part of *VA*'s conceptual world. This places *VA* in a much larger network of Noah traditions that develop in various directions in the DSS. Regarding the presence of Noah in *VA*, Peters (2008: 53) remarked: "Noah is named together with Levi and Moses as ones who offer up offerings, implying that later tradents saw his inclusion as a logical development in the trajectory." In this, Peters seems to be taking a wide view of the ancestral references in *VA*, not only the glimpse provided by the present fragment. Though nearly lacking all context, the preceding form בתרה ("after him") suggests either a chronological or, more likely, a genealogical setting (cf. 4Q547 9 10). If the latter, it is significant that *ALD* traces the origins of the priestly tradition to Noah (*ALD* 57; cf. *Jub.* 7:1–5). If Noah's role in the narrative of *VA* served analogous purposes, 4Q547 5 4 may hint at yet another avenue by which this Aramaic priestly tradition claimed and conferred authority for the priestly line by securing an antediluvian anchor for its identity. Reflecting on the aims of the scribes behind the three "sequential pseudepigrapha" associated with Levi, Qahat, and Amram, Stone (1999: 138) remarked that they "obviously found it very important that the priestly tradition they enfolded be rooted in remote antiquity," with a likely "specific connection of this tradition with Noah."

4.11.4. An Allusion to Jacob and the Sacrificial Activities of Levi (4Q547 8)

Additional references to sacrificial actions of the past, now with reference to the priestly duties of Levi and his lineage.

$$
\begin{aligned}
&[\ldots]\circ\,[\ldots]\ 1\\
&[\ldots]\mathring{\text{ע}}\text{ברה}\ \text{לוי}\ \text{קרב}\ \text{די}\ \mathring{\text{כ}}[\ldots]\ 2\\
&[\ldots]\text{אבנ}\mathring{\text{י}}\ \text{ד}\mathring{\text{י}}[\ldots]\text{מדב}\mathring{\text{ח}}\ \text{על}\ \text{לכה}\ \text{מרת}[\text{א}\ldots]\ 3\\
&[\ldots]\text{כ}^{\text{לוה}}[\ldots]\text{קורבנא}\mathring{\text{ל}}\mathring{\text{כ}}[\ldots]\ 4\\
&[\ldots]\circ[\ldots]\circ[\ldots]\ 5
\end{aligned}
$$

1. [...]...[...]
2. [...] all that Levi his son offered ...[...]
3. [...] I said to you, upon the altar [...] of stones [...]
4. [...a]ll the sacrifice [...]will be[...]
5. [...]...[...]...[...]

Textual, Scribal, and Material Notes
Primary images for transcription: PAM M43.567; B-295535; B-294991.

Commentary
Lines 2–4: *all that Levi his son offered ...[...] I said to you, upon the altar [...] of stones [...a]ll the sacrifice [...]will be.* Three forms in this fragment confirm the context of a sacerdotal description: קרב ("he offered"), מדבח ("altar"), and קורבנא ("the sacrifice"). Line 2 confirms that the officiant here was indeed לוי ("Levi"). However, since Levi is referred to as ברה ("his son"), this material also implies the existence of a Jacob tradition, or at least an allusion, in *VA*. In this regard, the present fragment provides an important linkage to the ancestral-priestly traditions of *ALD* and *WQ*. In the former, Jacob played a key role in the earthly inauguration of Levi's priesthood as well as in offering a tithe (*ALD* 9; cf. 1Q21 4). For the latter, Jacob was associated with foundational ancestral commands and virtues (4Q542 1 i 7, 11).

Like so many of the smaller fragments of *VA*, it is difficult to discern if the narrative context is revelatory dialogue or ancestral discourse. Line 3 confirms the fragment features first-person speech, perhaps by Amram, another ancestor, or an angel. As seen in the commentary to 4Q547 9 2–6, it is clear that the sacrifice on Mount Sinai, presumably by Aaron, was the final topic of the dream-vision. Yet, as noted above with respect to *ALD* and *WQ*, the Aramaic priestly literature is not short on this-worldly scenes of ancestral instruction relating to priestly practices. Ambiguities of narrative context aside, the present fragment confirms that instruction or revelation on priestly duties was likely a larger feature of *VA* than the fragmentary remains suggest.

4.11.5. Revelatory Sacrifice on Sinai and Amram Inscribing the Dream Vision (4Q547 9)

The final scene of Amram's dream-vision and awakening formula followed by a reference to the return to Canaan and genealogical reference to Miriam.

1 [...]ο א[...]
2 [...]פֿצית[...]
3 [...]ο בנה [...]
4 [...]בֿהר סיני י[ו]ם֯[...]
5 [...]ο[...]οο[...]כה רבא על מדבח נחש֯[...]
6 [...]ה֯ יתרם כהן מן כול בני עלמא באה֯[...]
7 [...]י֯א ובנוהי בתרה לכול דרי עלֿמין בקו֯[...]
8 [...] ואנה אתעירת מן שנת עיני וחזוא כתב֯[ת...]
9 [...]מ֯ן ארעכנען והוא לי כדי אמר֯[...]
10 [...]מֿרים ומן באת֯[רה]לקֿהֿת עשה֯[...]
11 [...]תֿין בע[...]הויתה [...]
12 [...]ο[...]οο[...]ה[...] vacat
BOTTOM MARGIN

1. [...] ... [...]
2. [...] I delivered [...]
3. [...]... he built [...]
4. [...] on Mount Sinai, a day [...]
5. [...]...[...]...[...]your great [...] upon the bronze altar [...]
6. [...]... will be exalted as priest more than all the sons of the world...[...]
7. [...]... and his sons after him for all eternal generations ...[...]
8. [...] Then I woke up from the sleep of my eyes and inscribed the vision [...]
9. [...] from the land of Canaan. So it happened to me when he said [...]
10. [...] Miriam and from afte[r him], Qahat, ten[...]
11. [...]...[...] you were [...]
12. [...]...[...]...[...]... vacat.

Textual, Scribal, and Material Notes
Primary images for transcription: PAM M43.567; B-295536; B-294992.

Line 7: There are traces of two partial characters at the beginning of the line, from the end of the word prior to ובנוהי ("and his sons"). Puech (2001: 388) reconstructed the form מש[יח here, introducing an anointing or messianic element to the text that is otherwise absent in *VA* and a lexical item unrepresented in Qumran Aramaic. As Cook (2015: 149) commented: "The letter identified as *he* is dubious (it appears to be an *aleph* instead), and the restoration [of Puech] is therefore unlikely."

Line 9: ארעכנען ("the land of Canaan") – The forms here are inscribed without a space between them.

Commentary
Lines 2–7: *I delivered [...]... he built [...] on Mount Sinai, a day [...]...[...]... [...]your great [...] upon the bronze altar [...]... will be exalted as priest more than all the sons of the world...[...]... and his sons after him for all eternal generations.* While there are significant gaps in the known content of Amram's dream-vision due to the fragmentary manuscript evidence, the awakening formula in line 8 confirms that lines 2–7 contain the final elements or scene of the revelation. This material, therefore, bookends 4Q544 1 10 // 4Q547 1–2 9, which contained the introductory formula and opening scene. The content here, however, is distinctly different from the symbolic tableau turned dualistic revelation that launched the dream-vision.

These lines contain a concentration of priestly terms and topics with both geographical and genealogical referents. Goldman (2020: 114–15) described the following materials as a "very brief rewriting of Exod. 24–29." While there may be some topical and terminological overlaps between this *VA* fragment and that larger stretch in Exodus, none are strong enough to confirm the former "rewrites" the latter in a direct or intentional way.

Lines 2–5 contain just enough scattered phrases to confirm that Amram's dream-vision involved a description or depiction of sacrificial activity (cf. Høgenhaven 2020: 132–33). It seems that the verb בנה ("he built") in line 3 likely refers to establishing sacrificial infrastructure, such as the מדבח נחש ("the bronze altar") of line 5. This presumably refers to the infrastructure of the tabernacle (cf. Exod. 38:30; 39:39; cf. 1 Kgs 8:64; 2 Kgs 16:14–15; 2 Chron. 1:5–6; 7:7; Ezek. 9:2). The extent of the sacrificial aspects of this reference are lost in the fragment. However, the very inclusion of a sacrificial scene within a dream-vision invites comparison with the Aramaic *New Jerusalem* fragments, which includes vivid sacrificial portrayals of a functioning priesthood in a likely future temple (Perrin 2015a: 177).

In view of the likely sacrificial content of these early lines, the reference to בהר סיני ("Mount Sinai") is perhaps related in some way to the projected chronology and cartography of the wilderness experience. As Høgenhaven (2020: 126) observed, hints of geography in both the visionary and narrative units indicate that "in VA the events of the exodus are still in the future." The form here is likely a Hebraism, as we would expect the form טור סיני ("Mount Sinai") in Aramaic (Puech 2001: 389), which occurs in the fragmentary text of 4Q556 1 2. The reference to Sinai here is unique in the Aramaic DSS yet in the context of *VA* likely relates to the Mosaic undertone of several fragments and references (4Q543 1a–b; 4Q545 1a i 7–9; 4 15). Of these materials, 4Q545 4 15 is arguably the most relevant and significant for the Sinai reference here as that fragment references Moses in close proximity to a theme of writtenness. While it would be tempting to draw that reference together with the present material to construct some tradition of a Mosaic revelation or writing in the context of Sinai, it is clear that whatever is inscribed in that text takes place בּאַרעָא ("in the land; 4Q545 4 15).

While no proper name for a priest survives, lines 6–7 likely allude to Aaron. Earlier in the account he seems to have been referenced by genealogical allusion for his position as seventh after Abraham (4Q545 4 18) and perhaps even by name in a likely fragment of the dream-vision (4Q546 8 2). It is also possible that the sacrificial traditions of the previous fragment related to Levi and his sons are also relevant here, yet the narrative context of that material was less certain (4Q547 8). 4Q547 9 describes the priestly figure and his progeny in lofty terms: he will be elevated as a priest above all others (line 6) and his sons will have an eternal position (line 7). In this way, *VA*'s perspective on the priesthood may relate to analogous concepts in both *ALD* and *WQ* as both advance rhetoric establishing the antiquity and ongoing nature of the priesthood (4Q213a 5 i 3; 4Q542 1 i 13).

Line 8: *Then I woke up from the sleep of my eyes and inscribed the vision.* This line features the awakening formula for the dream-vision. In addition to serving the narrative function of closing this unit, the formula also contributes to Amram's characterization and the claimed authority of *VA* in important ways. Here Amram is not only a seer with an established revelatory resume, he is also presented as a scribe. This adds to his authoritative and ancestral profile and puts him in the league of similar seer-scribes of the Aramaic texts, such as Daniel (Dan. 7:1) and Enoch (*1 En.* 40:8; 81:6; 82:1), who likewise committed aspects of their visionary experiences and learning to written form (Perrin 2015a: 111). Such references lead Flannery-Dailey (2004: 136–37) and Drawnel (2010a: 542–43) to conclude that there is a close association between scribal activity and revelatory knowledge in some Second Temple traditions, which likely extends from earlier prophetic models (Perrin 2015a: 111; cf. Nah. 1:1; Hab. 2:2). Note also that in Josephus, Amram's revelation and disclosure to Yochebed regarding the risk on Moses life in Egypt concludes with the formula at *Ant.* 2.217: Ταῦτα τῆς ὄψεως αὐτῷ δηλωσάσης περιεγερθεὶς ὁ Ἀμαράμης ἐδήλου τῇ Ἰωχαβέλῃ, γυνὴ δ' ἦν αὐτοῦ ("When the vision had informed him of these things, Amram awaked and told it to Jochebed, who was his wife"). This theme of Amram relating the revelation to his wife about the perils to the family in Egypt also finds an intriguing parallel to Abram's cedar-date palm revelation in *GenAp*, which he also relates to his wife upon awakening (1Q20 19 17–18).

Within the immediate context of *VA*, this scribal notation also anchors the pseudepigraphic claims of the work as the opening title already presented *VA* as the veritable textual remains of Amram's visionary experience. On this compositional strategy, see the commentary on 4Q543 1a–c 1–4.

Finally, Amram's awakening formula here exhibits degrees of philological parallels with several others in the Aramaic texts. As Caquot (1998: 24) noted, Amram's remark here finds a close parallel to the reference of Levi's awakening: אָנה אתעירת מן שנתי ("And] I awoke from my sleep"; 4Q213b 1 2). In similar turns of phrase, revelations of *GenAp* also include inflected *ithpeel* forms of (1Q20 19 17; 15 21).

Line 9: *from the land of Canaan. So it happened to me when he said.* Following the dream-vision experience while in Hebron, it seems that the narrative movement of *VA* here resumed with a likely notice of departure from Canaan (Høgenhaven 2020: 125). Given the emphasis on the travel constraints presented by the Egypt–Canaan–Philistia war, presumably this entailed Amram at last making the return journey to his kindred in Egypt. Neither the content nor identity of the third-person speaker referenced in the discourse marker at the end of the line are known. Recall that Qahat has already long departed from Amram (4Q543 3 1; 4Q545 1a–b ii 17; 4Q546 2 3). It is possible that the phrase is to be understood as referring to the fulfillment of words previously spoken. If this is the case, then Amram may describe here that his return to Egypt occurred as uttered, presumably by the *angelus interpres* of the dream-vision. As discussed in the commentary to 4Q543 15 1–3, there were hints that Amram's revelation included confirmation of his safe return home.

Line 10: *Miriam and from afte[r him], Qahat, ten.* The sequential marker באתֿ[רה ("afte[r him") and the cardinal number עשֿׂה ("ten") suggest a genealogical description or narrative notice. Recall that 4Q549 2 8–11 includes a fragmentary genealogy of Miriam's priestly offspring.

Chapter 5

CONCLUSION

5.1. *Pseudepigraphal Texts and Pseudepigraphic Traditions: Rethinking the "Trilogy" Question for* ALD, WQ, *and* VA

One of the widely accepted outcomes of more than seven decades of Dead Sea Scrolls research is that the world of Qumran is one that was formative to scripture yet from a time before the media forms, cultural catalysts, and confessional efforts that finalized the canons of Judaism and Christianity. The challenge now is discerning how to move beyond the truism that "the Bible did not yet exist" toward models for mapping the development of emerging traditions regardless of their place within or outside of later biblical collections.

In this regard, *ALD*, *WQ*, and *VA* presented an intriguing case for considering the generation of traditions around ancestral figures. In this concluding chapter, which reflects and draws upon the foregoing commentary, I explore three areas to provide both internal perspective and external context for a new approach to this group of Aramaic priestly pseudepigrapha. These areas and their driving questions are as follows:

1. Conceptual and compositional correlations: To what degree do the Aramaic Levi, Qahat, and Amram materials at Qumran exhibit shared ideas, terminology, or outlooks? Are the scribes creating the texts participating in similar compositional strategies or developing links between the texts to communicate their staged progression?
2. Codicological and contextual perspectives: Are there material or scribal indications in the Qumran witnesses to suggest that the Levi, Qahat, and Amram texts were created as a group or interacted with as a cluster?
3. Cultural precedents: Are there antecedent or emerging constructs available, either internal or external to ancient Jewish culture, that indicate a trend in clustering compositions in groups, particularly in a set of three?

Following a discussion of each item with key examples from the texts themselves, I bring these perspectives to bear on how we might rethink the grouping of *ALD*, *WQ*, and *VA* at different stages in the development, reception, and ongoing study of the materials. Using the metaphor of a constellation, I redescribe *ALD*, *WQ*, and *VA* as participants and representatives of an emerging Aramaic, pseudepigraphal, priestly tradition that takes shape in the mid-Second Temple period.

5.2. Conceptual and Compositional Correlations

To what degree do the Aramaic Levi, Qahat, and Amram materials at Qumran exhibit shared ideas, terminology, or outlooks? Are the scribes creating the texts participating in similar compositional strategies or developing links between the texts to communicate their staged progression?

This first criterion is already established in the history of research as an important metric for assessing both similarities and differences. It is based largely in literary criticism or theological analogies between the texts. However, a quick pulse check on shared themes or outlooks will not suffice. Rather, what matters most is that items are distinctive in their philological expression or application in a particular literary setting and/or for a focused ideological purpose. The Aramaic Levi, Qahat, and Amram materials exhibit a surprising number of common ideas and compositional features. While some items involve only two of the three texts, the collective force of the growing list of items draws the three together in degrees of relation.

5.2.1. Forming and Maintaining Internal Identity against Outsiders

The concern for affirming boundaries against outsiders is evident in both *ALD* and *WQ*. The priestly application of the rhetoric and terms of reference indicate the scribes behind the texts are likely drawing on and/or contributing to a shared construct. As noted by Greenfield, Stone, and Eshel (2004: 29; cf. Puech 2001: 259), נכרי ("stranger, foreigner") and כילא ("assimilators") are distinctive terms used for this purpose. In both texts, these relatively rare Aramaic terms occur in scenes portraying ancestral instruction about preserving identity against outsiders (cf. 4Q542 1 i 6; 4Q213 1 i 16; MS A, Cambr. f [*ALD* 91:9–10]). That is, both the terminology and setting are instructive. Both traditions also caution against becoming √בסר ("despised") in the eyes of others (4Q542 1 i 6; 4Q213 1 i 11 // MS A, Cambr. e [*ALD* 89:21]) and hint at the importance of retaining authority with respect to outsiders (4Q542 1 i 7) or caution against the loss of authority (MS A, Cambr. e [*ALD* 90:22–23]; 4Q213 1 i 12). While Tervanotko counted "attitudes towards strangers" among her discussion of thematic differences between the Levi and Qahat materials, it is arguably their shared terminology as well as its deployment in analogous settings that is most instructive of their continuity.

5.2.2. Endogamous Marriage for Preserving the Priestly Identity and Genealogy

The ideal of endogamy is both embodied and exemplified in memories of the priestly ancestors across all three texts (cf. Tervanotko 2014: 46). This ideal is advanced in other key Aramaic texts found at Qumran (Dimant 2017: 178–85; Perrin 2015b: 35–42) and other writings from the Second Temple period (Frevel 2011; Hayes 2002; Lange 2008a; 2008b). Both Levi and Amram are presented as models of endogamous unions (*ALD* 62; 4Q544 1 i 8). *Words of Qahat*'s rhetoric of avoiding intermixing with outsiders implies a similar commitment (4Q542 1 i 8–9). This emphasis likely intersects with the caution against sexual promiscuity, expressed using the shared terminology of זנו ("fornication") in both *ALD* and *WQ* (*ALD* 16 [MS A, Bodl. b 8 14–16]; πορνεία [MS E, Mt. Athos 18,2]; 4Q213a 1 13; 4Q542 3 i–ii 12). *Aramaic Levi Document* and *VA* address this concern with respect to daughters in the priestly line. In *ALD*, Levi's grandson Amram wed his aunt (i.e., Levi's daughter) Yochebed (cf. *ALD* 73–75). In *VA*, Amram's daughter Miriam marries her uncle Uzziel (i.e., Amram's brother; 4Q543 1a–c 5–7; 4Q545 1a i 4–8; 4Q546 1 3–4; 4Q547 1–2 7). Therefore, the three texts share a priestly application of endogamous marriage and exhibit a pattern for establishing this genealogy to include sons and daughters of the priestly line.

5.2.3. The Earthly Priestly Genealogy and its Otherworldly Counterpart

All three texts secure Abraham as the ancestral anchor and originator of the priestly tradition (*ALD* 8–61; 4Q542 1 i 11; 4Q545 4 18; cf. Puech 2001: 343; Perrin 2015a: 164–65). On this point, Jones (2020: 21–22) remarked the compositions "have extended the patriarchal genealogy by grafting the Levitical genealogy on it, thereby creating a single genealogical chain that runs from Abraham through that segment of the Levitical line that leads to Aaron, the prototypical priest (i.e., Qahat and Amram)."

This earthly authority, however, is also layered with an otherworldly one underscoring the eternality of the priestly line (Angel 2010: 54–55; cf. Milik 1978: 93). This shared concept is evident in the approximate terminology of an כהנות עלמא ("eternal priesthood") in 4Q213a 5 i–ii 3 and the reference to Aaron's election as כהן עלמין ("a priest forever") in 4Q545 4 19. *Words of Qahat* and *VA* also use closely paralleled idioms to reference the everlasting quality and blessing of the priestly line לכול דרי עלמין ("for all eternal generations"; 4Q542 1 i 4; 4Q547 9 7). *Aramaic Levi Document*, *WQ*, and *VA* extend this concept by claiming variations of divine mandates (cf. 4Q213a 5 i–ii 3; 4Q213b 1 1; 4Q542 1 ii 3–4; 4Q545 4 19). For *ALD* and *VA*, there is a strong case to be made for leveraging a celestial Melchizedek tradition to authorize the foundational priesthoods of the ancestors (see the commentary on 4Q213b 1 8; 4Q544 3 2; 4Q545 4 16). In sum, the Levi–Qahat–Amram group constructs an understanding that the priestly line's origins may be ancient yet they are enduring and in association with otherworldly offices.

5.2.4. *Command-Fulfillment and Transmitting Ancestral Knowledge through Generations*

The texts coordinate a chain of transmitting ancestral knowledge through narrative commands for instruction and the actualization of such injunctions in the next priestly generation. 4Q213 1 i 9–10 issued a call for instruction, which Levi fulfilled by passing on the inherited lore from Abraham (4Q213 1 i 9–10; MS E, Mt. Athos 18,2). *Words of Qahat* emphasized how Qahat too transmitted the ancestral knowledge to the next generation, particularly Amram. In this, he transmits not only knowledge but also affirms the injunction to instruct the priestly lineage is transgenerational (4Q542 1 ii 9–10). The connection with Levi, then, is both in the model of teaching and in the booklore inherited from him (4Q542 1 ii 11–13). *Visions of Amram*, in turn, features Amram commanding his children (4Q543 1a–c 2 // 4Q545 1a i 2, 11). At a closer level, the literary theme is presented with specific terminology. Each text repeatedly uses inflected forms of the verb פקד ("to command") in their instructional settings (*ALD* 82:6 [4Q213 1 i 3, rec.]; 4Q542 1 i 13; ii 10; 4Q543 1a–c 2; 4Q545 1a i 11). In this way, the three texts not only participate in a discourse of ancestral teaching, they generate it, and do so using shared terminology.

By presenting scenes of ancestral teaching *including* a call to teach the next generation, each text is sufficiently open-ended. This enables the growth of the tradition. Simply put, where *ALD* issues a call to teach the next heir of the heritage, *WQ* steps in to imagine and document this. As *WQ* exemplifies and emphasizes the necessity of teaching for the next generation, *VA* extends the tradition by ensuring this task was fulfilled in the life of the next ancestor. At face value, this trend is perhaps a shared motif. However, at the compositional level, this open-endedness and the unfulfilled injunctions to literally command the next generation are perhaps the clearest scribal mechanism that propelled the tradition. Research on the compositional development of pentateuchal traditions at Qumran affirmed that providing narrative fulfillments to previous commands was an important catalyst for the evolution of traditions even before the Samaritan Pentateuch (Tov 1985: 7; Falk 2007: 119; White Crawford 2008: 23–35, 124–25; Zahn 2011: 35–45, 155–56). In a similar vein, Tov (2008: 390) also observed commands and complementary fulfillments contributed to the incremental growth of the Greek Daniel traditions. Tov highlighted how the addition of the actualization of the divine command to chop down the tree in Dan. 4:14a (LXX) is akin to other instances of ensuring harmony between commands and fulfillments in Exodus 7–11 (SP) and Kish's command to Saul in 1 Sam. 9:3 (LXX[Luc] and Peshitta).

For our group of Aramaic priestly texts, genealogies matter not only for the identity of the priesthood, but for providing a chain of custody for the inherited tradition.

5.2.5. *Textual Relics and Revelatory Episodes Endorsing the Priestly Heritage*

One of the accents on scribalism found in the texts relates to how all three leading patriarchs in the texts are associated with the production or procurement of booklore (*ALD* 57–59; 4Q542 1 ii 12–13; 4Q543 1a–c 1; 4Q547 9 8). This is inextricably linked to ancestral scribal authority and textuality for the priestly profiles of Levi, Qahat, and Amram. But are there variations in how this is worked out? Perhaps.

Tervanotko (2014: 47) ranked the role of books in the transmission of each as a difference between the texts, since "Amram does not mention books in his admonition to his children in *VA*." However, this overlooks both key aspects of *VA*'s presentation in the larger complex of its pseudepigraphic attribution. The superscripted title of the work as well as the depiction of Amram inscribing his revelation clearly front the importance booklore in the generational model of knowledge production and transmission (4Q543 1a–c 1; 4Q545 1a i 1), which pairs also with Amram's activity of writing the revelation upon awakening (4Q547 9 8). On the form of *VA*'s title, see Perrin 2013: 109–11; and Popović 2017. The textuality of ancestral and inherited tradition, therefore, is essential to all three texts.

Aramaic Levi Document and *VA* also seem to utilize the dream-vision for similar purposes, to either positively endorse or negatively disqualify an ancestral line from the priestly genealogy. In *ALD* 64, the onomastics of Gershom's name are related to his being cast out of the running for the high priestly office. In *VA*, a large part of Amram's dream-vision focuses on the priestly role and position of Aaron, described in strikingly similar terms to Levi (cf. 4Q545 4 16–19; *ALD* 48, 51, 61; Perrin 2015a: 165). Therefore, these two share a common understanding of patriarchs as seers with access to divine knowledge on the future course of the priesthood.

5.2.6. *Pseudepigraphic Attribution and the Collective Cultivation of Priestly Profiles*

Notwithstanding the open question of genre, the three texts clearly embody a pseudepigraphic presentation by capturing the voices of priestly figures from the past. Levi's profile arguably develops out of both narratives and allusions in the Hebrew Scriptures (Gen. 34; 49:5–7; 1 Sam. 2:27; Mal. 2:2–5; cf. Kugel 1993: 33; VanderKam 1999: 519; Perrin 2015a: 152–56). Qahat and Amram, however, exist only as names in genealogies or among references to the duties of the priestly clans (see the individual text introductions for primary source references).

While pseudepigraphy is hardly a unique compositional feature in writings of the Second Temple period, the development of at least two priestly pseudepigrapha out of near blank canvases for two figures is rather striking. Furthermore, the profiles of Levi, Qahat, and Amram develop almost collaboratively as each text contributes to both a developing tradition and the formation of figures. For example, *ALD* 63–77 cultivates a preliminary profile for Qahat and Amram through expanded birth notices. Kugler (1996a: 117) commented that this section "establishes Levi's lineage and indicates how his seed became a priestly family." Similarly, *WQ* extends the importance of Levi's authority and Amram's position (4Q542 1 i 11; 1 ii 9, 11). Finally, *VA*, from the very opening words of the document, anchors its discourses in named references to both Levi and Qahat (4Q545 1 a i 1). It also casts Qahat as a character in travel narrative (4Q544 1 1; 4Q546 2 3).

In this regard, it is not only the priestly pseudepigraphic perspective of the individual texts that is suggestive but the way the three develop discourses that elevate the founding figures of the priestly lines that matters.

5.3. *Codicological Considerations*

Are there material or scribal indications in the Qumran witnesses to suggest that the Levi, Qahat, and Amram texts were created as a group or interacted with as a cluster?

This criterion adopts a material philological approach by studying features within the Qumran manuscripts that relate to a range of issues, including their material production, scribal development, or paratextual features.

5.3.1. *The Possibility of a Limited Number Scribal Hands in the Manuscripts*

Given the volume of manuscripts represented at Qumran, and presumably more which were lost through decay, it is statistically likely that some scribes either at Qumran or beyond copied multiple manuscripts found in the caves. For proposed portfolios of individual scribes, see Tov 2004: 20–24. The Aramaic Levi, Qahat, and Amram manuscripts have registered in these discussions in two ways.

The first is external and considers the similarity of their scripts with other known manuscripts at Qumran. Milik (1976: 5) proposed that the same scribe was responsible for 4QLevi^d (4Q214) and 4QEn^f (4Q207). Strugnell (Bonani et al. 1991: 28; see also Tov 2004: 23; Hogeterp 2010: 15 n. 83) proposed that our *WQ* manuscript (4Q542) was penned by the same scribe as 4QSam^c (4Q53), which is generally thought to be the same scribe responsible for 1QS, 1QSa, and 1QSb, and 4Q175 (cf. Ulrich 1979: 1; Cross et al. 2005: 247; Tov 2004: 24). If 4Q207 and 4Q214 were penned by the same copyist, it may be a departure point for exploring the profiles of traditionists at work within the Aramaic corpus. If 4Q542 was part of a larger roster of texts copied by the same scribe it is significant that all other items in that list are Hebrew. Both cases, however, are speculative.

The second direction is internal and relates to the possibility that some of the Qumran *ALD*, *WQ*, and *VA* manuscripts were produced by the same scribe. Stone and Greenfield (1996: 22) indicated that Cross opined 4QLevi^b (4Q213a) and 4QLevi^c (4Q213b) might have been written by the same scribe. Ultimately, their independent analysis concluded otherwise. Puech (2001: 259, 377) determined that the same scribe copied 4Q542 and 4Q547, which seems to be the case. Van der Schoor (forthcoming) recently argued that the paleographical profiles of the Cave Four *ALD* manuscripts exhibit a more limited degree of variation than often recognized, suggesting they may relate to only four manuscripts, not seven as traditionally counted.

The paleographical perspective on the Levi–Qahat–Amram fragments, therefore, suggests that at least two of the manuscripts were penned by the same hand (4Q542 and 4Q547). The question now is whether the scribal profiles of these manuscripts relate to any other material philological features of the fragments.

5.3.2. *Manuscript Profiles and Serial Pseudepigraphy*

The Levi, Qahat, and Amram Qumran scrolls are often unforgivingly fragmentary. Yet they retain some material features that at least open the question of the possibility that more than one composition featured on the same scroll. There are two key areas of evidence to consider.

The first is the tattered remains of stitching on the right edge of a sheet at the very outset of 4Q543 1a, immediately before the title of *VA* at the top of the column. The question is: what came before? While Milik's proposal technically pertained to the clustering of the text at the level of Greek translation and reception in early Christian circles, Puech (2001: 259) wondered if it was possible that 4Q543 1a retains the hinge once originally attached to a copy of *WQ*. When compounded with his view that 4Q542 and 4Q213 were similar in script, one finds the makings of a material case for securing a trilogy even at Qumran, though Puech is adequately cautious. We do not know if what came before was inscribed content, a handle sheet, or some other element.

The second regards 4Q542 and 4Q547—the two texts likely written by the same scribe—as potentially coming from the same scroll. Machiela (2021a) noted that these fragments have strikingly short columns, consisting of no more than thirteen lines, with similarly modest marginal measurements.[1] This line count is clear on 4Q542 given the preservation of margins and the full column of 4Q542 1 i. The fragments of 4Q547 require reconstruction for column measurements and line counts. However, 4Q547 seems to retain the upper and lower margins of the text, which includes 12 lines of extant material. Puech reconstructed (2001: 379) 4Q547 1–2 as a partial column of 13 lines, although these fragments are especially challenging. These similarities rank 4Q542 and 4Q547 in among the smaller scrolls in the entire Qumran corpus. For the other material measurements, see Puech 2001: 257–58, 375–76. Tov (2004: 84) summarized the data for scrolls with "small writing blocks" as follows: "The *average number of lines* per column in Qumran scrolls is probably twenty, with a height of approximately 14–15 cm

---

1. Thanks to Daniel Machiela for sharing an advance copy of the article.

5. Conclusion

(including top and bottom margins). Larger scrolls contained columns with 25 to as many as 60 lines. Scrolls of the smallest dimensions contained merely 5–13 lines and their height was similarly small."

The Aramaic texts at Qumran are diverse in their material quality, though several other items in the corpus also fit in this category. These include: 4QBirth of Noah[b] (4Q535, 6 lines), 4QJews in the Persian Court[a, b, d] (4Q550, 4Q550a, 4Q550c, between 7–8 lines), 4QRécit (4Q551, 8 lines), 4QList of False Prophets (4Q339 [Hebrew?], 9 lines), 4QAramaic Apocalypse (4Q246, 9 lines), 4QBrontologion (4Q318, 9 lines), 4QDan[e] (4Q116 [Hebrew], 9 lines), 4QEnGiants[c] (4Q531 22, 12 lines?), 4QBirth of Noah[c] (4Q536, 13 lines). For Tov's comprehensive list of line numbers for Qumran texts, see Tov (2004: 84–90).

Most significantly, however, this codicological case complements the paleographical association noted above to confirm that 4Q542 and 4Q547 were in fact inscribed on the same material object. This codicological association also requires a context in light of wider trends for composing or collecting texts and traditions on single scrolls in the Qumran Aramaic corpus. *Genesis Apocryphon* is a clear example of multiple pseudepigrapha associated with different ancestors included on the same scroll, in that case, with the surviving materials coincidentally relating to three verifiably first-person personae (Lamech, Noah, and Abram). The most instructive element of that scroll is the title of the Noah section at 1Q20 5 29 (see Steiner 1995). Lange (2003: 312) proposed that this feature may signify the Noah section was part of a "collection of different literary compositions." While the codicology of the Aramaic Enoch fragmentary manuscripts is complex (cf. Nickelsburg 2001: 81–108; Stuckenbruck 2007), at least three of the scrolls at Qumran included materials from multiple traditions attributed to, or associated with, Enoch (4Q204–4Q206). Elsewhere I have argued (Perrin 2021) that the Aramaic-Hebrew hybrid of Daniel is yet another example of collecting tales associated with the same figure onto a single piece of media (see esp. 4Q112 14; 4Q113 15, 16–18 i). Though its meaning in context is not entirely clear, the so-called *Birth of Noah* texts include a reference to gaining knowledge from תלתת ספריא ("three books") as a signal of the advanced learning for the youth (4Q534 1 i 5; for proposals on potential meaning of the reference, see Starcky 1963: 502; Carmignac 1965: 212; Fitzmyer 1965: 362; Grelot 1975: 492–93; Milik 1978: 94; cf. García Martínez 1992: 9; Puech 2001: 137–38). Of course, we could extend our data to consider instances of multi-text or merged-traditions on single scrolls in the Hebrew writings among the DSS (Tov 2004: 165–66).

With this criterion, we may conclude that there is at least one positive instance of a material connection between exemplars of the Qahat and Amram materials. The texts presently available do not indicate if there was a material association with the Levi materials. The contextual framework of the Aramaic corpus indicated that ancestral tales *could* co-exist on the same scroll in variations of serial pseudepigraphy. If some or all these materials did exist on the same scroll it would then challenge us to reframe our approach: these materials are not necessarily discrete literary compositions but literary units representing a larger priestly tradition. As such, we should not describe these writings as three different Jewish pseudepigraphal texts but as examples of the process of Jewish pseudepigraphy in a growing collection developed around the authority of priestly patriarchs.

5.3.3. *Marginalia in the Priestly Texts*

Manuscripts are more than the words on the page. In addition to considering the scribal and codicological character of the Qumran Levi, Qahat, and Amram materials, we can also gain glimpses of marginalia across the texts. The data are limited but provide a space for starting to think about interactions with the texts in antiquity. Of course, there are many unknown variables regarding when, where, why, and by whom marginalia were added to the texts in the transmission and reception processes.

Without minimizing these obstacles, at least one set of marginalia emerges as an intriguing feature in some of the texts. While marginal horizontal strokes or *paragraphos* (a small horizontal line with a hook) are not uncommon in the Hebrew texts at Qumran (Tov 2004: 180–87), there are but four occurrences in the Aramaic literature. At least three manuscripts of our Aramaic priestly texts include a marginal stroke to signal the shift in discourse. Such markings are found at: 4Q542 1 ii 8–9 (horizontal line); 4Q213 1 ii 11–12; 4Q213a 2 10–11 (both *paragraphos*). The only other occurrence of a paratextual stroke inserted between lines is found in a fragment of the *Book of Giants* at 4Q532 1 ii 6–7 (horizontal line).

García Martínez (2010: 337) undertook a preliminary comparison of scribal features in the Aramaic and Hebrew DSS and found that "there are no differences in the scribal practices among the two sorts of texts." While the scribal study of the Aramaic DSS is largely uncharted, separate studies by Machiela (2013) and myself (2021c) have indicated that though similar in scribal and material characters, there are important variations and gradations between the Hebrew and Aramaic texts. Among the items García Martínez (2010: 338) listed were uses of *paragraphos* signs in 4Q213a, 4Q542, and 4Q532, with the occurrence in 4Q214b unregistered in his data. While he is correct in noting the general similarity in representation of this feature—these forms of marginalia are relatively common in the larger Qumran collection—it is possible that the concentration of this style of marking in the Levi and Qahat texts is instructive. That is, given the paucity of this style of marking in the Aramaic texts, the concentration in our priestly pseudepigrapha is curious.

We could, of course, entertain the question of *when* the markings were added and *by whom*. If, on the one hand, the markings were included earlier in the life of these traditions, it may hint at a common scribal approach. If, on the other hand, the markings were included by a later reader, it may suggest at least the materials were interacted with in a common way. Both possibilities open still further questions of the social location of scribes and/or users of the manuscripts. Given the highly fragmentary nature of the materials and underdeveloped study of scribal features in the Aramaic DSS, little more can be said of these possibilities.

5.4. Cultural Contexts

Are there antecedent or emerging constructs available, either internal or external to ancient Jewish culture, that indicate a trend in clustering compositions in groups, particularly in a set of three?

There are several caveats to Milik's original proposal that demand methodological consideration before moving forward. His conception of a tripartite group was made largely on the basis of his understanding of the transmission and reception of patriarchal traditions in early Christian writings. This theory rests on the presupposition that both the Qahat and Amram materials were translated in Greek and circulated beyond the bounds of what we presently know of their limited reception. To be sure, we also have little secure knowledge of the translation and transmission history of *ALD*, save for its partial representation in Greek in a tenth-century codex (Greenfield and Stone 1979: 215). Further clouding the chronology required of this thesis is that the *Apostolic Constitutions* is a liturgical collection dated to the late fourth century CE (Nautlin 2014: 197–98). The issue here, then, is whether or not the concept of a trilogy as a defined cluster of texts would have been operative in the world of the production, transmission, or reception of *ALD*, *WQ*, and *VA*.

There are several areas of interrelated contexts that could factor into this aspect of the study. For example, there is the increasing trend in the Hebrew Scriptures for referencing groups or ancestral figures, not least in threes (e.g., Ezek. 14:14). Imagined booklore in the Aramaic texts as well as the material and codicological considerations of the DSS discussed above could also factor into cultural contextual considerations. Ancient Near Eastern first-person traditions could also provide another conversation partner, particularly those that engage in varieties of attribution to famed figures and embrace future outlooks (Davila 2013: 124; Longman 1991; Neujahr 2012).

To outline at least one area of context, I preliminarily explore but one of the relevant cultural spaces of which the Aramaic texts were a part: the Hellenistic world. The following is not an exhaustive consideration of this avenue of study. Rather, it illustrates the types of questions we can begin asking as we consider the context(s) of the Aramaic DSS.

5.4.1. *Emerging Sets of Literature or Performances in Classical Sources*

When it comes to their cultural contextualization, the Aramaic DSS have been predominantly studied in terms of their indebtedness to, influence by, or appropriation of Babylonian traditions. While this approach has resulted in some helpful insights into select topics and texts, less energy has been spent on recovering the interactions with traditions from the west. See, for example, the insightful studies of Ben Dov (2008); Drawnel (2004); a growing cluster of treatments on giants traditions in Cooley (2014); Frölich (2012); Goff (2009); Lemaire (2010); as well as research on Nabonidus traditions with an eye to Mesopotamian texts in Henze (1999); Kratz (2011); Perrin (forthcoming); and Waerzeggers (2017). Given the general date ranges of writings and witnesses among the Qumran Aramaic corpus from the mid-third century BCE to early first century CE, the Hellenistic and Graeco-Roman context is arguably more relevant for understanding the ideas and outlooks that were both formative to this literature and informed the way it was understood by audiences living in Judaea in the late Second Temple period under the auspices of Graeco-Roman powers.

To be sure, there have been inroads into this topic to demonstrate that the scribes of the Qumran Aramaic texts were indeed conversant in cultural lore and practices of this Mediterranean cultural context. Topics evidencing such cultural interactions include: views of female sexual pleasure as a sign of conception in *GenAp* 2 9–15 (Frölich 2011; van der Horst 2012), Ionian cartography and Noah's division of the earth in *GenAp* 16–17 (Machiela 2009: 87–90), patterns of four kingdoms historiography in Daniel 2, 7 and the aptly named Aramaic *Four Kingdoms* (4Q552–4Q553) (Perrin 2020), perceptions of pre-scientific knowledge such as physiognomy (Popović 2007), as well as first-person voices in light of the historiographical awareness of Hellenistic writers (Stuckenbruck 2011). While there is much uncharted territory in mapping the Hellenistic setting of both authors and audiences of the Aramaic DSS, studies in these areas have demonstrated the increasing importance of this topic for exploring how these Second Temple Jewish texts were informed by, and formed within, Hellenistic cultures of Judaea.

In this light, one essential area of investigation yet to register in studies on *ALD*, *WQ*, and *VA* is whether or not the clustering of ancestral lore or cultural media in groups occurred in the Hellenistic or Graeco-Roman worlds. As indicated above, this setting may be relevant both for rethinking the authorial aims of text production (were the scribes of the Levi, Qahat, and Amram texts creating a set of literature in view of patterns in the Hellenistic world?) and the reception or perception of these writings by audiences (were readers, hearers, or users of the texts understanding the group as having some unity in light of clusters of traditions in Hellenistic culture?). Arguably, the most pertinent materials for pressing into this new territory are provided by classical biographies and performances as well as lexical analyses of mentions of three-fold collections of writings.

Classical biographies of the fifth through fourth centuries BCE provide some evidence for emerging clusters. Xenophon of Athens (ca. 430–354 BC) was both prolific in writing memoirs, encomiums, and romances, as well as influential for the emerging biographical models of classical writers. Xenophon's memoirs in *Anabasis* (ca. late 380s BCE) are arguably the most relevant for the present topic. In this writing, Xenophon undertakes a detailed account of Cyrus the Younger and his three generals who attempted to topple the Persian throne of Artaxerxes II yet met their untimely deaths either in battle or execution. Given his position, Cyrus's account is the lengthiest of the lot. Following these, the synopses of the three generals are provided in sequence: Clearchus the Lacedaemonian, Proxenus the Boeotian, and Menon the Thessalian (*Anab.* 2.6.1–29). While it is possible that the treatment of three generals is merely incidental—there just happened to be three military leaders in the position—the work ends with mention of two other executed individuals. Agias the Arcadian and Socrates the Achean receive but passing reference (*Anab.* 2.6.30). In this way, Xenophon's treatment is possibly a cluster of three memorialized figures set under the umbrella of a fourth major figure, yet it is clear that his treatment of this triad involved their election from among a slightly larger group of candidates.

Though his work survives largely in fragments and served as a source for Plutarch's *Life of Pericles* (ca. 75 CE), Stesimbrotus of Thasus's (ca. 470—420 BCE) *On Themistocles, Thucydides, and Pericles* provides some hints of a reasonably unified threefold collection. The writing presents a triad of biographies of three Athenian military leaders, which, though not sequential in their lives and times, exhibit some unity. As Hägg observed, "[t]he writing is less concerned with slandering the three Athenian generals and statesman on political grounds than with showing their true characters by means of anecdotes" (Hägg 2012: 14). While there is some debate around how to best describe Stesimbrotus's work, there is a general recognition that it is biographical, perhaps even to be understood as a forerunner to the more fully developed Greek genre (for a scholarly proposal around the formative place of Stesimbrotus in the development of biographical literature, see Hägg 2012: 14 n. 13; 16 n. 22).

The examples from Xenophon and Stesimbrotus provide some point of reference for treatments of the memories of figures past in threes. However, Aeschylus's three tragedies in *The Oresteia* provides the strongest foundation for a Greek trilogy established in performance. The three plays plus a satyr (*Agamemnon*, *The Libation Bearers*, *The Eumenides*, with *Proteus*) are set against the backdrop of the Trojan War, an ancestral myth which audiences were familiar with not least from the *Iliad* and *Odyssey* and, thus, was enabled and extended by both playwright and performers beyond their Homeric origins. The trilogy consists of three self-contained tales that relate to an overarching epic, which are set around the lives of figures who lived sequentially over two generations, and are unified by a common thematic direction, namely asserting the need for a new *polis*. For more detailed synopses of the themes of each, see Goldhill (2004) and the complete commentary by Conacher (1987). For introduction and translation, see Fagles and Stanford (1976).

That Aeschylus's work was both well-known and favorably received is evident by the *The Oresteia*'s first-place prize at the 458 BCE Great Dionysian festival of Athens (Goldhill 2004: x). As Burian and Shapiro observed (2011: 3–4), the cultural currency of Aeschylus's tragedian trilogy extends into other literary and material culture: "to judge from such evidence as the references to *The Oresteia* in the comedies of Aristophanes and the reflection of at least two of its plays in vase painting, the Greeks themselves regarded this trilogy as among Aeschylus's greatest achievements" (Burian and Shapiro 2011: 3–4). While Aeschylus's trilogy is the only known surviving threefold play from this era, the commissioned writing and performance of trilogies of tragedies plus a satyr was a focal point of this annual festival of the *polis* (Goldhill 2004: 13). In this way, the performative aspect of cultural heritage in Athens as exemplified by the formal trilogy of *The Oresteia* is the clearest evidence for the existence of a trilogy in Hellenistic culture.

While none of these comparisons netted a clear analogy to the proposed triad of priestly texts, they did provide, even in outline, a cultural framework in the Hellenistic period for clustering aspects of cultural memory related to the recent or remote past in groups of three. This perspective, however, sends us back to re-consider the very premise of early proposals over the Aramaic Levi, Qahat, and Amram texts.

5.5. *Switching Metaphors: From Trilogy to Constellation*

Milik's initial impression of grouping the Levi, Qahat, and Amram materials was helpful to start the conversation on what were then newly available texts. Yet our growing knowledge of the Dead Sea Scrolls demands ongoing re-evaluation of earlier proposals. The development and application of the three criteria above resulted in both confirmations and questions related to if, how, and when the Aramaic Levi, Qahat, and Amram texts became a group.

Should we think of the group of texts as *conceived* as a group in their earliest Aramaic scribal settings? Possibly. The scribes of the Aramaic set of writings were active cultivators of traditions developed in the orbit of ancestral figures and often picked up on lingering loose-ends in traditions to drive the tradition forward. In this way, the chain of injunctions and actualizations of commanding the priestly generations in each text fits quite well with compositional techniques documented elsewhere in ancient Jewish scriptures (e.g., pre-Samaritan texts and "Additions" to Daniel). Similarly, there is some evidence of the convergence or collection of ancestral traditions, specifically Aramaic pseudepigrapha, on singular scrolls at Qumran (i.e., Enoch, *Genesis Apocryphon*, and Daniel). In light of this trend, the codicological indications that at least two of our priestly traditions, those associated with Qahat and Amram in 4Q542–4Q547, were inscribed on the same scroll takes on new significance. Collectively, these items challenge the way Levi, Qahat, and Amram materials have been understood as discrete *texts* and invite us to rethink how they perhaps function as representations of a larger priestly *tradition* oriented around three figures.

Should we rethink these writings as a group of *received* texts, not in early Christianity as Milik averred, but in the Second Temple period? Perhaps. Here the concentration and similarities of marginal markings in the priestly texts documented above may be one factor in helping understand how a culture of scribes and/or users interacted with the texts in similar ways. Similarly, by interrogating the larger cultural frameworks for clustering texts or traditions in the Hellenistic world, we may develop an etic approach by recovering the culturally conditioned cognitive frameworks that may have shaped ancient perceptions of developing groups of texts. In this way, Milik's suspicion of a priestly group of writings may have pressed in the right direction but the avenue he took to arrive at the conclusion was wrong. I admit, however, we need more work to firm up or refine the question of the earliest reception of our Aramaic pseudepigrapha. Of course, the Levi allusion in CD 4 14–19 indicates some Qumran Hebrew literature interacted with at least one area of priestly traditions associated with the figure of Levi. The relatedness of this reference to *ALD*, however, remains a point of debate (see Drawnel 2004: 214, 267; Eshel 2007).

Regardless of the unknowns of their ancient production and reception as a group, is it beneficial to study the Levi, Qahat, and Amram texts as a group? Absolutely. For all their diversity, there are discernable currents of continuity across clusters of texts in the Qumran Aramaic corpus. Most scholars agree on this. The converging interests that galvanize priestly identity internally and externally develop and articulate priestly traditions, and claim and confer authority in the Levi, Qahat, and Amram materials indicate that these writings provide a large-scope impression of priestly ideas and interests cultivated in Aramaic scribal cultures of ancient Judaism. As a collective, then, they achieve this overall impression better than as solo acts.

Exploring and articulating the development, transmission, and reception of ancient textual traditions is complex. As such, metaphors or analogies are at once essential yet unlikely to account for all the variables. From "trilogies," to "clusters," to "family portraits," and even "baklava," scholars have tried to find images and ideas that help capture the dynamic process and outcomes of the scribal activities in antiquity. For these additional metaphors, see Collins 2010a: 421–22; Machiela and Perrin 2014; Stone 2011: 151–54; and Ulrich 1994. Of course, every metaphor has its limits. Yet the notion of constellations of texts and growing traditions has a particular explanatory power even toward its eventual, and inevitable breakdown.

The metaphor of a constellation for organizing or arranging ideas hearkens to the philosophical work of Walter Benjamin, notably in *The Origins of German Trauerspiel*. Najman (2012) bridged Benjamin's notion of the constellation into studies on the formation of ancient Jew Levi–Qahat–Amram ish literature, with several others now also applying it to articulate either the generic forms or developmental processes of textual traditions in a pre-canonical age (Wright 2010: 295–95; Perrin 2015a: 227–33; Zahn 2020: 94–95). There are at least four aspects of this analogy that are useful and have a particular payoff for the Levi–Qahat–Amram group studied here. I explore these items below neither in a technical astrophysical sense nor from a theoretical perspective of genre theory—I know the limits of my interdisciplinary efforts! Rather, I deploy it here for heuristic purposes.

First, constellations are part of larger systems. This is not unlike the phenomenon of "asterisms," which are informal clusters of stars that may or may not be part of recognizable constellations. For our metaphor, this allows some fluidity for individual traditions to participate in more than one configuration. In this way, the Levi–Qahat–Amram constellation can exist in its own integrity but this recognition does not unnecessarily distance it from the larger multi-dimensional reality of materials. In this case, we can recognize the group as hanging together in a meaningful way while also underscoring that it is part of larger concentric worlds of texts and traditions: first the Aramaic writings represented at Qumran, then the wider ring of the Qumran collection. That is, while a given constellation in the sky might capture our attention, its context in a larger cosmos also matters. And membership within a constellation is not exclusive of involvement in other formations.

Second, constellations are configurations of individual items yet form representations that are more than the sum of these parts. The Levi, Qahat, and Amram materials can and do have value on their own. Yet studied together they form what appears to be a cohesive and generative group that gives voice to an emerging Aramaic priestly tradition of pseudepigrapha. Priestly knowledge, practice, tradition, and identity appears to be a key theme of several Aramaic texts at Qumran. As such, we can study these features in individual texts and then also stand back and articulate the overarching dynamics that relate to the larger network. That is, while the given stars of a constellation have their own brilliance and character, as a collective they present an image that helps guide and direct our understanding.

Third, the configurations and perceptions of constellations may change over time due to the vantage point of the viewer. As we learn more about the contents and shape of individual texts and the traditions in which they participate, we can re-chart or re-position the proximity of texts as needed. Whereas a trilogy, for example, locks texts into a book-based metaphor, the constellation approach is inherently more open. As noted above, there is value in studying these texts as a group. As we learn more about this group and the features that define it or distance it from others, we can increasingly determine the degrees of relation of the traditions and adjust them accordingly. That is, a chart of these constellations is not fixed and finalized but, like the universe of which they are a part, is open to incremental change.

Fourth, individual astral items and constellations are part of the larger, rapid inflation of an ever-expanding universe. The event colloquially known as "The Big Bang" is what resulted in our system and existence. The Aramaic DSS represent what appears to be a rather sudden burst of scribal creativity in the mid-Second Temple period. The causes of this scribal big bang are yet unknown, although the outcomes are evident. This collection includes a large group of ancient Jewish pseudepigrapha developed around the orbits of ancestral figures (e.g., Enoch, Noah, or Abraham) or new personae from the more recent past (e.g., Daniel or Tobit) all penned in Aramaic. The opportunity now is to press ahead in studying new stars, rethinking old ones, and to boldly go into emerging networks within the newly formed group. That is, as we increasingly map the stars of constellations in this space, we gain both a focused view of its features and work towards a better understanding of its beginnings.

Bibliography

Aeschylus. 1984. *The Oresteia*. Translated by Robert Fagles. New York: Penguin Books.
Alexander, Philip S. 1999. "The Demonology of the Dead Sea Scrolls." Pages 331–53 in *The Dead Sea Scrolls after Fifty Years: A Comprehensive Assessment*. Edited by Peter W. Flint and James C. VanderKam. Leiden: Brill.
Alexander, Philip S. 2011. "The Dualism of Heaven and Earth in Early Jewish Literature and Its Implications." Pages 169–85 in *Light Against Darkness: Dualism in Ancient Mediterranean Religion and the Contemporary World*. Edited by Armin Lange, Eric M. Meyers, Bennie H. Reynolds III, and Randall Styers, Randall. JAJSup 2. Göttingen: Vandenhoeck & Ruprecht.
Angel, Joseph L. 2010. *Otherworldly and Eschatological Priesthood in the Dead Sea Scrolls*. STDJ 86. Leiden: Brill.
Angel, Joseph L. 2014. "Reading the Book of Giants in Literary and Historical Context." *DSD* 21: 313–46.
Anderson, Gary A. 1992. "Sacrifice and Sacrificial Offerings: Old Testament." *The Anchor Yale Bible Dictionary* 5: 870–86.
Aschim, Anders. 2000. "Melchizedek and Levi." Pages 773–88 in *The Dead Sea Scrolls Fifty Years after Their Discovery: Proceedings of the Jerusalem Congress, July 20–25, 1997*. Edited by Lawrence H. Schiffman, Emanuel Tov, and James C. VanderKam. Jerusalem: Israel Museum.
Baarda, Tjitze. 1992. "The Shechem Episode in the Testament of Levi: A Comparison with Other Traditions." Pages 11–73 in *Sacred History and Sacred Texts in Early Judaism: A Symposium in Honour of A. S. van Der Woude*. Edited by Jan N. Bremmer, Florentino García Martínez, and A. S. van der Woude. CBET 5. Kampen: Pharos.
Bar, Shaul. 2001. *A Letter That Has Not Been Read: Dreams in the Hebrew Bible*. HUCM 25. Cincinnati: Hebrew Union College Press.
Bauckham, Richard. 1983. *Jude, 2 Peter*. WBC 50. Waco: Thomas Nelson.
Becker, Jürgen. 1970. *Untersuchungen zur Entstehungsgeschichte der Testamente der zwölf Patriarchen*. AGJU 8. Leiden: Brill.
Berger, Klaus. 1973. "Der Streit des guten und des bösen Engels um die Seele: Beobachtungen zu 4Q Amrb und Judas 9." *JSJ* 4: 1–18.
Bergman, J. 2003. "חָלַם." *TDOT* 4: 421–32.
Berlin, Adele. 2001. "The Book of Esther and Ancient Storytelling." *JBL* 120: 3–14.
Bockmuehl, Markus. 1989. *Revelation and Mystery in Ancient Judaism and Pauline Christianity*. WUNT 36. Tübingen: Mohr Siebeck.
Bohak, Gideon. 2013. "A New Genizah Fragment of the Aramaic Levi Document." Pages 101–114 in *From Cairo to Manchester: Studies in the Rylands Genizah Fragments*. Edited by Renate Smithuis and Philip S. Alexander. JSSSup 31. Oxford: Oxford University Press.

Bohak, Gideon. 2011. "A New Genizah Fragment of the Aramaic Levi Document." *Tarbiz* 79: 373–83.
Bonani, G., Israel Carmi, S. Ivy, Willy Wolfli, John Strugnell, and Magen I. Broshi. 1991. "Radiocarbon Dating of the Dead Sea Scrolls." *Atiqot* 20: 27–32.
Bremmer, Jan M. 2014. "Descents to Hell and Ascents to Heaven in Apocalyptic Literature." Pages 340–57 in *The Oxford Handbook of Apocalyptic Literature*. Edited by John J. Collins. Oxford: Oxford University Press.
Brooke, George. 1994. "Power to the Powerless: A Long-Lost Song of Miriam." *BAR* 20: 62–65.
Brooke, George. 2013. "Some Issues behind the Ethics in the Qumran Scrolls and Their Implications for New Testament Ethics." Pages 83–106 in *Early Christian Ethics in Interaction with Jewish and Greco-Roman Contexts*. Edited by Jan Willem van Henten and Joseph Verheyden. STAR 17. Leiden: Brill.
Brooks Johnson, Michael. 2018. "One Work or Three? A Proposal for Reading 1QS-1QSa-1QSb as a Composite Work." *DSD* 25: 141–77.
Brown, Raymond. 1968. *The Semitic Background of the Term "Mystery" in the New Testament*. Biblical Series 21. Philadelphia: Fortress Press.
Burchard, Christoph. 1965. "Review: Testamenta XII Patriarchum." *RevQ* 5: 281–84.
Burian, Peter, and Alan Shapiro, eds. 2011. *The Complete Aeschylus: The Oresteia*. Oxford: Oxford University Press.
Camp, Claudia. 2011. "Feminist and Gender-Critical Perspectives on the Biblical Ideology of Intermarriage." Pages 303–15 in *Mixed Marriages: Intermarriage and Group Identity in the Second Temple Period*. Edited by Christian Frevel. LHBOTS. New York: T&T Clark.
Caquot, André. 1995. "Grandeur et Pureté Du Sacerdoce: Remarques Sur Le Testament de Qahat (4Q542)." Pages 39–44 in *Solving Riddles and Untying Knots: Biblical, Epigraphic, and Semitic Studies in Honor of Jonas C. Greenfield*. Edited by Jonas C. Greenfield. Winona Lake, IN: Eisenbrauns.
Caquot, André. 1998. "Les testaments qoumrâniens des pères du sacerdoce." *RHPR* 78: 3–26.
Carmi, Israel. 2000. "Radiocarbon Dating of the Dead Sea Scrolls." Pages 881–88 in *The Dead Sea Scrolls Fifty Years after Their Discovery: Proceedings of the Jerusalem Congress, July 20–25, 1997*. Edited by Lawrence H. Schiffman, Emanuel Tov, and James C. VanderKam. Jerusalem: Israel Exploration Society in cooperation with The Shrine of the Book, Israel Museum.
Charles, R. H., and A. Cowley. 1907. "An Early Source of the Testaments of the Patriarchs." *JQR* 19: 566–83.
Charles, R. H. 1908. *The Greek Versions of the Testaments of the Twelve Patriarchs: Edited from Nine Mss. Together with the Variants of the Armenian and Slavonic Versions and Some Hebrew Fragments*. Oxford: Clarendon Press.
Charles, R. H. 1913. *The Apocrypha and Pseudepigrapha of the Old Testament in English: With Introductions and Critical Explanatory Notes to the Several Books, Volume 1*. Oxford: Clarendon Press.
Charles, R. H. 1913. *The Apocrypha and Pseudepigrapha of the Old Testament in English: With Introductions and Critical Explanatory Notes to the Several Books, Volume 2*. Oxford: Clarendon Press.
Coblentz Bautch, Kelley. 2006. "What Becomes of the Angels' 'Wives'? A Text-Critical Study of '1 Enoch' 19:2." *JBL* 125: 766–80.

Collins, John J. 1980. "The Epic of Theodotus and the Hellenism of the Hasmoneans." *HTR* 73: 91–104.
Collins, John J. 2010a. "Epilogue: Genre Analysis and the Dead Sea Scrolls." *DSD* 17: 418–30.
Collins, John J. 2010b. *The Scepter and the Star: Messianism in Light of the Dead Sea Scrolls*. 2nd ed. Grand Rapids: Eerdmans.
Collins, John J. 2011. "Reading for History in the Dead Sea Scrolls." *DSD* 18: 295–315.
Collins, John J. 2014. *Scriptures and Sectarianism: Essays on the Dead Sea Scrolls*. Grand Rapids: Eerdmans.
Conacher, Desmond J. 1989. *Aeschylus Oresteia: A Literary Commentary*. Toronto: University of Toronto Press.
Conczorowski, Benedikt J. 2011. "All the Same as Ezra? Conceptual Differences Between the Texts on Intermarriage in Genesis, Deuteronomy, and Ezra." Pages 89–108 in *Mixed Marriages: Intermarriage and Group Identity in the Second Temple Period*. Edited by Christian Frevel. LHBOTS. New York: T&T Clark.
Cook, Edward M. 1993. "Remarks on the Testament of Kohath from Qumran Cave 4." *JJS* 44: 205–19.
Cook, Edward M. 2007. "Voldemort at Qumran?" Ralph the Sacred River (Blog). http://www.ralphriver.blogspot.com/2007/08/voldemort-at-qumran.html.
Cook, Edward M. 2014. "Qumran Aramaic, Corpus Linguistics, and Aramaic Retroversion." *DSD* 21: 356–84.
Cook, Edward M. 2015. *Dictionary of Qumran Aramaic*. Winona Lake: Eisenbrauns.
Cooley, Jeff. 2014. "The Book of Giants and the Greek Gilgamesh." Pages 67–79 in *Windows to the Ancient World of the Hebrew Bible: Essays in Honor of Samuel Greengus*. Edited by Bill T. Arnold, Nancy Erickson, and John H. Walton. Winona Lake: Eisenbrauns.
Cross, Frank Moore Jr. 1961. "The Development of the Jewish Scripts." Pages 133–202 in *The Bible and the Ancient Near East: Essays in Honor of William Foxwell Albright*. New York: Doubleday.
Davila, James R. 2013. "Aramaic Levi: A New Translation and Introduction." Pages 121–42 in *Old Testament Pseudepigrapha: More Noncanonical Scriptures*. Edited by Richard Bauckham, James Davila, and Alexander Panayotov. Grand Rapids: Eerdmans.
Davis Bledsoe, Amanda M. 2016. "Throne Theophanies, Dream Visions, and Righteous (?) Seers: Daniel, the Book of Giants, and 1 Enoch Reconsidered." Pages 81–96 in *Ancient Tales of Giants from Qumran and Turfan: Contexts, Traditions, and Influences*. Edited by Matthew Goff, Loren Stuckenbruck, and Enrico Morano. WUNT 360. Tübingen: Mohr Siebeck.
Deasley, A. 2000. *The Shape of Qumran Theology*. Carlisle: Paternoster.
Dehandschutter, Boudewijn. 1974. "Le reve dans l'Apocryphe de la Genese." Pages 48–55 in *La littérature juive entre Tenach et Mishna: Quelques problèmes*. Edited by Willem Cornelis van Unnik. RechBib 9. Leiden: Brill.
Dimant, Devorah. 1983. "The Biography of Enoch and the Books of Enoch." *VT* 33: 14–29.
Dimant, Devorah. 1994. "Apocalyptic Texts at Qumran." Pages 175–91 in *The Community of the Renewed Covenant: The Notre Dame Symposium on the Dead Sea Scrolls*. Edited by Eugene C. Ulrich and James C. VanderKam. Notre Dame, IN: University of Notre Dame Press.

Dimant, Devorah. 2011. "Between Qumran Sectarian and Non-Sectarian Texts: The Case of Belial and Mastema." Pages 235–56 in *The Dead Sea Scrolls and Contemporary Culture: Proceedings of the International Conference held at the Israel Museum, Jerusalem (July 6–8, 2008)*. Edited by Adolfo D. Roitman, Lawrence H. Schiffman, and Shani Tzoref. STDJ 93. Leiden: Brill.

Dimant, Devorah. 2007. "The Qumran Aramaic Texts and the Qumran Community." Pages 197–205 in *Flores Florentino: Dead Sea Scrolls and Other Early Jewish Studies in Honour of Florentino García Martínez*. Edited by Athony Hilhorst, Émile Puech, and Eibert J. C. Tigchelaar. JSJS 122. Leiden: Brill.

Dimant, Devorah. 2017. *From Enoch to Tobit: Collected Studies in Ancient Jewish Literature*. FAT 114. Tübingen: Mohr Siebeck.

Dimant, Devorah. Forthcoming. "The Two-Ways Notion in the Qumran Texts." In *The Qumran Scrolls and Hellenistic Contexts: Papers from the 10th Meeting of the International Organization of Qumran Studies, Aberdeen 2019*. Edited by Bärry Hartog and Andrew B. Perrin, with the assistance of Shelby Bennett and Matthew Hama. STDJ. Leiden: Brill.

DiTommaso, Lorenzo. 2010. "Apocalypticism and the Aramaic Texts from Qumran." Pages 451–83 in *Aramaica Qumranica: Proceedings of the Conference on the Aramaic Texts from Qumran in Aix-en-Provence 30 June–2 July 2008*. Edited by Katell Berthelot and Daniel Stökl Ben Ezra. STDJ 94. Leiden: Brill.

Doudna, Gregory L. 1998–9. "Dating the Scrolls on the Basis of Radiocarbon Analysis." Pages 430–71 in vol. 1 of *The Dead Sea Scrolls After Fifty Years*. Edited by Peter W. Flint and James C. VanderKam. Leiden: Brill.

Drawnel, Henryk. 2004. *An Aramaic Wisdom Text from Qumran: A New Interpretation of the Levi Document*. JSJS 86. Leiden: Brill.

Drawnel, Henryk. 2005. "The Aramaic Levi Document: An Overview of Its Content and Problematics." *Scripta Judaica Cracoviensia* 3: 7–17.

Drawnel, Henryk. 2006. "The Literary Form and Didactic Content of the Admonitions (Testament) of Qahat." Pages 55–73 in *From 4QMMT to Resurrection: Mélanges qumraniens en hommage à Émile Puech*. Edited by Florentino García Martínez, Annette Steudel, and Eibert Tigchelaar. STDJ 61. Leiden: Brill.

Drawnel, Henryk. 2010a. "The Initial Narrative of the Visions of Amram and Its Literary Characteristics." *RevQ* 24: 517–54.

Drawnel, Henryk. 2010b. "Amram, Visions of." *EDEJ*, 326–27.

Drawnel, Henryk. Forthcoming. "The Manuscripts of the Aramaic Testament of Levi (Visions of Levi) as Interpreted by Józef T. Milik." *RevQ*.

Duke, Robert R. 2007. "Moses' Hebrew Name: The Evidence of the Vision of Amram." *DSD* 14: 34–48.

Duke, Robert R. 2010. *The Social Location of the Visions of Amram (4Q543–547)*. StBibLit 135. New York: Peter Lang Publishing.

Elledge, C. D. 2017. *Resurrection of the Dead in Early Judaism: 200 BCE–CE 200*. Oxford: Oxford University Press.

Eppel, Robert. 1937. "Les tables de la Loi et les tables celestes." *RHPR* 17: 401–12.

Eshel, Esther. 1999. "Demonology in Palestine in the Second Temple Period." [Hebrew] Jerusalem: Hebrew University.

Eshel, Esther. 2009. "The Dream Visions in the Noah Story of the Genesis Apocryphon and Related Texts." Pages 41–61 in *Northern Lights on the Dead Sea Scrolls: Proceedings of the Nordic Qumran Network 2003–2006*. Edited by Anders Klostergaard Petersen, Torleif Elgvin, Cecilia Wassen, Hanne von Weissenberg, and Mikael Winninge. STDJ 80. Leiden: Brill.

Eshel, Hanan, and Esther Eshel. 2003. "Separating Levi from Enoch: Response to 'Enoch, Levi, and Peter: Recipients of Revelation in Upper Galilee." Pages 458–68 in vol. 2 of *George W.E. Nickelsburg in Perspective: An Ongoing Dialogue of Learning*. Edited by Jacob Neusner and Alan J. Avery-Peck. JSJS 80. Leiden: Brill.

Eshel, Hanan. 2007. "The Damascus Document's 'Three Nets of Belial': A Reference to the Aramaic Levi Document?" Pages 243–55 in *Heavenly Tablets: Interpretation, Identity and Tradition in Ancient Judaism*. JSJS 119. Edited by Lynn LiDonnici and Andrea Lieber. Leiden: Brill.

Esztári, Réka and Ádám Vér. 2015. "The Voices of Ištar: Prophetesses and Female Ecstatics in the Neo-Assyrian Empire." Pages 3–39 in *Religion and Female Body in Ancient Judaism and Its Environments*. Edited by Géza G. Xeravits. Berlin: De Gruyter.

Fabry, Heinz-Josef. 2013. "יָדַע." *ThWQ* 2: 79–93.

Falk, Daniel K. 2007. *The Parabiblical Texts: Strategies for Extending the Scriptures in the Dead Sea Scrolls*. LSTS 63. CQS 8. London: T&T Clark.

Feldman, Ariel. 2013. "The Song of Miriam (4Q365 6a ii + 6c 1-7) Revisited." *JBL* 132: 905–11.

Feldman, Ariel. 2018. "Patriarchs in Aramaic Traditions." Pages 469–80 in *T&T Clark Companion to the Dead Sea Scrolls*. Edited by George J. Brooke and Charlotte Hempel. London: T&T Clark.

Feldman, Liane M. 2020. "Sanitized Sacrifice in Aramaic Levi's Law of the Priesthood." *JAJ* 11: 343–68.

Fitzmyer, Joseph A. 2000. *The Dead Sea Scrolls and Christian Origins*. SDSSRL. Grand Rapids: Eerdmans.

Fitzmyer, Joseph A. 2003. *Tobit*. CEJL. Berlin: De Gruyter.

Fitzmyer, Joseph A. 2004. *The Genesis Apocryphon of Qumran Cave 1 (1Q20): A Commentary*. 3rd ed. BO 18B. Rome: Editrice Pontificio Istituto Biblico.

Flannery-Dailey, Frances. 2004. *Dreamers, Scribes, and Priests: Jewish Dreams in the Hellenistic and Roman Eras*. JSJS 90. Leiden: Brill.

Flint, Peter W. 1997. *The Dead Sea Psalms Scrolls and the Book of Psalms*. STDJ 17. Leiden: Brill.

Frevel, Christian, ed. 2011. *Mixed Marriages: Intermarriage and Group Identity in the Second Temple Period*. LHBOTS. New York: T&T Clark.

Frey, Jörg. 2010. "On the Origins of the Genre of the 'Literary Testament': Farewell Discourses in the Qumran Library and Their Relevance for the History of the Genre." Pages 345–75 in *Aramaica Qumranica: Proceedings of the Conference on the Aramaic Texts from Qumran in Aix-en-Provence 30 June–2 July 2008*. Edited by Katell Berthelot and Daniel Stökl Ben Ezra. STDJ 94. Leiden: Brill.

Fröhlich, Ida. 2001. "Demons, Scribes, and Exorcists in Qumran." Pages 73–81 in *Essays in Honour of Alexander Fodor on His Sixtieth Birthday*. Edited by Kinga Dévényi and Tamás Iványi. Budapest: Eötvös Loránd University Chair for Arabic Studies.

Fröhlich, Ida. 2012. "Enmeduranki and Gilgamesh: Mesopotamian Figures in Aramaic Enoch Traditions." Pages 637–53 in *A Teacher for All Generations: Essays in Honor of James C. VanderKam*. Edited by Eric F. Mason et al. JSJS 153. Leiden: Brill.

Frymer-Kensky, Tikva. 2002. *Reading the Women of the Bible*. New York: Schocken Books.
García Martínez, Florentino. 1985. "4Q'Amram B I, 14: ¿Melki-reša o Melki-ṣedeq?" *RevQ* 12: 111–14.
García Martínez, Florentino. 1997. "The Heavenly Tablets in the Book of Jubilees." Pages 243–60 in *Studies in the Book of Jubilees*. Edited by Matthias Albani, Jörg Frey, and Armin Lange. TSAJ 65. Tübingen: Mohr Siebeck.
García Martínez, Florentino and Eibert J. C. Tigchelaar. 1998. *The Dead Sea Scrolls: Study Edition*. Leiden: Brill.
García Martínez, Florentino. 2010. "Scribal Practices in the Aramaic Literary Texts from Qumran." Pages 327–41 in *Myths, Martyrs, and Modernity: Studies in the History of Religions in Honour of Jan N. Bremmer*. Edited by Jitse Dijkstra, Justin Kroesen, and Yme Kuiper. SHR 127. Leiden: Brill.
García Martínez, Florentino. 2014. "Les rapports avec l'Ecriture des textes arameenes trouves a Qumran." Pages 19–40 in *Old Testament Pseudepigrapha and the Scriptures*. Edited by Eibert J. C. Tigchelaar. BETL 270. Leuven: Peeters.
Gladd, Benjamin. 2008. *Revealing the Mysterion: The Use of Mystery in Daniel and Second Temple Judaism with Its Bearing on First Corinthians*. BZNW 160. Berlin: De Gruyter.
Gnuse, Robert Karl. 1984. *The Dream Theophany of Samuel: Its Structure in Relation to Ancient Near Eastern Dreams and Its Theological Significance*. Lanham, MD: University Press of America.
Gnuse, Robert Karl. 1990. "The Jewish Dream Interpreter in a Foreign Court: The Recurring Use of a Theme in Jewish Literature." *JSP* 7: 29–53.
Goff, Matthew J. 2003. *The Worldly and Heavenly Wisdom of 4QInstruction*. STDJ 50. Leiden: Brill.
Goff, Matthew J. 2009. "Gilgamesh the Giant: The Qumran Book of Giants Appropriation of Gilgamesh Motifs." *DSD* 16: 221–53.
Goldhill, Simon. 2004. *Aeschylus, the Oresteia*. 2nd ed. Cambridge: Cambridge University Press.
Goldman, Liora. 2010. "Dualism in the Visions of Amram." *RevQ* 24: 421–32.
Goldman, Liora. 2013. "The Burial of the Fathers in the Visions of Amram from Qumran." Pages 231–49 in *Rewriting and Interpreting the Hebrew Bible: The Biblical Patriarchs in the Light of the Dead Sea Scrolls*. Edited by Devorah Dimant and Reinhard G. Kratz. BZAW 439. Berlin: Walter de Gruyter.
Goldman, Liora. 2020. "Between Aaron and Moses in 4QVisions of Amram." Pages 101–108 in *Vision, Narrative, and Wisdom in the Aramaic Texts from Qumran: Essays from the Copenhagen Symposium, 14–15 August, 2017*. Edited by Mette Bundvad and Kasper Siegismund with the collaboration of Melissa Sayyad Bach, Søren Holst, and Jesper Høgenhaven. STDJ 131. Leiden: Brill.
Greenfield, Jonas C., and Michael E. Stone. 1979. "Remarks on the Aramaic Testament of Levi from the Geniza." *RB* 86: 214–30.
Greenfield, Jonas C. 1988. "The Words of Levi Son of Jacob in Damascus Document IV, 15–19." *RevQ* 13: 319–22.
Greenfield, Jonas C., and Michael E. Stone. 1990. "Two Notes on the Aramaic Levi Document." Pages 153–61 in *Of Scribes and Scrolls: Studies on the Hebrew Bible, Intertestamental Judaism, and Christian Origins Presented to John Strugnell on the Occasion of His Sixtieth Birthday*. Edited by Harold W. Attridge, John J. Collins, and Thomas H. Tobin. Lanham, MD: University Press of America.

Greenfield, J., and M. Sokoloff. 1992. "The Contributions of Qumran Aramaic to the Aramaic Vocabulary." Pages 78–98 in *Studies in Qumran Aramaic*. Edited by Takamitsu Muraoka. AbrNSup 3. Louvain: Peeters.

Greenfield, Jonas C. 1993. "'Because He/She Did Not Know Letters': Remarks on a First Millennium C.E. Legal Expression." *Journal of the Ancient Near Eastern Society* 22: 39–44.

Greenfield, Jonas C., and Michael E. Stone. 1996. "Aramaic Levi Document." Pages 1–72 in *Qumran Cave 4 XVII: Parabiblical Texts: Part 3*. Edited by George Brooke, John Collins, Torleif Elgvin, Erik Larson, Carol Newsom, Émile Puech, Lawrence Schiffman, Michael Stone, and Julio Trebolle Barrera. DJD 22. Oxford: Clarendon Press.

Grelot, Pierre. 1956. "Notes sur le Testament Araméen de Lévi." *RB* 63: 391–406.

Gross, Andrew D. 2013a. "Testament of Kohath." Pages 1869–71 in vol. 2 of *Outside the Bible: Ancient Jewish Writings Related to Scripture*. Edited by Louis H. Feldman, James L. Kugel, and Lawrence H. Schiffman. Philadelphia: Jewish Publication Society.

Gross, Andrew D. 2013b. "Visions of Amram." Pages 1507–10 in vol. 2 of *Outside the Bible: Ancient Jewish Writings Related to Scripture*. Edited by Louis H. Feldman, James L. Kugel, and Lawrence H. Schiffman. Philadelphia: Jewish Publication Society.

Gruen, Erich S. 2013. "Did Ancient Identity Depend on Ethnicity? A Preliminary Probe." *Phoenix* 67: 1–22.

Gruen, Erich S. 2016. *The Construct of Identity in Hellenistic Judaism: Essays on Early Jewish Literature and History*. Berlin: Walter de Gruyter.

Hägg, Tomas. 2012. *The Art of Biography in Antiquity*. Cambridge: Cambridge University Press.

Halpern-Amaru, Betsy. 2005. "Burying the Fathers: Exegetical Strategies and Source Traditions in Jubilees 46." Pages 135–52 in *Reworking the Bible: Apocryphal and Related Texts at Qumran: Proceedings of a Joint Symposium by the Orion Center for the Study of the Dead Sea Scrolls and Associated Literature and the Hebrew University Institute for Advanced Studies Research Group on Qumran, 15–17 January 2002*. Edited by Esther G. Chazon, Devorah Dimant, and Ruth A. Clements. STDJ 58. Leiden: Brill.

Hamidović, David. 2013. "La transtextualite dans le livre de Michel (4Q529; 6Q23): Une etude du repertoire des motifs litteraires apocalyptiques sur Henoch, Daniel et les Jubiles." *Sem* 55: 117–37.

Harrington, Hannah K. 2000. "Purity." *EDSS* 2: 724–28.

Harrington, Hannah K. 2011. "Intermarriage in Qumran Texts." Pages 251–79 in *Mixed Marriages: Intermarriage and Group Identity in the Second Temple Period*. Edited by Christian Frevel. LHBOTS. New York: T&T Clark.

Hayes, Christine E. 1999. "Intermarriage and Impurity in Ancient Jewish Sources." *HTR* 92: 3–36.

Hayes, Christine E. 2002. *Gentile Impurities and Jewish Identities: Intermarriage and Conversion from the Bible to the Talmud*. Oxford: Oxford University Press.

Heger, Paul. 2014. "Genealogy and Holiness of Seed in Second Temple Judaism: Facts or Creative Supposition?" Pages 302–74 in *Women in the Bible, Qumran and Early Rabbinic Literature*. STDJ 110. Leiden: Brill.

Hieke, Thomas. 2005. "Endogamy in the Book of Tobit, Genesis, and Ezra– Nehemiah." Pages 103–20 in *The Book of Tobit*. Edited by Géza G. Xeravits and József Zsengellér. Leiden: Brill.

Hieke, Thomas. 2015. "Menstruation and Impurity: Regular Abstention from the Cult According to Leviticus 15: 19–24 and Some Examples for the Reception of the Biblical Text in Early Judaism." Pages 54–70 in *Religion and Female Body in Ancient Judaism and Its Environments*. Edited by Géza G. Xeravits. Berlin: Walter de Gruyter.

Hillel, Vered. 2018. "Aramaic Levi." Pages 261–63 in *T&T Clark Companion to the Dead Sea Scrolls*. Edited by George J. Brooke and Charlotte Hempel. London: T&T Clark.

Himmelfarb, Martha. 1993. *Ascent to Heaven in Jewish and Christian Apocalypses*. Oxford: Oxford University Press.

Himmelfarb, Martha. 2004. "Earthly Sacrifice and Heavenly Incense: The Law of the Priesthood in Aramaic Levi and Jubilees." Pages 103–22 in *Heavenly Realms and Earthly Realities in Late Antique Religions*. Edited by Ra'anan S. Boustan and Annette Yoshiko Reed. New York: Cambridge University Press.

Høgenhaven, Jesper. 2020. "Geography in the Visions of Amram." Pages 119–36 in *Vision, Narrative, and Wisdom in the Aramaic Texts from Qumran: Essays from the Copenhagen Symposium, 14–15 August, 2017*. Edited by Mette Bundvad and Kasper Siegismund with the collaboration of Melissa Sayyad Bach, Søren Holst, and Jesper Høgenhaven. STDJ 131. Leiden: Brill.

Hollander, Harm W., and Marinus de Jonge. 1985. *The Testaments of the Twelve Patriarchs: A Commentary*. SVTP 8. Leiden: Brill.

Holst, Søren. 2020. "Fragments and Forefathers: An Experiment with the Reconstruction of 4QVisions of Amram." Pages 137–152 in *Vision, Narrative, and Wisdom in the Aramaic Texts from Qumran: Essays from the Copenhagen Symposium, 14–15 August, 2017*. Edited by Mette Bundvad and Kasper Siegismund with the collaboration of Melissa Sayyad Bach, Søren Holst, and Jesper Høgenhaven. STDJ 131. Leiden: Brill.

Hultgård, Anders. 1977. *L'eschatologie des Testaments des Douze Patriarches: I Interprétation des textes*. Historia Religionum: Acta Universitatis Upsaliensis 6. Uppsala: Uppsala University Press.

Jonge, Marinus de. 1978. *The Testaments of the Twelve Patriarchs: A Critical Edition of the Greek Text*. PVTG 1. Leiden: Brill.

Jonge, Marinus de. 1998. "Levi in Aramaic Levi and in the Testament of Levi." Pages 71–89 in *Pseudepigraphic Perspectives: The Apocrypha and Pseudepigrapha in Light of the Dead Sea Scrolls: Proceedings of the International Symposium of the Orion Center for the Study of the Dead Sea Scrolls and Associated Literature, 12–14 January, 1997*. Edited by Esther G. Chazon, Michael Stone, and Avital Pinnick. STDJ 31. Leiden: Brill.

Jonge, Marinus de. 2003. *Pseudepigrapha of the Old Testament as Part of Christian Literature: The Case of the Testament of the Twelve Patriarchs and the Greek Life of Adam and Eve*. SVTP 18. Leiden: Brill.

Kapera, Zdzisław J. 2007. "Preliminary Information about Józef T. Milik's Unpublished Manuscripts of 'The Testament of Levi.'" *Polish Journal of Biblical Research* 6: 109–12.

Keady, Jessica M. 2017. *Vulnerability and Valor: A Gendered Analysis of Everyday Life in the Dead Sea Scrolls Communities*. LSTS 91. New York: T&T Clark.

Knoppers, Gary N. 2017. "Toward a Critical Edition of the Samaritan Pentateuch: Reflections on Issues and Methods." Pages 163–88 in *Reading the Bible in Ancient Traditions and Modern Editions: Studies in Memory of Peter W. Flint*. Edited by Andrew B. Perrin, Daniel K. Falk, and Kyung S. Baek. EJL 47. Atlanta: SBL Press.

Kobelski, Paul J. 1981. *Melchizedek and Melchireša'*. CBQMS 10. Washington, D.C.: The Catholic Biblical Association of America.
Koehler, Ludwig, Walter Baumgartner, Johann Jakob Stamm, and M. Richardson. 2000. *The Hebrew and Aramaic Lexicon of the Old Testament*. Leiden: Brill.
Kosmala, Hans. 1978. "The Three Nets of Belial: A Study in the Terminology of Qumran and the New Testament." *Annual of the Swedish Theological Institute* 4 (1965): 91–113. Repr. Pages 115–137 in *Studies, Essays, and Reviews* 2. Leiden: Brill.
Kőszeghy, Miklós. 2015. "The Female Body in Israel and Judah before the Exile." Pages 43–53 in *Religion and Female Body in Ancient Judaism and Its Environments*. Edited by Géza G. Xeravits. Berlin: Walter de Gruyter.
Kugel, James L. 1992. "The Story of Dinah in the Testament of Levi." *HTR* 85: 1–34.
Kugel, James L. 1993. "Levi's Elevation to the Priesthood in Second Temple Writings." *HTR* 86: 1–64.
Kugel, James L. 2012. "How Old Is the Aramaic Levi Document?" Pages 343–64 in *A Walk Through Jubilees: Studies in the Book of Jubilees and the World of Its Creation*. JSJS 156. Leiden: Brill.
Kugler, Robert A. 1996a. *From Patriarch to Priest: The Levi-Priestly Tradition from Aramaic Levi to Testament of Levi*. EJL 9. Atlanta: Scholars Press.
Kugler, Robert A. 1996b. "Some Further Evidence for the Samaritan Provenance of 'Aramaic Levi' ('1QTestLevi'; '4QTestLevi')." *RevQ* 17: 351–58.
Kugler, Robert A. 2008. "Whose Scripture? Whose Community? Reflections on the Dead Sea Scrolls Then and Now, by Way of Aramaic Levi." *Dead Sea Discoveries* 15: 5–23.
Kugler, Robert A. 2010. "Levi." Pages 884–85 in *The Eerdmans Dictionary of Early Judaism*. Edited by John J. Collins and Daniel C. Harlow. Grand Rapids: Eerdmans.
Lange, Armin, and Ulrike Mittmann-Richert. 2002. "Annotated List of the Texts from the Judaean Desert Classified by Content and Genre." Pages 115–64 in *The Texts from the Judaean Desert: Indices and an Introduction to the Discoveries in the Judaean Desert Series*. Edited by Emmanuel Tov. DJD 39. Oxford: Clarendon Press.
Lee, Peter. 2015. *Aramaic Poetry in Qumran*. Saarbrücken: Scholars' Press.
Lemaire, André. 2010. "Nabonide et Gilgamesh: L'araméen en Mésopotamie et à Qoumrân." Pages 125–44 in *Aramaica Qumranica: Proceedings of the Conference on the Aramaic Texts from Qumran in Aix-en-Provence, 30 June–2 July 2008*. Edited by Katell Berthelot and Daniel Stökl Ben Ezra. STDJ 94. Leiden: Brill.
Lichtenberger, Hermann. 2004. "Spirits and Demons in the Dead Sea Scrolls." Pages 14–21 in *The Holy Spirit and Christian Origins: Essays in Honor of James D. G. Dunn*. Edited by Graham N. Stanton, Bruce W. Longenecker, and S. C. Barton. Grand Rapids: Eerdmans.
Lim, Timothy H. 2000. "The Qumran Scrolls, Multilingualism, and Biblical Interpretation." Pages 57–73 in *Religion in the Dead Sea Scrolls*. Edited by John J. Collins and Robert Kugler. SDSSRL. Grand Rapids: Eerdmans.
Lim, Timothy H. 2009. "Towards a Description of the Sectarian Matrix." Pages 7–31 in *Echoes from the Caves: Qumran and the New Testament*. Edited by Florentino García Martínez. STDJ 85. Leiden: Brill.
Lim, Timothy H. 2013. *The Formation of the Jewish Canon*. New Haven: Yale University Press.
Loader, William. 2009. *The Dead Sea Scrolls on Sexuality*. Grand Rapids: Eerdmans.

Loader, William. 2011. *The Pseudepigrapha on Sexuality: Attitudes towards Sexuality in Apocalypses, Testaments, Legends, Wisdom, and Related Literature*. Grand Rapids: Eerdmans.
Machiela, Daniel A. 2009. *The Dead Sea Genesis Apocryphon: A New Text and Translation with Introduction and Special Treatment of Columns 13–17*. STDJ 79. Leiden: Brill.
Machiela, Daniel A. 2010. "Genesis Revealed: The Apocalyptic Apocryphon from Qumran Cave 1." Pages 205–21 in *Qumran Cave 1 Revisited: Texts from Cave 1 Sixty Years after Their Discovery: Proceedings of the Sixth Meeting of the IOQS in Ljubljana*. Edited by Daniel K. Falk, Sarianna Metso, Donald W. Parry, and Eibert J. C. Tigchelaar. STDJ 91. Leiden: Brill.
Machiela, Daniel A. 2012. "On the Importance of Being Abram: Genesis Apocryphon 18, Jubilees 10:1–13:4, and Further Thoughts on Literary Relationship." Pages 715–36 in vol. 2 of *A Teacher for All Generations: Essays in Honor of James C. VanderKam*. Edited by Eric Mason, Samuel I. Thomas, Alison Schofield, and Eugene Ulrich. JSJS 153. Leiden: Brill.
Machiela, Daniel A. 2013. "Lord or God? Tobit and the Tetragrammaton." *CBQ* 75: 463–72.
Machiela, Daniel A., and Andrew B. Perrin. 2014. "Tobit and the *Genesis Apocryphon*: Toward a Family Portrait." *JBL* 133: 111–32.
Machiela, Daniel A. 2015. "The Aramaic Dead Sea Scrolls: Coherence and Context in the Library of Qumran." Pages 244–58 in *The Dead Sea Scrolls at Qumran and the Concept of a Library*. Edited by Sidnie White Crawford and Cecilia Wassen. STDJ 116. Leiden: Brill.
Machiela, Daniel A. 2017. "Charity as a Theme in Some Qumran Aramaic Texts." Paper presented at the International Meeting of the Society of Biblical Literature. Berlin, August 10.
Machiela, Daniel A., and James C. VanderKam. 2018. "Genesis Apocryphon." Pages 1–147 in *The Dead Sea Scrolls: Hebrew, Aramaic, and Greek Texts with English Translations: Genesis Apocryphon and Related Documents*. Edited by James H. Charlesworth, Henry W. Morisada Rietz, and Loren L. Johns. Tübingen: Mohr Siebeck.
Machiela, Daniel A. 2021a. "Is the Testament of Qahat Part of the Visions of Amram? Material and Literary Considerations of 4Q542 and 4Q547." *JSJ* 52 (1): 27–38.
Machiela, Daniel A. 2021b. "Some Proposed Connections between the Visions of Amram and the Four Kingdoms in View of the Aramaic Literature from Qumran." *DSD* 28 (2): 226–45.
Maier, Johann. 1995. *Die Qumran-Essener: Die Texte vom Toten Meer, Band II: Die Texte der Höhle 4*. Stuttgart: UTB.
Milik, J. T. 1955a. "1Q21. Testament de Lévi." Pages 87–91 in *Qumran Cave I*. Edited by Dominique Barthélemy and Józef Tadeusz Milik. DJD 1. Oxford: Clarendon.
Milik, J. T. 1955b. "Le Testament de Lévi en Araméen: Fragment de la Grotte 4 de Qumrân." *RB* 62: 398–406.
Milik, J. T. 1971. "Problèmes de la littérature hénochique à la lumière des fragments araméens de Qumrân." *HTR* 64: 333–78.
Milik, J. T. 1972a. "4QVisions de 'Amram et Une Citation d'Origene." *RB* 79: 77–97.
Milik, J. T. 1972b. "Milkî-ṣedeq et Milkî-reša' dans les anciens ecrits juifs et chretiens." *JJS* 23: 95–144.

Milik, J. T. 1976. *The Books of Enoch: Aramaic Fragments of Qumran Cave 4*. Oxford: Clarendon Press.
Milik, J. T. 1978. "Écrits Prééséniens de Qumrân: D'Hénoch à Amram." Pages 91–106 in *Qumrân: Sa Piété, Sa Théologie et Son Milieu*. Edited by M. Delcor. BETL 46. Paris: Duculot.
Milik, J. T. 1992. "Les modèles araméens du livre d'Esther dans la Grotte 4 de Qumrân." *RevQ* 15: 321–99.
Miller, Geoffrey D. 2016. "Canonicity and Gender Roles: Tobit and Judith as Test Cases." *Bib* 97: 199–221.
Mroczek, Eva. 2016. *The Literary Imagination in Jewish Antiquity*. New York: Oxford University Press.
Muraoka, T. 2011. *A Grammar of Qumran Aramaic*. ANESSup 38. Leuven: Peeters.
Najman, Hindy. 2000. "Torah of Moses: Pseudonymous Attribution in Second Temple Writings." Pages 202–16 in *The Interpretation of Scripture in Early Judaism and Christianity: Studies in Language and Tradition*. Edited by Craig A. Evans. LSTS 33. Sheffield: Sheffield Academic Press.
Najman, Hindy. 2012. "The Idea of Biblical Genre: From Discourse to Constellation." Pages 307–21 in *Prayer and Poetry in the Dead Sea Scrolls and Related Literature: Essays in Honor of Eileen Schuller on the Occasion of Her 65th Birthday*. Edited by Jeremy Penner, Ken M. Penner, and Cecilia Wassen. STDJ 98. Leiden: Brill.
Najman, Hindy, and Nicole Hilton. 2018. "Revelation." Pages 481–90 in *T&T Clark Companion to the Dead Sea Scrolls*. Edited by George J. Brooke and Charlotte Hempel. London: T&T Clark.
Nautlin, P. 2014. "Apostolic Constitutions." *Encyclopedia of Ancient Christianity* 1: 197–98. Downer's Grove: IVP.
Naveh, Joseph. 1998. "Fragments of an Aramaic Magic Book from Qumran." *IEJ* 48: 252–61.
Neujahr, Matthew. 2012. *Predicting the Past in the Ancient Near East: Mantic Historiography in Ancient Mesopotamia, Judah, and the Mediterranean World*. BJS 354. Rhode Island: Brown University Press.
Newsom, Carol A. 1990. "'Sectually Explicit' Literature from Qumran." Pages 167–187 in *The Hebrew Bible and Its Interpreters*. Biblical and Judaic Studies from the University of California, San Diego 1. Winona Lake, IN: Eisenbrauns.
Nickelsburg, George W. E. 2001. *1 Enoch: A Commentary on the Book of 1 Enoch*. Hermeneia. Minneapolis: Fortress.
Nickelsburg, George W. E., and James C. VanderKam. 2012. *1 Enoch: The Hermeneia Translation*. 2nd ed. Minneapolis: Fortress.
Noegel, Scott B. 2007. *Nocturnal Ciphers: The Allusive Language of Dreams in the Ancient Near East*. AOS 89. New Haven: American Oriental Society.
Nordheim, Eckhard von. 1980. *Die Lehre der Alten: II. Das Testament als Literaturgattung im Judentum der hellenistisch-römischen Zeit*. ALGHJ 13. Leiden: Brill.
Norin, Stig. 2013. "The Aramaic Levi—Comparing the Qumran Fragments with the Genizah Text." *SJOT* 27: 118–30.
Oppenheim, A. Leo. 1956. *The Interpretation of Dreams in the Ancient Near East: With a Translation of an Assyrian Dream-Book*. TAPS 46. Philadelphia: The American Philosophical Society.

Pakkala, Juha. 2011. "Intermarriage and Group Identity in the Ezra Tradition" Pages 78–88 in *Mixed Marriages: Intermarriage and Group Identity in the Second Temple Period.* Edited by Christian Frevel. LHBOTS. New York: T&T Clark.

Palmer, Carmen. 2018. *Converts in the Dead Sea Scrolls: The Gēr and Mutable Ethnicity: Converts in the Dead Sea Scrolls.* STDJ 126. Leiden: Brill.

Pass, Herman L., and John Arendzen. 1900. "Fragment of and Aramaic Text of the Testament of Levi." *JQR* 12: 651–61.

Paul, Shalom M. 1973. "Heavenly Tablets and the Book of Life." *JANESCU* 5: 345–54.

Pearse, Holly A. 2004. "The Guide and the Seducer: The Dualism of 4QVisions of 'Amram." MA thesis, McMaster University.

Penner, Ken M. 2014. "Did the Midrash of Shemihazai and Azael Use the Book of Giants?" Pages 15–45 in *Sacra Scriptura: How "Non-Canonical" Texts Functioned in Early Judaism and Early Christianity.* Edited by James A. Charlesworth, Lee Martin McDonald, and Blake A. Jurgens. JCTCRS 20. London: T&T Clark.

Penney, Douglas L., and Michael O. Wise. 1994. "By the Power of Beelzebub: An Aramaic Incantation Formula from Qumran (4Q560)." *JBL* 113: 627–50.

Perrin, Andrew B. 2013. "Capturing the Voices of Pseudepigraphic Personae: On the Form and Function of Incipits in the Aramaic Dead Sea Scrolls." *DSD* 20: 98–123.

Perrin, Andrew B. 2015a. *The Dynamics of Dream-Vision Revelation in the Aramaic Dead Sea Scrolls.* JAJSup 19. Göttingen: Vandenhoeck & Ruprecht.

Perrin, Andrew B. 2015b. "Tobit's Context and Contacts in the Qumran Aramaic Anthology." *JSP* 25: 23–51.

Perrin, Andrew B. 2017a. "The Textual Forms of Aramaic Levi Document at Qumran." Pages 431–52 in *Reading the Bible in Ancient Traditions and Modern Editions: Studies in Memory of Peter W. Flint.* Edited by Andrew B. Perrin, Daniel K. Falk, and Kyung S. Baek. EJL 47. SBL Press.

Perrin, Andrew B., and Matthew J. Hama. 2017b [2006]. "4Q548 (Dualistic Fragments in Aramaic)." *The Online Critical Pseudepigrapha.* Edited by Ian W. Scott, Ken M. Penner, and David M. Miller. Atlanta: Society of Biblical Literature. http://pseudepigrapha.org/docs/intro/4Q548.

Perrin, Andrew B. 2018a. "The Aramaic Imagination: Incubating Apocalyptic Thought and Genre in Dream-Visions Among the Qumran Aramaic Texts." Pages 110–40 in *Apocalyptic Thinking in Early Judaism: Engaging with John Collins' The Apocalyptic Imagination.* JSJS 182. Edited by Sidnie White Crawford and Cecilia Wassen. Leiden: Brill.

Perrin, Andrew B. 2018b. "Writing about 'Books' within Scrolls: Portrayals of Scribal Craft and Written Tradition in the Aramaic Dead Sea Scrolls." Paper presented at the international meeting of the Society of Biblical Literature, Helsinki, August 1.

Perrin, Andrew B. 2020a. "Expressions of Empire and Four Kingdoms Patterns in the Aramaic Dead Sea Scrolls." Pages 96–120 in *Four Kingdoms Motifs before and beyond the Book of Daniel.* Edited by Andrew B. Perrin and Loren T. Stuckenbruck with the assistance of Shelby Bennett and Matthew Hama. TBN 28. Leiden: Brill.

Perrin, Andrew B. 2020b. "Greek Gospels and Aramaic Dead Sea Scrolls: Compositional, Conceptual, and Cultural Intersections." *Open Theology* 6: 440–56.

Perrin, Andrew B., and Brandon Diggins. 2020c. "Variant Readings in the Aramaic Dead Sea Scrolls: A Tool for Ongoing Research on the Textual Status and Linguistic Setting of Ancient Jewish Aramaic Literature." Pages 93–118 in *Dead Sea Scrolls, Revise and Repeat: New Methods and Perspectives on the Dead Sea Scrolls.* Edited by Carmen Palmer, Andrew R. Krause, Eileen Schuller, and John Screnock. EJL 52. Atlanta: SBL Press.

Perrin, Andrew B. 2021. "Redrafting the Architecture of Daniel Traditions in the Hebrew Scriptures and Dead Sea Scrolls." *JTS* 72: 44–71.

Perrin, Andrew B. Forthcoming. "Charting Constellations of Aramaic Jewish Pseudepigrapha." *Proceedings of the 2019 Meeting of the International Organization for Qumran Studies, University of Aberdeen, August 4–8, 2019.* Edited by Bärry Hartog and Andrew B. Perrin, with the assistance of Shelby Bennett and Matthew Hama. STDJ. Leiden: Brill.

Perrin, Andrew B. Forthcoming. "Daniel Traditions and the Qumran Movement? Reconsidering the Interface between Texts, Traditions, Identities, and Movements." *Re-Imagining Apocalypticism: Apocalypses, Apocalyptic Literature, and the Dead Sea Scrolls.* Edited by Lorenzo DiTommaso and Matthew Goff. EJL. Atlanta: SBL Press.

Perrin, Andrew B. Forthcoming. "Symptoms and Symbols, Prayers and Portents: Diagnostic Physiognomy and the Diviner in the Aramaic Prayer of Nabonidus (4Q242)." *Proceedings of the Aramaic Science in Qumran Conference, Pázmány Péter Catholic University Budapest, May 15–16, 2018.* Edited by Ida Fröhlich. Ancient Cultures of Knowledge. Tübingen: Mohr Siebeck.

Peters, Dorothy M. 2008. *Noah Traditions in the Dead Sea Scrolls: Conversations and Controversies of Antiquity.* EJL 26. Atlanta: SBL Press.

Philonenko, Marc. 1993. "'Melkireša' et Melkira': Note sur les Visions de 'Amram." *Sem* 41: 159–62.

Popović, Mladen. 2007. *Reading the Human Body: Physiognomics and Astrology in the Dead Sea Scrolls and Hellenistic-Early Roman Period Judaism.* STDJ 67. Leiden: Brill.

Popović, Mladen. 2017. "Pseudepigraphy and a Scribal Sense of the Past in the Ancient Mediterranean: A Copy of the Book of the Words of the Vision of Amram." Pages 308–318 in *Is There a Text in this Cave? Studies in the Textuality of the Dead Sea Scrolls in Honour of George J. Brooke.* Edited by Ariel Feldman, Maria Cioată, and Charlotte Hempel. STDJ 119. Leiden: Brill.

Puech, Émile. 1991, "Le Testament de Qahat en Araméen de La Grotte 4 ('4QTQah')." *RevQ* 15: 23–54.

Puech, Émile. 2001. *Discoveries in the Judaean Desert: XXXI: Qumrân Grotte 4: XXII: Textes Araméens Premiere Partie: 4Q529–549.* DJD 31. Oxford: Clarendon Press.

Puech, Émile. 2002. "Le 'Testament de Lévi' en araméen de la Geniza du Caire." *RevQ* 20: 511–56.

Pummer, Reinhard. 1982. "Genesis 34 in Jewish Writing of Hellenistic and Roman Periods." *HTR* 75: 177–88.

Rabin, Chaim. 1954. *The Zadokite Documents: I. The Admonition. II. The Laws.* Oxford: Clarendon Press.

Rad, Gerhard von, and James L. Crenshaw. 1976. "The Joseph Narrative and Ancient Wisdom." Pages 439–47 in *Studies in Ancient Israelite Wisdom.* Edited by James L. Crenshaw. New York: Ktav Publishing House.

Ravid, Liora. 1999. "The Special Terminology of the Heavenly Tablets in the Book of Jubilees)." *Tarbiz* 68: 463–71 (Hebrew).

Reynolds, Bennie H. 2013. "Understanding the Demonologies of the Dead Sea Scrolls: Accomplishments and Directions for the Future: Understanding the Demonologies of the Dead Sea Scrolls." *Religion Compass* 7: 103–14.

Rothenbusch, Ralf. 2011. "The Question of Mixed Marriages Between the Poles of Diaspora and Homeland: Observations in Ezra-Nehemiah." Pages 60–77 in *Mixed Marriages: Intermarriage and Group Identity in the Second Temple Period.* Edited by Christian Frevel. LHBOTS. New York: T&T Clark.

Satlow, Michael L. 2001. *Jewish Marriage in Antiquity*. Princeton: Princeton University Press.

Schattner-Rieser, Ursula. 2004. *L'araméen Des Manuscrits de La Mer Morte: I. Grammaire*. Instruments Pour l'étude Des Langues de l'Orient Ancien 5. Prahins: Éditions du Zèbre.

Schattner-Rieser, Ursula. 2007. "J. T. Milik's Monograph on the Testament of Levi and the Reconstructed Aramaic Text of the Prayer of Levi and the Vision of Levi's Ascent to Heaven from Qumran Caves 4 and 1." *QC* 15: 139–55.

Schattner-Rieser, Ursula. 2011. "Levi in the Third Sky: On the 'Ascent to Heaven' Legends within Their Near Eastern Context and J. T. Milik's Unpublished Version of the Aramaic Levi Document." Pages 801–19 in vol. 2 of *The Dead Sea Scrolls In Context: Integrating the Dead Sea Scrolls in the Study of Ancient Texts, Languages, and Cultures*. Edited by Armin Lange, Emanuel Tov, and Matthias Weigold in association with Bennie H. Reynold III. VTSup 140. Leiden: Brill.

Schechter, Solomon. 1910. *Documents of Jewish Sectaries:* Vol. 1 of *Fragments of a Zadokite Work*. Cambridge: Cambridge University Press.

Schiffman, Lawrence H. 2005. "Sacrificial Halakhah in the Fragments of the Aramaic Levi Document from Qumran, the Cairo Genizah, and Mt. Athos Monastery." Pages 177–202 in *Reworking the Bible: Apocryphal and Related Texts at Qumran. Proceedings of a Joint Symposium by the Orion Center for the Study of the Dead Sea Scrolls and Associated Literature and the Hebrew University Institute for Advanced Studies Research Group on Qumran, 15–17 January, 2002*. Edited by Esther G. Chazon, Devorah Dimant, Ruth A. Clements, and Florentino García Martínez. STDJ 58. Leiden: Brill.

Schöpflin, Karin. 2015. "Women's Roles in the Narrative and Theology of the Book of Tobit." Pages 173–85 in *Religion and Female Body in Ancient Judaism and Its Environments*. Edited by Géza G. Xeravits. Berlin: Walter de Gruyter.

Schuller, Eileen M. 1994. "Women in the Dead Sea Scrolls." Annals of the New York Academy of Sciences 722: 115–31.

Schuller, Eileen M., and Carol A. Newsom. 2012. *The Hodayot (Thanksgiving psalms): A Study Edition of 1QH^a*. EJL 36. Atlanta: SBL.

Schwiderski, Dirk, ed. 2004. *Die Alt-Und Reichsaramäischen Inschriften: Band 2: Texte Und Bibliographie*. FSBP 2. Berlin: Walter de Gruyter.

Schwiderski, Dirk, ed. 2008. *Die Alt-Und Reichsaramäischen Inschriften: Band 1: Konkordanz*. FSBP 4. Berlin: Walter de Gruyter.

Segal, Michael. 2016. *Dreams, Riddles, and Visions: Textual, Contextual, and Intertextual Approaches to the Book of Daniel*. BZAW 455. Berlin: Walter de Gruyter.

Schoor, van der, Hanneke. Forthcoming. "The Assessment of Variation: The Case of the Aramaic Levi Document." *DSD*.

Southwood, Katherine. 2011. "An Ethnic Affair? Ezra's Intermarriage Crisis Against a Context of 'Self-Ascription' and 'Ascription of Others.'" Pages 46–59 in *Mixed Marriages: Intermarriage and Group Identity in the Second Temple Period*. Edited by Christian Frevel. LHBOTS. New York: T&T Clark.

Stadel, Christian. 2008. *Hebraismen in den aramäischen Texten vom Toten Meer*. Schriften der Hochschule für Jüdische Studien Heidelberg 11. Heidelberg: Universitätsverlag Winter Heidelberg.

Stadel, Christian. 2016. "קשׁט." *ThWQ* 3: 516–20.

Starcky, J. 1956. "Le travail d'édition des fragments manuscrits de Qumrân." *RB* 63: 49–67.
Starcky, J. 1963. "Les quatre étapes du messianisme à Qumran." *RB* 70: 481–505.
Stone, Michael E. 1984. *Jewish Writings of the Second Temple Period: Apocrypha, Pseudepigrapha, Qumran Sectarian Writings, Philo, Josephus*. CRINT, vol. 2. Minneapolis: Fortress Press.
Stone, Michael E., and Jonas C. Greenfield. 1993. "Prayer of Levi." *JBL* 112: 247–66.
Stone, Michael E. 1996. "The Dead Sea Scrolls and the Pseudepigrapha." *DSD* 3: 270–95.
Stone, Michael E. 1999. "The Axis of History at Qumran." Pages 133–49 in *Pseudepigraphic Perspectives: The Apocrypha and Pseudepigrapha in Light of the Dead Sea Scrolls: Proceedings of the International Symposium of the Orion Center for the Study of the Dead Sea Scrolls and Associated Literature, 12–14 January, 1997*. Edited by Esther G. Chazon and Michael E. Stone with the collaboration of Avital Pinnick. STDJ 31. Leiden: Brill.
Stone, Michael E. 2002. "Aramaic Levi in Its Contexts." *JSQ* 9: 307–26.
Stone, Michael E. 2011. *Ancient Judaism: New Visions and Views*. Grand Rapids: Eerdmans.
Stone, Michael E., and Esther Eshel. 2013. "Aramaic Levi Document." Pages 1490–1510 in vol. 2 of *Outside the Bible: Ancient Jewish Writings Related to Scripture*. Edited by Louis H. Feldman, James L. Kugel, and Lawrence H. Schiffman. Philadelphia: Jewish Publication Society.
Strawn, Brent A. 2016. "תָּמַם." *ThWQ* 3: 1135–43.
Stuckenbruck, Loren T. 1997. *The Book of Giants from Qumran: Texts, Translation, and Commentary*. TSAJ 63. Tübingen: Mohr Siebeck.
Stuckenbruck, Loren T. 1997. "The Throne-Theophany of the Book of Giants: Some New Light on the Background of Daniel 7." Pages 211–20 in *The Scrolls and the Scriptures: Qumran after Fifty Years*. Edited by Stanley E. Porter and Craig A. Evans. JSPSup 26. Sheffield: Sheffield Academic Press.
Stuckenbruck, Loren T. 2014. *The Myth of Rebellious Angels: Studies in Second Temple Judaism and New Testament Texts*. WUNT 335. Tübingen: Mohr Siebeck.
Suter, David W. 1979. "Fallen Angel, Fallen Priest: The Problem of Family Purity in 1 Enoch." *HUCA* 50: 115–35.
Suter, David W. 2003. "Why Galilee? Galilean Regionalism in the Interpretation of 1 Enoch 6–16." *Hen* 25: 167–212.
Tervanotko, Hanna. 2014. "A Trilogy of Testaments? The Status of the Testament of Qahat versus Texts Attributed to Levi and Amram." Pages 41–59 in *Old Testament Pseudepigrapha and the Scriptures*. Edited by Eibert J. C. Tigchelaar. BETL 270. Leuven: Peeters.
Tervanotko, Hanna. 2015a. "Gendered Beauty: on the Portrayal of Beautiful Men and Women in the Hebrew Bible." Pages 43–52 in *So Good, So, Beautiful: Studies in Psalms, Ethics, Aesthetics, and Hermeneutics*. Edited by Peter Tomson and Jaap de Lange. Gorichem: Narratio.
Tervanotko, Hanna. 2015b. "Members of Levite Family and Ideal Marriages in Aramaic Levi Document, Visions of Amram, and Jubilees." *RevQ* 106: 155–76.
Tervanotko, Hanna. 2016. *Denying Her Voice: The Figure of Miriam in Ancient Jewish Literature*. JAJSup 23. Göttingen: Vandenhoeck & Ruprecht.
Thomas, Samuel I. 2009. *The "Mysteries" of Qumran*. EJL 25. Leiden: Brill.

Thomas, Samuel I. 2010. "Esoteric Knowledge in Qumran Aramaic Texts." Pages 403–32 in *Aramaica Qumranica: Proceedings of the Conference on the Aramaic Texts from Qumran in Aix-en-Provence, 30 June–2 July 2008.* Edited by Katell Berthelot and Daniel Stökl Ben Ezra. STDJ 94. Leiden: Brill.

Tigchelaar, Eibert. 2002. "In Search of the Scribe of 1QS." Pages 339–52 in *Emanuel: Studies in Hebrew Bible, Septuagint, and Dead Sea Scrolls in Honor of Emanuel Tov.* Edited by Shalom M. Paul, Robert A. Kraft, Lawrence H. Schiffman, and Weston W. Fields. VTSup 94. Leiden: Brill.

Tigchelaar, Eibert. 2007. "The Imaginal Context and the Visionary of the Aramaic New Jerusalem." Pages 257–70 in *Flores Florentino: Dead Sea Scrolls and Other Early Jewish Studies in Honour of Florentino García Martínez.* Edited by Anthony Hilhorst, Émile Puech, and Eibert J. C. Tigchelaar. JSJS 122. Leiden: Brill.

Tigchelaar, Eibert. 2010. "Aramaic Texts from Qumran and the Authoritativeness of Hebrew Scriptures: Preliminary Observations." Pages 155–71 in *Authoritative Scriptures in Ancient Judaism.* Edited by Mladen Popović. JSJS 141. Leiden: Brill.

Tiller, Patrick A. 1997. "The 'Eternal Planting' in the Dead Sea Scrolls." *DSD* 4: 312–35.

Tov, Emanuel. 1985. "The Nature and Background of Harmonizations in Biblical Manuscripts." *JSOT* 31: 3–29.

Tov, Emanuel. 1997. "The Scribes of the Texts Found in the Judean Desert." Pages 131–52 in *The Quest for Context and Meaning: Studies in Biblical Intertextuality in Honor of James A. Sanders.* Edited by Craig A. Evans and Shemaryahu Talmon. BibInt 28. Leiden: Brill.

Tov, Emanuel. 2004. *Scribal Practices and Approaches Reflected in the Texts Found in the Judean Desert.* STDJ 54. Leiden: Brill.

Trehuedic, Kévin. 2010. "Le visions du testament d'Amram A–E; F (?); G (?): 4Q543–4Q544–5Q545–4Q546– 4Q547–4Q548 (?)–4Q549 (?)." Pages 207–30 in *Exode, Lévitique, Nombres, Édition et traduction des manuscrits hébreux, araméens et grecs.* Edited by Katell Berthelot and Thierry Legrand. La Bibliothèque de Qumrân 2. Paris: Editions du Cerf.

Trotter, Jonathan R. 2012. "The Tradition of the Throne Vision in the Second Temple Period: Daniel 7:9–10, '1 Enoch' 14:18–23, and the 'Book of Giants' (4Q530)." *RevQ* 25: 451–66.

Ulrich, Eugene C. 1979. "4QSam^c: A Fragmentary Manuscript of 2 Samuel 14–15 from the Scribe of the Serek Hay-Yaḥad (1QS)." *BASOR* 235: 1–25.

Ulrich, Eugene C. 1994. "The Bible in the Making: The Scriptures at Qumran." Pages 77–93 in *The Community of the Renewed Covenant: the Notre Dame Symposium on the Dead Sea Scrolls.* Edited by Eugene Ulrich and James C. VanderKam. CJA 10. Notre Dame: University of Notre Dame Press.

Uusimäki, Elisa. 2021. "In Search of Virtue: Ancestral Inheritance in the Testament of Qahat." *Biblical Interpretation* 29: 206–28.

Van de Water, Rick. 2000. "Reconsidering Palaeographic and Radiocarbon Dating of the Dead Sea Scrolls." *RevQ* 19: 423–39.

VanderKam, James C. 1997. "The Origins and Purposes of the Book of Jubilees." Pages 3–24 in *Studies in the Book of Jubilees.* Edited by Matthias Albani, Jörg Frey, and Armin Lange. TSAJ 65. Tübingen: Mohr Siebeck.

VanderKam, James C. 1998. "Authoritative Literature in the Dead Sea Scrolls." *DSD* 5: 382–402.

VanderKam, James C., and Peter W. Flint. 2002. *The Meaning of the Dead Sea Scrolls: Their Significance for Understanding the Bible, Judaism, Jesus, and Christianity.* New York: HarperCollins.

VanderKam, James C. 2010. "Jubilees 46:6–47:1 and 4QVisions of Amram." *DSD* 17: 141–58.

VanderKam, James C. 2018. *Jubilees 1–21.* Hermeneia. Minneapolis: Fortress.

Vermes, Geza. *The Dead Sea Scrolls in English.* 4th ed. Sheffield: Sheffield Academic Press, 1995.

Walsh, Matthew. 2019. *Angels Associated with Israel in the Dead Sea Scrolls.* WUNT 2. Tübingen: Mohr Siebeck.

Wassen, Cecilia. 2005. *Women in the Damascus Document.* AcBib 21. Atlanta: SBL, 2005.

Wechsler, Michael G. 2000. "Two Para-Biblical Novellae from Qumran Cave 4: A Reevaluation of 4Q550." *DSD* 7: 130–72.

White Crawford, Sidnie A. 1992. "4Q364 & 365: A Preliminary Report." Pages 217–28 in *The Madrid Qumran Congress: Proceedings of the International Congress on the Dead Sea Scrolls, Madrid 18-21 March, 1991.* Vol. 1. Edited by Julio Trebolle Barrera and Luis Vegas Montaner. STDJ 12. Leiden: Brill.

White Crawford, Sidnie A. 1996. "Has *Esther* Been Found at Qumran? *4QProto-Esther* and the *Esther* Corpus." *RevQ* 17: 307–25.

White Crawford, Sidnie A. 2003. "Traditions about Miriam in the Qumran Scrolls." Pages 33–44 in *Women and Judaism.* Edited by L. J. Greenspoon, R. Simkins, and J. Cahan. SJC 14. Omaha: Creighton University Press.

White Crawford, Sidnie. 2008. *Rewriting Scripture in Second Temple Times.* SDSSRL. Grand Rapids: Eerdmans.

White Crawford, Sidnie A. 2014. "Rewritten Scriptures as a Clue to Scribal Traditions in the Second Temple Period." Pages 105–17 in *Rewritten Bible after Fifty Years: Texts, Terms, or Techniques? A Last Dialogue with Geza Vermes.* Edited by József Zsengellér. JSJS 166. Leiden: Brill.

White Crawford, Sidnie A. 2015. "There is Much Wisdom in Her: The Matriarchs in the Qumran Library." Pages 133–52 in *Celebrate Her for the Fruit of Her Hands: Essays in Honor of Carol L. Meyers.* Winona Lake, IN: Eisenbrauns.

White Crawford, Sidnie A. 2016. "The Qumran Collection as a Scribal Library." Pages 109–31 in *The Dead Sea Scrolls at Qumran and the Concept of a Library.* Edited by Sidnie White Crawford and Cecilia Wassen. Leiden: Brill.

Williamson, H. G. M. 1985. *Ezra and Nehemiah.* WBC 16. Waco: Thomas Nelson.

Wills, Lawrence M. 1990. *The Jew in the Court of the Foreign King: Ancient Jewish Court Legends.* Minneapolis: Fortress.

Winslow, Karen S. 2011. "Mixed Marriages in Torah Narratives." Pages 132–49 in *Mixed Marriages: Intermarriage and Group Identity in the Second Temple Period.* Edited by Christian Frevel. LHBOTS. New York: T&T Clark.

Wright, Benjamin G. 2010. "Joining the Club: A Suggestion about Genre in Early Jewish Texts." *DSD* 17: 289–314.

Wright, Benjamin G., and Suzanne M. Edwards. 2015. "'She Undid Him with the Beauty of Her Face' (Jdt 16.6): Reading Women's Bodies in Early Jewish Literature." Pages 73–108 in *Religion and Female Body in Ancient Judaism and Its Environments.* Edited by Géza G. Xeravits. Berlin: Walter de Gruyter.

Yarbro Collins, Adela. 1996. *Cosmology and Eschatology in Jewish and Christian Apocalypticism.* JSJS 50. Leiden: Brill.

Young, Kyle. 2020. "Product Received: Influence of the 'Old in the New' on the Formulation of Theologies of 'the' Septuagint." Pages 71–91 in *Towards a Theology of the Septuagint: Stellenbosch Congress on the Septuagint, 2018*. Edited by Johann Cook and Martin Rösel. SCS. Atlanta: SBL Press.

Zahn, Molly M. 2011. *Rethinking Rewritten Scripture: Composition and Exegesis in the 4QReworked Pentateuch Manuscripts*. STDJ 95. Leiden: Brill.

Zanella, Francesco. 2016. "צָדַק." *ThWQ* 3: 383–93.

Zsengellér, József. 2015. "Judith as a Female David: Beauty and Body in Religious Context." Pages 186–211 in *Religion and Female Body in Ancient Judaism and Its Environments*. Edited by Géza G. Xeravits. Berlin: Walter de Gruyter.

Index of References

Hebrew Bible/Old Testament

Genesis
1:2	112
5:22–24	115
7:11	112
9:21	115
12:2	51
13:14–17	174
13:16	51
14:18	60
15:5	51
16:10	51
17:7	51
18:2	145
21:33	92
22:17	51
28:16	59
28:22	59
31:10	145
31:12	145
31:47	116
34	8, 53, 55, 208
34:30–31	8
37:6–10	39
37:11	59
42:4	59
42:7	59
45:8	31
46:11	81, 84, 153
49	8
49:5–7	8, 208
49:5	19

Exodus
1:6	29
1:8	29
2:10	171
6:16	81, 153
6:18	81, 122, 138
6:20	72, 122
6:22	138, 139
7–11	207
9:29	44
14:31	49
15:5	113
15:20–21	139
15:20	191
17:10–12	139
23:20	172
24–29	201
24:14	139
29:40–41	65
30:19	63
30:21	63
31:2	139
32:13	49
32:26–29	8
38:30	201
39:39	201
40:12	50
40:15	56, 106
40:31	63

Leviticus
1	15, 64
1:3–9	65
1:9	65
1:12	16, 76
1:17	16, 76
2:13	64
3:5	16, 76
4:12	16, 76
6:12	16, 76
8:6	50
10:4	138
10:10–11	116
14:6	16, 76
14:49–52	16, 76
16:20	105
18:7–20	140
18:12	73
19:19	96
20:20	73
22:10–12	96
23:13	65
23:42–24:2	77

Numbers
3:10–38	96
3:17	81, 153
3:19	81, 122, 138
3:27	81
3:29	81
3:30	81, 138
4:2	81
4:4	81
4:15	81
4:18	81
4:34	81
4:37	81
6	92
6:25–27	91
7:9	81
10:21	81
12:1–15	139

Numbers (cont.)		2 Samuel		2 Chronicles	
15:1–10	65	21:8	52	1:5–6	201
15:9–10	65			4:6	65
16:1	81	1 Kings		7:7	201
16:9–10	50	3:6	100	15:3	116
18:4–7	96	3:15	59	16:4	52
18:21–28	59	4:12	52	17:7–9	116
19:6	16, 76	8:38	44	19:4–11	116
20:1	139	8:64	201	20:19	81
20:16	172	15:20	52	29:12	81
25:7–13	8	19:16	52	34:12	81
25:13	56, 106,			35:3	116
	110	2 Kings		36:15	172
26:9	122	6:21	31		
26:57–58	81	9:7	49	Ezra	
26:57	81, 153	13:14	31	5:6	136
26:58	122	15:29	52	6:1–2	37
26:59	72, 139	16:14–15	201	6:2–12	64, 65
28:7–21	65			6:9	64
		1 Chronicles		7:10–11	116
Deuteronomy		2:19	139	7:11	136
22:9	96	5:29	139	7:18	93
24:8–9	139	6:1	81	7:25	38
29:9	37	6:2–3	122	9:5	44
33:10	31, 116	6:2	81		
34:5	49	6:16	81	Nehemiah	
		6:18	81, 122	10:34	16, 77
Joshua		6:22	81	13:31	16, 77
5:13	145	6:38	81		
14:1	37	6:39	81	Esther	
21:4	81	6:49	49	3:14	136
21:5	81	6:61	81	4:8	136
21:10	81	6:66	81	8:13	136
21:20	81	6:70	81		
21:26	81	9:29	65	Job	
23:2	37	9:32	81	1–2	48
24:29	49	12:33	100	1:13	44
		15:5	81	19:15	96
Judges		20:19	81	23:7	103
7:22	52	21:1	48	25:4	39
		23:6	81, 153	31:27	39
1 Samuel		23:12–13	122	35:8	104
2:27	14, 115,	23:12	81	42:6	143
	208	24:20	122		
9:3	207	29:12	81	Psalms	
18:19	52	34:12	81	12:2	100
				28:2	44

73:13	100	38:17	49	10:5	145
78:70	49	40–48	34	10:13	162
104:6	113	40:38	65	10:21	162, 193
106:37	197	43:22–24	64	11:36	91
110:4	168	43:24	65	11:38	121
119:133	48	44:13	50	12:1	162, 193
134:2	44	45:17	65	12:4	37
148:3	39	48:11	50		
154	44			*Hosea*	
		Daniel		4:2	105
Proverbs		2	214		
1:3–4	105	2:18	179	*Amos*	
3:15	32	2:19	179	7:4	112
4:6–7	34	2:22	92		
6:16–19	105	2:27	179	*Jonah*	
8:21	32	2:28	179	2:5	112
8:27–28	113	2:29	179		
14:1	34	2:30	179	*Micah*	
15:33	31	2:40	152	3:11	37
16:16	32	2:44	110	6:4	139
20:9	100	2:47	91, 179	6:8	47, 105
		3:7	38		
Ecclesiastes		3:31	38	*Nahum*	
7:12	34	4:2	156	1:1	202
		4:5	52, 182		
Isaiah		4:9	156, 179	*Habakkuk*	
9:2	41	4:14	207	2:2	202
11:2	17	4:27	99, 104		
13:10	35	4:31	44	*Haggai*	
22:6	35	5:19	38	1:13	172
24:17	45	5:23	93		
40:28	92	6:18	59	*Zechariah*	
44:26	172	6:23	117	1–6	145
51:10	113	6:26	38	1:6	49
		7	91, 214	1:18	145
Jeremiah		7:1	37, 52,	2:1	145
7:9	105		156, 202	3	157
26:5	49	7:7	146, 159,	3:1–2	48
30:14	111		182	5:1	145
31:26	59	7:9	146	5:9	145
		7:10	91, 193	6:1	145
Ezekiel		7:12	38		
8:5	145	7:28	59	*Malachi*	
9:2	201	8:3	145	2:2–5	208
14:14	213	8:16	163	2:5–8	110
31:15	112	9:10	49	2:5–6	115
36:23	92	9:21	163	2:5	14

Malachi (cont.)
2:6	14
2:7	31, 116, 172

NEW TESTAMENT
Matthew
1:24	59
15:19	45
23:23	47

Luke
1:79	42

John
8:12	41
11:41	44
12:35	41

Romans
16:26	92

Ephesians
4:19	47

Colossians
2:2–3	32

Hebrews
7	168
7:4	95
7:8–9	95
11:22	29

1 Peter
2:5–9	25

1 John
2:11	41

Jude
9	156

Revelation
1:6	25
1:14	146
5:10	25

APOCRYPHA/DEUTERO-CANONICAL BOOKS
1 Esdras
4:58	44

Tobit
1:1–2	137
1:1	148
1:3	41, 188
1:9	138
1:18–20	153
2:3–8	153
3:11	44
3:14	99
3:15	101
4:7	104
4:12	45, 95, 138, 155
5:1	106
5:16	163
6:8–9	163
6:8	183, 197
6:12	138, 172
6:15	197
6:16–18	163
6:16	106, 197
6:17	197
6:18	197
7:9	148
8:3	163
13	34, 121
13:11	142
13:12	110
13:20	105
14:2	99, 104
14:3	106
14:4	110
14:8	94
14:9	94
14:12	153

Additions to Esther
A 11	59

Wisdom of Solomon
7:14	35
10:13–14	32

Ecclesiasticus
29:11–12	35
40:18	32
41:12	32
44–50	95
45:17	31
45:18	96
47:17	116

Letter of Jeremiah
6:1	136
60	39

1 Maccabees
2:42	3

PSEUDEPIGRAPHA
1 Enoch
1:4	92
1:8	92
1:9	162
2:1	164
6:6	162
6:7	162
6:8	162
9:1	53, 162
10:1–3	104
10:11	162
10:16	51, 104
13:8	145
13:9	52
14	91
14:1	103, 136, 137
14:12	53
14:20	146
14:22	91
18:8–12	166
20:5	162
21:5	162
22:1–14	112
24:6	162
25:7–27	166
33:2–3	53
33:3	162
34:2–3	53
35:1	53

36:2	53	*2 Baruch*		*Demetrius*	
40:7	48	5:1	92	2.19	*123*
40:8	202	37:1	59	3	139
40:9	162				
41:9	48	*2 Enoch*		*Eupolemus*	
53:3	48	1:3	59	4:5	193
54:6	48, 162	2:2	94		
60:4–5	162	2:4	94	*Ezekiel the Tragedian*	
62:1	145	36:4	94	18–26	139
65:6	48	39:3	94		
68:2–4	162	39:8	94	*History of the Rechabites*	
69:14	162	40:1	94	8:1	193
71:3	162	47:1	94	16:14	193
71:8–9	162	50:5	35		
72:1	162	53:1	94	*Joseph and Aseneth*	
80:1	162			11:19	44
81:1–2	193	*3 Enoch*		23:14	55
81:6	202	1:3	123		
82:1	202	26:12	193	*Jubilees*	
83:1	106	28:7	146	1:16	104
83:3	52	49:5	123	1:29	193
85:2	106			3:10	193
87:2	145	*4 Baruch*		3:31	193
89:2	145	6:2	44	4:5	193
89:5	184			4:15	165
89:12	148	*4 Ezra*		4:17	30
89:30	159	3:1	59	4:21–22	165
90:40	59	4·1	162	4:32	193
91:1	106	5:14	59	4:33	155
91:13	110	5:20	162	5:1–6	165
91:14	41, 104	9:38	59	5:13	193
91:18	41	10:25	59	6:1–3	65
91:19	94	10:28	162	6:17	193
93:2–10	104	14:24	193	7:1–5	198
93:2	106, 193			7:3–5	16, 66
93:10	30, 47, 51, 116	*4 Maccabees*		7:34	94
		7:19	95	7:39	94
93:11	105	16:25	95	8:3	165
94:1	41, 104, 106, 114			10:1–13	165
		Apocalypse of Abraham		11:4–5	165
103:2	193	11:2	146	13:16	92
106:1	106			14:17	59
106:10	146	*Artapanus*		16:18	25
106:19	193	3:26	193	16:26	104
106:2	146			20:6	94
107:1	94, 113	*Assumption of Moses*		21:5	94
		10:17	92	21:11	64

Jubilees (cont.)
21:12–14	16, 78
21:12	78
21:16	63
21:24	104
22:16–25	99
25:3	94
30–32	178
30:5–7	54
31:15	37
32:1	13, 58
32:2	59
32:3	60
32:36	59
34:15	29
34:20	70
36:6	104
40:9	48
44:14	81, 153
45:15	115, 153
46	154, 155
46:2	48
46:6–10	153
46:9–47:1	131
46:10	154
47:1	122
47:4	139
50:5	48

Liber Antiquitatum Biblicarum
2:10	94
9:3–14	122
9:7–8	179
9:10	139, 142, 191
12:5	193
12:10	193
19:7	193
20:8	139
22:5	193
26:12–13	193
26:15	193
54:1	193
54:5	193

Lives of the Prophets
2:14	193

Questions of Ezra
1:14–15	156

Sibylline Oracles
3:257	193
4:166	44

Testament of Abraham
13:9–14 A	156
17:12–16	152

Testament of Asher
1:1	136

Testament of Dan
2:1	94
6:1	94

Testament of Gad
1:1	136
3:1	94

Testament of Job
1:5–6	8

Testament of Joseph
1:1	136

Testament of Judah
13:1	94
14:1	94
17:1	94
21:2–4	25

Testament of Levi
2:3	50, 52
2:4–5	44
2:5–5:7	13, 130
2:6–10	13
2:9	58
4:2	13
4:3	92
5:1	53
5:2	13, 56, 58
5:3–4	13, 54
5:4	193
6–7	54
6:2	59
6:8–7:1	55
8	13, 130
8:1–18	13
8:4	79
8:11	24
8:14	24
8:18	58
8:19	59
9:3	60
9:5–14	99
9:11	63
9:12	78
9:14	65
10:1	94
11:1	70
11:4–6	81
13:1	94
13:2	14, 30
13:5	94
13:9	31
14:1–3	39
14:1	40, 94
18:3	92
18:14	102
19:1	94

Testament of Naphtali
1:1	136
5:1–7:1	130

Testament of Reuben
1:1	136
3:9	94

Testament of Simeon
1:1	29
3:1	94
5:2	94
7:1	94

Testament of Zebulun		27		62, 67		89	28, 97
1:1	136	28		63, 65, 118		89:21	205
5:5	94	29		79		90	28, 98
10:1	94	30		63, 64, 66, 91		90:22–23	205
						91	29, 31, 96
DEAD SEA SCROLLS		31		15		91:9–10	205
ALD		37–40a		65		93–94	67
1a	45	42–44		65		93	29
3	91	42–45		65		94	29
4–6	13, 25	48		178, 208		96	34
4	25, 26	49–50		101		98	67
6	25	49		178		104	67
7–9	57	50		98, 99			
7	56	51		178, 208		*CD*	
8–61	206	52		65		*(Damascus Document)*	
8	101	57–59		116, 208		3 3–4	101
9	26, 60, 91, 199	57		15, 198		4 14–19	17, 45, 217
		61		178, 208		4 15–18	47
11–61	98	62		138, 155, 206		4 15	49
11–13	101			209		5 7–11	139
11:3	71	63–67					
12	148	63		70, 71		*1QHa*	
13	91, 106	64		74, 208		4 25–26	93
		65		72		9 9–22	93
13, 15	15	66		70, 81		9 25–26	193
14	79	67		24, 37, 71		9 29	157
14:8	94	68		72		9 36	157
15b–16	51	69–73		69		11 18, 32–33	112
16	17, 47, 121, 205	69		70, 71		12 15	100
		70		72		12 31	157
16:14	94	71		67, 70, 72		12 33	157
17	101	73–75		205		13 13	157
18	49, 99	73		70 138		13 17	157
19	63	74		81		14 14	157
20–23	61, 62	75		72, 155		14 18	104
21	63	76		71		16 7	104
22–27	75	77		72		18 30	157
22	15, 101	81–82		29		19 9	157
23–25	68	82–95		26		22 25	48
23–25a	78	82		106, 118		25 34–27 3	180
24–25	67, 68	83b		141			
25	68	84		106		*1QM*	
25a–b	61, 62	85		103, 104		1 8	104
25a	15	86		28		5 9	121
25b–30	65	88–91		67		5 14	121
26–30	62	88		30, 38, 114		11 2	92

1QM (cont.)		2 22	92	20 8	148		
12 12–13	121	5 9	94, 103	20 9	138		
13 10	100	5 20	114	20 12–15	45		
13 12	41	5 21	179	20 12	91		
14 16	91	5 25	179	20 13–16	93		
18 6	91	5 29	37, 136, 211	20 13	93		
				20 16	91, 164		
1QpHab		6 1–6	103	20 17	164		
10 13	141	6 2–6	188	20 20	164		
		6 3	41	20 25	93		
1QS		6 4	30	20 26–28	183		
3 21	41	6 6	98, 100	20 26	164		
4 1	41	6 7–10	138	20 27	138		
4 2–8	47	6 7	155	20 28	164		
4 3–6	105	6 9	197	20 34	138		
4 3	100	6 11	164	21 2	91		
4 16–20	165	6 12	59, 179	21 8–19	174		
4 21	100	7 2	39, 164	21 8	156		
4 23–24	100	7 7	93	21 9	145		
4 23	100	10 13–17	65	21 10–22	153		
4 25–26	93	10 16	66	21 13–14	174		
6	157	10 17	16, 64	21 20	91		
8 5	104	11 15–12 1	115	22 3	153		
9 14	104	11 13	102	22 15	91		
11	157	12 16	118	22 16	91, 93		
11 10	41	12 17	91, 93	22 18	93		
11 7–9	104	12 19–15 21	92	22 21	91, 93		
15	157	12 19	52	22 27	109, 156		
20	157	12 21	91	22 32	45		
		14 13	104				
1QSb		14 19	179	*1Q21*			
4 27	92	14 20	179	1 2	13, 37, 38, 119, 148		
		15 14	164				
1Q20		15 18	38	1 3	91		
0 7	97	15 21	59, 202	3 1	13		
0 12	114	15 24	91	3 3	56		
0 18	92	16–17	214, 214	4	59		
1 2	179	16 12	95	4 1	56, 57		
1 3	179	19 8	92	4 5	62, 75		
1 7	179	19 15–16	121				
2 9	45	19 17–18	202	*1Q23*			
2 9–15	214	19 17	59, 202	29 1	163		
2 10	103	19 18	182	31 3	193		
2 13	45	19 25–26	37				
2 16	164	19 25	15, 30, 103, 118	*2Q20*			
2 18	103			1 2	48		
2 19–22	103	20 7	30				

Index of References

2Q26		4 i 19	138	*4Q205*	
1 1–3	193	4 ii 6	172	1 xii	166
		4 ii 9	164, 197	2 i 26	148
4Q112		4 ii 12	106	2 ii 29	159
3 ii, 4–6 18	156	4 ii 13	164, 197		
				4Q206	
4Q113		*4Q198*		4 i 19	184
1 5	211	1 1	99, 104		
16–18 i	211	1 2	106	*4Q209*	
		1 6	110	7 iii 6	39
4Q156					
2 4	105	*4Q200*		*4Q210*	
		1 ii 5	44	1 iii 3, 7	39
		2 9	32		
4Q177				*4Q212*	
12–13 i 5	100	*4Q201*		1 ii 15	102
		1 i 5	92	1 ii 17	110, 142
4Q180		1 ii 10	102	1 ii 18	41
1 3	193	1 iv 5	179	1 ii 19	94
		1 v 4	142	1 iv 12	116
4Q181				1 iv 13	30, 47
1 1	157	*4Q202*		1 iv 18	110, 142
		1 iii 14	91, 92	1 iv 22	41, 104
4Q184		1 iv 6	164	1 v 16	105
4 4	157			1 v 24	114
		4Q203		1 v 25	41, 104
4Q185		4 3	163		
1–2 i 9	157	7a 5	163	*4Q213*	
		7a 7	164	1–2 ii 4	121
4Q196		7b ii 2	193	1, 2	11
2 1	148	8 1–5	36	1 i	74, 103
6 8	44	8 3–5	136, 137	1 i 3, rec.	207
6 9	99	8 3	193	1 i 6	205
6 10	101	9 3	45, 179	1 i 7–11	11
10 1	104			1 i 7	99, 104
11 2	106	*4Q204*		1 i 8	48
14 i 5	164, 197	1 i 18	164	1 i 9–10	114, 207
14 i 12	164, 197	1 i 29	102	1 i 9	47, 74, 114
14 i 8	106	1 iv 9	103	1 i 10	14
17 i 5	91	1 vi 3–4	145	1 i 11–12	14
17 ii 8	105	1 vi 8	164	1 i 11	97, 205
17 ii 15	110, 142	1 viii	166	1 i 12	47, 74, 205
18 15	91	4 4	93	1 i 14	12
18 16	106	5 ii 26	179	1 i 16	96, 205
		5 ii 28	94, 113	1 ii–2	73, 74, 79, 80
4Q197		5 ii 29	114		
4 i 13	164, 183, 197			1 ii–2 6	75, 80

4Q213 (cont.)		2 14–18	13	2–3 5	47	
1 ii–2 8–9	14	2 14–15	58	2–3 i	127	
1 ii–2 8	14	2 14	15	2–3 i 1–6	172, 190	
1 ii–2 9	14	2 15	156	2–3 ii	32, 79	
1 ii–2 10–11	12, 51, 109, 196	2 18	58, 119, 164	2–3 ii 5	14, 30, 35	
1 ii–2 12	15, 116	3–4	13	2–3 ii 6	35	
1 ii–2 15	13, 24, 119, 148	3–4 3	101	2 ii 6	14	
1 ii 9	12	3–4 5	101	*4Q214b*		
1 ii 11–12	212	3–4 6	38	2–3	15, 68	
2	11	3–4 7	110, 178	2–3, 4, 5–6 i 2–6	15	
2 9	74	3–4 8	59, 60	2–3 5	68	
2 13	11	3–4 13–16	189	2–3 8	62	
2 15	11	3 12	114	2–6 i	61, 62, 67	
3–5	26	3 17	142	2–6 i 4–6	16	
3–4	10	3 18	105	2–6 i 6–9	65	
3	11	5 i–ii 3	110, 206	5–6 i	62, 68	
3 2	11	5 i 3	13, 106, 178, 202	7 1	57	
4 1, 6–7	16	6 1	13, 58	8	32, 73	
4 2	10			8 1	35, 121	
4 5	12, 16, 45, 104	*4Q213b*		8 2	35	
4 6	48	1 1	13, 22, 53, 206	8 3	35, 47	
4 8–9	11	1 2	202	*4Q223–224*		
4 8	97	1 4	26, 56	1 i 2	157	
4	11	1 5	24	2 iv 3	157	
5	11	1 6	13, 56, 176, 178	*4Q227*		
5 1–2	11	1 8	206	2 3	157	
6	11	2 10–11	12, 196	*4Q242*		
		8 3	14	1–3 1	136	
4Q213a				1–3 1–3	138	
1–2	10, 11	*4Q214*				
1 8–12	1	1–2	75	*4Q243*		
1 10	93	1 i 13–14	31	1 2	91	
1 12	17, 41, 104	1 7	68	6	37	
1 13	12, 17, 23, 121, 205	2	15	7 3	41	
1 14	15, 30	2 2–8	79	9 1	40	
1 17	17, 41, 42, 164, 168	2 6	118	13 2	164, 197	
		2 10	15	24 1	113	
1 18	93	3	58			
2 6	93	3 2 12		*4Q244*		
2 10–11	34, 83, 109, 212	*4Q214a*		1–3 1	148	
2 11–13	21	1	75	12 2	164, 197	
2 13	21	1 1	78	12 4	137	

4Q245		4Q377		4Q423	
1 i 4	37	2 i 9	139	4 3	157
1 i 5	81	2 ii 10–11	172	8 2	157

4Q246		4Q381		4Q434	
1 ii 1–2	39	76–77 2	157	1 ii 2	157
1 ii 4–6	112				
1 ii 5	41, 104	4Q382		4Q491	
1 ii 9	112	40 1	157	8–10 i 13	91
				16 3	25
4Q251		4Q385			
17 2–3	139	2 5	157	4Q496	
				3 7	105
4Q252		4Q386			
1 5	112	1 i 4	157	4Q501	
		1 ii 2	157	1 1	96
4Q258					
13 2	157	4Q389		4Q504	
		1 6	137	1–2 iv 9–10	92
4Q259				1–2 iv 14	193
3 10	104	4Q392		7 9	32
		1 4	157		
4Q264		1 6	157	4Q510	
1 2	157			1 2	91
		4Q401			
4Q280		11 3	168	4Q511	
2 2	42			26 3	157
		4Q403			
4Q318		1 ii 26	91	4Q525	
8 7	148			2 iii 3	121
		4Q405		5 7–8	96
4Q364		4–5 2 [rec. 4Q403 1 i 34]			
4 b–e ii 22	145		91	4Q529	
		14–15 i 3	91	1 1–4	162
4Q365				1 1	37, 136, 164
6b 5–6	139	4Q408			
6a ii + 6 c 1–7	139	1 1	157	1 6–7	92
23 10	77	4Q413		1 6	37
23 4–11	77	1–2 2	157	1 11	92
23 4–12	16			1 12	92
		4Q416		19 25–26	37
4Q370		1 12	112		
1 i 4	112			4Q530	
		4Q418		2 i + 3 4	197
4Q372		55 11	157	2 ii 6–12	36
2 3	112	81 i 11–13	104	2 ii + 6–12	163
				2 ii + 6–12 2	119, 163

4Q530 (cont.)		1 + 2 + 3 3	114	1 i 10	189
2 ii + 6– 12 4	59	1 ii + 2 16	112	1 i 11	83, 84, 199, 206, 209
		6 1	112		
		15 1	38		
2 ii + 6– 12 8	121			1 i 12–13	48, 84
		4Q538		1 i 12	29, 36, 84
2 ii + 6– 12 17	91	1–2 4	164	1 i 13	84, 85, 202, 207
2 ii + 6– 12 20	182	*4Q539*		1 ii	83
2 ii + 6– 12 23–24	92	2–3 2	114	1 ii 1–8	85
				1 ii 1	31
2 ii 6 14	36	*4Q541*		1 ii 2	83
7 ii	163	7 4	30	1 ii 3–4	56, 206
15 2	163	9 i 4	113	1 ii 4	83, 142
		13 3	104	1 ii 5	85
4Q531		24 ii 5	102, 148	1 ii 6–7	85
2 + 3 1	39	24 ii 6	102	1 ii 6	41
2 + 3 9	148			1 ii 8–9	12, 51, 83, 196, 212
2 + 3 10	30	*4Q540*			
7 2	163	1 1–2	76	1 ii 9–10	207
7 1–4	163			1 ii 9–13	15, 36, 84
22 9	163	*4Q542*		1 ii 9–12	82
46 1	163	1 i–ii 12	45, 82	1 ii 9	83, 84, 85, 209
		1 i 1–ii 1	85		
4Q532		1 i–ii, 2, 3	82	1 ii 10–13	84
1 ii 6–7	109, 212	1 i	82, 210	1 ii 10	83, 207
2 7	164	1 i 1–ii 9	84	1 ii 11–13	207
		1 i 1–2	50	1 ii 11	83, 209
4Q534		1 i 1	56, 133, 161, 168, 178	1 ii 12–13	208
1 i 2	146			1 ii 12	51
1 i 5	211			2	82
1 i 7	179	1 i 2	45, 83	2 5	83
1 i 8	30, 38, 45, 179	1 i 3	148	2 11–12	85
		1 i 4–6	1	2 11	164
1 i 9–10	197	1 i 4–5	84	3	82
1 i 10	141	1 i 4	29, 192, 206	3 i–ii 12	47, 206
7 1	30			3 i	82, 83
		1 i 5–13	55	3 ii 12	17
4Q536		1 i 5–7	87		
2 i + 3 5	30	1 i 5	32, 36, 83	*4Q543*	
2 i + 3 8	179	1 i 6–9	94	1a	124, 125, 210
2 i + 3 9	179	1 i 6	205		
2 i + 3 12	179	1 i 7–8	84	1a–b	201
		1 i 7	199, 205	1a–b4	164
4Q537		1 i 8–9	205	1 a–c	73, 169, 170, 185, 190
1 + 2 + 3 0	91	1 i 9	158		
1 + 2 + 3 3–5	193	1 i 10–11	148		

Index of References

1a–c 1–4	17, 124, 129, 171, 202	1 i 8	206	1 a i 1	81, 126, 153, 208
		1	125, 143, 144, 173,	1 a i 2	106, 114, 207
1a–c 1	15, 36, 53, 116, 126, 208		174, 194, 195	1 a i 3	137
		1 1–3	174	1 a i 4–8	84, 206
1a–c 2–4	183	1 1–2	174	1 a i 4–5	138
1a–c 2	106, 114, 207	1 1	81, 209	1 a i 4	134, 137
		1 3–8	147	1 a i 4 15	148
1a–c 3–4	129	1 3–7	175	1 a i 5	127, 135
1a–c 4–5	171	1 6	186	1 a i 7–9	135, 148, 201
1a–c 5–7	84, 127, 171, 190, 205	1 7	143		
		1 8	84, 128, 138, 143	1 a i 8–9	140, 148
				1 a i 8	126, 127
2a–b	127, 169, 172, 173, 177	1 10	201	1 a i 9	118, 142, 164, 189
		1 11–12	128, 145		
		1 12	119	1 a i 11	106, 114, 207
2a–b 2	30	1 13–14	128		
2a–b 4	176, 184	1 13	129, 145, 182	1a–b	186
2a–b 5	174			1a–b ii	185, 186, 194
2a–b 7–9	170, 174	1 14	145		
3	149, 173, 185, 186	2–3	119, 197	1a–b ii 11	142, 143, 149, 153
		2	128, 186, 187		
3 1	203			1a–b ii 11–13	153
4	149, 194	2 13	42, 49, 93, 128, 183, 187	1a–b ii 14	154
4 4	128			1a–b ii 17	150, 153, 203
5–9	149, 187, 194	2 14–16	128	1a–b ii 18	154
5–9 4	159	2 15–16	119, 194	4	13, 58, 60, 128
5–9 5	128, 129	2 15	187, 188		
5–9 6	152, 156, 159	2 16	128	4 14–15	193
		3	128, 133	4 15	127, 184, 201, 202
5–9 7	152	3 1	119		
5–9 8	152, 159	3 2	128, 178, 206	4 16–19	168, 208
10 1	119			4 16	60, 66, 126, 127, 190, 191, 206
10 2	160				
14	167	*4Q545*			
15	192	1 i 5	115		
15 1–3	203	1a 1	73	4 17	142
16	127, 177, 192	1a 14	141	4 18	101, 127, 189, 202, 206
		1a 15	141		
16 2–4	93	1 a i	133, 134, 140, 142, 185		
22 2	91, 161			4 19	57, 168, 206
4Q544		1 a i 1–4	18, 124, 129	6	196, 197
1–2	187, 188			11 1	126
1–2 12–13	144				

4Q546		3 4–5	125	*4Q553*	
1	73, 124, 129, 133, 169	4 i 4	158, 166	1 i 2	172
		5 3	40	3 + 2 ii + 4 5	157
		6 2	125	3 + 2 ii + 4 6	38
1 1–2	18, 183	6 4	168	3 + 2 ii + 4 1–7	156
1 2	134	8–9	189		
1 3–4	84, 206	8 4	125		
1 3	134	9 2–7	177	*4Q554*	
1 4	94	9 4	126, 127, 148	1 i 17	156
2	142, 143, 149, 173	9 6–7	106, 168	2 i 16	197
2 1	118, 155	9 7	94, 110, 113, 142, 206	*4Q556*	
2 3	81, 153, 154, 203, 209			1 2	201
		9 8	15, 36, 53, 59, 116, 136, 176, 193, 208	*4Q558*	
2 4	154			88 1	91
4	167				
5 2	168			*4Q559*	
8 2	127, 171, 176, 202	9 10	191	3 4	171
		12 7	143	4 1	171
8 5	45, 93				
10 1–2	148	*4Q548*		*4Q560*	
12 2	94, 168	1 ii–2 5	93	1 i 3	148
12 3	126, 171, 183	1 ii–2 5	104	1 i 5	148
		1 ii–2 7–8	188	1 ii 5	164
12 4	179	1 ii–2 8	113	1 ii 6	164, 183
14	125	1 ii–2 10–16	168		
14 1	94, 114	2 6	105	*4Q561*	
14 2	147, 148	9 8	126	11 9	59
14 4	94, 106, 114				
		4Q547		*4Q564*	
16	94	9 8	176	1 ii 2	197
20 2	177				
		4Q549		*4Q569*	
4Q547		2 1	139	1–2 9	106
1–2	143, 149, 173, 210	2 8–11	203		
		2 9	139	*4Q574*	
1–2 6–8	128			1 4–5	53
1–2 6–7	143	*4Q550*		1 8	30
1–2 6	150	1–2	37		
1–2 7	84, 125, 138, 205	2 2	101	*4Q577*	
		2 4	37	7 4	157
1–2 9	156	5 + 5a 3–4	37		
1–2 12	161			*4Q582*	
2	144	*4Q552*		1 5	25
3	180, 181	6 10	91		
3 1	181				

Index of References

6Q8		3 4	13 16, 66	4:2	65
1 2	163	4 4 14	81	4:3	16, 64
1 3–5	163	6 6 15–17	139		
1 4	163			**Babylonian Talmud**	
2 1	121	Philo		*Baba Batra*	
		On Agriculture		15b	139
11Q5 (11QPsa)		80–81	139		
19 15	48			*Giṭin*	
23 3–4	44	*Allegorical Interpretation*		83a	140
		1.76	139		
11Q5		2.66–67	139	*Šabbat*	
24 15	157			77b	113
		On the Preliminary			
11Q6		*Studies*		*Sanhedrin*	
4–5	16 48	24.131	122	76b	140
11Q10		*On the Contemplative*		*Soṭah*	
A11 2	41	*Life*		11b–12a	139
2 4	96	87	139		
7a 8	103			*Yebamot*	
9 8	39	Josephus		62b	140
19 1	39	*Jewish Antiquities*		100a	157
26 3	104	3.54	139		
30 2	30	4.78	139	*Jerusalem Talmud*	
30 5	164	13.301	20	*Baba Batra*	
30 6	112	2.10–223	122	1:7, 15b	8
33 7	30	2.199–200	153		
37 4	30	2.212–15	139	Tosefta	
37 8	143	2.215–17	142	*Sukkah*	
		2.217	202	3:24	66
11Q11		2.221	139		
4 7	112	2.226	139	**Targumic Texts**	
		3.2.4	127, 139	*Samaritan Targum*	
11Q18	*(New*	3.9.1	65	*Genesis*	
	Jerusalem)	3.105	139	13:7	157
1 2	165	3.227	16, 64		
1 3	16, 65			*Targum of the Prophets*	
1 3 2	64, 65	*Jewish War*		*Ezekiel*	
1 3 4–5	16, 66	1.70	20	*16:10*	*159*
1 3 5	66				
1 3 28	64	Mishnah		*Targum Neofiti*	
		Sukkah		*Genesis*	
11Q19 (Temple Scroll)		4:9	66	15:13	97
23 1–3	16, 77			20:5	105
34 7–14	65	*Tamid*		49:30	96
34 9–11	64	2:3	77		
34 9–12	16	4:1–3	65		

Exodus
12:38   99

Deuteronomy
18:11   197

Targum Onqelos
Genesis
27:42   181

Exodus
12:45   97

Targum Ps.-Jonathan
Leviticus
19:19   96

Numbers
34:11   96

Targum Job
2:9   8
31:35   157
38:40   181

Targum 1 Chronicles
16:22   101
17:8   101

Targum CG Genesis
48:4   96

Targum Habakkuk
1:7   159

Targum J. 1 Samuel
23:9   181

Targum Jonah
28:22   111

Targum Proverbs
22:1   101

Targum Psalms
35:1   157

Targum Qohelet
6:3   101
6:4   101
7:1   101
9:8   101
10:1   101

OTHER RABBINIC WORKS
Deuteronomy Rabbah
11:10   156

Exodus Rabbah
32:2   172

Genesis Rabbah
19:12   139
57:4   8

Numbers Rabbah
16:1   172

Ginza Rabbah
229:2   159

Leviticus Rabbah
1:1   172

Pesh. Psalms
58.6   197

Pesh. Judges
5.30   159

CLASSICAL AND ANCIENT CHRISTIAN LITERATURE
Apostolic Constitutions
VI 16.3   2

Artemidorus
Onirocritica
1.1–2   156
4.1   156

Augustine
City of God
7   29

Xenophon
Anabasis
2.6.1–29   214
2.6.30   215

NEW TESTAMENT APOCRYPHA AND PSEUDEPIGRAPHA
Vision of Paul
14–17   156

OSTRACA
97   172

MANUSCRIPTS AND OTHER TEXTS
MS A, Bodl.
a VII 1.5   148
a 8 2   26
a 8 16–17   24
b 8 7–8, 13–14   15
b 8 7   106
a 8 7   58
a 8 8–9   56
a 8 8   58
b 11   79
a 8 18   58
a 8 20   58
a 8 22–23   99
b 8 14–16   45
b 8 21   49
b 9 2   76
c 9 9   61, 76
c 9 13   76
c 9 13–23   68
c 9 15–16   76
c 9 19   68
c 9 18   78
c 9 20   68, 78
c 9 23   68
d 9 4   63

Index of References

d 9 7	63	*MS Koutloumousiou*		B–294989	195
d 9 9	118	39	9	B–294992	198
d 9 11	79			B–294994	196
d 9 12	63	*Aramaic Aḥiqar*		B–294995	195
d 9 14–15	63	tradition		B–295085	54
		col. 1, line 1		B–295086	56
MS A, Cambr.		recto; cf. col. 3,		B–295087	57
c 7 1	24	lines 35–36,		B–295402	28, 34
c 7 2	70	42	30	B–295403	38
c 7 7	38	col. 2,		B–295404	40
c 7 17	69	line 19	30	B–295405	34
c 7 19	70			B–295406	42
f 6 4–6	32	*Dead Sea Scrolls*		B–295425	44, 51
f 6 8	29	*Manuscript Images*		B–295531	198
f 6 9	96	M41.405	28, 34, 44,	B–295533	195
f 6 10	96		51	B–295536	198
f 6 11–12	96	M41.512	181	B–295538	196
		M41.941	170	B–295539	195
f 6 23	74	M41.945	68, 69, 74,	B–295639	54
e 6 5	118		76, 79	B–295640	56
e 6 9	106	M42.363	51, 54, 56,	B–295641	57
e 6 10–11	103		57	B–295984	28, 29, 34
e 6 12	104	M43.241	28, 34, 38,	B–295985	38
e 6 14	28		40, 42, 44	B–295986	40
e 6 17	30	M43.242	44, 51, 54,	B–295987	34
e 6 20	28		56, 57, 61,	B–295988	42
e 6 21	97		62, 66	B–295997	44, 51
e 8 17	28	M43.260	68, 69, 74,	B–359457	181
f 6 23	34		76, 78, 80	B–359458	181
f 15 15	29	M43.565	89, 108,	B–359459	174
			117, 120	B–359460	174
Ms Heb		M43.566	174, 175,	B–359463	182
c 27 f 56	9		181, 182	B–359464	182
		M43.567	195, 196,	B–359467	175
Mount Athos Text			198, 200	B–359468	175
MS E		M43.571	150, 160,	B–359469	181
2,3	9		167	B–359470	181
2,3 1	44, 45	M43.577	134, 141,	B–359479	117
2,3 10–11 7	45		143, 144	B–359480	117
2,3 10–11 9	47, 48	M43.578	146, 147	B–359481	120
18,2	49, 51, 61,	M43.586	185–93	B–359482	120
	63, 68, 74,	M43.610	54	B–359984	54
	76, 78, 106			B–359985	54
18,2 15a	51	B–281216	44, 51	B–361394	76
18,2 19	51	B–294987	198	B–361395	76

Dead Sea Scrolls Manuscript Images (cont.)

B–361398	69, 74	B–361887	141	B–363315	189
B–361399	69, 74	B–361888	141	B–363318	188
B–361402	80	B–361889	141	B–363319	188
B–361403	80	B–361890	141	B–363320	190
B–361775	146	B–361891	141	B–363321	190
B–361772	147	B–361892	143	B–363334	193
B–361773	147	B–361893	143	B–363335	193
B–361774	146	B–361894	144	B–366681	61
B–361796	144	B–361895	144	B–366682	61
B–361797	144	B–361898	143	B–366683	62
B–361806	144	B–361899	143	B–366684	62
B–361807	144	B–363262	167	B–366685	66
B–361812	144	B–363263	167	B–366686	66
B–361813	144	B–363264	160	B–370770	170, 174
B–361814	144	B–363265	160	B–370771	170, 174
B–361815	144	B–363296	192	B–370774	89, 108
B–361816	144	B–363297	192	B–370775	89, 108
B–361817	144	B–363300	185	B–370880	150
B–361880	134	B–363301	185	B–370881	150
B–361881	134	B–363302	186	B–371305	147
B–361886	141	B–363303	186	B–371317	68, 74, 76, 78, 80
		B–363304	187	B–371436	61
		B–363305	187		
		B–363314	189		

Index of Authors

Alexander, P. S. 49, 166
Anderson, G. A. 64
Angel, J. L. 13, 48, 50, 52, 58, 66, 93, 119, 131, 145, 146, 151, 152, 158, 159, 161, 166, 171, 172, 176, 178, 199, 206
Arendzen, J. 9
Aschim, A. 180

Baarda, T. 52
Bar, S. 44, 52, 59, 92, 182
Bauckham, R. 157
Becker, J. 21, 22
Berger, K. 156
Bergman, J. 52
Bockmuehl, M. 179
Bohak, G. 9
Bonani, G. 87, 209
Bremmer, J. M. 166
Brooke, G. 105, 139
Brown, R. 179
Burchard, C. 18
Burian, P. 215

Camp, C. 138
Caquot, A. 92, 96, 97, 202
Carmi, I. 87
Charles, R. H. 9, 46, 62
Collins, J. J. 55, 111, 113, 156, 180, 217
Conacher, D. J. 215
Cook, E. M. 3, 31, 40, 54, 78, 82, 87, 89, 90, 92–94, 96, 97, 99, 102, 105, 108-109, 111, 113, 117, 144, 151, 152, 157, 159–61, 167, 181, 197, 200
Cooley, J. 163, 213
Cross, F. M. 12, 209, 210

Davila, J. R. 13, 18, 19, 78, 167, 213
Davis Bledsoe, A. M. 91
Deasley, A. 105

Dehandschutter, B. 156
Dimant, D. 36, 49, 85, 91, 115, 127, 129, 158, 167, 206
DiTommaso, L. 85
Doudna, G. L. 20
Drawnel, H. 3, 6, 9–11, 13–15, 18, 19, 22–26, 28–32, 34, 36, 37, 39–42, 44–49, 52, 54, 56, 58–65, 67–74, 76, 78–80, 86, 87, 97, 98, 129, 131, 137, 176, 202, 213, 217
Duke, R. R. 21, 123, 124, 129, 131, 134, 135, 140–42, 146, 150–52, 158–61, 171, 172, 174, 175, 181, 183–86, 188–90, 192, 193, 195, 196

Elledge, C. D. 111
Eppel, R. 193
Eshel, E. 3, 9, 11, 13, 16, 19, 22, 24, 28–32, 34–37, 40, 41, 44–48, 52, 58, 65, 67, 71, 72, 74, 78, 162, 176, 178, 205, 217

Fabry, H.-J. 92
Falk, D. K. 207
Feldman, L. M. 16, 65, 79, 95, 114, 139
Fitzmyer, J. A. 11, 20, 82, 92, 94, 109, 123, 151, 152, 155, 156, 160, 161, 167, 211
Flannery-Dailey, F. 44, 52, 156, 158, 202
Flint, P. W. 48, 111, 113
Frevel, C. 206
Frey, J. 18, 86, 129, 132, 136
Fröhlich, I. 162–63

García Martínez, F. 11, 36, 58, 82, 89, 90, 108, 109, 111, 123, 127, 141, 146, 147, 150–52, 159, 160, 167, 174, 175, 181, 185, 186, 193, 196, 211, 212
Gladd, B. 179

Gnuse, R. K. 31, 52
Goff, M. J. 163, 179, 213
Goldhill, S. 215
Goldman, L. 4, 129, 138, 142, 152, 153, 155, 156, 158, 172, 175, 184, 189, 201
Greenfield, J. C. 3, 9–13, 16, 18–20, 22, 24, 26, 28–32, 34–37, 39–48, 54, 56–58, 60–63, 65, 67–69, 71, 72, 74–76, 78–80, 97, 106, 152, 157, 176, 178, 205, 210, 213
Grelot, P. 10, 26, 211
Gross, A. D. 87

Hägg, T. 215
Halpern-Amaru, B. 131
Hama, M. J. 105, 124
Harrington, H. K. 11, 82, 109, 123, 151, 152, 160, 161, 167
Hayes, C. E. 206
Hillel, V. 18, 19, 22
Himmelfarb, M. 64, 166
Høgenhaven, J. 129, 142, 154, 155, 166, 175, 176, 184, 201, 203
Hollander, H. W. 3, 52
Holst, S. 5
Hultgård, A. 21, 22

Jonge M. de 3, 6, 9, 13, 22, 52, 129

Kapera, Z. J. 3, 11
Knoppers, G. N. 21
Kobelski, P. J. 123, 129, 151, 152, 156, 160, 167
Kosmala, H. 46
Kugel, J. L. 3, 8, 13, 14, 20, 22, 52, 60, 208
Kugler, R. A. 11, 13, 15, 18–22, 35, 40, 47, 54, 58–60, 70, 77, 209

Lange, A. 19, 86, 129, 206, 211
Lee, P. 29, 85, 86, 96, 98, 103, 116
Lemaire, A. 163, 213
Lichtenberger, H. 162

Machiela, D. A. 6, 20, 86, 91, 92, 99, 115, 124, 157, 179, 210, 212, 214, 217
Maier, J. 151
Milik, J. T. 2, 3, 10, 11, 13, 17–21, 23, 25, 39, 40, 52, 81, 82, 85, 91, 92, 109, 111, 113, 123, 129, 151, 152, 156, 158, 160, 162, 167, 206, 209–211, 213, 216
Mittmann-Richert, U. 19, 86
Mroczek, E. 48
Muraoka, T. 91, 93, 98, 113, 120, 150, 151

Najman, H. 77, 92, 217
Nautlin, P. 213
Naveh, J. 164
Neujahr, M. 213
Newsom, C. A. 93, 99, 132
Nickelsburg, G. W. E. 6, 52, 104, 211
Noegel, S. B. 52
Nordheim, E. von 129, 136
Norin, S. 20, 78

Oppenheim, A. L. 52, 156, 182

Palmer, C. 98
Pass, H. L. 9, 33, 38, 106, 107, 113
Paul, S. M. 156, 193
Pearse, H. A. 132, 158
Penner, K. M. 91
Penney, D. L. 164
Perrin, A. B. 13, 14, 24, 26, 36, 52–54, 59, 60, 62, 66, 67, 74, 77, 85, 86, 91, 92, 101, 105, 106, 115, 124, 130, 134, 136, 145, 151, 152, 156, 158, 159, 163, 167, 168, 177, 179, 180, 182, 189, 191, 193, 201, 202, 206, 208, 211, 213, 214, 217
Peters, D. M. 198
Philonenko, M. 129, 156
Popović, M. 135, 158, 208, 214
Puech, E. 3, 57, 60, 82, 83, 87, 89–91, 93–95, 97, 99–102, 105, 108, 109, 111, 113, 116–18, 120, 121, 123–25, 131, 134, 135, 139, 141–44, 146, 150–52, 154, 157, 160, 162, 164, 167, 169–71, 174–79, 181, 183–86, 188–93, 195–97, 200, 201, 205–6, 210, 211
Pummer, R. 55

Rabin, C. 46
Rad, G. von 31
Ravid, L. 193
Reynolds, B. H. 49, 162

Schattner-Rieser, U. 3, 11, 13, 19, 20, 23, 58, 91, 93
Schiffman, L. H. 15, 65
Schoor, H. van der 12, 210
Schuller, E. M. 93
Schwiderski, D. 6, 101
Segal, M. 31, 165
Sokoloff, M. 152, 157
Stadel, C. 30, 35, 37, 91–93, 95, 97, 100, 103, 106, 113, 117, 157, 184
Starcky, J. 2, 211
Stone, M. E. 3, 9–13, 16, 18–20, 22, 24, 26, 28–32, 34–37, 39–45, 47, 48, 54, 56–58, 60–63, 65, 67–69, 71, 72, 74–76, 78–80, 97, 106, 130, 176, 178, 198, 205, 209, 213, 217
Stuckenbruck, L. T. 45, 48, 49, 83, 91, 112, 119, 162, 163, 165, 211, 214
Suter, D. W. 52

Tervanotko, H. 4, 85, 139, 179, 191, 205, 206, 208
Thomas, S. I. 179, 191
Tigchelaar, E. 11, 36, 58, 82, 89, 90, 108, 109, 123, 127, 141, 146, 147, 150–52, 160, 174, 175, 181, 185, 186, 196

Tiller, P. A. 104
Tov, E. 11, 82, 109, 120, 123, 198, 207, 209–212
Trotter, J. R. 91

Ulrich, E. C. 209, 217
Uusimäki, E. 83, 85, 99, 100, 105

Van de Water, R. 87
VanderKam, J. C. 6, 20, 21, 46, 92, 131, 153–55, 175, 208
Vermes, G. 151

Walsh, M. 132, 162, 168
White Crawford, S. A. 139–40, 207
Williamson, H. G. M. 77
Wright, B. G. 165, 217

Yarbro Collins, A. 166
Young, K. 39, 47

Zahn, M. M. 207, 217
Zanella, F. 105

www.ingramcontent.com/pod-product-compliance
Lightning Source LLC
Chambersburg PA
CBHW062130300426
44115CB00012BA/1877